THE SPIRIT AND THE MIND

Essays in Informed Pentecostalism

To honor Dr. Donald N. Bowdle
Presented on his 65th Birthday

Edited by

Terry L. Cross
Emerson B. Powery

University Press of America,® Inc.
Lanham • New York • Oxford

BR
50
.S673
2000

Copyright 2000 by
University Press of America, ® Inc.
4720 Boston Way
Lanham, Maryland 20706

12 Hid's Copse Rd.
Cumnor Hill, Oxford OX2 9JJ

All rights reserved
Printed in the United States of America
British Library Cataloging in Publication Information Available

Library of Congress Cataloging-in-Publication Data

The spirit and the mind: essays in informed Pentecostalism /
edited by Terry L. Cross, Emerson B. Powery.
p.cm
"To honor Dr. Donald N. Bowdle, presented on his 65th birthday."
Includes bibliographical references.
1.   Theology. 2. Pentecostalism. 3. Bible—Criticism,
interpretation, etc. I. Bowdle, Donald N. II. Cross, Terry L.
III.   Powery, Emerson B.
BR50.S673   2000   270.8'2—dc21   99-086326

ISBN 0-7618-1627-5 (cloth: alk. ppr.)
ISBN 0-7618-1628-3 (pbk: alk. ppr.)

♾[TM] The paper used in this publication meets the minimum
requirements of American National Standard for Information
Sciences—Permanence of Paper for Printed Library Materials,
ANSI Z39.48—1984

Donald N. Bowdle, Ph.D., Th.D.

CONTENTS

II. HISTORICAL & THEOLOGICAL STUDIES

III. PRACTICAL STUDIES

CONTRIBUTORS

French L. Arrington (Ph.D., St. Louis University) is Professor of New Testament Greek and Exegesis, Church of God Theological Seminary.

Bob R. Bayles (Ph.D., Trinity Evangelical Divinity School) is Assistant Professor of Christian Education, Lee University.

Faye S. Bodley is an M.Div. student at Gordon-Conwell Theological Seminary.

R. Jerome Boone (D.Min., Columbia Theological Seminary) is Dean, School of Religion, and Professor of Old Testament, Lee University.

Donald N. Bowdle (Ph.D., Bob Jones University; Th.D., Union Theological Seminary, Virginia) is Professor of History and Religion, Lee University.

Charles W. Conn (Litt.D., Lee College) is President Emeritus, Lee University; Historian of the Church of God; General Overseer of the Church of God, 1966-1970.

Charles Paul Conn (Ph.D., Emory University) is President, and Professor of Psychology, Lee University.

Terry L. Cross (Ph.D., Princeton Theological Seminary) is Assistant Dean, School of Religion; Director of Graduate Studies in Religion; Associate Professor of Theology and Philosophy, Lee University.

Jerald Daffe (D.Min., Western Conservative Baptist Seminary) is Professor of Pastoral Ministry, Lee University.

Carolyn Dirksen (Ph.D., University of Arizona) is Vice-President for Academic Affairs, and Professor of English, Lee University.

Michael E. Fuller (Ph.D. candidate, University of Durham) is Instructor in Biblical Studies, Lee University.

Daniel Hoffman (Ph.D., Miami University, Ohio) is Assistant Professor of History, Lee University.

Cheryl Bridges Johns (Ph.D., Southern Baptist Theological Seminary) is Associate Professor of Discipleship and Christian Formation, Church of God Theological Seminary.

Lee R. Martin (D.Th. candidate, University of South Africa) is Instructor of Hebrew and Old Testament, Church of God Theological Seminary.

Rickie D. Moore (Ph.D., Vanderbilt University) is Professor of Old Testament Studies, Church of God Theological Seminary.

Karen Carroll Mundy (Ph.D., University of Tennessee) is Professor of Sociology, Lee University.

Emerson B. Powery (Ph.D., Duke University) is Assistant Professor of New Testament, Lee University.

David G. Roebuck (Ph.D., Vanderbilt University) is Director of the Hal Bernard Dixon, Jr. Pentecostal Research Center, and Assistant Professor of Religion, Lee University.

William A. Simmons (Ph.D., University of St. Andrews, Scotland) is Associate Professor of New Testament, Lee University.

John Sims (Ph.D., Florida State University) is President, European Bible Seminary, Rudersberg, Germany; Professor of History and Religion, Lee University (on leave).

John Christopher Thomas (Ph.D., University of Sheffield, England) is Professor of New Testament, Church of God Theological Seminary.

Ridley Usherwood (D.Min., Columbia Theological Seminary) is Associate Professor of Intercultural Studies, Lee University.

Sabord Woods (Ph.D., University of Tennessee) is Professor of English, Lee University.

Foreword

The demand for excellence is at the heart of Dr. Donald N. Bowdle's legacy. In a culture where the expedient is preferred over the excellent, Don Bowdle continues to hone his trade. In an academy where technical skills increasingly dominate the theoretical, Don Bowdle continues to promote the humanities. In a church where overnight schemes have re-placed theological reasoning, Don Bowdle continues to foster a passion for thinking as a spiritual discipline.

As Bowdle frequently ruminated within the classroom, everyone has 20-20 hindsight; so now we also see more clearly as we glance back at the development of our own theological journeys. One key figure in our early intellectual development was Dr. Bowdle, who challenged us by modeling for us a Christian thinker. The interaction with pertinent and challenging themes was timely. Equally important, his life as a teacher provided an example of one option—exemplified by few within our theological circle—for our callings. His approach to the intellectual life is appropriately cap-tured in Bernard's statement:

> *Some seek knowledge for the sake of knowledge: that is curiosity; others seek knowledge that they may themselves be known: that is vanity; but there are still others who seek knowledge in order to serve and edify others, and that is charity* (Bernard of Clairvaux).

Furthermore, we would be remiss if we failed to recognize that Don Bowdle is not only a wonderful mentor in the theological discipline but also a disciple of the (arguably) quintessential sport, baseball. When we recall the consistency of Bowdle's own teaching career, one player, whose own record characterizes the persistent life, comes immediately to mind. Despite illness or injury, this particular individual performed his duties at a high level of expertise in more consecutive games (2,362!) than any other player in the history of Major League Baseball. It is fitting that this player has played his entire career with the Baltimore Orioles, Don's favorite team. Don Bowdle is the Cal Ripken, Jr. of Lee University's team.

It may seem strange to some readers that we have chosen a title that appears conflicting, especially for Pentecostalism. What does the spirit have to do with the mind? Part of Dr. Bowdle's legacy is in answer to that question. "Spirit and Mind" are not set here as a dichotomy. Dr. Bowdle would not allow for that. As one of the authors within this collection states, "(Don Bowdle) was the first person to convince me that intellect need not be in conflict with the Spirit. That gift, given again and again to countless fledgling intellectuals, is at the heart of Dr. Bowdle's legacy."[1] This title seems fitting because we have discovered that truth for ourselves, partly through his work among us.

As for the subtitle of the book, "Informed Pentecostalism," several of our authors will provide definitions of what this phrase means, including the honoree himself—from whom we derived the phrase. It is not our intention in this foreword to attempt another description of what we think informed Pentecostalism is, although our own depiction admittedly might be a variation of those described within this collection. It will suffice us, within this limited space, to repeat Walter Hollenweger's response to Harvey Cox's (*Fire from Heaven*) omission of the ability of Pentecostal scholars to think theologically:

> They learn the discipline of scholarly research without confusing theological work with the gospel. It is true that sometimes they have problems in convincing their fellow Pentecostals that theological thinking and scholarly research can also be a gift of the Spirit. But Pentecostalism is not comprised merely of a singing and praying crowd of enthusiastic believers and practical doers, as one might guess from Harvey Cox's book. There are a growing number of Pentecostal theologians who ask the very question which is at the heart of Cox's book: Why do the mind and the heart have to be such antagonists, the one trying to force the other in?[2]

We believe the mind and heart cooperate in offering a reflection on what it means to be confronted by the reality of God through the Spirit. Precisely how they cooperate and the specific role of each has yet to be fleshed out among Pentecostals. Several directions for this relationship will be offered in the following essays. We believe an "informed Pentecostalism" will need to have such a discussion concerning the role of reason and the role of experience in Christian living and thought. Along with a myriad of other scholarly Pentecostal reflections, we offer this collection in honor of Don Bowdle as one response to Hollenweger's question concerning the relation of the mind and heart.

---

[1]Carolyn Dirksen, "Dr. Donald N. Bowdle: An Informed Pentecostal," 4 (n. 9).

[2]"Fire from Heaven: The Testimony by Harvey Cox," *PNEUMA: The Journal of the Society for Pentecostal Studies* 20/2 (Fall 1998): 201-202.

Donald Bowdle has been educated in a variety of disciplines: New Testament, theology, and church history. He has taught courses as diverse as Western Civilization and New Testament Greek, Old Testament Survey and the Gospel of John, Systematic Theology and the Book of Revelation. In many respects, Dr. Bowdle is a "renaissance man." While most *Festschriften* focus narrowly on a specific area of the honoree's expertise, this *Festschrift* offers a broad panoply of topics. We feel this best represents the expansive interests of Dr. Bowdle as well as reflects the variety of fields that his students and colleagues have pursued.

Dr. Bowdle has taught in biblical studies for almost forty years at Lee University. Anyone who has been a student in his biblical classes recognizes that he is an expert exegete and interpreter of the Scriptures. To honor his love of God's Word, we have presented a group of essays in biblical studies.

Dr. Bowdle has also taught systematic theology for over twenty years. His grasp of nuanced theological points and his ability to synthesize a vast array of theologians' views have captured the minds of many doctrinal neophytes. To honor his passion for good theology, we have offered a collection of essays in theological studies.

Dr. Bowdle has taught the history of Christianity for over twenty years as well. His ability to highlight significant trends and yet note the smallest vital detail of an historical epoch has stirred many students to study further the historical life of the Church. To honor his zeal for history, we have presented a collection of historical essays.

Finally, Dr. Bowdle has been thoroughly involved in the life of the church. His desire to see a ministry that was well trained in Bible and theology has left a marked legacy on churches throughout the world. To honor his heart for ministry and the Church, we have offered a collection of essays that examine the practical application of the theological enterprise.

These are a kaleidoscope of essays. Some are obviously Pentecostal; others have no clear connection to the Pentecostal movement. Informed Pentecostalism is not interested only in things Pentecostal. It wants to serve the entire church and the cause of Christ. Informed Pentecostalism wants to advance the study of religion, theology, and the Bible through excellence in academic pursuits. Thus, the reader will find Christian scholars portraying a kind of Christian humanism, which Bowdle espouses in his essay explaining informed Pentecostalism.

In addition, these are a variety of authors. Some writers have been students, some have been colleagues, and some have been both. We believe readers will be informed, challenged, and pleased with this collection. We hope that we have reflected appropriately the legacy of Don Bowdle's life and informed Pentecostalism.

A project of this nature is not possible to complete without the assistance of numerous competent people. We appreciate the participation of the authors who willingly assisted us and the financial support of Lee University in honoring Don Bowdle. President Paul Conn and Dean Jerome Boone have promoted the project with enthusiasm from its outset. Thanks are due to Dale Coulter and Dan Hoffman who graciously read initial, selected drafts. Also we owe a special thanks to three of our (and Don's) students: Cailin Chrismer has worked diligently with the project since its inception. Her numerous gifts, including grammatical skills and technical expertise, were essential throughout; Crip Stephenson's attention to detail in proof-reading is unmatched; Darcy Abbott, a recent graduate, began the arduous task of compiling the bibliography. Also, we wish to thank Peter Cooper at the University Press of America for accepting the collection, despite the changing market for volumes of this nature. We have used Turabian's 6th edition as a guide except for biblical abbreviations, for which we used the format of the Society of Biblical Literature. Finally we extend thanks to our wives (Linda and Kimberly) for maintaining a semblance of order in the lives of our families in our frequent absences, both physical and mental, during this period.

Terry L. Cross
Emerson B. Powery

The Editors

A Letter to the Reader

Dr. Paul Conn, President, Lee University

The publication of a *Festschrift* is a rare occasion for a college or university. It is, in fact, a recognition bestowed more sparingly than even the awarding of honorary doctorates or the naming of campus buildings. In its eighty-year history, Lee University has only once before, in 1980, produced such a volume.

It is not surprising, then, that **the person** honored by this book is an individual whose impact on the life of our institution is virtually unequaled. Dr. Donald N. Bowdle returned to his alma mater in 1962 as a young intellectual trailblazer and stayed to become, by the end of the century, the distinguished senior member of an increasingly excellent faculty. During that lifetime of service, he has been neither merely an observer of the institution's development, nor merely a participant in it, but a prime mover and catalyst during the entire journey.

This volume is a collection of papers written by men and women who, in various ways, primarily as students and colleagues, have personally witnessed and enjoyed Bowdle's unique blend of intellectual, spiritual, and relational refinement. It should be noted that these papers are not the work of the university itself, in any corporate sense, but of individuals, and the views contained in them express individual perspectives rather than an official university position.

The **timing** of the publication of this volume is suggestive of Lee's emergence, as we begin the new century as a fully-developed university, which is responding to the need of the church for intellectual and theological leadership. Later this year, the Lee University School of Religion will begin offering graduate degrees, joining the other three schools of the university. A faculty has been assembled that brings to the classroom men and women with finely tuned theological minds and an instinct for teaching. Students arrive in greater numbers each year to study with this superb faculty, and increasingly they seek graduate training that bears the distinctive Lee University trademarks of excellence and intellectual boldness.

The willingness and ability to provide "leadership of ideas" is not a new thing for Lee University. Since its quite humble beginnings in 1918, this institution has led the Church of God as its flagship institution. It has trained generation after generation of ministers, missionaries, and theological scholars. It has not merely served but led the church intellectually, never so far ahead of the curve as to lose the confidence of the denominational mainstream, but always bold enough to challenge the conventional thinking of any given generation. That is the role of a denominational university: to serve faithfully, but to serve by leading and not by pandering to the regressive impulses, which occasionally assert themselves in denominational life.

The **theme** of this volume is also appropriate, both to the time as well as for the person who is being honored. This is a period in which Pentecostalism is being defined in a sometimes bewildering variety of ways. It is a very large tent, under which are gathered, at least periodically, a diverse group of people: newcomers and old-timers, the renegade and the orthodox, those who would embrace as a holy mantle the label "fundamentalist" and those who would shun it as insulting, Catholic and anti-Catholic, inclusive and isolationist. It is a period in which to call oneself Pentecostal is to join a huge happy flood; at the same time, however, one is given pause: with what and with whom does one identify oneself, theologically and intellectually, by membership in such a club?

Lee University has no ambivalence about its identity as a Pentecostal institution. We are Pentecostal in the most biblically pure sense of the word. Not just our historic antecedents, but our present daily reality, gives us the confidence to embrace our Pentecostal faith. In embracing it, however, we also are working at the subtler and more difficult work of defining it, in a manner that has theological and experiential integrity. To define what it means to be Pentecostal in one's own life is not just the right but the responsibility of a university community, which would call itself Pentecostal.

In this task, we reject a narrow and narcissistic commitment to learn and draw inspiration only from those ideas and individuals which are "distinctively Pentecostal." We will not discard or ignore the vast storehouse of intellectual and biblical resources that can inform us, and through which God can teach us, as we seek to understand what it means to be Pentecostal in the 21st Century.

Like so many of my colleagues at Lee and elsewhere, I am personally a Pentecostal today in large measure through the influence of Don Bowdle. When I was a student at Lee Bible College in the 1960's, seeking to resolve the inevitable dissonance of my own personal development in a religious subculture which I approached with both love and caution, I saw in Dr. Bowdle a model of "informed Pentecostalism." He had a worldview that was faithful to scripture and to what we called the "full gospel," while still open to whatever God might teach him from the rich history of the church. Don Bowdle's brand of Pentecostalism resonated with me in those student days; it seemed consistent, intellectually and at a deeply personal spiritual level, with the larger context of the whole Bible, rightly divided.

It is to such a Pentecostalism that we at Lee University aspire. It is Pentecostalism without anger, Pentecostalism without cheap sensationalism, Pentecostalism without obsessive denominationalism, Pentecostalism without self-righteous impulse to exclude those of a slightly different hue or stripe. It is Pentecostalism without "oneupmanship," without need to identify itself as the highest rung on the ecclesiastical ladder. It is Pentecostalism that centers on Jesus Christ, which understands the Upper Room not as an ecclesiastical museum, but as a staging area for those who would take the love of Christ to the world. It is Pentecostalism with the humility to acknowledge that we have much to learn from others. It is informed Pentecostalism, which does not call attention to itself but to Jesus Christ.

Don Bowdle does not perfectly embody that ideal, nor do any of us, nor does Lee University. But we are energized by the aspiration to understand and reflect, better and better, this type of Pentecostalism. That a book with such a theme should honor a man who has consistently led in that quest, and that it should be produced by a university which is stepping up to lead the Pentecostal community theologically and educationally, is triply appropriate.

Dr. Donald N. Bowdle:
An Informed Pentecostal

Carolyn Dirksen[*]

Mild-mannered, soft-spoken, gentle, and gentlemanly, Dr. Donald N. Bowdle fits no one's stereotype of a revolutionary. He is conservative in lifestyle, measured in speech, temperate in manner, and unerringly thoughtful in demeanor; yet through his long career as a writer and teacher, he has contributed to a quiet revolution in the beliefs and attitudes of the Church of God. He has explored and expounded upon the uncharted terrain of Pentecostal theology in ways few others have attempted, and he has quietly battled for an environment within the denomination which is open to and respectful of liberal education. As he points out in his essay in this volume, "Informed Pentecostalism: An Alternative Paradigm,"[1] Pentecostalism has been at odds with intellectualism since its inception, emphasizing the validity of the emotions and remaining skeptical of the mind. Against that backdrop, Bowdle—a third-generation Pentecostal and member of the Church of God—has consistently gone against the grain by developing his mind and his heart, balancing relationship and reason, and unfalteringly pointing his students toward life as informed Pentecostals.

Because Pentecostal theology has not been fully explored, and because Pentecostalism is a composite of origins and orientations,[2] Bowdle's work has sometimes placed him in the center of debate. In a subculture

---

[*]Carolyn Dirksen (Ph.D., University of Arizona). Vice-President for Academic Affairs; Professor of English, Lee University.

[1]Donald N. Bowdle, "Informed Pentecostalism: An Alternative Paradigm," 9-19.

[2]Donald N. Bowdle "Holiness in the Highlands: A Profile of the Church of God in Appalachia," *Christianity in Appalachia: Profiles in Regional Pluralism,* ed. Bill J. Leonard. (Knoxville, TN: University of Tennessee Press, 1999), 243.

that respects experience and emotion, his quest for evermore education has also at times been either puzzling or misunderstood. For all his mild-mannered professorial ways, he has never shrunk from the fray. Now, as he approaches 65 and completes 45 years of ministry, his legacy is clear: Donald N. Bowdle has done as much as any one individual to articulate Pentecostal theology and to make the Pentecostal context a hospitable environment for the life of the mind. Generations of his students have experienced the liberation of the liberal arts and have learned through his teaching and his example, that God loves good stewards of the intellect.

Born and raised in Easton, Maryland, Bowdle began life as the son of a former schoolteacher and a bakery truck driver. His first interest in learning came from his mother, Katherine Kline Bowdle, a devout Christian who introduced him both to books and to Christ. Although his father, Nelson, was not to become a Christian until late in life, Bowdle's grandparents, Robert Elmer and Effie Legates Bowdle were among the first Pentecostals in Maryland, and Effie was a licensed minister.

Don attended his first Church of God service when he was two weeks old and became a Christian at age 13. Two years later he received the baptism in the Holy Spirit and was called into ministry. Pursuing that calling, Bowdle came to Lee College in the fall of 1953 and began a career in higher education that would span four decades. "My primary role models in those early days at Lee were Hollis Gause and Elmer Odom, both teachers in religion; Dorcas Sharp Headley, my English teacher; and Robert Humbertson who taught speech," Bowdle remembers.[3] Through their serious dedication to their work and scholarship, these four helped Bowdle begin to see the possibility of integrating faith and learning and of becoming a Christian who was faithful in the development of his mind.[4]

In 1955, while still a student at Lee, Bowdle married Nancy Lee George. Raised in the same Maryland town, they had come to Lee together as freshmen, and Nancy would be by Don's side as he pursued his numerous degrees.[5] Graduating from Lee in 1957, Bowdle found that his options for graduate study were limited since Lee at that time was not accredited. He

---

[3]Dr. Hollis Gause served on the Lee faculty and administration from the late 1940s to 1975 when he went to the Church of God Seminary as its first dean/director. Elmer Odom served as a member of the Lee faculty until his retirement. He passed away in 1989. Dorcas Headley left Lee in the mid 1960s but is still an English teacher and strong supporter of Lee and its mission.

[4]"Conversations on Camera," Charles W. Conn (Cleveland, TN: Lee University Pentecostal Resource Center, 21 April 1999).

[5]Nancy worked at the Church of God Publishing House while Don began his teaching career. She completed her Bachelor of Arts degree from Lee in 1991. The Bowdles had two children, Keven and Karen (LaBelle), and four grandchildren. Keven's children are Garrett and Jackson, and Karen's are Noah and Summer Grace.

enrolled at Bob Jones University where he completed the M.A. and, in 1961, a Ph.D. in New Testament Text and Theology. This achievement made Bowdle one of the first ministers in the Church of God to attain a doctorate in religion. At Bob Jones, Bowdle was introduced to the writings of John Calvin. Calvin's theological insights made a lasting impression on Bowdle's life and thought, and Calvin's influence permeates much of Bowdle's own writing and teaching.

With his Ph.D. in hand, Bowdle's greatest desire was to return to Lee to teach. "Lee had some excellent teachers, but it wasn't a great college, and I knew it had the potential to become one. I wanted to contribute what I could to making it better."[6] Then Lee President Ray H. Hughes hired Bowdle to begin teaching in the fall of 1962, leaving a year in the interim. Bowdle decided to continue his studies and completed a Th.M. in Ancient and Medieval Studies at Princeton Theological Seminary.

Fortuitously, he attended Princeton Seminary during the 150th anniversary of the seminary and, to commemorate that occasion, Karl Barth was invited to the campus for a series of lectures. Already familiar with Barth's work, Bowdle was spellbound with these presentations and added Barth to his list of those having a significant influence on his thinking. "Hearing Barth deliver that lecture series was the highlight of my academic career," he comments. "Although there is much in Barth's theology with which contemporary Evangelicals might disagree, he swung the pendulum back from liberalism and stopped theology in its tracks for 25 years."[7] Bruce Metzger, noted expert on the New Testament, was also a strong influence on Bowdle during his time at Princeton Seminary.

From Princeton, Bowdle came to the Lee College faculty. With three graduate degrees, one from an Ivy League school, he was already something of an anomaly, and he attracted a loyal following of students eager to expand their intellectual horizons. Since that moment, his influence on the college and the young people of its sponsoring denomination has been inestimable. In 1964 Bowdle was ordained as a Church of God minister. Teaching both history and theology, he constantly felt a need for further study and research, so in 1966 he entered a Th.D. program at Union Theological Seminary in Virginia where he completed a degree in 19th Century American Social and Religious Thought.[8]

Returning to Lee in the fall of 1969, Bowdle brought all his new information and skills to bear on his teaching and assumed new leadership

---

[6]Donald N. Bowdle, interview by author, Cleveland, TN, 30 June 1999.

[7]"Conversations on Camera."

[8]The title of his Th.D. dissertation is "Evangelism and Ecumenism in Nineteenth Century America: A Study in the Life and Literature of Samuel Irenaeus Prime, 1812-1885" (1970).

roles at the institution.[9] At this time, Lee was in transition. Formerly a
four-year Bible college with a two-year junior college division, it had become a four-year liberal arts college in 1968.[10] Although some were reluctant to make the change, fearing that the role of religious studies might be
compromised, Bowdle was a whole-hearted supporter of the new structure. "I thought it was the right thing to do," he remembers. "I was de-
lighted when we merged into one school."[11] Always a believer in the
value of the liberal arts, Bowdle has commented, "The liberal arts, . . .
informed by the Word of God, [are] the building blocks of a Christian
worldview."[12]

As evidence of his influence on campus, Bowdle was asked to articulate the college's new mission statement, putting into words Lee's institutional purpose. In that document he reiterated his belief that

> there is a positive correlation between scholarship and whole-
> ness; that one must approach all of learning with a sense of
> privilege and responsibility under God; that truth is truth
> wherever it is found, whether test tube, literary masterpiece
> or Holy Scripture; that appropriate integration of truth is
> both intellectual and behavioral in nature; and that the pursuit
> and application of truth is, indeed, "ministry."[13]

Still part of the Lee University mission statement, this declaration reflects
Bowdle's recognition of the inseparability of faith and learning and offi-
cially documents the profound effect of his thinking on the nature and
identity of the institution.

In 1971, Bowdle edited *Ellicott's Bible Commentary: In One Volume*
for Zondervan Publishing House, clearly demonstrating his skill as an
editor and his insight into scripture. In 1972, he published his favorite

---

[9]I first met Dr. Bowdle when he came back to campus with his second doctorate. As a second-year faculty member, I was in awe of him from his reputation
alone, but when I met and worked with him, I found him to be a most amiable
colleague. Having been brought up in a church context that was not hospitable to
the development of the mind, I was spellbound by his accomplishments, and it
was his calm, reassuring presence that first gave me the idea that it might not be
preposterous for a Church of God "girl" to go for a Ph.D. Although I met him at
a time when women in the professions were not always welcomed, he treated me
with the highest professional respect and gave me great confidence in my place and
in my abilities. He was the first person to convince me that the intellect need not
be in conflict with the Spirit. That gift, given again and again to countless fledgling
intellectuals, is at the heart of Dr. Bowdle's legacy.
[10]Charles W. Conn, *Like a Mighty Army* (Cleveland, TN: Pathway Press,
1996), 341.
[11]Interview by author.
[12]"Informed Pentecostalism," 12.
[13]*Lee University Undergraduate Catalog* (1999-2000), 8.

work to date, *Redemption Accomplished and Applied* (Cleveland, TN: Pathway Press). This small book, commissioned by the Department of Youth and Christian Education as a Church Training Course manual, left a distinct mark on the development of the denomination's theology and created one of the more memorable debates about Bowdle's theological tenets. Bowdle's explanation that sanctification is gradual rather than instantaneous created so much controversy that it took more than a year for the General Executive Council to approve the manuscript for publication. During the revision process, Bowdle added documentation and scriptural references, but he did not back down from his original position.

Once it was published, the response to the book was also heated. Bowdle tells of one pastor who began reading the chapter on sanctification and became so angry that he threw the book against the wall and let it lie on the floor for a week. He began reading it again with the same reaction. Finally, after controlling his emotions but not his curiosity, he finished the chapter and was convinced. He called Dr. Bowdle, whom he had never met, and invited him to come to his church to teach the book. Since then, Bowdle has preached in that church more than forty times. Over the years, *Redemption Accomplished and Applied* has become one of the best-selling texts in the church training course series.[14]

After spending the next few years in administrative positions including department chair and Dean of the Division of Religion, Bowdle suffered a severe heart attack in 1977. Through the pain and trauma of that event, he became determined to focus his time on the things he loved most, his family, teaching, and writing; and he withdrew from administration. In 1980, Bowdle organized and edited a *Festschrift* in honor of Charles W. Conn to commemorate his tenth year as president of Lee. Entitled *The Promise and the Power: Essays on the Motivations, Developments, and Prospects of the Ministries of the Church of God,*[15] the collection brought together some of the best writers in the Pentecostal tradition with reflections on the history and development of various elements of Pentecostalism. Essays in that volume have provided the groundwork for a significant amount of subsequent research into the Pentecostal movement.

A life-long learner with a passion for books and scholarship, Bowdle again returned to his studies in 1984-85, this time as a post-doctoral fellow at Yale where he studied under Jaroslav Pelikan. Again, in 1988-89, he took a sabbatical from Lee and sampled a smorgasbord of courses in theology and history at Edinburgh University in Scotland. While at New College in Edinburgh, Bowdle presented lectures on "Philip Schaff's Assessment of the Development of a National Character: '*America*,' 1855"

[14]Interview by author.
[15]Cleveland, TN: Pathway Press, 1980.

and "Pragmatism or Providence?: A Case Study in Ecumenism in Nineteenth-Century America."[16] "Giving those lectures was a real highlight
for me," he remembers. "There were people there from a variety of different
disciplines, and we all sat around a long table and discussed the ideas."[17]

In 1990, a tragedy occurred in Dr. Bowdle's life when his wife Nancy
was diagnosed with Lou Gehrig's disease. Bringing about gradual debili-
tation and ultimately resulting in the failure of the involuntary muscles,
the disease lasted for two more years before Nancy's death in 1992. "During that time, I would not have been able to continue teaching had it not
been for the care I received from the Lee family, especially the women's
club, Sigma Nu Sigma, and from our friends at the Westmore Church of
God."[18] It was also during this time that Bowdle began to cling ever more
tightly to the teachings of John Calvin. "You can believe something in
your head," Bowdle comments," but when something tragic happens, you
learn to believe it in your heart. Wesley is a good theologian for sunny
days; but when it's raining, you want Calvin."[19] During the months of
Nancy's degenerative illness, the Bowdles were particularly strengthened
by Calvin's teachings about God's sovereignty. "I never felt closer to the
Lord than when I was serving Nancy," Bowdle remembers.[20]

After Nancy's death, Bowdle took a summer off from teaching at Lee
and traveled more than 6,000 miles preaching and teaching in local churches.
In 1994, Bowdle married Jean Eversole Cooley whom he describes as having "a richness and quietness of spirit." Don met Jean at Lee where she
served as secretary to the Vice President for Academic Affairs, and they
were married on campus in the Alumni Park gazebo. [21]

Although his work has always been centered at Lee, Don's ministry
has taken him to more than forty foreign countries where he has taught
Bible and theology. He is a frequent lecturer at the Han Young Theological University in Seoul, Korea, and also presented a lecture at Zaporozhye
State University, Ukraine, in 1993. In addition, he has traveled the high-
ways and back roads of America preaching in a wide variety of churches.
His influence has also been felt through the publication of more than
twenty-five articles in the Church of God *Evangel* and his editorship of
the *Academic Forum.*

---

[16]"Conversations on Camera."
[17]Interview by author.
[18]"Conversations on Camera."
[19]Interview by author.
[20]Ibid.
[21]"Conversations on Camera." Jean has one daughter, Dianna Cooley Puhr, who
was a student at Lee when the Bowdles were married. "Dianna was a welcome
child to me," Bowdle comments.

Bowdle's two most recent works, "Holiness in the Highlands"[22] and "Informed Pentecostalism: An Alternative Paradigm" in this volume, clearly assert that the quiet revolutionary has not lost his vision. In "Holiness in the Highlands," he suggests an agenda for the Church of God:

> Theological education of the laity, discipleship formation, inclusion of women and ethnic minorities in administrative services, stewardship of social concern, pursuit of a balanced spirituality, denial of a distracting glossocentrism, repentance of any debilitating secularization of holiness—such are the matters which the Church of God must address with great intentionality.[23]

In "Informed Pentecostalism," he further calls for an affirmation of Christian Humanism and a reconsideration of the Pentecostal heritage. As these essays clearly demonstrate, Bowdle does not seek controversy for its own sake. His goal is always to raise issues for the consideration of the denomination that will foster constructive dialogue and bring about positive change.

Don Bowdle's ministry has impacted literally thousands of people—directly as they sat in his classes or read his published works and indirectly as his former students ministered to them from their pulpits. Gradually, his influence, like water flowing over a stone, has modified the contours of Lee University and the Church of God. During his 45 years of ministry, he has contributed to an environment on campus and in the wider church in which issues like those above can be comfortably raised and discussed. He has been instrumental in bringing Lee from its origins as a sectarian Bible school to a Christ-centered liberal arts university, and he has done much to lay the groundwork for respect of the intellect within the Church of God. Hundreds of younger intellectuals in ministry, like Terry Cross and Emerson Powery, who have organized and edited this volume, recognize their debt to him as do all who have the privilege of working with him daily in the enterprise of shaping the next generation of church leaders. Donald N. Bowdle's unflinching integrity, intimidating intellect, and undaunted courage blend perfectly with his sweet spirit and warm congeniality to make him the consummate professor. Mentor, colleague, and friend, he has given Lee University and the Church of God an incredible gift: the complete focus of his passion, his intelligence, and his heart.

---

[22]"Holiness in the Highlands," 243-56.
[23]Ibid., 252.

Informed Pentecostalism:
An Alternative Paradigm

Donald N. Bowdle[*]

Pentecostalism is a coat of many colors.[1] As I have observed else-where,[2] no one person ever should presume to speak for the movement, nor any single denomination pretend fully to represent it, so diverse is it in both thought and practice. International in its range, Pentecostalism wears many faces, speaks a variety of languages, and indulges a multiplicity of styles of expression. Perhaps for these very reasons, no adequate *Kulturgeschichte* of the movement is likely to be written.[3]

The commitments which follow have issued from forty-five years of ministry and observation in the fifty United States and in forty other countries on five continents. Thirty-eight of these years have been in-vested in both undergraduate and graduate students whom God has given me at Lee University. There I have done what I love best: lecturing, directing seminars, and otherwise engaging young minds preparing to live, in one way or another, as Christian professionals in the world. These

[*]Donald N. Bowdle (Ph.D., Bob Jones University; Th.D., Union Theological Seminary, VA). Professor of History and Religion, Lee University.
[1]J. S. Whale has employed the expression "coat of many colours" in reference to the diversity of modern Protestantism. *(The Protestant Tradition* [Cambridge: Cambridge University Press, 1955], 177.) Here it is apropos to Pentecostalism.

By "Pentecostalism" I refer throughout this essay to the traditional/historical Pentecostal movement as per its established denominational representations, no-tably the Church of God, but neither to Oneness Pentecostalism nor to the more recent variety of Charismatic expressions.

[2]"Holiness in the Highlands: A Profile of the Church of God," in *Christianity in Appalachia: Profiles in Regional Pluralism*, ed. Bill J. Leonard (Knoxville: The University of Tennessee Press, 1999), 243.

[3]See Walter J. Hollenweger, *The Pentecostals* (London: SCM Press, 1972), passim.

commitments are my very own, offered candidly and charitably and as an invitation for dialogue to those who really care about fostering a quality Pentecostalism.[4]

Those who minister in the academy understand that the legacy and lore of an institution are, indeed, but the lengthening shadows of the men and women who serve it. It is especially incumbent upon those whose call is the theological enterprise to be respectful of tradition yet sufficiently self-assured to articulate an alternative paradigm in the interests of re-newal and relevance.

An informed Pentecostalism is such an alternative paradigm. The scandal of the Pentecostal mind has been its reluctance—even refusal—to engage the culture on its own grounds in the finest tradition of the Christian faith.[5] Several conditions may have conjoined in yesteryear to occasion such a posture: inherent timidity of humble socioeconomic ori-gins, imminent expectations of premillennial eschatology, and tension within the Body of Christ created by a particularistic view of the work of the Holy Spirit. But traditional/historical Pentecostalism is now without excuse. Contemporary ministry requires "baptized brains" as well as baptized hearts and hands.

Nor is "informed Pentecostalism" oxymoronic! The Holy Spirit would have us discern that there is a positive correlation between scholarship and wholeness, whether personal or societal, and that one must approach all learning with a sense of privilege and responsibility under God. From this perspective, then, let us explore the relevant questions: How may the scandal of the Pentecostal mind be arrested?[6] What comprises the alter-native paradigm of which we speak? What are the components of an informed Pentecostalism? What are the urgent theological considerations of a quality Pentecostalism?

---

[4]If readers object to the expression "quality Pentecostalism," they are reminded here that the Apostle Paul chided the Corinthians for accepting anything less than that.

[5]See, e.g., *The Epistle to Diognetus*, chaps. 5, 6; Aurelius Augustine, *The City of God*, bk. 19; John Calvin, *Institutes of the Christian Religion*, IV.20; C. S. Lewis, *Mere Christianity*, bk. 3; H. Richard Niebuhr, *Christ and Culture*, chap. 6.

[6]All of the essays herein represent the cutting edge of an informed Pentecostalism. The reader is encouraged, at this juncture, to give careful attention to the contribu-tion of Cheryl Bridges Johns. Johns explores aspects of "the Pentecostal mind" in terms of epistemology and worldview, and dialogues with Mark A. Noll's criti-cism of the nature of Pentecostalism and what he considers indicative of the "lack of mind" found within the movement.

I. Affirming a Christian Humanism

Pentecostals are long overdue a radical attitude adjustment respecting the academy. Defining ourselves largely in negative terms, and too often in counterpoise with the culture, we have pridefully announced our self-alienation from the academy and its perceived dubious influences. But in doing so, we have precluded the enormous benefits of perhaps the most powerful creative force in the life of historic Christianity.

Humanism is a devotion to the humanities (*humanitas*) and commonly traced to the Renaissance and its revival of interest in the Greek and Roman classics. It addresses the urgent universal query: What does it mean to be human? A celebration of humanity, humanism is an ethic that affirms the inestimable dignity of humankind and aims at its highest self-realization. The essential themes of humanism are personal selfhood, persons in community, and everything in the material world that, fully respected and properly husbanded, enriches human existence.

Christian humanism elevates the discussion to the gracious intention of God toward the human cause. It proceeds from the *imago Dei* in humankind (Genesis 1:26, 27) and culminates in an incarnational theology (John 1:14), necessary postulates to a truly authentic humanity. Relation to God, then, not the capacity for reason, is what distinguishes the human creature from the rest of the created order. By relation to God are meant both enhancement of temporal existence and assurance of eternal life through the salvific work of Christ.[7]

Misconstruing the humanism of the Renaissance with the secular humanism of the Enlightenment,[8] Pentecostals have generally concluded

---

[7]See J. I. Packer and Thomas Howard, *The True Humanism* (Waco: Word Books, 1985). But cf. Francis A. Schaeffer, *How Should We Then Live? The Rise and Decline of Western Thought* (Old Tappan, NJ: Fleming H. Revell, 1976). Karl Barth vigorously reaffirmed the divine immanence in the historical Jesus, the Man for us (*The Humanity of God* [Richmond: John Knox Press, 1960]).

[8]In their fine work *The Case for Christian Humanism*, Franklin and Shaw insist that "nothing is basically wrong with the term *humanism*, but it is the victim of an erratic history of connotation." They remind us that while the developmental stream of classical-Christian humanism did not divide abruptly into secular and Christian rivulets, an incipient secular humanism can be identified from the late-Renaissance period, as Desiderius Erasmus and the Protestant Reformers contended that *pietas* be wedded to *humanitas*. (R. William Franklin and Joseph M. Shaw, *The Case for Christian Humanism* [Grand Rapids: Wm. B. Eerdmans Publishing Co., 1991], xi, 18-23.) See E. Harris Harbison, *The Christian Scholar in the Age of the Reformation* (New York: Charles Scribner's Sons, 1956); Charles Norris Cochrane, *Christianity and Classical Culture; A Study of Thought and Action from Augustus to Augustine* (New York: Oxford University Press, 1957). Jaroslav Pelikan and Donald G. Bloesch urge that Protestant scholars "rediscover" the Patristics, a literary treasury for the *whole* Christian Church.

that Christian humanism is a contradiction of terms. But the Christian scholar—the Christian humanist, if you will—seeks truth no less than the scholar who makes no profession of faith in Christ. Truth is truth no matter where it is found, whether test tube, literary masterpiece, or Holy Scripture; and truth is truth no matter by whom it is found. The informed Pentecostal understands that scholarship cannot be compartmentalized into secular and sacred pursuits because the whole of it is a holy calling.

Pentecostals must make peace with the academy and understand that Jesus is Lord of learning, too. Accessing the enormous resources of the academy, we will be prepared to explore an integration of faith and learning that is both intellectual and behavioral in nature and to experience that wholeness of self to which allusion has been made earlier. The liberal arts are liberating arts and, informed by the Word of God, the building blocks of a Christian worldview.[9]

II. Reconsidering the Pentecostal Heritage: Continuity/Discontinuity

The Pentecostal Movement is largely ahistorical in perceiving itself in the scheme of things. It recognizes its antecedents in the Holiness revivals

---

The term "secular" derives from the Latin *saeculum*, meaning "world" or "age." A secular humanist is one who, maintaining that the material world and the present time alone are coextensive with reality, necessarily depreciates metaphysics, revelation, and accountability. See Peter Gay, *The Enlightenment: An Interpretation. The Rise of Modern Paganism* (New York: Vintage Books, 1968). The German *Aufklärung* well expresses this mood.

[9]It should be remembered that the academy birthed the Protestant Reformation. Reminiscences of Wycliffe, Tyndale, Luther, Bucer, Melanchthon, and Calvin clearly support the thesis. Each employed the lectern as well as the pulpit from which to call for a new understanding of salvific and ecclesial concerns. This company imbibed the spirit of the Renaissance, but Melanchthon and Calvin among them excelled in humanist learning. With Bucer and Luther they were heirs to the scholarly provisions of Reuchlin and Erasmus. See the excellent Reformation studies by Roland H. Bainton, William J. Bouwsma, Hans J. Hillerbrand, Johan Huizinga, and, more recently, Alister E. McGrath.

The reader would do well to note how Erasmus, the eminent Christian humanist, employed his scholarly insights in addressing the culture in general and the political sector in particular. See *The Education of a Christian Prince*, published in 1516 and dedicated to the future Emperor Charles V of the Holy Roman Empire. I am reminded here of Boorstin's comment that in the humanities, unlike the sciences, the latest works are not necessarily the best. This applies to all the older sources cited herein, whether they are ancient texts or simply texts that are not "current." See Daniel J. Boorstin, "Reference Notes" in *The Seekers: The Story of Man's Continuing Quest to Understand His World* (New York: Random House, 1988), 261.

of the late-nineteenth century, but its Reformation heritage somehow seems to elude it. Discussion of these relationships is an exercise in continuity/discontinuity.

Contemporary Pentecostalism maintains a significant continuity with the Reformation tradition of the sixteenth century. It embraces the principal tenets of the Reformers: justification by faith alone, the authority of Scripture alone, and the privilege of individual interpretation of Scripture, that is, disassociation from the dictates of any ecclesiastical magisterium, including the individual priesthood of the believer. It is, furthermore, Trinitarian in its doctrine of God and Christocentric in its missionary expression. These components of European Reformation heritage comprised the substance of Christianity in colonial America, especially through Puritan and Anglican influence, and throughout the early national period.

Holiness revivalism and the separatist phenomenon in *post-bellum* America have been explored by numerous scholars in the field.[10] While no single reason suffices for their emergence, a plausible scenario is (1) a *reaction* against naturalism, socialism, "Romanism," and Protestant theological liberalism, as represented by the Social Gospel movement, (2) a *reaffirmation* of the devotional life vis-à-vis the perceived spiritual impoverishment of those bodies from which the defections occurred and their attendant resistance to revivalism, and (3) a *reconstruction* within some segments of conservative-evangelical scholarship to accommodate a premillennial eschatology.[11] Both Wesleyan and Reformed (Keswick) persuasions made their respective contributions to the Holiness enterprise.

But, notwithstanding doctrinal and practical affinities, there developed a fundamental discontinuity of Pentecostalism with both Wesleyan and Keswick models of conservative-evangelical Christianity. This discontinuity was occasioned by the stigmatizing experience of tongues-speaking, which Pentecostals maintained was available to those in whose lives sanctification had become evident.[12] Indeed, Pentecostals regarded their distinctive emphasis as but an extension of the earlier Holiness

---

[10]See Bowdle, "Holiness in the Highlands," 252-53, n. 3, for a complex of reasons, each with some justification, by a variety of historians of religion in America, notably Sydney E. Ahlstrom, Martin E. Marty, Lefferts A. Loetscher, William W. Sweet, and Richard Hofstadter. Vinson Synan (*The Holiness-Pentecostal Movement in the United States* [Grand Rapids: Wm. B. Eerdmans Publishing Co., 1971]) writes, sympathetically, that the Holiness schism constituted the religious counterpart of the political and economic revolt of the populists.

[11]The matter is discussed further, especially in the Appalachian context, by Bowdle, "Holiness in the Highlands," 244-45.

[12]For comment on the sustained debate on the doctrine of sanctification, see Bowdle, "Holiness in the Highlands," 254, n. 18.

concepts and thought of themselves as different from other Holiness believers only in the further experience they had graciously received.[13]

An informed Pentecostalism will understand, then, that its roots are Christian, Protestant, conservative-evangelical, and Holiness (both Wesleyan and Keswick) in nature, and it should respect and appreciate those roots. But it is incumbent upon Pentecostalism that it not permit any particularistic view of the work of the Holy Spirit to intrude upon that heritage so as to define it in any exclusive manner. Pentecostalism must reject with great intentionality any narcissism of personal experience that would suggest it is a "third force"[14]—alongside Roman Catholicism and Protestantism—and thus an alternative form of Christianity. Indeed, the Body of Christ need suffer no further fracturing![15]

III. Critiquing Pentecostal Pneumatology

It has been suggested, pejoratively, that Pentecostalism is an experience in search of a theology. The earliest Pentecostals did take their faith seriously, as commitment to the Scriptures as the very Word of God would evidence. Evangelism was given top priority, however, given limited means and an urgent message. Theological formulation was forthcoming, nevertheless, sometimes deliberately and at other times defensively, often in *ad hoc* fashion but always painfully slowly. Regrettably, evangelism and biblical and theological scholarship frequently were perceived as counterpoised.

Biblical and theological scholarship has developed belatedly and unevenly in Pentecostalism, covering the spectrum from suspicion to toleration to cultivation. Periods of passivity and "pockets" of resistance to

---

[13]For an incisive and convincing discussion of such tensions in Appalachia— prior even to Azusa Street—see Charles W. Conn, *Like a Mighty Army: A History of the Church of God, 1886-1995,* definitive ed. (Cleveland, TN: Pathway Press, 1996).

[14]"Third force" was first assigned to Pentecostalism by Henry P. Van Dusen in "Caribbean Holiday," *Christian Century* 72 (17 August, 1955): 946-48. But cf. Allen H. Anderson and Walter J. Hollenweger, eds., *Pentecostals After A Century: Global Perspectives on a Movement in Transition* (Sheffield: University of Sheffield Press, 1999).

[15]Note Conn's excellent statement: "There is but a hair's breadth between the current of conviction and the shoals of bigotry. Many a church has begun with the simple faith that its organization is divinely ordained, only to end behind walls of its own ecclesiolatry. An aggressively evangelistic church is in danger of such absorption with its own affairs that it loses its outside perspective and looks askance at all others than itself. Sometimes this is done to the point of doubting the sincerity, fitness, or divine acceptance of others" (*Like a Mighty Army,* 312).

formal scholarship may, no doubt, be attributed to long-standing antipathy to the academy, yet Pentecostals have sustained a predisposition toward more general and informal learning. The formal theological enterprise among Pentecostals, an urgent and belated ministry, must seek to transcend the inhibiting collage of perceptions and commitments that long have characterized the Pentecostal mind.

An informed Pentecostalism will, by all means, critique the whole of pneumatology. It will affirm the biblical and disavow any "feeling theology" born of an emotionalism that too long has complicated the Pentecostal venue. Such a critique will be sensitive and charitable, yet no less determined and impartial. No sterile exercise, an informed pentecostalism will enhance discipleship and Christian formation among ministry and laity alike because both will better discern the theological meaning of what they are doing and better relate the faith to the wider dimensions of life and mission in fresh, authentic, and relevant terms.

What comprises such an agenda? For those to whom an informed Pentecostalism really matters, I offer here five continuing concerns in the interests of any constructive dialogue that might be forthcoming. Let us visit them or revisit them, whichever may be the case, respectively, for the reader.

1. Baptism in the Holy Spirit has no salvific significance.

Regeneration by the Holy Spirit, a prior demonstration of God's grace, is the immediate and indispensable salvific act in the believer's life. This is abundantly attested in Scripture (see, e.g., John 3:3-7; Romans 8:9, 11; 1 Corinthians 12:13; Ephesians 2:1, 5; 1 Peter 1:23; 2 Peter 1:4). Regeneration admits of two dimensions: first, concurrent with justification, there is the impartation of new life to the soul (new birth) by the direct agency of the Holy Spirit, effecting immediately a filial relationship with the Father; secondly, there is the bearing of fruit appropriate to this new life because of the indwelling presence and sustaining work of that same Holy Spirit (see Galatians 5:22, 23).[16]

---

[16]All Christians are indwelt by the Holy Spirit, whether or not they have been baptized in the Holy Spirit, notwithstanding three passages which Pentecostals have often taken to the contrary: first, while Matthew 25:1-10 does use oil as emblematic of the Holy Spirit, the writer is referring to regeneration, not to Spirit baptism, as necessary to the rapture of the Church; secondly, the Greek text of John 14:17 may better be rendered "He is with you [παρ' ὑμῖν μένει] and he is in you [καὶ ἐν ὑμῖν ἐστίν]" than "He is with you [παρ' ὑμῖν μένει] and shall be in you [καὶ ἐν ὑμῖν ἔσται]," countering any teaching of mere presence of the Holy Spirit at regeneration but possession later at Spirit baptism; thirdly, the divine pledge in Jeremiah 31:31-33 of a future internal work of the Holy Spirit is prophetic of God's dealing with national Israel, not a denial that Old Testament saints had then experienced the Holy Spirit.

Baptism in the Holy Spirit relates not to salvation but to service. It is a post-salvation experience in the Holy Spirit (the doctrine of subsequence, John 7:37-39; Acts 19:2) available to every believer. While Old Testament saints were justified and regenerated[17]—not saved provisionally or "on credit"—because of the *eternal* sacrifice, in God's purview, of the *eternal* Christ according to the *eternal* plan (see Acts 2:23; Ephesians 1:4-6; Revelation 13:8), there is no experience in the Old Testament tantamount to a Spirit baptism as per the New Testament.

A divine endowment whereby to enhance the believer's personal witness for Christ, baptism in the Holy Spirit focuses on the mandate for mission in Matthew 28:18-20. It clarifies a point which cessationists apparently overlook, that is, if the Great Commission is still in force, then the power whereby to discharge it must still be current.

2. Spirit baptism and Spirit fulness are not coextensive.

A presumptuous Pentecostalism long has contended that "Spirit baptism" and "Spirit fulness" are synonymous, and that non-Pentecostals are but "nominal" Christians. It is true that on the Day of Pentecost, all believers in the Upper Room were "filled with the Holy Spirit" (Acts 2:4) at a point in time. But consider the injunction of Ephesians 5:18: ". . . Be filled with the Spirit." The Greek text here employs the present imperative verb πληροῦσθε, teaching a continual filling with the Spirit. The word "filled" is deliberately and instructively relative in nature, that is, How full is full? Does not regeneration render one Spirit-filled as much as Spirit baptism renders one Spirit-filled?

No experience of grace elevates one believer above another in the Body of Christ. Any notion to the contrary is divisive and evinces the spirit of the world. Nor is any one believer in possession of all the fulness of the Spirit. Fulness of the Spirit is that for which one strives in the devotional life, and it may be demonstrated in ways that do not correspond to estimations and expectations in Pentecostalism. We must beware the pathology of traditionalism!

3. A distracting glossocentrism has become the defining experience of Pentecostalism.

Tongues-speaking has long been regarded by Pentecostals as the consummatory spiritual experience. Unfortunately, a glossocentrism has come to characterize the movement and, to its detriment, to render it a spiritual imbalance that only the Holy Spirit can rectify. This is not an appeal for adherents to become *less* Pentecostal but *more* Pentecostal,

---

[17]This position maintains continuity between the Testaments, compatibility between law and grace, and continuum of salvation history. The inferior ethic sometimes demonstrated by Old Testament saints may be accounted for by the paucity of the sanctifying work of the Holy Spirit, as everywhere taught and expected in the New Testament.

that is, to revisit the Pentecostal model projected in the Scriptures and to adjust present perceptions and practices thereby.

According to the instruction of Jesus himself, baptism in the Holy Spirit is, in essence, the divine dynamic whereby to facilitate the believer's witness (Luke 24:45-49; Acts 1:8). It is urgent to note that while tongues were *evidence*, witness is *essence*. To confuse one with the other is to reduplicate the Pentecostal improprieties at Corinth, where the Apostle Paul cites tongues as the least of the gifts of grace. An informed Pentecostalism simply will not magnify what the Apostle abridged.

Glossocentrism, then, is counterproductive to the divine intention, distracting the Pentecostal fellowship from its larger responsibilities in Christian service. Really, the paramount criterion for Pentecostal activity is the presence of the Holy Spirit in renewing power in whatever circumstance requires it.[18]

4. A debilitating secularization of holiness has too much affected the current Pentecostal denominationalism.

A secularization of holiness has become the spiritual "Achilles' heel" of much of contemporary Pentecostalism. It represents a compromise with culture that may prove to be the ultimate liability to those who fail to discern it and lack the will to address it. This malady is manifested by all those who, substituting style for substance, measure effectiveness in kingdom work in terms of numbers, finances, buildings, and programs. Far from an appeal to "the good old days" when legalism prevailed, this is a call to a maturity in worship that denies the "glitz" of much media Pentecostalism, a responsibility in stewardship of resources that is indicative of social concern, and a commitment to creative evangelism.

Any "gospel" of health and wealth is in direct contradiction to the priorities of Jesus and the solicitations of Scripture. "Really no gospel at all," as the Apostle Paul would phrase it in another connection (Galatians 1:7), such a secularization of holiness has a debilitating and derogating effect upon all that the truly spiritual life commends. One cannot so believe and so act and, at the same time, cultivate the fruit of the Spirit in his/her life, a much-neglected teaching in Pentecostal circles.

An informed Pentecostalism will discern these inhibiting conventions and will sound the warning with both determination and discretion. It has no option.

---

[18]Some outside the Pentecostal tradition have encouraged us to broaden our reflection theologically on the glossolalia phenomenon. See, e.g., Richard Lovelace, "Baptism in the Holy Spirit and the Evangelical Tradition," in *Faces of Renewal*, ed. Paul Elbert (Peabody, MA: Hendrickson Publishers, 1988); and James H. Smylie, "Testing the Spirits in the American Context: Great Awakenings, Pentecostalism, and the Charismatic Movement," *Interpretation* 33 (January 1979): 32-46.

5. Pentecostal scholarship is often unnecessarily at variance with the wider community of theological enterprise.

Pentecostal scholars who labor in the academy are the *avant-garde* in the movement. They are informed, discriminating, and creative in their pursuit of matters incident to the ministry of the mind to which God has called them. Committed Pentecostals, they reflect academic odysseys that include a plethora of influences both within and without the (academic) community of faith.

The eclectic nature of their academic sojourneyings necessarily means that Pentecostal scholars have been enriched intellectually by the challenges and engagements from those outside the Pentecostal camp. In the virtually impossible task of assuring that they themselves do not reflect that same eclecticism in their own work, some seem to have tried, too conspicuously, to create for Pentecostal theology a distinctive and detached identity. In doing so, they may have depreciated the conservative-evangelical tradition that planted the very seed and tended the very soil in which Pentecostalism germinated.

But is there really any distinctive and detached Pentecostal theology? Apart from commitment to baptism in the Holy Spirit and the spiritual pursuits issuing from that experience, is there a need to reexamine every component of the historic Christian faith and to judge it—even to reconstruct it—according to the canons of a "Pentecostal hermeneutic"?

Scholarship is best conducted in community with, never in isolation from, other heads and hearts. The Body of Christ has, as it were, a corporate mind that none dare disregard or derogate. Only when so conducted can theology be that "most thankful and *happy* science" that Karl Barth has commended to us.[19] The informed Pentecostal knows this.

Appropriate Postscript

My colleagues, each of whom I respect immensely, have honored me by their contributions to this *Festschrift*. I am deeply indebted to Drs. Terry Cross and Emerson Powery for executing this substantial project with efficiency and style, notwithstanding the myriad demands on their own time and energies in an exciting university context where it is a joy to minister.

I would request the reader to judge my particular essay in the same spirit that Aurelius Augustine anticipated for his own work a millennium

---

[19]Karl Barth, *Evangelical Theology: An Introduction*, trans. Grover Foley (New York: Holt, Rinehart and Winston, 1963), 12. Jürgen Moltmann and Miroslav Volf also have committed conspicuously to theology constructed in community.

and a half ago: "... Those who think I have said too much, and those who think I have said too little, I ask to forgive me."[20]

---

[20]Quoted in the preface to *The Education of a Christian Prince by Desiderius Erasmus*, trans. and notated by Lester K. Born (New York: W. W. Norton & Company, Inc., 1936), vii.

I. Biblical Studies

Where Are the Descendants of Abraham?: Finding the Source of a Missing Link in Genesis

Lee R. Martin[*]

Introduction

Genesis records the creative activity of God. Through his Word, God creates the universe: "Let there be light," and light came into being. Through his Word, he creates the first human: "Let us make *adam*," and *adam* is created. Through his Word, he creates for himself a people, the people of Israel: "I will make you a great nation," God says to Abram, and in the face of impossibility he makes that Word a reality. The creative Word of God is especially evident in chapters one and twelve of Genesis, which give an account of the "two crucial beginnings for the Bible."[1]

As Genesis chronicles this creative activity of God from the beginning of the universe through the end of the life of Joseph, the narrative is both unified[2] and carried forward by the repetition of the phrase "These are the descendants of. . . ." This phrase is widely known as the *Toledot* Formula, since the Hebrew word translated "descendants of" is תּוֹלְדוֹת (*toledot*).

---

[*]Lee R. Martin (Doctoral Candidate in Old Testament, University of South Africa). Instructor of Hebrew and Old Testament, Church of God Theological Seminary.

[1]Walter Brueggemann, "Genesis," in *The Books of the Bible*, vol. 1, ed. Bernhard W. Anderson (New York: Charles Scribner's Sons, 1989), 21. Brueggemann adds that both Israel and the world "exist only because God speaks" (22).

[2]Brevard Childs, *Introduction to the Old Testament as Scripture* (Philadelphia: Fortress Press, 1979). Childs says the *Toledot* Formula functions to "structure the book of Genesis into a unified composition and to make clear the nature of the unity which is intended," 146.

This *Toledot* Formula occurs ten times in Genesis:[3]

2:4	These are the descendants of Heaven and Earth.
5:1	These are the descendants of Adam.
6:9	These are the descendants of Noah.
10:1	These are the descendants of Noah's Sons.
11:10	These are the descendants of Shem.
11:27	These are the descendants of Terah.
25:12	These are the descendants of Ishmael.
25:19	These are the descendants of Isaac.
36:1	These are the descendants of Esau.
37:2	These are the descendants of Jacob.

The *Toledot* Formula appears to be a literary device that signals the beginning of each new section within the book of Genesis. While scholars recognize the presence of this literary device, they have not been able to come to an agreement regarding its specific meaning, its literary function, its relative importance, or its theological implications. Although some commentators have chosen to make the *Toledot* Formula the basis for their outline of Genesis,[4] others downplay its importance as a primary structural marker. These commentators choose to organize the book according to preexistent sources, individual narratives, or prominent characters.[5]

---

[3]The phrase actually occurs eleven times, but the descendants of Esau seem to be listed in the fashion of a *Part A* and *Part B* (Gen 36:1, 9). Therefore, this study will assume that ten sections use the *Toledot* Formula, as is common among commentators. An exception is Kenneth A. Mathews, who insists on making two separate sections from the Esau genealogies. See his *Genesis 1-11:26*, The New American Commentary (n.p.: Broadman & Holman Publishers, 1996), 27-28. In any case, the questions regarding Esau's genealogy have little or no bearing on this study.

[4]E.g., Mathews, *Genesis,* 31; Gordon J. Wenham, *Genesis 1-15*, Word Biblical Commentary (Waco, TX: Word Books, 1987), xxii; and C. F. Keil and F. Delitzsch, *The Pentateuch*, vol. 1 of Biblical Commentary on the Old Testament, trans. James Martin (Grand Rapids: Wm. B. Eerdmans, n.d.), 5-6.

[5]See, e.g., Walter Brueggemann (*Genesis*, Interpretation: A Bible Commentary for Teaching and Preaching [Atlanta: John Knox, 1982], viii-ix) who outlines Genesis in four parts: 1) The "Pre-History;" 2) Abraham Narrative; 3) Jacob Narrative; and 4) Joseph Narrative. See also Gerhard von Rad (*Genesis*, in Old Testament Library, ed. Peter R. Ackroyd, James Barr, and John Bright, [Philadelphia: Westminster, 1972], 5-6); and Hermann Gunkel (*Genesis* [Macon, GA: Mercer University Press, 1997], trans. Gunkel, et al. from the 3rd edition, [Göttingen: Vandenhoeck & Ruprecht, 1910; 1st edition, 1901], [1]-[2]) who divide the book into individual narratives, based on Source, Form, and Tradition Criticism. Gunkel makes 74 such divisions. Surprisingly, John Sailhamer, who is usually attentive to details of literary structure, gives virtually no attention to the *Toledot* Formula. See his "Genesis," in *The Expositor's Bible Commentary* (Grand

This study will be organized around several interrelated questions: 1) Does the term תּוֹלְדוֹת have the same meaning throughout the book of Genesis?; 2) Is it possible that 2:4a ("These are the descendants of heaven and earth") is a conclusion to the creation story of chapter one rather than a heading for chapter two?; 3) If the *Toledot* Formula functions as a heading for each new section in Genesis, why does chapter one not begin with this heading?; 4) What is the function of the *Toledot* Formula within the canonical shape of the book of Genesis?; and 5) Where are the descendants of Abraham? The listing above shows that the *Toledot* Formula occurs for every major person in Genesis, except for Abraham. Abraham's *Toledot* Formula is a missing link in Genesis.

This essay intends to show that the *Toledot* Formula traces an unbroken line of descendants through which the will of God is enacted. The *Toledot* Formula introduces every major section in Genesis except for those beginning at chapter one and chapter twelve. There is no *Toledot* Formula at these places because they each represent the creative Word of God. Gen 12 is a new creation parallel to Gen 1. In Gen 1, God creates the world for himself; and in Gen 12, he creates his people, Israel.[6] Thus, the literary structure of Genesis shows that God is the source of this missing link at Gen 12.

I. The Meaning of the Hebrew Word תּוֹלְדוֹת

The *Toledot* Formula introduces a genealogy in 5:1; 10:1; 11:10; 25:12 and 36:1 (cf. also Num 3:1 and Ruth 4:18). In these places it clearly means "These are the descendants of." On the other hand, it seems to introduce a narrative in 2:4; 6:9; 11:27; 25:19; and 37:2. In these places, the translation "descendants" does not seem fitting. Therefore, English versions differ in their treatment of the phrase. The King James Version is consistent in translating the word תּוֹלְדוֹת as "generations," causing some confusion, because דּוֹר is the usual word for "generation" and is found seven times in Genesis. The New Revised Standard Version translates תּוֹלְדוֹת as "descendants" except for 2:4 ("generations") and 37:2 ("story of the family"). The New International Version consistently translates the *Toledot* Formula, "This is the account of."

Apparently, there is no clear English equivalent to the Hebrew תּוֹלְדוֹת, a word that means "that which is birthed, descendants, progeny." It is derived from the verb ילד, which means "to give birth, to beget." Other

Rapids: Zondervan, 1990).
[6]Brueggemann, *Genesis*, 22. It is somewhat surprising that although Brueggemann argues for the creative act of God in Gen 12, he does not develop the comparison with ch. 1, and he does not make a connection to the *Toledot* Formula.

words derived from יָלַד are יֶלֶד ("child"), יַלְדוּת ("childhood"), יָלִיד ("born"),
and מוֹלֶדֶת ("relatives").[7] The verb יָלַד can mean "bring forth," referring
figuratively to events or happenings rather than to people (for example,
Prov 27:1, ". . . you do not know what a day may bring forth;" and Job
15:35, "They conceive mischief and bring forth evil"). Figuratively, then,
the noun תּוֹלֵדוֹת can also refer to events as well as to people. Thus תּוֹלֵדוֹת
always means "that which is brought forth" or "that which proceeds from,"
in the sense of descendants (genealogy) or in the sense of important
events or event-sequences (narratives). However, even the five *Toledot*
Formulas that introduce narrative material contain genealogies in some
form within the narrative.[8] Therefore, it is not necessary to posit different
meanings for the *Toledot* Formula. It always means "that which is birthed"
(either literally or figuratively).[9] The *Toledot* Formula, then, may be translated, "These are the descendants of" (NRSV) or "These are the generations of" (KJV). The translation, "This is the account of" (NIV), may be
acceptable, as long as "account" does not imply "origin."

II. The Descendants of Heaven and Earth

The most problematic occurrence of the *Toledot* Formula is found in
Genesis 2:4. The verse reads, "These are the descendants of heaven and
earth when they were created, in the day that Yahweh God made the earth
and heaven." Based on Source Criticism, some scholars believe that 2:4a
serves as the conclusion of the preceding creation story, rather than the
superscription for what follows. As such, it would be translated, "This

---

[7]See Harris, Archer, & Waltke, *Theological Wordbook of the Old Testament*,
(Chicago: Moody Press, 1980), 1:378-80; and Abraham Even-Shoshan, "תּוֹלֵדוֹת,"
in *A New Concordance of the Bible* (Jerusalem: Kiryat Sepher, 1989), 1223.

[8]Adam, Eve, plants, and animals are brought forth in chapter 2; Noah's sons are
named in 6:10; Terah's sons are named in 11:27; Esau and Jacob are born in chapter
25; and Jacob's descendants are listed in chapter 46.

[9]Cf. Harris, *Theological Wordbook*, 1:380; Childs, *Scripture*, 145; Umberto
Cassuto, *A Commentary on the Book of Genesis*, 2 vols., trans. Israel Abrahams
(Jerusalem: Magnes Press, 1964), 1:97; Victor P. Hamilton, *Genesis Chapters 1-
17*, The New International Commentary on the Old Testament (Grand Rapids:
William B. Eerdmans, 1990), 4; John Skinner, *A Critical and Exegetical Commen-
tary on Genesis,* vol. 1, The International Critical Commentary, ed. S. R. Driver,
A. Plummer, and C. A. Briggs (Edinburgh: T. & T. Clark, 1910), 4-5; and M. H.
Woudstra, "The *Toledot* of the Book of Genesis and Their Redemptive-Historical
Significance," *Calvin Theological Journal* 5 (1970): 187. Contra William L. Holladay,
"תּוֹלֵדוֹה," in *A Concise Hebrew and Aramaic Lexicon of the Old Testament* (Leiden:
Netherlands: E. J. Brill, 1971; reprint, Grand Rapids: Eerdmans, 1976), 387, who
incorrectly allows for the meaning "origin" for Gen 2:4. The Hebrew word יַחַשׂ
means "genealogical list" (see Neh 7:5).

was the origin of Heaven and Earth."[10] Source critics conclude that the *Toledot* Formula is a device of P, as is the creation narrative of chapter one. The creation account of chapter 2, however, is from J.[11] Therefore, 2:4a is the conclusion of P's creation narrative and forms an *inclusio* with 1:1.[12] Gunkel, while accepting the conclusions regarding P and J, insists that the *Toledot* Formula is always a superscription. Thus, he claims that 2:4a must have been displaced and should come before Gen 1:1 as an introduction to P's account of creation.[13]

Several factors indicate that 2:4 should not be divided and relocated, but that it should remain intact and function as the superscription for the subsequent narrative of Adam and Eve. First, Gen 2:4 contains a chiasm, and must be held together as a unit.[14]

The chiasm is: a   heaven
                  b   earth
                  c   created
                  c'   made
                  b'   earth
                  a' heaven

Second, the *Toledot* Formula should be allowed to serve its usual function as a superscription,[15] in which the Hebrew תּוֹלְדוֹת means

---

[10]von Rad, *Genesis,* 63. Evidently, von Rad ignores the fact that although the Hebrew תּוֹלְדוֹת is found 39 times in the OT, it never means "origin." See Keil, *Pentateuch,* 71.

[11]Cf. Skinner, *Genesis,* 40-41; and von Rad, *Genesis,* 63.

[12]Clyde T. Francisco, "Genesis," in *The Broadman Bible Commentary* (Nashville: Broadman Press, 1969), 101; cf. Sailhamer, 10.

[13]See Gunkel (*Genesis,* 103), where he extracts 2:4a and discusses it before 1:1. Cf. Claus Westermann, *Genesis 1-11: A Commentary,* trans. J. Scullion (Minneapolis: Augsburg, 1986), 8.

[14]Cf. Nahum Sarna, *Genesis,* in *Jewish Publication Society Torah Commentary,* (New York: Jewish Publication Society, 1989), 17; Alviero Niccacci, *The Syntax of the Verb in Classical Hebrew Prose,* trans. W. G. E. Watson, JSOTSuppl 86 (Sheffield: JSOT Press, 1990), 200, n26; Wenham, *Genesis,* 46; and Mathews, *Genesis,* 35.

[15] Cf. W. Gunther Plaut, *Genesis* (New York: Union of the American Hebrew Congregations, 1974), 19; Derek Kidner, *Genesis: an Introduction and Commentary,* Tyndale Old Testament Commentaries, gen. ed. D. J. Wiseman (Downers Grove, IL: InterVarsity, 1967), 59; Wenham, *Genesis,* xxi; Childs, *Scripture,* 145; Woudstra, *"Toledot,"* 187-88; Keil, *Pentateuch,* 70-71; Cassuto, *Genesis,* 97; and Skinner, *Genesis,* 71. See Hamilton, *Genesis,* 2-10; and Mathews, *Genesis,* 26-41, for very detailed and helpful critiques of the various approaches to the structure of Genesis, including the view of P. J. Wiseman (*New Discoveries in Babylonia About Genesis* [London: Marshall, 1936]), that the *Toledot* Formulas are colophons. Wiseman's approach is improved by Dale S. DeWitt ("The Generations of Genesis," *Evangelical Quarterly* 48 [Oct-Dec 1976]: 196-211); but it still seems forced and unbelievable.

"descendants, progeny" or "that which is brought forth."[16] Third, the
Hebrew Masorah indicates that 2:4 begins the second of 45 *sidarim* (major
divisions) within the book of Genesis.[17] Fourth, in spite of a long and
complex history of tradition, the final form of the text must be given high
priority. Wenham maintains that "source-critical considerations cannot
override redactional indicators."[18] Serious attention must be given to the
canonical form of the text.[19]

Genesis 2:4, therefore, introduces the subsequent narrative, in which
Adam, Eve, plants, and animals are brought forth from the dust of the
earth. After the creation of Heaven and Earth in chapter one, that creation
serves as "patriarchal ancestor,"[20] producing humans, plants, and animals. The concept of heaven and earth bringing forth progeny is either
stated or alluded to in other OT passages, for example, "Drop down, ye
heavens, from above, and let the skies pour down righteousness: let the
earth open, and let them bring forth salvation, and let righteousness spring
up together" (Isa 45:8); and "I will betroth you to me in faithfulness; and
you shall know the LORD. And in that day, says the LORD, I will answer
the heavens and they shall answer the earth; and the earth shall answer
the grain, the wine, and the oil, and they shall answer Jezreel" (Hos 2:20-
22); and "Thus says God the LORD, Who created the heavens and stretched
them out, Who spread out the earth and its offspring" (Isa 42:5, NASB).

The *Toledot* Formula links together the creation account of chapter
one with the different creation account of chapter two and indicates that
the two accounts have different purposes. By way of analogy, Gen 1 is to
Gen 2 as a father is to his children.[21] Chapter one is the origin of the

---

[16]According to Rabbinic tradition (*b. Yoma* 54b), Rabbi Eliezer the Great translates *toledot* of Gen 2:4 as "offspring," not "origin."
[17]See Page H. Kelley, Daniel S. Mynatt, and Timothy G. Crawford, *The Masorah
of* Biblia Hebraica Stuttgartensia (Grand Rapids: William B. Eerdmans Publishing
Co., 1998), 155, for an explanation of the *sidarim*.
[18]Wenham, *Genesis,* 256.
[19]Childs, *Scripture,* 142-45. Cf. Brueggemann, *Genesis,* 107; and Robert Cohn,
"Narrative Structure and Canonical Perspective in Genesis, *Journal for the Study
of the Old Testament* 25 (1983): 3.
[20]Josef Schreiner, "יָלַד" in *Theological Dictionary of the Old Testament,* ed. G.
Johannes Botterweck and Helmer Ringgren, vol. 6, trans. David E. Green (Grand
Rapids: William B. Eerdmans Publishing Co., 1964), 80. See also Childs, *Scripture,* 149-50, who uses similar terminology. It is interesting that in Greek mythol-
ogy, Uranos (Heaven) and Gaea (Earth) give birth to the twelve Titans. An
objection has been registered that there are no descendants of Heaven listed, but cf.
Num 3:1, where Moses and Aaron are named in the heading, but only Aaron's
descendants are listed.
[21]Childs, *Scripture,* 150. Childs points out that his interpretation of the *Toledot*
Formula explains the juxtaposition of the two creation accounts. The accounts are
not parallel, but are assigned different tasks.

creation, and chapter two is the natural development of that creation. The repetition of humanity's creation/formation (1:27 and 2:7) presents no problem, because a similar kind of repetition is found in other sections of Genesis. The sections seem to overlap in time. Humanity is created in 1:27 and 2:7; Seth is born in 4:25 and 5:3; Noah's sons are named in 5:32 and 6:10; Canaan is mentioned in 9:18 and 10:6; Arphaxad is listed in 10:22 and 11:10; Abram is born in 11:26 and 11:27; Isaac is born in 21:3 and 25:19; and the 12 sons of Jacob are listed in 35:23-26 and 46:8-25.

The book of Genesis cannot begin with the *Toledot* Formula, because the creation is not a "theogony or divine cosmogony that views creation as an act of begetting and birth."[22] God creates by his Word.[23] He "calls into being that which does not exist" (Rom 4:17 NASB). Genesis 1 affirms that "the world was created by the word of God" (Heb 11:3 RSV).

III. The Function of the *Toledot* Formula

Throughout Genesis, the *Toledot* Formula is a heading for the account that follows. These headings function "to trace an unbroken line of descendants from Adam to Jacob, and at the same time to provide a framework in which to incorporate the narrative traditions of the patriarchs."[24] The *Toledot* Formula acts as a link, or a hinge,[25] holding together each overlapping section within the book.

Although the sections of Genesis overlap chronologically, each new *Toledot* Formula occurs according to a recognizable pattern. A new section begins only when the story of the previous father has come to a close (usually he has died).[26] In 2:1 God stops creating and rests, and 2:4 begins the descendants of creation (Adam). The story of Adam ends in 4:25,[27] and the following genealogy leads to Noah's father, Lamech, who dies in 5:32. Noah's descendants are the subject of the next section, and Noah dies in 9:29. The descendants of Noah's sons are given next, and each son is followed genealogically past his time of death. Shem's progeny are the subject of the next section, which is a linear genealogy that leads far past Shem's lifetime. The section beginning at 11:27 details the descendants of

---

[22]Schreiner, "יֶלֶד," 80.

[23]See Brueggemann, *Genesis*, 18. His commentary on Genesis is a powerful and moving exposition of Genesis from the perspective of the call/speech of God.

[24]Childs, *Scripture,* 146.

[25]Mathews, *Genesis,* 33.

[26]The death itself may not be mentioned, but in every case the chronology will show that the person has died.

[27]5:1-5 jumps backward in time to restate Adam's creation and the birth of Seth. Although Adam's death is recounted in 5:5, the ending of chap. 4 with Seth demonstrates that the time of Adam's significance is past.

Terah, who dies at 11:32.[28] In 25:8, Abraham dies, and the *Toledot* Formula for Ishmael follows immediately. Ishmael dies in 25:17, just before the beginning of the section for Isaac's descendants in 25:19. In 35:29 Isaac dies, and the Esau section begins at 36:1. Esau's genealogy is followed to its end (36:43), just before Jacob's section begins in 37:2. Jacob lives until near the end of Genesis and dies after he has blessed his children (49:33). There are no further *toledot* sections, because Genesis comes to a close.

As the book of Genesis traces the line of the chosen family, each *Toledot* Formula progressively narrows the focus of the story.[29] Heaven and Earth produce humanity, plants, and animals; but only humanity continues as part of the story of Genesis. From humanity comes the genealogy of Adam, but the focus is narrowed to Noah. Noah's sons are Shem, Ham, and Japheth, but only Shem's line will continue the story.[30] From Shem's line, Terah is the chosen one; and of Terah's three sons, only Abraham receives the call of God (But where is the *toledot* heading for Abraham?). Abraham has two sons, but the promise is carried over only to Isaac.[31] Of Isaac's two sons, Jacob is recipient of the inheritance. At this point the narrowing ends, and all of Jacob's descendants are part of the continuing story. The genealogy has reached the point where all of the subsequent descendants are recipients of God's promise. Thus, in every section but Jacob's, the most important descendants are listed, and one descendant is singled out to continue the story of Genesis.

IV. The Descendants of Abraham?

The listing above shows that the *Toledot* Formula occurs for every major person in Genesis, except for Abraham. Every indicator suggests

---

[28]A section chronicling the descendants of Abraham is expected here, but there is a gap from 11:31 to 25:12 before the next *Toledot* Formula is found. Abraham is the only patriarch without a *toledot* section.

[29]Wenham, *Genesis*, xxi; cf. Childs, *Scripture*, 153; Woudstra, *"Toledot,"* 187; and Claus Westermann, *Handbook to the Old Testament*, trans. and ed. Robert Boyd (Minneapolis, MN: Augsburg Publishing House, 1967), 24. For a discussion of the theological implications of the genealogies themselves, see Robert B. Robinson, "Literary Functions of the Genealogies of Genesis" *Catholic Biblical Quarterly* 48 (October 1986): 595-608; David J. A. Clines, *The Themes of the Pentateuch*, JSOTSuppl 10 (Sheffield: JSOT Press, 1978): 66-68; Childs, 152-53; and Brueggemann, "Genesis," 52.

[30]The descendants of Ham and Japheth are listed as a side branch whose lines come to a conclusion in the table of nations. The story of Genesis continues with the line of Shem.

[31]The descendants of both Ishmael and Esau are listed as side branches, whose lines come to a conclusion outside the perimeter of the promise. After their genealogy is given, the story moves on without them.

that Gen 12:1 should have a heading that reads, "These are the descendants of Abram." So, why is Abraham's *Toledot* Formula missing?

Skinner and others argue that the main character of a section is not necessarily the person who is mentioned in the *Toledot* Formula.[32] For example, in the section headed with Isaac's name, Jacob is the main character; and in the section named after Jacob, Joseph is the main character. So, in the Terah section, Abraham is expected to be the main character. This observation, however, does not explain the absence of Abraham's *Toledot* Formula, because every other patriarch does have a *Toledot* Formula, even though he may not be the primary character in the section headed by his own name. Furthermore, the pattern is not consistent, because Noah is the main character in the section named after him.

Woudstra declares that there is no *Toledot* Formula for Abraham because the author of Genesis is only concerned "to show where ways begin to part," for example, Terah, Ishmael, Isaac, Esau, and Jacob.[33] It is very difficult, however, to imagine a parting of the ways that could be more extreme than Gen 12. In fact, according to Brueggemann, the break between 11:32 and 12:1 is a "major break" and may be the "most important structural break in the Old Testament."[34] Clines declares that the Abraham material "clearly" begins a new section.[35] The following evidence indicates that 12:1 should begin a new section: 1) The literary pattern is parallel to the beginnings of the other sections of Genesis. The Terah section should end after 11:32, which records his death. The next *Toledot* Formula comes an unprecedented fourteen chapters later. In 11:27, Abram is born; in 11:32, Terah dies; and in 12:1, the reader would expect the text to say, "These are the descendants of Abram;" 2) The grammar of 12:1 points to a new beginning. The Hebrew text begins with a resumptive *wayyiqtol*: "The LORD had said to Abram. . . ."[36] This speech to Abram occurs sixty years before the death of Terah in the previous verse. This backward movement in 12:1 would suggest to the reader a break in the narrative, because, without exception, each section of Genesis overlaps the previous section. Each new *Toledot* Formula moves backward chronologically,

---

[32]Skinner, *Genesis,* 40. See also Mathews, *Genesis,* 38; Hamilton, *Genesis,* 9-10.

[33]Woudstra, *"Toledot,"* 188.

[34]Brueggemann, *Genesis,* 116.

[35]Clines, *Pentateuch,* 77

[36]This verb form, sometimes called "vav-consecutive," is not chronologically consecutive in this verse. This usage of the *wayyiqtol* is called the pluperfect by Bruce K. Waltke and Michael O'Connor, *An Introduction to Biblical Hebrew Syntax* (Winona Lake, IN: Eisenbrauns, 1990), 552-53. See Paul Joüon, *A Grammar of Biblical Hebrew,* 2 vols., trans. and rev. T. Muraoka (Rome: Pontifical Biblical Institute, 1991), 2:390, who shows that *wayyiqtol* can begin a new narrative. Cf. Niccacci, *Syntax,* 47.

resuming the story at a time previous to the end of the preceding section; 3) Jewish tradition includes a break between 11:32 and 12:1. The Hebrew Masorah indicates that Gen 12:1 is the beginning of the tenth of the *sidarim* for Genesis;[37] and 4) The "character of the material in chaps. 1-11 is markedly different from that in chaps. 12 onward."[38] Chapters 1-11 have a universal perspective, while chapters 12-50 focus only on Israel. Chapters 1-11 tell the story of all nations, but chapters 12-50 relate the story of one nation.[39] Robert L. Cohn proposes that the Abraham narratives are different from the primeval stories in several ways. He argues that in the Abraham narratives God rewards rather than punishes, that the narrator is no longer omniscient, that conflict is between persons rather than between God and humans, and that ethical decisions are no longer in black and white.[40] There is also a "clear-cut division between chs. 11 and 12,"[41] in that chapters 1-11 tell of people who have land but are losing it, and chapters 12-50 tell of people who have no land, but are moving toward it in anticipation.[42] This difference is illustrated by the use of the Hebrew word אֶרֶץ (land). In chapters 1-11, אֶרֶץ usually refers to the whole earth, but in chapters 12-50 it refers to the land of Canaan. Another word (אֲדָמָה) begins to be used in 12:3 to refer to the earth. Furthermore, the break that comes with Abram is so great, that God is no longer called "God" but is called "the God of Abraham."[43]

V. The Source of the Missing Link in Genesis

If the call of Abram presents a major break in the Genesis story, and literary indicators suggest that a new *Toledot* Formula is called for at 12:1, then why is it missing? There is no *Toledot* Formula at Gen 12:1 because it is parallel to Gen 1:1. Both chapter one and chapter twelve represent the creative Word of God. In Gen 1, God creates the world for himself; and in Gen 12, he "wants to create a people—Israel—for himself."[44] When discussing the structure of chapters 1-11, Brueggemann says, "If the point were pressed to complete the symmetry, we should juxtapose 12:1-4 as the

---

[37]See note 17.

[38]Wenham, *Genesis,* xxii. Cf. Westermann, *Handbook,* 29. Westermann divides Genesis at chapter 12.

[39]Cf. Brueggemann, "Genesis," 21, 35.

[40]Cohn, "Narrative," 6-8.

[41]Hamilton, *Genesis,* 11.

[42]Walter Brueggemann, *The Land: Place as a Gift, Promise, and Challenge in the Biblical Faith* (Philadelphia: Fortress Press, 1977), 15.

[43]E.g., Gen 26:24, along with eleven other places.

[44]Gunkel, *Genesis,* 163.

counterpart of chapter 1."[45] The barren state of Abram and Sarai is parallel to the dark, formless void of Gen 1:2. This major break in Genesis has its source in God, not in Abram. Abram and Sarai do not choose to be childless. They do not choose to run out of options. They do not choose darkness and barrenness; but out of the darkness, God speaks light; and out of barrenness, God speaks life. "The one who calls the worlds into being now makes a second call."[46] He calls to Abram: "I will make you . . .," reminiscent of "Let us make . . ." (1:26). He gives the land to Abram, just as he gives it to Adam (1:28). He blesses Abram, just as he blesses Adam (1:28). These similarities suggest to the reader that chapter 12 is a new creation, parallel to Gen 1. The missing *Toledot* Formula causes a "shift in expectancy"[47] that serves to heighten the impact of Gen 12.

Where are the descendants of Abraham? They are the people that God creates by his Word. The creation theme is prominent in the OT,[48] for example, when God declares himself to be the creator of Israel: "thus saith the LORD that created thee" (Isa 43:1). Malachi agrees that God is creator of his people: "Have we not all one father? [Abraham?] hath not one God created us?" (Mal 2:10). The theme of God as creator of his people is appropriated in NT texts. Paul declares, "We are his workmanship, created in Christ Jesus unto good works" (Eph 2:10). The creation motif may also suggest that the descendants of Abraham are not born by natural means; they are born "not of blood, nor of the will of the flesh, nor of the will of man, but of God" (John 1:13). The descendants of Abraham are created to be a great nation (Gen 12:2), a nation, "Which in time past *were* not a people, but *are* now the people of God" (1 Pet 2:10).

Where are the descendants of Abraham? They are not limited to Ishmael and Isaac, but they include all of Israel through all time. Even though Isaac is Jacob's natural father, God declares to Jacob, " I *am* the LORD God of Abraham thy father, and the God of Isaac" (Gen 28:13). To Joshua, God says, "I took your father Abraham from the other side of the flood, and led him throughout all the land of Canaan" (Josh 24:3). Isaiah invites all of Israel, "Look unto Abraham your father, and unto Sarah *that* bare you: for I called him alone, and blessed him, and increased him" (Isa 51:2). Mary, the mother of Jesus, rejoices when she remembers "The oath which he sware to our father Abraham" (Luke 1:73). Jesus proclaims, "Your father

---

[45]Brueggemann, *Genesis*, 22. Brueggeman, however, does not press the point and does not observe the parallels that are mentioned in this essay.
[46]Brueggemann, *Genesis*, 105.
[47]Cf. Eugene A. Nida, J. P. Louw, A. H. Snyman, and J. v. W. Cronje, *Style and Discourse* (Cape Town: Bible Society, 1983), 36-37.
[48]See Brueggemann, "Genesis," 40-42, where he describes the important role of the Abraham traditions on later texts, both OT and NT.

Abraham rejoiced to see my day" (John 8:56); and Stephen preaches, "The God of glory appeared unto our father Abraham" (Acts 7:2).

Where are the descendants of Abraham? They are everywhere; they are innumerable. Throughout the book of Genesis, the *Toledot* Formula identifies the person or persons who will fulfill God's purposes and inherit God's promises. It is impossible, however, to list Abraham's descendants, because God promised, "I will multiply thy seed as the stars of the heaven, and as the sand which is upon the sea shore" (22:17). The Genesis writer can name Adam's descendants; he can name Noah's descendants; he can name Shem's descendants, as well as those of Terah, Ishmael, Isaac, Esau, and Jacob. Yet he cannot begin to name the descendents of Abraham. Abraham is the Father of the faithful. The tradition of Abraham as father is used explicitly in the NT by Paul, who Christianizes the tradition. He declares that Abraham is the "father of us all" (Rom 4:16), and that, "they which are of faith, the same are the children of Abraham" (Gal 3:7).[49]

Where are the descendants of Abraham? They are found wherever anyone relinquishes the safety of country, relatives, and home. When the reader of Genesis reaches 12:1, he/she expects to read, "These are the descendants of" (*toledot*) but finds instead, "Leave your people" (*moledet*, a word meaning "relatives" that comes from the same root as *toledot*). This may be a play on words, where *moledet* alludes to the expected *toledot*. Abram is called to leave his country, his relatives, and his family. His faithful obedience is extolled in the NT by the writer of Hebrews, who writes that Abraham "obeyed, and he went out, not knowing whither he went" (Heb 11:8). Abraham's abandonment may also be echoed in the Gospel of Luke, where Jesus says, "Whosoever he be of you that forsaketh not all that he hath, he cannot be my disciple" (Luke 14:33). God calls Abram to abandon his life and walk toward death, for "expulsion is like death."[50] The descendants of Abraham display the same abandonment, because "Whosoever shall seek to save his life shall lose it; and whosoever shall lose his life shall preserve it" (Luke 17:33).

Where are the descendants of Abraham? The story of Abraham's descendants will never end, because the descendants of Abraham are those who, like Abraham, respond to the call of God with faith and obedience, those who are thus generated not by natural descent but by the Word of God, those who forsake all to follow him, those who "seek for a city which hath foundations, whose builder and maker is God" (Heb 11:10).

---

[49]It was Gal 3:7 that led to the conception of this study.
[50]Gunkel, 163.

Raw Prayer and Refined Theology: "You Have Not Spoken Straight to Me, As My Servant Job Has"

Rickie D. Moore[*]

Introduction

This opportunity to honor my former teacher, Donald N. Bowdle, is indeed an honor for me. Twenty-five years ago I sat as one of his students in a course on Old Testament wisdom literature. There he opened our minds to an appreciation of the ancient wisdom tradition by using the resources of its primary modern counterpart, academic scholarship. Yet Donald Bowdle utilized more than scholarship, even as he aimed for more than just our minds. He modeled for us a blending of scholarship and spirituality, indeed of mind and Spirit. In his own way, he strove to keep the two together against the powerful forces that ever tend to drive the two apart. And so he informed *and inspired* many of us along this same course.

For me, this life-long course included pursuing (at his particular encouragement) advanced study in the Old Testament, to include its wisdom literature. In this endeavor I had to face for myself those powerful forces that threaten to divorce spirituality from scholarship, criticism from confession, piety from theology, wisdom from prayer, talking *about* God from talking *to* God. I found these divisive propensities at work not only around me, but even *within* me. But more than that, I came to find these clashing forces not just in my own contemporary context but also in the ancient

[*]Rickie D. Moore (Ph.D., Vanderbilt University). Professor of Old Testament Studies, Church of God Theological Seminary.

biblical text, particularly in Old Testament wisdom literature,[1] and especially in the book of Job.[2] What I have found there has been extremely
helpful to me in coming to my own integration of scholarship and spirituality, of mind and Spirit. I offer a small but representative example of my
discoveries here as a tribute to my former teacher in the hope of contributing in some small way to the pursuit of inspired wisdom, such as Donald
Bowdle has encouraged in so many of us.

I. Translating Job 42:7

This essay focuses on a single verse at the end of the book of Job.
Similar to most English translations, the *New International Version* renders it:

> After the LORD had said these things to Job, he said to
> Eliphaz the Temanite, "I am angry with you and your two
> friends, because you have not spoken of me what is right, as
> my servant Job has" (42:7).

Obviously, this verse is crucial to the meaning of the book of Job, because
it registers the crux of God's judgment on the entire proceedings between
Job and his friends—an exchange covering most of the book, more than
three dozen chapters. Even though God confronts Job before this verse
with a lengthy discourse (chs. 38-41), which reduces Job to humble confession and contrition (42:1-6), the bottom line of God's judgment is this
succinct verdict in 42:7 that draws a sharp contrast between Job and his
friends on the matter of what they had not, but Job had, done.[3]
    The friends receive condemnation; Job receives commendation. But
what exactly had Job done that his friends had not done? Clearly it has to
do with speaking. The second-person plural perfect of the common verb
דבר ("to speak") has left no doubt about this. The only fuss for most
translators and commentators has been over how to read the term, נכונה
("what is right"), which comes after the immediately following prepositional phrase, אלי ("of me"). The term נכונה belongs to the root כון, which
has to do with being firm, established, right, upright, straight.[4] The root

―――――――――

[1]R. D. Moore, "A Home for the Alien: Worldly Wisdom and Covenantal
Confession in Proverbs 30:1-9," *Zeitschrift für die alttestamentliche Wissenschaft*
106 (1994), 96-107.
    [2]R. D. Moore, "The Integrity of Job," *Catholic Biblical Quarterly* 45/1 (1983):
17-31.
    [3]The crucial phrase is repeated in the following verse, 42:8.
    [4]*A Hebrew and English Lexicon of the Old Testament,* ed. F. Brown, S. R.
Driver, and C. A. Briggs (Oxford: Clarendon Press, 1907), s.v.; *Lexicon Veteris*

yields such common vocabulary as the adjective כֵּן ("right/honest," also used adverbially), the noun מָכוֹן ("place"), and the noun מְכוֹנָה ("base/pedestal"). The not-so-common feminine, singular participial form found in Job 42:7 has here been translated against this background. It has been taken either as an object[5] or an adverbial modifier[6] of the verb דבר, but either way the renderings produce the sense that what separates Job and his friends is the matter of the *rightness of their speech about God,* in other words, the *correctness of their theology.*[7]

Much comment has been generated, however, by the felt need to explain how Job's speech about God could be right and that of his friends not right. Throughout their debate it is the friends' theology, not Job's, that is hard to fault. They vigorously defend the orthodox doctrines of theology, while Job defiantly questions and even denies the justness of God.[8]

The conventional way to get 42:7 to square with this fact has been to explain that Job had been more accurate in addressing the overall theological scope of the issue at hand, as he challenged an overly narrow and rigid application of divine retribution.[9] This scholarly view trades heavily

Testamenti Libros, ed. L. Koehler and W. Baumgartner (Leiden: E. J. Brill, 1958), s.v.; and *The Dictionary of Classical Hebrew,* vol. 4, ed. D. J. A. Clines (Sheffield: Sheffield Academic Press, 1998), s.v.

[5]Both KJV and the Jewish Publication Society Translation render it "the thing that is right"; NIV, RSV, NRSV, and NASB all render it "what is right"; and NJPS renders it "the truth."

[6]BDB, 373, proposes reading it "correctly," citing Sirach 5:11 as a parallel adverbial use of the feminine participle. Translations following an adverbial reading are NAB ("rightly") and NEB ("as you ought").

[7]On this sense for 42:7, then, there is a wide consensus, despite the expected minor variations in wording of translations.

[8]Of course, for many this dissonance contributes to the historical critical conclusion that the poetic dialogue does not cohere with the prose narrative and that the two have been artifically combined in a way that has fallen short of reconciling the dissonance. See e.g., N. H. Tur-Sinai, *The Book of Job* (Jerusalem: Kiryat Sefer, 1967), 579 and M. H. Pope, *Job: A New Translation with Introduction and Commentary,* Anchor Bible vol. 15 (Garden City: Doubleday, 1965), 350.

[9]Advocates of this view, which are too many to enumerate, include H. H. Rowley, *Job,* New Century Bible (London: Marshall, Morgan & Scott), 267; R. Gordis, *The Book of Job* (New York: Jewish Theological Seminary, 1978), 494; N. C. Habel, *The Book of Job,* OTL (Philadelphia: Westminster, 1985), 583; and J. E. Hartley, *The Book of Job,* NICOT (Grand Rapids: Eerdmans, 1988), 539. Recently this conventional approach has been taken up in a fresh and expanded way by famed Latin American theologian Gustavo Gutiérrez, *On Job: God-Talk and the Suffering of the Innocent,* trans. from the Spanish by M. T. O'Connell (New York: Orbis, 1987). In his words, "God's approval evidently refers to Job's speeches as a whole, to the entire way he has followed" (11). I will discuss below the details of Gutiérrez's approach and its similarities and differences to my own.

on how the friends had been *wrong about Job*. But 42:7, according to the
accepted translation, specifies that it was *"about God"* that the friends
had been wrong.[10] And so the specificity on this point strains against the
theological generality of the conventional explanation.

An ancient way of alleviating this strain, it appears, shows up in a
variant reading of 42:7 found in several Hebrew manuscripts, which has
God faulting the friends for speaking "against my servant (בעבדי) Job."[11]
As an apparent move to avoid the more difficult reading of the Masoretic
Text, this variant has little to commend it.

One modern way of addressing the strain of 42:7 has appeared in the
form of an "ironic" interpretation of the book of Job that is found to hinge
on this verse.[12] This view assumes that the poetic dialogue between Job
and his friends was inserted into an older prose story (now the prologue
and epilogue) not just to augment it, as the common historical critical
approach has maintained,[13] but to impose on it an ironic twist. According
to this "ironic" approach, God's verdict in the prose epilogue had originally commended the pious speech of Job as depicted in the prologue ("In
all this Job neither sinned nor charged God foolishly," 1:22). But now a
poet, so goes the argument, has inserted a dialogue, in which Job has
repeatedly charged God with being unjust, so that God's final verdict in
the prose epilogue now ironically vindicates Job's charges against him!
In effect, this view has God saying, "Job has spoken *right* about *my* being
wrong!"

---

[10]This also undercuts the attempt by a few scholars (e.g., C. H. Mackintosh,
Job and His Friends [New York: Loizeau Brothers, n.d.], 66-67), to argue that
Job's right speech about God refers only to Job's confession in 42:1-6 and not to
anything said earlier, despite the fact that, in his confession, it is *about himself, not
God,* that Job speaks in a new way. For other evidence against this view, see the
keen comments of E. Good (*In Turns of Tempest: A Reading of Job* [Stanford, CA:
Stanford University Press, 1990], 380-82), who points out that God's verdict in
42:7 is introduced with the words, "after the LORD had spoken these words to
Job," as if to bypass any reference to what Job had just spoken in 42:1-6.

[11]See the textual note in *Biblia Hebraica Stuttgartensia* and also Gordis, *The
Book of Job,* 494.

[12]See D. Robertson, "The Book of Job: A Literary Study," *Soundings* 56
(1973): 446-84; and J. G. Williams, "You Have not Spoken Truth of Me: Mystery and Irony in Job," *ZAW* 83 (1971): 231-55, whose publication, though
earlier, notes Robertson's then unpublished article.

[13]This now common historical critical view (cf. note 8) that the poetic dialogue
between Job and his friends was inserted into a much older prose "folk tale" can be
traced from J. Wellhausen (in a review of A. Dillman, *Das Buch Hiob*), *Jahrbücher
für deutsche Theologie* 16 (1871): 555-58. For a list of a number of others who
have supported this position, see S. Terrien, "Job," *Interpreter's Bible,* vol. 3
(New York: Abingdon, 1954), 885.

This interpretation, though clever, nevertheless falters. It presupposes that the poet's irony is motivated by a desire to undermine a simplistic and rigid doctrine of retribution in the prose story—a doctrinal position that is simply not to be found there upon closer examination. There is nothing simplistic and rigid in this way, for instance, in Job's words, "Shall we receive good from the hand of God and not receive evil?" (2:10).[14] There seems to be enough literary and theological depth in the prose materials[15] that, if a poet had indeed so appropriated irony to subvert the theological intent of the prose, the prose narrative, through centuries of interpretation, must be credited with combining with the poetry in a way that, *even more ironically,* subverts recognition of the poet's irony! But even if there is too much irony here to be believed, the "ironic" reading of Job nevertheless sharply poses the problematic nature of God's words in 42:7 with respect to the dialogue of Job.

A striking solution to the foregoing difficulties encountered in the interpretation of Job 42:7 can be found by following another rendering of the verse—one that modern scholarship has scarcely considered. It entails an alternative reading of the prepositional phrase אֵלַי. The modern consensus, as noted earlier, has been to translate it "of/about me" or "concerning me,"[16] so that the entire phrase yields something like, "you have not spoken right *about me.*" However, the simplest rendering of this very common preposition with pronominal suffix is not "*about* me" but rather "*to* me," as indeed it *is* rendered in most of its approximately 300 occurrences in Hebrew Scripture.[17] The Hebrew preposition that would be typical for yielding "about" or "concerning" is עַל.[18] Granted, it is grammatically possible for אֶל to be used in this sense, "equivalent to עַל."[19] However, it is only context that would demand opting for this secondary sense of אֵלַי over the primary sense, "to me."

Interestingly, although modern scholarship has assumed this contextual demand for Job 42:7, it has not always been taken for granted. In the ancient versions one finds renderings of this prepositional phrase in Job 42:7 that make room for its primary sense. The Septuagint reads ἐνώπιόν

---

[14]See my discussion in "Integrity of Job," 18-20.

[15]See D. J. A. Clines, "False Naivety in the Prologue to Job," *Hebrew Annual Review* 9 (1985): 127-36.

[16]So all of the translations mentioned in notes 5 and 6.

[17]See S. Mandelkern, *Veteris Testamenti Concordantiae Hebraica Atque Chaldaicae* (Tel Aviv: Schocken, 1978), 80-81 and BDB, 39-41.

[18]See BDB, 754, and R. J. Williams, *Hebrew Syntax: An Outline,* 2nd ed. (Toronto: University of Toronto Press, 1976), 51.

[19]Williams, *Hebrew Syntax,* 53. He lists as examples: 1 Sam 4:19; 15:35 and 2 Sam 24:16. See also BDB, 41, where it is noted that the use of אל in the sense of על, although not plentiful anywhere, shows up more in the following books: 1 & 2 Sam, 1 & 2 Kgs, Jer, and Ezek.

μου, "before me." The Syriac and Vulgate follow suit. The Aramaic Targum of Job reads לותי, "with me."[20] In all these cases, the phrase and (consequently) the verse are translated in a way that points to the issue of speaking not merely *about* God but *to* God.[21] On the other hand, among modern translators and commentators I have found only two scholars— and only one in this century—who have advocated the primary sense for אֵלַי in Job 42:7.[22]

When the actual context of the book of Job is considered in relation to the translation "to me" in Job 42:7, one can find some striking correspondence. This translation, of course, has God making an explicit reference to prayer. It is clearly the case that Job prays repeatedly during the course of his interaction with his friends, while they, on the other hand, are never seen addressing God a single time.[23] They speak profusely *about* God,

---

[20]These versional readings are noted and dismissed without argument in S. R. Driver and G. B. Gray, *The Book of Job,* ICC (Edinburgh: T& T Clark, 1921), 348. See also E. Dhorme, *A Commentary on the Book of Job,* trans. H. Knight (Nashville: Thomas Nelson, 1984), 648.

[21]The Targum's "with me" obviously conveys this more directly, whereas "before me" in the Septuagint textual tradition readily includes the sense of speaking *to* God, but not necessarily so. Its rendering could be taken to indicate *speaking in God's presence* without necessarily speaking directly *to* God. It is difficult to explain how the Septuagint would have come to translate אֵלַי as "before me," since this translation lacks the grammatical precedence one can find for "about me." The Hebrew לפני would be the expected source for "before me," and in the absence of any Hebrew manuscript basis for this, one wonders whether the Septuagint here may have been representing a Greek impulse to make more room (in the book as well as the verse) for the sense of speaking *about* God versus speaking *to* God—an impulse that modern scholarship has followed to the point of excluding *any* room for the sense of speaking *to* God. Another pre-modern scholar who observed the plain reading of the Hebrew, "to me," in Job 42:7 is Saadiah Gaon, the famous Jewish philosopher who lived in Babylonia in the eighth century AD. However, he departs slightly from the primary sense of the following phrase to get: "as to my servant Job." See *The Book of Theodicy: Translation and Commentary on the Book of Job by Saadiah Ben Joseph Al-Fayumi,* trans. from Arabic by L. E. Goodman (New Haven: Yale University Press, 1988), 412.

[22]K. F. R. Budde, *Das Buch Hiob* (Göttingen: Vandenhoeck & Ruprecht, 1896), s.v., whose translation, "zu mir," is acknowledged by Driver and Gray *(Book of Job,* 348) only for the purpose of summarily dismissing it along with Budde's defense that "all human speech has God for its hearer, and is directed towards Him." The other scholar is Eugene Peterson in his "dynamic equivalence" translation, *The Message: The Wisdom Books* (Colorado Springs, CO: NavPress, 1996), whose rendering encompasses both of the given senses of אֵלַי: "You haven't been honest either with me or about me—not the way my friend Job has."

[23]This is carefully observed, detailed, and discussed by D. Patrick, "Job's Address of God," *ZAW* 91 (1979): 268-82. After noting that "Job's three companions never address God," he proceeds to note Job's direct address of God in

and they even speak *about speaking to God,*[24] but only Job breaks out beyond the boundaries of inter-human dialogue to address God directly. In fact, Job is *too direct,* in another sense of the term, for the theological sensibilities of his friends. Indeed, this seems to be what sparks their dispute with Job in the first place. Job's lament in chapter 3 boldly challenges God, and this brings an end to the comforters' seven days of silence (and comfort!) and a beginning to their counter-challenge of Job.[25] Thus, in the dialogue, Job is distinct from his friends not only in that he speaks to God and they do not, but also in that he dares to speak to God with a bold, confrontive, and challenging directness, which they reject on theological principle. The words of God in Job 42:7 can thus be seen to fit this contrast between Job and his friends *perfectly.* The friends "have not spoken *to* God," as Job has, neither have they, like Job, spoken to him *"firmly"* (following the most basic nuance of the root כּוּן[26] or *"straight"* to use a contemporary colloquialism[27] of a term also identified as a basic nuance of כּוּן).[28] God's verdict, on both counts, is thus aptly expressed: "you have not spoken straight to me, as my servant Job has."[29]

Seeing "right prayer" as the decisive issue here fits well with the immediate context of 42:7, for in the very next verse and in consequence to what God has just said, God tells Eliphaz and his friends to go with sacrificial offerings and "let my servant Job pray for you." The consequential relation between the two verses, then, is that, since only Job has prayed right

---

the following verses: 7:7,8,12-14,16,17-21; 9:27-28,30-31; 10:2-14,16-17,18,20; 13:19,20-27; 14:3,5-6,13,15-17,19-20; 16:7,8; 17:3,4; and 30:20-23.

[24]See 5:8; 8:5; 11:13; 15:4; and 22:27. In each of these cases the friends speak condescendingly to Job about how he should speak to God.

[25]See my discussion in "Integrity of Job," 21-30.

[26]Again, see BDB, 465. Lamontte Luker, a friend and Old Testament colleague, first suggested such a translation of this verse to me in a personal letter in March 1985. He proposed, "For you have not spoken firmly to me as my servant, Job." Although it was a long time before I took up this proposal and began to see its striking relevance for the whole book, I gratefully acknowledge Monte Luker's responsibility for planting the seed that grew into the thesis of this study.

[27]See *The Oxford Encyclopedic English Dictionary,* 3rd ed. (New York: Oxford University Press, 1996), s.v., which notes this usage of "straight": (of a verbal attack) delivered in a frank or direct manner.

[28]See *Lexicon Veteris Testamenti Libros,* 426.

[29]I am not choosing this nuance of "straight" in a way that intends to rule out the sense of "correct" or "right." Job's "straight" speaking to God, as it was characterized by the drama of the dialogue, is now characterized by a single term which confirms it as "right." What could keep the ambiguity and possiblities that are alive in the Hebrew term from functioning in this way?: Job's "straight" speaking is finally declared to have been "right," and his speaking that all along had been "right" is acknowledged to have been "straight." Thus the term can at once convey that the *straight* speaking was *right,* and the *right* speaking was *straight.*

and they have not, they now need Job to pray for them. The rest of verse
eight includes a repeating of God's words in verse seven, as if to underscore the tight consequential connection: "for to him (that is, Job when he
prays) I will show favor and not deal with you according to your folly,
since you have not spoken straight to me, as my servant Job has." The
immediate context of 42:7 thus reinforces what we saw in the larger context
of the book: the friends' "straight"[30] God-talk has separated them from
talking *straight to* God.

There is even more to be said for how a reference to prayer in 42:7
relates strategically to the entire book of Job. This comes into view in light
of the important work of Claus Westermann on the structure of the book of
Job—a work first published over two decades ago.[31] In this form-critical
study, Westermann points out that lament is structurally the controlling
genre of the book.[32] He observes that the dialogue between Job and his
friends (chaps. 4-27) is framed by laments of Job (chaps. 3 and 29-31),
"which stand outside the disputation and are strictly laments, lacking any
sort of address to the friends."[33] For Westermann, "this means that the
dialogue stands *within* the lament. The lament has both the first and the
last word."[34] Job's lament turns away from the friends and opens up to
direct address of God. In fact, the last word of Job's lament (chaps. 29-31),
so Westermann notes, "leads up to a summoning of God" (31:35-37).[35] Yet
more than this, Westermann observes that "this divine-human interaction
is never totally interrupted in the middle section (chaps. 4-27), but rather is
continued in Job's laments, which are components of his speech in the
dialogue section."[36] On this basis, Westermann concludes that "there is
only one way to see the whole of the Book of Job: the encompassing

---

[30]I use "straight" here with double *entendre*, in the sense of both "straight down
the line of established dogma" and "straight without deviation," (i.e., uninter-
rupted talking *about* God without ever talking *to* God). Again, I am playing on the
ambiguity of the English word in a way that I do not take to be irrelevant to the
characterization of the discourse of the friends in the book of Job.

[31]*Der Aufbau des Buches Hiob* (Stuttgart: Cawler Verlag, 1977), translated into
English as *The Structure of the Book of Job: A Form-Critical Analysis,* trans. C. A.
Muenchow (Philadelphia: Fortress, 1981).

[32]*Structure of Job,* 1-15. Even before Westermann, the argument that Job
should be viewed as a paradigm for an answered lament was advanced by H. Gese,
*Lehre und Wirklichkeit in der alten Weisheit: Studien zu den Spruchen Salomos
und zu dem Buche Hiob* (Tübingen: J. C. B. Mohr, 1958), 63-78. Westermann
mentions a number of others who have also emphasized the importance of the
lament form as a dominating feature of the book of Job (13-14).

[33]Ibid., 4.
[34]Ibid., emphasis added.
[35]Ibid., 6.
[36]Ibid. All of this is detailed in Patrick, "Job's Address of God," 268-72. See
biblical references in note 23.

confrontation is that between Job and God, while within this confrontation stands the one between the friends and Job."[37]

One could even add to Westermann's observation on how Job's laments frame the dialogue that these laments are themselves framed by a
prose narrative featuring intercession for his children as Job's first action
(1:5) and prayer for his friends as his last (42:9-10). Indeed, prayer is
primary from beginning to end.

Westermann's observations set in sharp relief the fact that the
disputation initiated (chap. 4) and carried forward by Job's friends, appears
(in the context of the entire dialogue section) as something of an
interruption or an intrusion upon a more primary dialogue between Job
and God. In fact, the friends' disputation is more than intrusion; it is
intentional opposition prompted by and targeted against Job's course of
prayer. From beginning to end, Job seeks a hearing with God; he calls for
it explicitly again and again.[38] However, the dispute of his friends forces
Job to press his cry to God against and through their decrying objections.
Their *refined theology* is pitted not only against the daring content of
Job's theology but, even more essentially, against the form it takes in *raw
prayer to God.*

Westermann's study helps us see the *decisive place of prayer* in the
genre and structure of the book of Job and the *decisive struggle over
prayer* in the dramatic unfolding of the book. Yet Westermann does not
connect this with or even notice the *decisive reference to prayer* at the
end of the book.[39] We can see, however, that a reference to prayer in Job
42:7 is not only permitted by the grammar of the verse, it is also favored by
the context of the book. Indeed, it speaks for the whole message of the
book with summarizing decisiveness.

II. Broader Implicatons and Conclusions

The reference to prayer in Job 42:7 and its relationship to the book of
Job, as illuminated in this study, have even broader implications. These
are not unrelated to implications which Westermann saw for his study. He
acknowledged that his findings on the dominance of lament in the book of
Job had significant import for the question of its common classification as
wisdom literature. He noted that the wisdom classification of Job "has

---

[37]Ibid., 5.

[38]See 10:2; 12:4; 13:3,15,22-24; 14:15; 16:19-21; 19:25-27; 23:3-10; 30:20; and
31:35-37.

[39]The same is true for the other scholars, previously noted (Gutiérrez, Patrick,
and Gese), who have drawn attention in significant ways to the prime role of
prayer in the book of Job.

clearly exerted a pervasive, perhaps even controlling influence upon nine-teenth- and twentieth-century exegesis,"[40] particularly in the way it has predisposed "most modern interpretations [to] proceed on the assump-tion that the Book of Job deals with a 'problem.'"[41] Westermann meant by this that these modern scholars have viewed the book in terms of a discus-sion of "theoretical" rather than "existential" character,[42] or, as he went on to express it, an "inquiry" that treats "suffering, or more precisely, the suffering of a just man [as an] object of thought."[43] Westermann noticed how this has obscured the fact that more "fundamentally the book treats an existential question" primarily by means of the "existential process" of lament.[44]

To Westermann's observations I would have some of my own to add. His apt characterization of modern scholarship's dominant way of approaching the book of Job corresponds strikingly to the friends' approach to the problem of Job. Specifically, modern scholars approach the book as a theoretical "discussion of a problem," without giving weight to the claims of particular, existential experience; and that is how the friends press their disputation with Job. Again, modern scholars look right past the pronounced emphasis on lament; and the friends do likewise with respect to Job. Such correspondence could be explained in terms of the "controlling influence" of the "wisdom" categorization on both modern interpretation (as Westermann noted) and the friends' interpretation of the problem of Job (as I have just indicated). However, I do not believe this explanation goes deep enough with respect to modern interpretation. Which is the more fundamental truth?: (1) that the wisdom categorization of Job has influenced its modern interpretation, or rather (2) that modern interpretation has influenced the wisdom categorization of Job? I submit it is the latter. Modern scholarship has interpreted the book the way the friends interpret Job's problem because of the bent of the former's own "wisdom" tradition. What Westermann regards as issuing from modern interpretation's wisdom classification of Job (namely, elevating theoretical inquiry over existential experience and raising discourse that treats reality as an "object of thought" over discourse that addresses the particularity and concreteness of human experience) can be seen to issue *from modern interpretation itself,* that is, *from its very mode of interpreting*—one that is in obvious ways parallel to the ancient wisdom tradition represented by Job's friends.

---

[40] *Structure of Job,* 1.

[41] Ibid.

[42] Ibid., 2.

[43] Ibid.

[44] Ibid., 2-3. And the book does this, Westermann further emphasized, by depicting a particular event of a particular person (6-8).

This leads to an important implication. The modern criticism of the book of Job and its underlying hermeneutic, which thus have lined up with the friends' criticism of Job, cannot escape the counter criticism, which the end of the book delivers against the friends and the wisdom tradition they represent! The statement, "you have not spoken right," indicts the friends' refined theological discourse, but it also, by extension, implicates the modern scholarly discourse, which has followed suit by downplaying and looking past the lament of Job. It has done this, I would submit, even to the point of *translating it out* of God's final verdict in Job 42:7.[45] However, the point of the verse and the book is finally inescapable: not speaking "right" *about* [God]" has to do with not speaking "straight" *to* [God]"—something that both ancient wisdom and modern criticism have tended to crowd out of their purviews.[46]

My point has been to challenge modern scholarship's translation of a verse and thereby extend Westermann's challenge against "most modern interpretations" of the book of Job. Yet in so doing, I have come to the point of showing how the book and the given verse themselves pose a challenge to modern criticism itself, particularly as the latter is applied to theological discourse. Gustavo Gutiérrez has recently done something similar in his book, *On Job*.[47] Focusing like myself on Job 42:7, but following modern scholarship's translation of it, he argues that this verse identifies "speaking correctly about God" as the key issue of the book[48] and "talk about God" or "God-talk" as what theology is.[49] By these terms, Gutiérrez places Job's example of right God-talk over against modern theology.[50] Job's experience reveals, as Gutiérrez points out, that language about God cannot be valid if it becomes separated from that which speaks from and for the experience of those suffering unjustly or innocently—what Gutiérrez calls "the language of prophecy."[51] Gutiérrez goes on to argue from Job's example that language about God that succeeds on this count will inevitably lead to what he calls "the language of contemplation" or speech that

---

[45]Earlier I raised the issue about the contextual demand for translating אֵלַי "about me" rather than its primary sense "to me." I submit that the contextual demand, which modern scholarship has routinely assumed, turns out to be the demand of modern scholarship's own conceptual context imposed on the text.

[46]On the limited place of prayer in Old Testament wisdom literature see J. L. Crenshaw, "The Restraint of Reason, the Humility of Prayer," in chap. 9 of his *Urgent Advice and Probing Questions: Collected Writings on Old Testament Wisdom* (Macon, GA: Mercer, 1995), 206-21.

[47]Cited in note 9.

[48]*On Job,* 11.

[49]Ibid., xi.

[50]Ibid., xvii-xix.

[51]Ibid., 16, 19-49.

entails the experience of worship and encounter with God.[52] He specifically mentions speaking *to* God in contrast to speaking merely *about* God,[53] although he never notices how Job 42:7 speaks directly to this point. On both counts Job's right God-talk, as brought forward by Gutiérrez's rich liberationist perspective, delivers a profound critique and challenge against modern theology.

My own perspective as a Pentecostal leads me to resonate deeply with Gutiérrez's liberating study, *On Job.* Pentecostalism, which itself has become so prominent in Latin America, undoubtedly has become so because of its deep lineage in the discourse of the oppressed.[54] Especially prominent in this discourse has been lament—the focus of the present study and something that my Pentecostal experience certainly has given me deep resources for seeing in Job.

Larry McQueen has recently shown the originating, generative role of lament in the Pentecostal movement and faith experience.[55] My attestation of this leads me to take issue with Gutiérrez's inclination to view prayer ("the language of contemplation") in terms of a "second stage" to which right language *about* God will eventually lead.[56] This view stops short of what I see in Job—a man for whom prayer is both the beginning and end of all God-talk,[57] (1) so that talking *about* God takes place *within* the experience of talking *to* God and not apart from it; (2) so that talking to God is not rendered subsequent and secondary to theology, but it is primary, unto the point of challenging the very formulation (endorsed by Gutiérrez), which defines theology as "talk *about* God;"[58] (3) so that theology becomes embedded in worship, thus becoming worship once again;[59] (4) so that talking *about* God and talking *to* God come together so intimately that a single term (like אֲלַי in the Hebrew!) could refer to them both at the same time!

[52]Ibid., 16, 51-103.

[53]Ibid., 54. Gutiérrez cites the observation of Patrick, "Job's Address of God," 269, that the friends never speak *to* God, as Job does, but only *about* him.

[54]See C. Bridges Johns, *Pentecostal Formation: A Pedagogy among the Oppressed,* JPTS 2 (Sheffield: Sheffield Academic Press, 1993), esp. 119-29.

[55]L. McQueen, *Joel and the Spirit: The Cry of a Prophetic Hermeneutic,* JPTS 8 (Sheffield: Sheffield Academic Press, 1995): 76-82.

[56]See *On Job,* 88. At one point Gutiérrez says, "Talk about God presupposes and, at the same time, leads to a living encounter with God" (17), but overall his study emphasizes the "gradual maturation [of God-talk] as the book moves along" (17) especially in terms of the "shift" from "the language of prophecy" to the "language of contemplation" (see esp. 16 and 88).

[57]Again, cf. Westermann, *Structure of Job,* 4.

[58]*On Job,* xi (emphasis added).

[59]I am indebted here to my teacher and colleague, R. Hollis Gause, who has richly expounded this definition and approach to theology for many years at the Church of God Theological Seminary.

This is the way it was with Job, for whom the fear of the LORD[60] was the beginning (Job 1:1) as well as the end (Job 28:28; 42:5-6) of wisdom, and also for the apostle Paul and a long line of early theologians, for whom such integration was not so unusual, prior to the re-fashioning of theology in the image and form of Greek metaphysics.[61]

Yet forms, formulas, and formulations of refined theology incessantly get raised up in ways that threaten to shut down prayer. The book of Job shows that this is not just a modern problem. Job also shows that it is a problem that can become the provoking catalyst for the form-shattering, breakthrough experience of lament[62]—what Pentecostals have long called "praying through."[63]

Job prays through. It takes God-talk that is straight and firm—firm enough to break through our forms and speak to the One who is no form,[64] the One who breaks all forms,[65] the One who breaks us. Yet the One who

---

[60]Deuteronomy grounds the Old Testament experience of fear of the LORD in the theophanic encounter of Israel at Horeb or Sinai (Deut 5, esp. 5:20-26). Fear of the LORD is widely accepted as the quintessential response of Hebrew worship.

[61]The role of Thomas Aquinas in this was undoubtedly major and set the stage for modern theology's commitment and attachment to Greek metaphysics. Interestingly, Aquinas' commentary on the book of Job, and Job 42:7 in particular, reflects both his philosophical orientation in relation to this larger role and also his direct influence on reading (and translating!) Job 42:7 in terms of a reference to theology rather than prayer. His commentary on the Latin text at this point reads: "*you have not spoken what is right before Me, **that is, faithful dogmas,** as has My servant Job.*" *Thomas Aquinas: The Literal Exposition on Job, A Scriptural Commentary Concerning Providence,* trans. A. Damico; Ed. M.D. Yaffe (Atlanta: Scholars Press, 1989), 471.

[62]See the recent study of Job by K. J. Dell, *The Book of Job as Skeptical Literature,* BZAW (Berlin: de Gruyter, 1991), who advances the compelling thesis that inherent in the very form of Job is an intentional pattern and programmatic effort to alter, parody, or deconstruct established literary forms in order to contest their claims. Dell takes note of my study, "Integrity of Job," where I show how Job's opening lament of chap. 3 is a direct counterpoint of his confession of faith in 1:21. This study and more recent spadework in the book of Psalms, as it has been informed by my Pentecostal experience, have convinced me that breaking conventional language forms is a key element in the nature and dynamic of lament.

[63]McQueen, *Joel and the Spirit,* 76-77.

[64]As Deut 4:15 says, "Therefore take good heed to yourselves. Since you saw no form on the day that the LORD spoke to you at Horeb out of the midst of the fire" (RSV).

[65]Immediately after highlighting the prohibition against making "a graven image in the form of anything," Deut 4:24 says, "For the LORD your God is a devouring fire, a jealous God" (RSV).

has broken me is the One who has spoken to me, revealing that I have spoken *straight to Him.*[66]

> Let the words of my mouth
> and the meditation of my heart
> be before your face,
> O LORD, my strength and my redeemer
> *(Psalm 19:15).*[67]

[66]I am grateful to my colleague, Chris Thomas, for his dialogue and encouragement during the writing of this article, also for his reading of the manuscript and helping me settle on the title.

The Role of the Holy Spirit in the Construction of the Second Temple

R. Jerome Boone[*]

The work of the Spirit of God is evident in the whole of Scripture from Genesis to Revelation. We read of the Spirit's work in creation in the opening verses of Genesis (1:2). We hear the Spirit calling humankind to partake of the water of life in the last chapter of Revelation (22:17). Even though the Spirit is evident in both testaments of the Bible, the person and work of the Spirit is primarily illuminated by the New Testament. Only about one half of the Old Testament books mention the Spirit of God. As B. B. Warfield observed, there is no clear rhyme or reason to when the Spirit is mentioned in the Old Testament.[1] There is no reference to the Spirit in Leviticus, but he is mentioned in Numbers. There is no mention of the Spirit in Joshua and Ruth, but he is discussed in Judges and Samuel. Ezra does not refer to the Spirit, but Nehemiah does. There is no mention of the Spirit in Jeremiah, but abundant references to the Spirit occur in Isaiah and Ezekiel.

My purpose in this essay is to describe the role of the Holy Spirit in the construction of the Second Temple. I will discuss this topic in a broader perspective than the physical rebuilding of the temple. As Gordon Fee has pointed out, the prophets speak of the divine presence of the Spirit of God as effecting all aspects of the restoration period.[2] The Spirit made possible the construction of the Second Temple by bringing Israel

---

[*]R. Jerome Boone (D.Min., Columbia Theological Seminary). Dean, School of Religion; Professor of Old Testament, Lee University.

[1]Benjamin B. Warfield, *Biblical and Theological Studies* (Philadelphia: Presbyterian and Reformed Publishing Company, 1952), 127-28.

[2]Gordon D. Fee, *God's Empowering Presence: The Holy Spirit in the Letters of Paul* (Peabody, MA: Hendrickson Publishers, Inc., 1994), 909.

back to Canaan. The Spirit transformed the hearts and spirits of the repatriated Jews so that Yahweh could dwell among them. Then, the Spirit
inspired the rebuilding of the temple and enabled Israel to overcome the
negative circumstances and formidable obstacles which threatened to
prevent the temple's construction. In the end, the Spirit had empowered
the construction of the Second Temple so that Yahweh could be among
his covenant people in the land of promise.

The limited discussion of the person and work of the Holy Spirit in the
Old Testament has caused a division among scholars concerning the role
of the Spirit in the lives of Old Testament saints. Scholars in the reformed
tradition tend to emphasize the work of the Spirit in the Old Testament in
ways analogous to that described in the New Testament.[3] Other scholars
would agree with the assertion of Michael Green: "On the whole, you had
to be someone special in the Old Testament days to have the Spirit of
God."[4] An early significant work on the Holy Spirit from a Pentecostal
perspective does not deal with the role of the Holy Spirit in the post-exilic
community in any significant way.[5] A more contemporary work on the
Spirit of God in the Old Testament recognizes the importance of the Spirit
in the post-monarchy era.[6]

The limited references to the Holy Spirit in the Old Testament compared
to those of the New Testament is often explained by a scheme of
progressive revelation. While it is impossible to defend a strictly linear
progressive revelation of the person and work of the Holy Spirit in the Old
Testament, there is evidence that Israel's comprehension of the Spirit
became increasingly clearer toward the end of the Old Testament period.
The Old Testament reaches a certain theological astuteness in the late
monarchy and post-monarchy periods and begins to understand that
Yahweh's work in the world is done by his Spirit. It is not the sophistication
of the New Testament but it is in that direction. The book of Nehemiah, for
instance, reflects on Israel's history and describes God's activity in the
Mosaic period as being done by his "good Spirit" (9:20). Later, in the same
reflection, it is said concerning God: "Thou didst bear with them [Israel]
for many years, and admonished them by Thy Spirit through Thy prophets"

---

[3]Gary Fredricks, "Rethinking the Role of the Holy Spirit in the Lives of Old
Testament Believers," *Trinity Journal* 9 (Spring, 1988): 82-83.

[4]Michael Green, *I Believe in the Holy Spirit* (London: Hodder and Stoughton,
1975), 28. Gary Fredricks' "Rethinking the Role of the Holy Spirit in the Lives of
Old Testament Believers" lists a number of scholars who agree with this premise,
including Stanley Horton, Morris A. Inch, Fredrick Dale Brunner, Leon Morris,
Millard J. Erickson, T. E. McComiskey, C. K. Barrett, and James D. G. Dunn.

[5]Stanley Horton, *What the Bible Says About the Holy Spirit* (Springfield, MO:
Gospel Publishing House, 1976).

[6]Wilf Hildebrandt, *An Old Testament Theology of the Spirit of God* (Peabody,
MA: Hendrickson Publishers, Inc., 1995).

(9:30).[7] The testimony of the book of Nehemiah is interpreting the past. The earlier literature describes the activity of God in Israel in a more direct way. It is God who speaks to Moses at Mt. Horeb and Moses who speaks to Israel. It is the word of the Lord that came to the prophets and the prophets communicated it to Israel. The religious leaders in Nehemiah's day, however, understood the role of God's Spirit in this divine-human activity. The same pattern of interpretation is seen in Isaiah 63:7-14. The rebellion of Israel in the wilderness is said to have "grieved His Holy Spirit" (63:10). Forty years later, "the Spirit of the Lord gave them rest" (63:14).

Walther Eichrodt considers the re-interpretation of God's activity in Israel's history as the work of the Spirit to be a crucial development in Old Testament theology.[8] The re-interpretation of the past illustrates Israel's developing perception of the Spirit of God "as a so-called *hypostasis*, that is to say, a separate entity which acts of its own motion, and is of itself concerned with human affairs."[9] This does not mean that the Spirit is somehow divorced from God. Rather, he acquires "a kind of mediatory position between God and man . . . a man's attitude toward it determines his attitude toward God; disobedience to the Holy Spirit grieves it and causes it to withdraw, with a result that the flow of divine life is cut off."[10]

A direct result of Israel's perception of the Spirit in the post-monarchy period is a more comprehensive understanding of the Spirit's work in the community of faith.[11] The workings of God in Israel are no longer seen only in the miraculous, mighty acts of God; the Spirit of God is understood to be actively involved in the daily lives of men and women in the community. Both Jeremiah (31:31-34) and Ezekiel (36:26-28) describe the spiritual transformation of the sinful pre-exilic community as the work of changing the hearts of the people. Ezekiel goes further than Jeremiah in ascribing this work and transformation to the Spirit of God. Ezekiel goes on to describe the work of God's Spirit in bringing the nation of Israel back to its ancestral homeland (37:1-14).

The post-exilic period is noticeably void of overt, miraculous acts of God, with the possible exception of the release of Israel from the exile. In the words of the literature of the period, it was a "day of small things" (Zech 4:10). And yet, Israel was warned not to despise "the day of small things" because Yahweh was at work in it. The skeptics would surely

---

[7]All scripture references are to the New American Standard Bible (NASB), copyright 1963, unless otherwise noted.
[8]Walther Eichrodt, *Theology of the Old Testament*, vol. 2, trans. J. A. Baker (Philadelphia: The Westminster Press, 1967), 60-68.
[9]Ibid., 60.
[10]Ibid.
[11]Ibid., 58.

have asked: where is God in this day of small things? The answer is "I am with you . . . . My Spirit is abiding in your midst" (Hag 2:4-5). The restoration of Israel and the temple was "not by might nor by power, but by My [God's] Spirit" (Zech 4:6).

The destruction of the Solomonic Temple by the Babylonians and the subsequent exile of the nation of Israel precipitated a severe theological crisis in Israel's faith. The temple was the pivotal link between Israel and Yahweh. It was the earthly dwelling place of Israel's God. It was the place where Yahweh was worshiped. It was the place where salvation was obtained by sacrifice on Yahweh's altar. In essence, the temple was the icon of covenant relationship.

Consequently, the restoration of Israel as a nation in the early Persian period led to the rebuilding of the temple as a first priority. The temple was rebuilt before the capital city of Jerusalem was restored. The repatriated Jews of the post-exilic era began immediately to rebuild the temple upon their return to the land (Ezra 3). Unfortunately, the restoration of the temple encountered heavy opposition from Israel's enemies and was held up for fourteen or fifteen years (534-520 BC; Ezra 4). The lengthy interruption in the restoration of the temple caused the loss of enthusiasm for the project and a general spiritual decline among the people. The prophets Haggai and Zechariah challenged the post-exilic community to complete the temple. Under the leadership of Zerubbabel, the governor, and Joshua, the high priest, the temple was rebuilt. It was completed on March 12, 515 BC, in the sixth year of King Darius of Persia.[12]

I. The Work of the Spirit in the Restoration of the Temple Builders

According to Ezekiel, it was the Spirit of God who provided the occasion for rebuilding the temple (Ezek 37). The first phase of the Spirit's involvement in the reconstruction of the temple was the national restoration of the temple builders—Israel. Ezekiel 37 prophesies the restoration event. The prophet seems to use the Hebrew term *ruach* with a double entendre. The complex definition of the Hebrew word as breath and spirit is utilized. The creation imagery of the prophecy (vv. 1-10) certainly draws on the concept of breath in *ruach*. God created Adam in Genesis 2 in a two-step process, forming his body and then breathing life into him. The prophet depicts God re-creating the nation of Israel in the same manner. The bodies are formed (37:4-8) and then Ezekiel prophesies to the *ruach* and the *ruach* enters the dead bodies, bringing them life (37:9-10). The

---

[12]Raymond P. Dillard and Tremper Longmann, III, *An Introduction to the Old Testament* (Grand Rapids: Zondervan Publishing House, 1994), 429.

ruach in verses 5, 6, 8 and 10 is surely the "breath of life," apart from which there is no life (Eccl 12:7).[13]

The double entendre attached to *ruach* is apparent at v. 14 when the Lord declares: "I will put My Spirit [*Ruach*] within you, and you will come to life, and I will place you on your own land." The emphasis of vv. 11-14 is on the "supernatural, life-giving power of Yahweh,"[14] mediated through His Spirit given to Israel. Walther Zimmerli notes that "it is remarkable that the reference here [v. 14] is explicitly to 'my spirit' . . . that is, the spirit of Yahweh."[15] It is not simply the breath of Yahweh that gives life; it is the Spirit of God that will restore Israel to national life.[16]

The national restoration of Israel described in vv. 1-14 is related to the more significant event of covenant renewal in the last part of Ezekiel 37 (vv. 24-28). The national restoration of Israel is part and parcel of covenant renewal. A return to the land of Canaan was an important aspect of the restoration of covenant blessings. The covenant emphasis of the passage is evident in the covenant formula stated in v. 27: "I will be their God, and they will be My people." As a consequence of covenant renewal, Yahweh will dwell among his people again. On three different occasions in this short pericope, God promises to establish his sanctuary —the temple—among His people:

> v. 26 "I... will set My sanctuary in their midst forever."
> v. 27 "My dwelling place also will be with them."
> v. 28 "My sanctuary is in their midst forever."

Ezekiel's prophecy makes it clear that national restoration was an aspect of covenant renewal that would result in Yahweh dwelling among his people. It is not surprising, then, that the prophecies of Ezekiel include a major vision about the rebuilding of the Temple (40-48). Within the context of the vision, Ezekiel "narrates the return of God's presence to the new temple" (43:1-12).[17]

Another way in which the Spirit of God was involved in the construction of the Second Temple was in the spiritual renewal of the temple builders. Without this transformation, there would have been no need for temple reconstruction. We have already noted the relationship between covenant renewal and temple. Yahweh's intention was to dwell among his covenant people (Ezek 37:24-28). Covenant renewal necessitated spiritual

---

[13]Hildebrandt, *Old Testament Theology*, 97.

[14]Ibid.

[15]Walther Zimmerli, *Ezekiel 2: A Commentary on the Book of the Prophet Ezekiel, Chapters 25-48* (Philadelphia: Fortress Press, 1983), 263.

[16]Warfield, *Biblical and Theological Studies*, 149.

[17]Hildebrandt, *Old Testament Theology*, 49.

renewal. Once again, it is Ezekiel who prophecies the role of the Spirit in Israel's spiritual transformation.

Ezekiel's earliest prophecies anticipate the work of God in Israel's spiritual renewal:

> 11:17 Therefore say, "Thus says the Lord God, 'I shall gather you from the peoples and assemble you out of the countries among which you have been scattered, and I shall give you the land of Israel. 18 When they come there, they will remove all its detestable things and all its abominations from it. 19 And I shall give them one heart, and shall put a new spirit within them. And take the heart of stone out of their flesh and give them a heart of flesh, 20 that they may walk in My statutes and keep My ordinances, and do them. Then they will be My people, and I shall be their God.'"

God's initiative does not preclude Israel's responsibility in that God commands Israel to participate in the event of spiritual renewal:

> 18:30 "Therefore I will judge you, O house of Israel, each according to his conduct," declares the Lord God. "Repent and turn away from all your transgressions, so that iniquity may not become a stumbling block to you. 31 Cast away from you all your transgressions which you have committed, and make yourselves a new heart and a new spirit! For why will you die, O house of Israel? 32 For I have no pleasure in the death of anyone who dies," declares the Lord God. "Therefore, repent and live."

The distinction between a new spirit which is *given* (11:19) and one which is *gotten* (18:31) does not contradict God's grace. "Renewal and repentance come through reception of God's *ruach*."[18]

Ezekiel reaches the summit of his prophecies about the renewing work of God's Spirit in 36:26-28. The context of the prophecy emphasizes God's grace in Israel's renewal. Israel, through its own disobedience was unclean (36:16-18). The righteous consequence of Israel's disobedience was exile and destruction (3:18-19). In contrast to Israel's disobedience and impurity, Yahweh will renew Israel for his own name sake (36:22). Israel's filthiness will be cleansed by God's clean water (36:25). The legal imagery

---

[18]Dale Moody, *Spirit of the Living God* (Philadelphia: The Westminster Press, 1968), 22. Spiritual renewal is God's initiative, as Paul makes clear in Titus 3:5: "He saved us, not on the basis of deeds which we have done in righteousness, but according to His mercy, by the washing of regeneration and renewing by the Holy Spirit." Nevertheless, it calls for human cooperation. In the words of Paul, one must "walk in a manner worthy of the calling with which you have been called" (Eph 4:1).

of Leviticus 11-15 pervades the passage with images of ritual purification. Once the purification is complete, God will take an extraordinary step to ensure that the old impurity does not return. Yahweh will put a new heart and a new spirit in his people.[19]

> 36:26 Moreover, I will give you a new heart and put a new spirit within you; and I will remove the heart of stone from your flesh and give you a heart of flesh. 27 And I will put My Spirit within you and cause you to walk in My statutes, and you will be careful to observe My ordinances. 28 And you will live in the land that I gave to your forefathers; so you will be My people, and I will be your God.

It would be a mistake to classify this prophecy with others like Joel 2:28-32 and relegate it to the future eschatological age of the Spirit, ushered in at Pentecost (Acts 2).[20] Ezekiel is prophesying about a work of the Spirit that would be active in the post-exilic community of faith. The prophet envisions a work of God's Spirit which would "empower Israel for obedience."[21] Some scholars have supposed that this prophecy cannot refer to the Old Testament period because the Spirit was not "in" Old Testament saints. However, Gary Fredricks argues convincingly that Jesus' remarks to his disciples in John 14:16-17 that the Spirit would be "in" them does not mean that the Holy Spirit was not in Old Testament saints (cf. Luke 1:41,67).[22]

The transformation of Israel from an habitually disobedient people to the new people of God will be accomplished by the gift of a new heart and a new spirit. The terms heart and spirit are not precise biological or psychological components of humankind. They are aspects of the human person. As John Taylor observes:

> The *heart* includes the mind and the will, as well as the emotions; it is in fact the seat of the personality, the inmost nature of man. The *spirit* is the impulse which drives the man and regulates his desires, his thoughts and his conduct.[23]

The heart and the spirit are interconnected. Israel's past reflected a compound problem. Its "heart of stone" (36:26) was insensitive to the will

---

[19]Hildebrandt, *Old Testament Theology of the Spirit of God*, 95.

[20]Charles Lee Feinburg, *The Prophecy of Ezekiel: The Glory of the Lord* (Chicago: Moody Press, 1969), 209.

[21]Bruce Vawter and Leslie J. Hoppe, *A New Heart: A Commentary on the Book of Ezekiel* (Grand Rapids: Wm. B. Eerdmans Publishing Co., 1991), 163.

[22]Fredricks, "Rethinking the Role of the Holy Spirit," 87-97.

[23]John B. Taylor, *Ezekiel: An Introduction and Commentary* (London: The Tyndale Press, 1969), 232.

of God. It was rebellious and stubborn. Israel's *ruach* had formerly been
a "spirit of harlotry" (Hos 5:4), an impulse toward covenant unfaithful-
ness. The compound nature of Israel's problem rendered the nation impo-
tent to do good. It did not have to be this way. H.W. Wolff calls attention
to the neutrality of the human *ruach*.[24] Some Israelites, like Caleb, had a
different *ruach*; they chose to obey Yahweh (Num 14:24). Consequently,
we find the psalmist praying, "renew a steadfast spirit within me...sustain
me with a willing spirit" (Ps 51:10,12).

The psalmist's prayer would be actualized in the restored Israel. God
would change Israel's disposition by removing the "heart of stone" and
creating a "heart of flesh" in its place (Ezek 36:26). Just as the "coming of
the Ruach of the Lord upon Saul 'gave him another heart'" (1 Sam 10:9),
the Spirit would create a new heart in Israel.[25] The "new heart" would be
sensitive and responsive to the will of God. Jeremiah, who also prophesies about this transformation (Jer 31:31-34), says that God's law will be
written on this new heart (31:33). Because the law will be internalized, it
will no longer be necessary for Israelites to teach each other the law. The
new heart, full of the knowledge of God's law, will enable every Israelite to
"know God" (Jer 31:34).[26]

God will energize Israel's new heart with a new spirit. The former
"spirit of harlotry" (Hos 5:4) will be replaced by a *ruach* which derives
from Yahweh, himself. "I will put My Spirit within you..." is the prophetic
promise (Ezek 36:27). The Spirit of Yahweh will empower Israel to live
according to God's laws and statutes. As William Dyrness points out,
"the Spirit becomes the new foundation of personal life for the people of
God."[27] There is a broader fulfillment of this prophetic word that comes in
the future. However, the Old Testament believer knew the presence of the
Lord as communicated by his Spirit.[28]

Ezekiel's expectation of the Spirit's work in Israel finds a final expression after his prophecy against Gog and Magog (38-39). Ezekiel affirms
that, regardless of possible threats against Israel, Yahweh will pour out his
Spirit upon the people (39:29). Ezekiel's prophetic word is paralleled by
other prophets (Isa 32:15, 44:3; Joel 2:28-29).

---

[24]Hans Walter Wolff, *Anthropology of the Old Testament*, trans. Maragret Kohl
(Philadelphia: Fortress Press, 1974), 37-38.

[25]Moody, *Spirit of the Living God*, 21.

[26]Elmer A. Martens, *God's Design: A Focus on Old Testament Theology*, 2d ed.
(Grand Rapids: Baker Books, 1994), 87-102. Elmer Martens discusses the impli-
cations of what it means to know God in his chapter on the knowledge of God in
Israel.

[27]William Dyrness, *Themes in Old Testament Theology* (Downers Grove, IL:
InterVarsity Press, 1979), 207.

[28]Ibid., 208.

II. The Work of the Spirit in the Restoration of the Temple

Unfortunately, the scarcity of information from the Persian period leaves us without much knowledge about the details of the Spirit's work. The primary sources for the temple reconstruction are Ezra, Haggai and Zechariah. Ezra does not mention the Spirit in its account. Haggai and Zechariah give brief accounts of the Spirit's involvement in the restored nation of Israel. Haggai is the most informative account of the Spirit's role in the actual rebuilding of the temple.

The book of Haggai opens with the declaration of God's indictment against Israel for not rebuilding the temple in the post-exilic era. The prophecy is dated to the first day of the sixth month in the second year of King Darius, the Persian king. Based on the Persian chronological system, the prophecy would have occurred on August 19, 520 BC.[29] Nothing in the prophecy explains Israel's shortcoming except the implication that Israel was focused on its own concerns of rebuilding private homes while the Lord's house lay in ruins. The prophecy ends as fragmentary as it begins. It is obvious that the post-exilic community responded in obedience to God's word through Haggai (1:14-15). The Lord promised to bless them for their obedience in committing to rebuild the temple.

If the reign of Darius had been Israel's first opportunity to rebuild the temple, there would not have been a divine indictment against the people. The truth is that Israel had failed to follow through on an earlier opportunity to rebuild the temple during the reign of Cyrus the Great.

Ezra contextualizes Haggai's message by recording Cyrus' restoration policy toward Israel and Israel's early attempt to rebuild the temple. Ezra records the event from a distinctive perspective. He understands the political reality of Persian authority as the channel for divine benevolence and blessing. For Ezra, as Sara Japhet has pointed out:

> Those who actualize the divine history of Israel are the kings of Persia. All of God's favors toward His people -- the building of the temple, the return of the exiles, the establishment of the cult, the enforcement of the Torah and its commandments—reach the people through the mediation of the kings of Persia, "whose spirit the Lord stirred up." God does not bring about the history of His people by direct intervention nor by the mediation of the leaders and personages of Israel alone, but rather through indirect action in which the kings of Persia play an indispensable role.[30]

---

[29]Dillard and Longmann, *An Introduction to the Old Testament*, 429.

[30]Sara Japhet, "Sheshbazzar and Zerubbabel Against the Background of the Historical and Religious Tendencies of Ezra-Nehemiah," *Zeitschrift für die Alttestamentliche Wissenschaft* 94 (1982): 73.

According to Ezra, Cyrus, acting under the sovereignty of Yahweh, appointed Sheshbazzar to lead the Jewish exiles back to their ancestral homeland sometime around 538 BC. Cyrus authorized the rebuilding of the temple (Ezra 1:1-4) and restored the former temple treasure—stolen by the Babylonians—to the Jews for use in the new temple. The Jewish exiles who were not planning to return to Canaan donated gold, silver, and other goods. Under Sheshbazzar's authority, about 50,000 Jews returned from the Babylonian exile to rebuild the nation of Judah and the temple (Ezra 2:1-65).

The earliest attempt to rebuild the temple failed. Israel's neighbors opposed the rebuilding effort and managed to stop it. The Samaritans, in particular, are singled out for condemnation for their role in opposing the temple reconstruction (Ezra 4). The repatriated Jews abandoned the temple project for about fifteen years. It was the second year of Darius' reign (520 BC) when God raised up Haggai, the prophet, to call Israel back to the task of rebuilding the temple (Hag 1:1).

Haggai's prophetic mission becomes the occasion for a pivotal revelation of the Spirit's work in the temple building community. The task of rebuilding was difficult at best. The enemies of Israel continued to oppose its reconstruction. The resources for building were limited. The task was physically demanding. The overall mood of the temple builders seems to have been discouragement (Hag 2:1-9). In the midst of the despair, God breaks into the situation with a prophetic revelation:

> "But now take courage, Zerubbabel," declares the Lord, "take courage also, Joshua son of Jehozadak, the high priest, and all you people of the land take courage," declares the Lord, "and work; for I am with you," says the Lord of hosts. "As for the promise which I made you when you came out of Egypt, My Spirit is abiding in your midst; do not fear!" (vv. 4-5)

The phrase "I am with you" (v.4) is loaded with meaning.[31] It guarantees divine presence and support for the task which is given. The phrase has a strong tradition in crisis contexts. At Bethel, God assured Jacob, "I am with you" (Gen 28:15) to preserve and protect you. When God called prophets, he often assured them of his empowering presence to carry out their ministries (Moses, Exod 3:12; Jeremiah, 1:8,19). Gideon, a judge, was promised divine presence in effecting the deliverance of Israel from its enemies (Judg 6:16). The prophet Amos gives the promise of divine presence to the righteous of Israel (Amos 5:14).[32]

---

[31]The discussion from this point to the conclusion is taken verbatim from my commentary on Haggai, which will be published by Sheffield Press in the near future.

[32]The phrase even occurs in the New Testament as a part of Jesus' promise to his disciples (Matt 28:20).

The occurence of the phrase, "I am with you" in the book of Haggai is not surprising. In fact, the phrase occurs twice in the book (1:13; 2:4).[33] The historical context of Haggai's ministry parallels the earlier uses of this phrase in numerous ways. Haggai's audience had been called or commissioned for a task. The circumstances surrounding the task were threatening. There was resistance or objection to the task from the called ones. All of these elements commonly occur in prophetic call narratives.[34]

The occurence of the phrase, "I am with you," does not suggest, in and of itself, a clear revelation of the Spirit's work. In Haggai, however, the phrase is paralleled by the statement "My Spirit is abiding in your presence..." (2:5). The parallel statement opens the way to a much fuller understanding of how the promise of divine presence should be interpreted in Haggai 1:13 and 2:4. The word "abides" (2:5) is a Hebrew participle denoting continuous action.[35] The thrust of the statement is, "My Spirit will always remain among you."[36]

The important issue for our purpose concerns the role of the Spirit in the community of temple builders as he is continually among them. Pieter Verhoef is right in asserting that the function of the Spirit in Haggai is not renewal.[37] The Spirit is not described as "within you" as in Ezekiel 36:26,27. He is among Israel "to encourage and to assure them."[38] The Spirit's work of renewal was already a reality in Israel's experience. It is evident in the post-exilic community's response to Haggai's initial call to rebuild the temple. The leaders and the people "obeyed the voice of the Lord their God" (Hag 1:12). The response is in stark contrast to the pre-exilic community which disobeyed the words of the prophets so often that it led to national destruction and exile.

The role of the Spirit in Haggai's day is a clear indication that personal (Ezek 36:26-28) and national renewal (Ezek 37:1-14) were not a panacea for Israel's inconsistent relationship with God. What Israel needed and received was the "abiding" presence of the Spirit to sponsor and empower daily obedience to God's will. Commitment to God is sometimes overwhelmed by frustrating and threatening circumstances.[39] A vital role of

[33]Some commentators argue that the phrase is an editorial insertion in 1:13; see Pieter A. Verhoef, *The Books of Haggai and Malachi: New International Commentary on the Old Testament* (Grand Rapids: Wm. B. Eerdmans Publishing Company, 1987), 84, for a rebuttal to this view.

[34]Norman Habel, "The Form and Significance of the Call Narratives," *Zeitschrift für die Alttestamentliche Wissenschaft* (1965): 297-323.

[35]Verhoef, *The Books of Haggai and Malachi*, 100.

[36]Ibid.

[37]Ibid.

[38]Hildebrandt, *Old Testament Theology*, 100.

[39]Hans Walter Wolff, *Haggai: A Commentary* (Minneapolis: Augsburg Publishing House, 1988), 59-62.

the Spirit in the construction of the Second Temple was to energize continually the human spirits of the Jews in order to bring the task to completion. The *ruach* of the Lord is "animating vigor and strengthening presence."[40] Thus, the admonition, "do not fear!" (2:5), and the statement that
"the Lord stirred up the spirit of Zerubbabel . . . Joshua . . . and all the
remnant of the people" (1:14).

The continual presence of the Holy Spirit as strengthening presence
is a new experience for Israel in the post-exilic period.[41] It is not new in the
sense that Israelites never experienced it before. The numerous occurances
of the phrase, "I am with you" in the Old Testament would argue against
such a conclusion. What is new is that this becomes the common experience of the community of faith. The abiding presence of the Spirit is no
longer limited to those with a special anointing. It is no longer existent
only in episodic events. Now, it is the normative experience of God's
people. Walther Eichrodt calls this *"the central miracle of the new age."*[42]
In this context, the Spirit expresses himself as a separate entity from God
who is "of [himself] . . . concerned with human affairs."[43]

The Spirit, as a separate entity, becomes a mediator between humankind and God.[44] He is never separated from God but becomes a personal
subject bearing divine attributes. Consequently, the Spirit is the Holy
Spirit of God. As God's Spirit, he is the efficacious power of God among
Israel and the world. The concept of God's activity in Israel expands from
that of power working externally and periodically upon persons to power
working internally and continually in the personal lives of all God's people.[45]

The announcement and the promise of the Spirit's empowering presence (Hag 2:5) is contextualized by the task of rebuilding the temple. The
narrative of the book of Haggai, in conjunction with Ezra 1-6 and the
prophecy of Zechariah, reveals what a difficult project this was. The
circumstances surrounding the building project were so oppressive that
the post-exilic community had abandoned the task earlier. The revival of
the rebuilding effort in 520 BC encountered both external and internal
opposition. The external opposition is described as a "great mountain"
(Zech 4:6). The internal opposition came from the older members of the
community who could remember Solomon's glorious temple. The memory
of past glory brought complaints about the seemingly insignificant temple
being built (Hag 2:1-3).

---

[40]Ibid., 80.
[41]Eichrodt, *Theology of the Old Testament*, 59-62.
[42]Ibid., 59.
[43]Ibid., 60.
[44]Ibid.
[45]Ibid., 59.

The fundamental challenge for the post-exilic community was the same issue that confronts the people of God in all generations. How do we do the will of God in the face of overwhelming opposition? The answer is obvious in the messages of Haggai and Zechariah: "be courageous!" (Hag 2:4; Zech 8:9, 13). The verb is translated variously as "be strong" or "stand fast." In the prophecy of Haggai, "be courageous" best communicates the message. The command is justified by the *ki* clause "for/because I am with you" (2:4). God was present in his abiding Spirit (2:5). The empowering presence of Yahweh is evident in a reverse way when Moses warned Israel not to fight against the Canaanites because "Yahweh will not be with you" (Num 14:44). The Israelites, against the counsel of Moses, went to war against the Canaanites and suffered defeat (14:45). On the other hand, Moses (Exod 3:12) and Gideon (Judg 6:12), assured of God's empowering presence, led Israel to victory over their enemies. God, in speaking to Israel in Haggai's day, is surely drawing on a long tradition of empowering presence.[46]

It is interesting that a historical precedent for the empowering presence of Yahweh is given in the text of Haggai: "as for the promise which I made you when you came out of Egypt" (2:5a). The reference is believed by many scholars to be a gloss. Verhoef notes that:

> The consensus of scholarly opinion is that this phrase must be considered a gloss, because (1) it is wanting in the LXX, Vetus Latina, and Peshitta; (2) no attempt to construe this phrase with the surrounding context has proven satisfactory; and (3) it breaks the connection between two clauses in vv. 4 and 5 that were evidently meant to be parallel, viz. "I am with you" (v. 4) and "my Spirit will always remain among you (v. 5)."[47]

It is possible that a scribe made a marginal reference to the promise of divine presence given to Israel after the Exodus (Exod 29:45) and that it was later incorporated into the text of Haggai.[48] The insertion does not alter the message of the text. It only provides commentary.

The magnitude of what is being revealed about the work of the Spirit in Haggai 2:4-5 is stated more succinctly in Zechariah. The prophet Zechariah was contemporary with Haggai and also prophesied about the reconstruction of the Second Temple (4:6-10; 6:9-15; 8:9-13). It was

---

[46]The apostle Paul continued to draw on that tradition, acknowledging his own weakness in which the grace of God was always more than sufficient (2 Cor 12:9).

[47]Verhoef, *The Books of Haggai and Malachi*, 99.

[48]Joyce G. Baldwin, *Haggai, Zechariah, Malachi: An Introduction and Commentary* (London: InterVarsity, 1974), 47.

Zechariah who delivered a strong word of encouragement to Zerubbabel, the governor and leader of the temple restoration project:

> 4:6 Then he answered and said to me, "This is the word of the Lord to Zerubbabel saying, 'Not by might nor by power, but by My Spirit,' says the Lord of hosts. 7 'What are you, O great mountain? Before Zerubbabel you will become a plain; and he will bring forth the top stone with shouts of "Grace, grace to it!"'"

The message to Zerubbabel is clear and exciting: the abiding presence of the Spirit will guarantee the accomplishment of God's will. The obstacles must have been formidable. They are described metaphorically as a "great mountain" (4:7). The term is not literal. The problem was not mounds of rubble which impeded the building program.[49] Ezra (3-6) relates the manifold problems which plagued the rebuilding of the temple. The metaphor of "great mountain" is used to characterize the opposition as a whole.[50] The guarantee of Spirit enablement is that "before Zerubbabel, you [great mountain] will become a plain" (4:7). The mountain of obstacles will be leveled; the temple will be rebuilt. The hands of Zerubbabel "will finish it" (4:9).

The emphatic message in this word of assurance and encouragement to Zerubbabel is that it is the Spirit who will work through him to achieve the task of temple construction. The completion of the temple is not dependent upon human resources. It is "not by might nor by power" (4:6) that Yahweh's temple will be built. The term "might" is used of military strength.[51] The word " power" is used to describe the strength of load carriers.[52] The two terms combine to make a comprehensive statement about the inadequacy of human efforts alone. In juxtaposition to the impotence of human resources is the all-powerful nature of God's Spirit. The Spirit of God, who empowered the work of the wilderness Tabernacle (Exod 35), will bring the Second Temple to completion.

---

[49]Ibid., 121.

[50]Carol L. Meyers and Eric M. Meyers (*Haggai and Zechariah 1-8,* Anchor Bible vol. 25B [Garden City: Doubleday & Company, Inc., 1987]) argue that the great mountain is Mt. Zion. The leveling of the mountain is understood to refer to the ancient process of temple building upon a "platform" of leveled earth (244-48). The interpretation is unconvincing in view of the context of the prophecy.

[51]Baldwin, *Haggai, Zechariah, Malachi*, 121.

[52]Ibid.

Conclusion

It is apparent that the Old Testament reached a significant degree of theological awareness in its understanding of the work of the Holy Spirit in the post-monarchy period. It is evident in the way that the narratives reflect upon Israel's history and describe the work of the Spirit in those earlier days. It is also evident in the way that they depict the Spirit of Yahweh as separate and distinct from Him, although not as an autonomous entity. The new work of the Spirit is anticipated by the pre-exilic and exilic prophets (especially Ezekiel) but described by the post-monarchy prophets (especially Haggai and Zechariah). The Spirit is clearly the efficacious power of God at work in Israel and the world. The Spirit sponsors and facilitates the construction of the Second Temple in numerous ways. The Spirit restores the temple builders to the land of Canaan (Ezek 37). The Spirit transforms the hearts and spirits of the Jews in the post-exilic community so that the covenant relationship between God and Israel can be restored (Ezek 36). The Spirit abides in the community of faith to inspire and to empower the people to do God's will, of which the construction of the Second Temple is the primary illustration (Hag 2:4-5).

The Davidic Messiah in Early Jewish Literature

Michael E. Fuller[*][1]

I. Introduction: Methodology, Terminology, and Purpose

In the history of scholarship, the study of (the) messiah[2] in early Jewish literature[3] has been hampered by unclear criteria and methodological approaches. Thus it is appropriate to begin this investigation into the *Davidic* messiah with some brief remarks regarding methodology and terminology. In the past some scholars have used "messianic" to characterize eschatological texts or ideas, even when no messiah or other future redeemer is mentioned in a text.[4] Likewise, "messiah" has been used to

---

[*]Michael E. Fuller (Ph.D. candidate, University of Durham). Instructor in Biblical Studies, Lee University.

[1]It is with great pleasure that I contribute this study in honor of Professor Donald Bowdle. As a Christian scholar and teacher, he has provided a high benchmark of piety and excellence for his students. I am grateful for his instruction and guidance that have remained with me throughout the years.

[2]The lower case spelling is used to signify the diversity and complexity of ideas of messianic language (i.e., the explicit appearance of "messiah" or "christ" in a text) in early Jewish literature. As noted below, in most cases, messianic language may be either non-technical or applied to a variety of figures.

[3]While the literature of Second Temple or Early Judaism may include writings from the sixth century BC to the third century AD, this study is primarily interested in the OT, apocryphal, pseudepigraphical, and the DS (Dead Sea) writings from the third century BC to the first century AD. This era encompasses the advent of hellenism into Palestine, the birth of Christianity, and the destruction of the Second temple and its aftermath.

[4]Joseph Klausner, *The Messianic Idea in Israel*, (London: Allen and Unwin, 1956), 9; Sigmund Mowinkel, *He That Cometh*: *The Messiah Concept in the Old Testament and Later Judaism* (Nashville: Abingdon, 1956); Gershom Scholem,

label any redeemer figure in a writing, even in the absence of explicit messianic terminology. It is important to note, however, that the presence of משיח or χριστός ("messiah," "anointed [one]") alone does not signify an eschatological redeemer. In early Jewish literature משיח or χριστός is most often used to denote someone or something as "anointed" without any hint of future or ultimate importance. For instance, in the Dead Sea Scrolls (DSS) משיח occurs in several places that refer to (OT) prophets or prophecy (CD-A [*Damascus Document*] 2.12-13;[5] 5.21-6:1;[6] 1QM [*War Scroll*] 11.7-8).[7] Thus CD-A 5.21-6.1 reads:

> And the land became desolate, for they spoke rebelliously against God's ordinances (מצות) (which were given) through the hand of Moses and through the holy anointed ones (במשיחי הקודש).[8] And they prophesied falsely . . . .[9]

Two other passages which mention anointed figures are 4Q375 (*Apocryphon of Moses*) and 4Q376 (*Liturgy of the Three Tongues of Fire*). Both (4Q375, col. 1.9; 4Q376, col. 1.2) describe anointed priests in their respective cultic/ceremonial contexts.[10] Neither of these passages cast the priest as a special figure of Israel's salvation.[11] Several other scrolls, as well, speak of "anointed" ones in contexts that apparently have little or no obvious eschatological overtones.[12]

The Messianic Idea in Judaism (New York: Schocken, 1971); G. Vermes, "Messianism," in *History of the Jewish People in the Age of Jesus Christ (175 BC - AD 135)* by Emil Schürer, trans. T. A. Burkill et al, rev. and ed. G. Vermes and F. Miller (Edinburgh: Clark, 1979), 489-555.

[5]Par.: 4Q266 [4QDᵃ], frag. 2, 2.12 (formerly, 4Q267 [4QDᵇ]).

[6]Par.: 4Q266 [4QDᵃ], frag. 3, 2.17 (formerly, 4Q267 [4QDᵇ]); 6Q15 [6QD], frag. 3.4.

[7]4Q287 (*4QBerakoth*ᵇ) and 4QDᵉ, frag. 9,2.14 probably refer to slander or rebellion against the prophets, although the writer may have in mind "anointed" prophets/visionaries *within the DS Community* and not within the OT.

[8]Such texts witness to the OT already being conceived of as the Law and the Prophets, although the content of these two divisions of scripture is not indicated.

[9]All translations are mine unless otherwise noted.

[10]4Q376 is highly fragmentary and more difficult to assess. Col 3:1-3 does mention the Prince of the Congregation and "his enemies." Therefore this passage may pertain to preparations for the eschatological war between Israel and the Kittim. 1QM, col. 9.8 speaks of the danger of the priests profaning their "priestly anointing" with the dead and the blood on the battlefield. 4Q521, frag. 8.9 refers to "all his anointed ones" in a context that has priestly connotations: [... וכל כלי קודשו...] (4Q521 frag. 8.9).

[11]However, as demonstrated below, some DSS passages may indeed portray (a) priest(s) in this fashion.

[12]See 4Q254, frag. 4.1 ("the two sons of the oil of the anointing"; see Zech 4:14); 4Q381 ("and I, your anointed": [David?]; 4Q377 (". . . Moses, his anointed"), etc.

Since מֹשִׁיחַ does not in itself operate as a technical term meaning "messiah," its interpretation must be determined by other factors within the text. Even when מֹשִׁיחַ does signify a future savior, and thus may be translated messiah, it still must be qualified by the interpreter since a number of eschatological, messianic figures appear in early Jewish literature.[13] In this study, "messiah" is used to identify a future *Davidic ruler* only when he is explicitly referred to as מֹשִׁיחַ or χριστός in a text or directly connected with "messiah" by other appellations or terms within the writing or corpus of genetically related writings.[14] Of particular interest is the characterization of the figure of the text in question. How is he portrayed? And what are his role and duties? In the study of particular passages from Second Temple Judaism, both the diverse as well as the common expectations surrounding a Davidic messianic figure are brought into clearer focus.

---

[13]Since "messiah" is such an "amorphous and fluid" term (James H. Charlesworth, "From Messianology to Christology: Problems and Prospects," in *The Messiah: Developments in Earliest Judaism and Christianity*, ed. Charlesworth [Minneapolis: Fortress, 1992], 10), this may explain why references to messiah(s) or anointed figure(s) usually appear with attributives, in genitival phrases, construct states, or in conjunction with other titles and appellations. Even when מֹשִׁיחַ appears in the absolute and clearly designates an eschatological figure, such as in the DSS, the *Psalms of Solomon,* and the NT, the term appears alongside associate titles or alternative identifications. William Scott Green, ("Introduction: Messiah in Judaism: Rethinking the Question," 4, in *Judaisms and their Messiahs at the Turn of the Christian Era* [Cambridge: Cambridge University Press, 1990]) argues that "[t]he New Testament's gingerly application of multiple titles suggests a crisis of classification, the dilemma of a signified without a signifier." However, as argued in this study, the diverse use of "messiah," in both "routine" and eschatological contexts, probably makes further qualification necessary, even in early Jewish literature.

[14]The work of Jacob Neusner, William S. Green, and Ernst Frerichs, eds., (*Judaisms and their Messiahs at the Turn of the Christian Era* [Cambridge: Cambridge University Press, 1990]) and James H. Charlesworth, ed., (*The Messiah: Developments in Earliest Judaism and Christianity* [Minneapolis: Fortress, 1992]) have resulted in tighter methodological controls in the study of messiah. (Charlesworth's volume originated from papers given in 1987 at *The First Princeton Symposium on Judaism and Christian Origins*.) John J.Collins (*The Scepter and the Star: The Messiahs of the Dead Sea Scrolls and other Ancient Jewish Literature* [New York: Doubleday, 1995], 11-19, 60) broadens the definition of "messiah" to include Davidic figures and others who can be terminologically linked in related texts to "messiah." This modification results primarily from the DSS, where a redeemer may be identified by multiple titles, including "messiah." While this means of identifying "messiah(s)" is appropriate, it must be used cautiously, since it can (wrongfully) perpetuate the notion that "messiah" was the dominant category by which (an) eschatological redeemer(s) was referred.

II. The Davidic messiah in early Jewish literature

The expectation of a Davidic messiah is not often found in the literature of Early Judaism. While in Daniel 9:25-26, two figures are referred to
as משיח in the absolute state, neither is specified as a Davidic redeemer.[15]
There is no mention of a Davidic messiah in the OT Apocrypha,[16] and in
the OT Pseudepigrapha, only two documents[17] mention such a figure
(*Psalms of Solomon*; *4 Ezra*). Several documents among the DSS refer to
a Davidic messiah, but often different epithets are used for the figure as
well. This analysis begins with the *Psalms of Solomon*, proceeds to the
Dead Sea Scrolls, and then finishes with the *4 Ezra*. The book of *4 Ezra* is
treated last since it is the only document from the literature that refers to a
Davidic messiah in the wake of the Second temple destruction, and thus
may testify to certain modifications of the concept of messiah.

A. The Psalms of Solomon

While the hope for a Davidic messiah is not common in the literature of
Second Temple Judaism, there are texts that do indeed demonstrate that
some Jews attached great importance to a Davidic figure in the hope for
Israel's restoration. A *locus classicus* for the study of messianism occurs

---

[15]The "anointed one" in Dan 9:25 probably corresponds either to the governor
Zerubbabel or the high priest Joshua of the sixth century return and restoration,
while the anointed one who is "cut off" in 9:26 is usually interpreted as the murder
of the high priest Onias III in the mid-second century BC (2 Macc 4:33-35), so J.
J. M. Roberts, "The Old Testament's Contribution to Messianic Expectations,"
in *The Messiah: Developments in Earliest Judaism and Christianity*, ed. James H.
Charlesworth (Minneapolis: Fortress, 1992), 40-41. For Onias III's murder, see
Victor Tcherikover, *Hellenistic Civilization and the Jews* (New York: Atheneum,
1970), 172.

[16]Cf. 1 Macc 2:57; Sir 47:22.

[17]Some references to a messiah in the writings of the Pseudepigrapha are not
explicitly connected with David (e.g., *2 Baruch*, the *Similitudes* [*1 Enoch* 36-71];
3 Enoch). Other occurrences are in documents that are either of a late date and/or
have undergone intensive Christian redaction (e.g., *Apocalypse of Zephaniah*, *Apocalypse of Elijah*, *Apocalypse of Sedrach*, *Ascension of Isaiah*, *Odes of Solomon*,
etc.). The pseudepigraphical writings of *2 Baruch*, *4 Ezra*, *1 Enoch* 37-71 [the
Similitudes], probably date from the mid to late first century AD and are of much
value in evaluating the (re)formulations of messianic expectations which occurred
in the wake of the Jerusalem's destruction, a formative milieu of Christianty's
conception of Jesus. There are traditions about the messiah in these documents
which predate their penning.

in the *Psalms of Solomon* (*Pss.Sol.*) (17:21-46;18:5-8).[18] At three different points a future χριστός[19] is mentioned (*Pss.Sol.* 17:32; 18:5,7).

Pss.Sol. 17:32	*Pss.Sol.* 18:5	*Pss.Sol.* 18:6
καὶ βασιλεὺς αὐτῶν χριστὸς κύριος.[20] And their king [will be] the Lord messiah.	καθαρίσαι ὁ θεὸς Ισραηλ εἰς ἡμέραν ἐλέους ἐν εὐλογία εἰς ἡμέραν ἐκλογῆς ἐν ἀνάξει χριστοῦ αὐτοῦ May God cleanse Israel for a day of mercy with blessing for the appointed day when his messiah will reign.	μακάριοι οἳ γενόμενοι ἐν ταῖς ἡμέραις ἐκείναις . . . (7) ὑπὸ 'ράβδον παιδείς Χριστοῦ κυρίου ἐν φόβω θεοῦ αὐτοῦ ἐν σοφία πνεύματος καὶ δικαιοσύνης καὶ ἰσχύος 18:8a χατευθῦναι ἄνδρα ἐν ἔργοις δικαιοσύνης φόβω θεοῦ Blessed are the ones who will be in those days . . . under the rod of discipline of the Lord's messiah in fear of his God in wisdom of spirit and of righteousness and strength to lead people in works of righteousness in (the) fear of God.

[18]The *Psalms of Solomon* is a pseudepigraphical writing that dates from the middle part of first century BC. It is located, as well, in some versions of the LXX. *Psalms of Solomon* 2, 8, 17 make clear allusions to the events regarding Aristobulus II and Hyrcanus II and the invasion of Pompey (e.g., *Pss.Sol.* 2:2; 8:16-28). *Pss.Sol.* 2:26 refers to Pompey's death in 48 BC. See George W.E. Nickelsburg, *Jewish Literature Between the Bible and the Mishnah* (Philadelphia: Fortress, 1981), 195-98, 203-12.

[19]Syr.: mšyh'

[20]The reading of "the Lord's messiah" is disputed. Although both the Syriac (mšyh' mrn') and the Greek support it, largely on the basis of 18:7 (χριστοῦ κυρίου [the]Lord's anointed) and the belief that χριστὸς κύριος reflects the Hebrew *Vorlage*: משיח אדון, the emendation χριστὸς κυρίου is suggested. See Joseph L. Trafton, *The Syriac Version of the Psalms of Solomon: A Critical Evaluation,* SBL Septuagint and Cognate Studies Series 11 (Atlanta: Scholars Press, 1985), 177.

In the *Psalms of Solomon* the messiah is integrally linked to God's promise of eternal kingship to David (17:4). This promise and the charge that others have wrongfully usurped the Davidic throne (17:5c-6) form the basis of the appeal: "See Lord, and raise up for them their king, (the) son of David, in the time which you know, O God, to rule over (τοῦ βασιλεῦσαι) your servant, Israel" (*Pss.Sol.* 17:21). The messiah's kingship[21] is developed between the opposing poles of the kingship of God and the rule of the corrupt Jewish regime (17:5-20) and that of the foreign conqueror.[22] The kingship of God is intrinsically tied to that of his anointed regent.[23] As God is called "king" (17:1, 34, 46), so is the earthly ruler (17:4, 21, 32, 42).[24] In applying the same title to both God and the messiah, the writer blurs clear, categorical distinctions between the figures.[25] While the messianic king is certainly subordinate to God the king, it is not the writer's aim to downplay the significance of the earthly regent. Rather, the main point is that, unlike Israel's corrupt rulers and foreign powers, the future Davidic regent has been anointed *by God* to restore Israel and will manifest and inaugurate the deity's rule.[26]

In contradistinction to some restoration passages in early Jewish literature, the messiah in the *Psalms of Solomon* is depicted as the sole agent of all aspects of Israel's re-establishment. He alone procures the kingdom (17:21-32) and then reigns over it (17:32-44). The *chief aim* of Israel's reconstitution is to bring the land and the people into *a state of*

---

[21]The focus on kingship in *Psalms of Solomon* 17 is underlined by the vocabulary found therein: nine of the fifteen occurrences of βασιλεὺς (*Pss.Sol.* 17:1(2x),4,20,21,32 (2x),34,42,46; cf. 2:30(2x),32; 5:11,19) in the *psalms* are here; three of the four references to βασιλεία (*Pss.Sol.* 17:3; 5:18)/βασιλείον (*Pss.Sol.* 17:4,6) are in this chapter, and βασιλεύω is found only in 17:21.

[22]*Psalms of Solomon* 17 begins and ends with a declaration of the Lord as the eternal king (βασιλεὺς) (17:1,46, also 17:34), while the Jewish ruling body (βασιλείον) is denounced as sinful and illegitimate (17:5-6,20b). The gentile ruler is described as lawless (17:11) as well as the Jewish king (17:20). Immediately prefacing the writer's cry for a new king (17:21) is the charge in 17:20: ὁ βασιλεὺς ἐν παρανομίᾳ ("The king was lawless").

[23]If the absolute reading of "lord" is to be retained in regard to the messianic figure, this would be another shared appellation between the king and deity; see PsSol 17:1,4,21: God as Lord; 17:32d: king as lord.

[24]Moreover, both the deity-king and the future king are said to rule eternally (17:1,46; 17:4).

[25]This does not mean that the royal figure is portrayed as supernatural or a deity per se. As in other kingships in the ancient and hellenized Near East, the king was closely associated with the patron deity. The OT reflects this as well (e.g., Psalms 2:6-7 and 2 Samuel 7). Later in *Psalms of Solomon* 17, the author characterizes the words of the king ὡς λόγοι ἁγίων ἐν μέσῳ λαῶν ἡγιασμένων (*Pss.Sol.* 17:43c), a possible angelic designation.

[26]Nickelsburg (*Jewish Literature,* 208) notes: "As God's vicar and agent on earth, the king shares in, or embodies, divine qualities."

holiness/righteousness. All the components of the restoration—(1) eradication of Gentiles and sinners from the land, (2) regathering of the tribes,
(3) submission of the nations, and (4) the cleansing of Jerusalem—are
integrally related to this objective and carried out by the messianic king.[27]
Psalms of Solomon 17:32 forms an *inclusio* with 17:21, serving as a re-
statement of the messiah's kingship and the kingdom that he will establish
17:21-32: "And he will be a righteous king, and there will be no
unrighteousness in his days in their midst because all of them will be holy
and their king will be the Lord's messiah" (17:32).

Psalms of Solomon 17:32 also marks the beginning of the next section
(17:32-44), which follows up the *establishment* of the kingdom with a
portrayal of the new messianic *reign* that will be implemented over the
reconstituted Israel. While the restoration process initially involves some
degree of violence in the overthrow of the ruling powers and the expulsion
of foreigners from the land (PsSol 17:22-25),[28] the reign itself is characterized by holiness and a strong anti-war component. The king will not rely
on weaponry or violence in his domain over Israel and the nations.[29]
Rather, he will rely upon God.[30] He is portrayed as a righteous, sage-king,
with special emphasis upon his word and blessing in maintaining the
purity of the restored Israel.[31]

The writer's insistence on the messiah's absolute reliance upon God is
a leitmotif in the *Psalms of Solomon* of 17 and 18. For this understanding,
the author is deeply indebted to Isaiah (Isa 11:1-4). It is noteworthy to
point out here that Isaiah 11 plays an important part in the conception of
the messiah elsewhere in early Jewish literature (below):

> Isa 11:1) A shoot shall go out from the stump of Jesse, and a
> sprout shall spring from his roots. (2) And the Spirit of God

---

[27]The messiah inaugurates the restoration as a warrior-king who eradicates all
sinners and the gentiles (17:22-5) from Jerusalem. The elimination of the "unrighteous" ones (17:22) from the land is matched positively by his regathering of the
tribes, "a holy people" (17:26a, 43bc, 44c). The tribes are to be distributed upon
the ethnically cleansed land (17:28b) according to their (ancient) tribal allotments
(17:28a). The future regent will return Jerusalem to its ancient state holiness
(17:30b) (καὶ καθαριεῖ Ιερουσαλημ ἐν ἁγιασμῷ ὡς καὶ τὸ ἀπ᾽ ἀρχῆς).
Ruled over by a righteous, Davidic king, who has cleaned the city from gentiles and
sinners and filled her with righteous Jews, Jerusalem will become the "glorious"
capital of the world. The nations that ruled over Israel will become submissive to
her (17:30a). In their pilgrimages to acknowledge Israel and the Jewish deity's
supremacy, they will return the diaspora Jews to behold the city of God (17:31).
[28]But he does so without weaponry (*Pss.Sol.* 17:24b).
[29]The kingship of the messiah will be in opposition to the foreign powers who
have "laid waste the land of Israel" (17:11-20; 2:1-29; 8:1-22).
[30]Cf. the description of the gentile ruler, Pompey, in *Pss.Sol.* 2:28-29.
[31]This emphasis runs throughout 17:33-44.

> shall rest upon him (and) the Spirit of wisdom and understanding (and) the Spirit of counsel and strength (and) the Spirit of knowledge and the fear of God. (3) And he shall delight in the fear of God. And he shall not judge by the sight of his eyes or decide by the hearing of his ears, (4) but shall judge the poor with righteousness and shall decide with equity the afflicted of the earth. He shall strike the earth with the rod of his mouth and with the breath of his lips he shall kill the wicked.[32]

In the initial purging of gentiles and sinners from the land of Israel, the messiah is expected to be "undergirded" by God with "strength," "wisdom," and "righteousness" (*Pss.Sol.* 17:22-23; cf. Isa 11:2) as he eradicates the unrighteous nations "with an iron rod" (*Pss.Sol.* 17:24a; cf. Isa 11:4c; Psalm 2:9) and "the word of his mouth" (17:24b; cf. Isa 11:4c [LXX]).[33] In the description of the messianic reign, (17:32-44), the royal figure again "strikes the earth with the word of his mouth," this time as an indication of "mercy" and "blessing" to the submissive gentiles and righteous people (17:35a; cf. 17:24b; Isa 11:4c [LXX]). It probably also denotes the ongoing cleansing, which is the chief characteristic of the messiah's rule, since the implications of sin and unrighteous are Israel's desecration and destruction. Unlike other kings who rule by their own military and political might, the writer is careful to stress that the Davidic king's power originates from God. Drawing from Isaiah 11, the writer claims that God will make the king "powerful in the holy Spirit and wise in the counsel of understanding with strength and righteousness" (17:37; Isa 11:2). In similar terms the psalmist in 18:6-7 looks forward to the reign ("rod") of discipline of the messiah, who "in the fear of his God, in the wisdom of the Spirit and of righteousness and strength" (18:7; Isa 11:2-3) "will direct Israel in righteousness and the fear of God" (18:8; Isa 11:2-3). This portrayal of the Davidic king— as one who was chosen by God and empowered by him alone through the holy Spirit and wisdom—is the fundamental basis for the writer's primary claim that the expected Davidic ruler is, in fact, the Lord's messiah.

In *Psalms of Solomon* 17-18 the writer makes several crucial claims about the future king: (1) He will be a "Son of David" since God's promise

---

[32]Translation based on RSV.

[33]From his attributes of "strength," "wisdom," and "righteousness" (17:22) six infinitival phrases (17:22-4) underscore the destructive power of the warrior-king in the initial holy war: θραῦσαι ("to shatter"); καθαρίσαι ("to cleanse"); ἐξῶσαι ("to expel"); ἐκτρῖψαι ("to root out"); συντρῖψαι ("to crush"); ὀλεθρεῦσαι ("to destroy"). There is, however, no mention of the Spirit in this section, a point which is critical to Isaiah 11. The fact that the destruction of the enemies occurs through the "word of his mouth" (17:24) does not lessen the violent portrayal of the king's activities in 17:22-5. It simply stresses the fact that he is uniquely enabled by God to render destruction.

to David has eternal validity and hope for future restoration. (2) The messiah's appearance will signify the inauguration of Israel's restoration, which takes place in the eradicating of all gentiles and sinners from the land of Israel, gathering the tribes into the land, submission of the nations, and the renewing of Jerusalem to the state of her ancient holiness. (3) The messianic king's primary task is the establishment and maintenance of righteousness and holiness. (4) The Davidic king shuns all other exterior means of power; he is utterly reliant on God, and through his Spirit, wisdom, and strength rules Israel in righteousness.

B. The Dead Sea Scrolls

The identification of a particular eschatological figure *as a Davidic messiah* in the DSS sometimes depends on the correlation of several (related) terms and references from the various writings. [34] However, while such connections are critical in evaluating the numerous epithets in the scrolls, it is often lost in the discussion that only one (extant) text in the DSS identifies a future *Davidic* king *explicitly* as (the) משיח. 4Q252 (*Commentary on Genesis[a]*)[35] col. 5.1-4 reads:

[לו]א יסור שליט משבט יהודה בהיות לישראל ממשל
[לוא י]כרת יושב כסא לדויד כי המחקק היא ברית המלכות
[ואל]פי ישראל המה הדגלים vacant צד בוא משיח הצדק צמח
דויד כי לו ולזרעו נתנה ברית מלכות עמו עד דורות עולם

(1) A ruler (שליט) shall [no]t depart from the tribe (שבט) of Judah. When there is for Israel dominion (ממשל), (2) [there will not c]ease someone who sits on the throne of David. For 'the staff' (המחקק) is the covenant of the kingdom (ברית המלכות), (3) [and the thousa]nds of Israel, these are 'the feet' (or divisions). Until the messiah of righteousness (משי הצדק) comes, the Branch of (4) David (צמח דויד). For to him and to his descendants the covenant of the kingdom of his people has been given until eternal generations.

As the title of this text implies, it is from a larger work (4Q252-254) that contains pesharim,[36] or interpretations, on parts of Genesis. The passage above comes from a section of that work which apparently interpreted

---

[34] For Collins' assessment of the coordinating terms that relate to a Davidic figure, see *The Scepter*, 11-19, 56-73. Also see the introduction of this paper.

[35] George J. Brooke, et al, *Qumran Cave 4: Parabiblical Texts, Part 3,* DJD 17, (Oxford: Clarendon, 1996), 185-207.

[36] The classification of this work as pesher is debated. See Ida Fröhlich, "Themes, Structure and Genre of Pesher Genesis," *Jewish Quarterly Review* 85 (1994): 81-99.

portions[37] of Jacob's dying testament (Gen 49:1-33) to his twelve sons
(= the twelve tribes of Israel). This particular passage concerns Gen 49:10,
Jacob's testament to Judah:

> The scepter (שבט) shall not depart from Judah, nor the staff
> (ומחקק) from between his feet (רגליו), until he comes
> צד כי־יבא to whom it belongs (שילה).[38] And to him shall be
> the obedience (יקהת) of the peoples (Gen 49:10).

The writer reads Gen 49:10 in conjunction with Jer 33:15-17, which
refers to "the Branch of righteousness" (cf. 4Q252, lines 3-4) and one who
"will not cease for David . . . sitting on the throne of the house of Israel"
(cf. 4Q252, line 2). The "scepter," "the coming one," "the righteous
Branch," and "the enthroned one" are all connected to the hope for a
Davidic ruler in 4Q252. The promise of a future Davidic king is a crucial
component of the writer's messianic conception and is the basis for his
belief in Israel's restoration. The advent of the messiah is expected to
occur in tandem with Israel's dominion (ממשל). This connection is found
in the *Psalms of Solomon* and 4Q161 (below) as well. In addition to his
Davidic lineage, the messiah is defined in terms of "righteousness"
(משיח הצדק), which suggests that like the *Psalms of Solomon* 17-18, the
establishment and maintenance of righteousness may be a dominant feature of the messiah's reign over Israel.[39] This aspect is also evident in line
5, which mentions that "he will [...] observe the Torah with the men of the
Community."

Specific and elaborate details of the messiah's role and duties in Israel's
restoration are minimal in 4Q252. It is plausible that in 4Q252, the writer
simply presents the messiah's enthronement as the climatic finale of Israel's
restoration, rather than as the *instrument* of it. However, if George J.
Brooke is correct in reading הדגלים ("divisions")[40] rather than הרגלים
("feet," cf. Gen 49:10) in line 3, this might imply a more specific role for the
messiah in Israel's dominion. In most cases in the scrolls, particularly in

---

[37]The commentary on the tribes may have been selective. Only portions of
Jacob's testament to Reuben, the firstborn son (4Q252, col. 4.3-7), Judah (col. 5),
and possibly Naphtali (col. 6) are extant in 4QpGen.

[38]For interpretations and proposed emendations of שילה see *A Hebrew and
English Lexicon of the Old Testament,* ed. F. Brown, S.R. Driver, and C.A. Briggs
(Oxford: Clarendon Press, 1907), 1010, col. 1. Possibly the text refers to "tribute" (NRSV) to be paid to the king by the nations or to the coming of Shiloh. The
writer of 4Q252 has obviously understood the reference messianically.

[39]A small fragment of 1Q30 mentions a " holy messiah." There are too many
lacunae to make an interpretation.

[40]Brooke (*Parabiblical,* 205) says a computer enhancement makes the dalet
"certain."

the 1QM (*War Scroll*),[41] הדגלים refers to the divisions of infantry battal-
ions or standards of the tribes of war. The association of this term with the
Davidic king could suggest a militant-messiah who would lead an
eschatological assault. This picture is consistent with some depictions of
the Davidic messiah in early Jewish literature (*Psalms of Solomon* 17-18;
4Q161; 4Q285). Nonetheless this interpretation of the messiah in 4Q252
rests on scanty evidence from the text itself and certainly is not the writer's
emphasis.

In 4Q252 Israel's restoration has special significance to the members
of the DS Community. The reference to "the thousands" (line 3) identifies
the ones in Israel over whom the messiah will rule. While the phrase ("the
thousands") may emphasize the magnitude of the kingdom,[42] it is more
likely that it designates those within the DS group. Lines 5-6 refer to the
"men of the Community" (אנשי היחד) and the כנסת אנשי ("the assembly of
the men of . . ."). Both אנשי היחד and כנסת אנשי are *termini technici* in the
scrolls and refer to the membership and hierarchy of the group. Moreover,
in other places in the scrolls, the epithet "the thousands" is used to denote a layer of the Community's membership as well.[43] Therefore, this
suggests that 4Q252 claims that the DSS Community is the true heir of
Israel's restoration.[44] The full picture of the Community's eschatological
expectations cannot be ascertained from this single document, but it is
clear that for this author, it will include (at least) (1) a Davidic king,[45] (2)

---

[41]1QM 1.14; 3.6; 4.10; 5.5; 12.17; 11QT 21.5; cf. 4Q405, frags. 20-22.14,
which refers to the divisions of the gods/angels around God's throne.

[42]See Dan 7:10.

[43]1QSa (*The Rule of the Congregation*), col.1.6-14 pertains to the initiation
process of new inductees into the Community. Lines 13-14 report that when a
member is thirty years old he can take his place "among the leaders of the thousands of Israel" (בראשי אלפי ישראל). More interesting, in light of the presence
of the messiah in 4Q252, is col. 2.14-15 of 1QSa, where the writer designates the
table positions of the "leaders [of thousands of Israel"] when the messiah comes
(cf. 4Q252, col. 5.3-4). Lastly, 11QT (Temple Scroll) col. 19.16 stipulates the
sacrifices and offering that the "leaders of the thousands of Israel" should give. In
all cases, as far as I can determine, where אלפ occurs in a plural construct state, it
is preceded by "leaders" in the construct state as well, and always refers explicitly
to the DSS Community. The reconstructed ואל[פי in line 3 might well be
emended to רואשי אל[פי]. For the relationship of the Temple Scroll to the
Community and the other DSS, see Hartmut Stegemann, *The Library of Qumran:
On the Essenes, Qumran, John the Baptist, and Jesus* (Grand Rapids: Eerdmans,
1998), 96; Yigael Yadin, *The Temple Scroll: The Hidden Law of the Dead Sea Sect*
(London: Weidenfeld and Nicolson, 1985).

[44]These lines (5-6) may be a commentary on the last portion of Gen 49:10:
". . . to whom it belongs. And to him shall be the obedience (יקהת) of the
peoples."

[45]The writer of 4Q252 does not understand the promise to pertain to a single

Israel's dominion, and (3) Torah observance, the latter of which is already being modeled in the DS group.

The identification of a future messiah as the "Branch of David" is found in three other places in the DSS: 4Q161 (*4QIsaiah Pesher*[a]), 4Q285 (*4QWar Scroll*[g]), and 4Q174 (*4QFlorilegium*). 4Q174[46] (frags. 1-3, 1.1-19) is a composition which interprets various OT texts in view of "the end of days" (אחרית הימים) (lines 2,12,15).[47] Lines 10-13 concern the Davidic messiah:

> (10) And (2 Sam 7:12-14) 'YHWH de[clares] to you that he will build for you a house. And I will raise up your seed after you and establish the throne of his kingdom 11) [forev]er. I will be a father to him and he will be a son to me.' He is the 'Branch of David' (צמח דויד) who will arise with the Interpreter of the Law (דורש התורה) who (12) [will rise up] in Zi[on in] the last days (בא]חרית הימים), as it is written: (Amos 9:11) 'I will raise up the tabernacle of David (סוכת דויד) which has fallen.' This (refers to) 'the tabernacle of (13) David' which has fallen,' who will arise to save Israel (להושיע את ישראל).

The reference to a Davidic ruler occurs within a large block of material (4Q174, frags. 1-3, 1.1-13) that pertains to the interpretation of 2 Sam 7:10-14. Of special interest to the writer in this section of *Florilegium* are the multiple meanings of "house" (בית) (2 Sam 7:11,13). Scholars usually note that this term is associated in the text with two[48] or three temples:[49] the eschatological sanctuary that Yahweh will build "in the end of days" (lines 2-3), the first sanctuary, which was destroyed (lines 5-6), and the "sanctuary of man" (line 6b).[50] The "house" of the messiah in line 10,

---

royal figure who will live forever, but rather one who will be the first in the eternal line ("his descendants") of Davidic kings. Nonetheless, the advent of the first messianic king is seen as the decisive and pivotal point of the restoration or dominion of Israel.

[46]See John M. Allegro, *Qumran Cave 4: I (4Q158-4Q186)*, DJD 5 (Oxford: Clarendon, 1968), 53-57 (hereafter *Cave 4*).

[47]For the "end of days," see Annette Steudel, "אחרית הימים in the Texts from Qumran," *Revue de Qumran* 16 (1993): 225-46.

[48]Michael O. Wise, "4QFlorilegium and the Temple of Adam," *Revue de Qumran* 15 (1991): 103-32.

[49]This is the majority viewpoint as offered by George J. Brooke, *Exegesis at Qumran: 4QFlorilegium in its Jewish Context*, JSOTSS 29 (Sheffield: JSOT, 1985), 193; Collins, *The Scepter*, 106-09; Devorah Dimant, "Qumran Sectarian Literature," in *Jewish Writings of the Second Temple Period: Apocrypha, Pseudepigrapha, Qumran Sectarian Writings, Philo, Josephus*, ed. Michael E. Stone (Philadelphia: Van Gorcum, 1984), 518-21.

[50]It is possible that the "sanctuary of man" (מקדש אדם) is to be equated with

however, is a continuation on this theme in *Florilegium*.[51] In this section
the author mentions some important components of Israel's restoration.
These include God's building of the eschatological, eternal temple (lines
1-3) (cf. Ex 15:17-18), the prohibition of Israel's enemies, foreigners, bas-
tards, and proselytes (lines 3-4) from entering the temple, the emergence
of a holy people— a "temple of man" (מקדש אדם) (line 6)—and the arrival
of the Davidic and priestly figures.[52]

The Davidic messiah is said to be the "house"[53] and the "son"[54] of 2
Samuel 7:13-14. He is referred to as "the Branch of David"[55] and will
"arrive with the Interpreter of the Law in Zi[on in] the end of days." The
writer's interpretation of the "Branch of David" draws upon Amos 9:11,
which foretells the "raising of the tabernacle of David that has fallen."[56]
The Davidic messiah's fundamental duty is put in succinct terms:
יעמוד להושיע את ישראל ("he will arise to save Israel"). Although the
importance of the priestly figure cannot be denied in the scrolls, it is
noteworthy that only the Davidic king is portrayed in *Florilegium* as the
restorer of Israel. The messianic salvation of Israel is not elaborated, but
in light of the preceding lines (4-9), his eschatological activities may concern

---

the eschatological temple that God will build with his own hands. But it is more
likely that the writer refers to three, perhaps four temples or houses: the
eschatological sanctuary, the sanctuary of the Community, the former sanctuary,
(and the house of David, the messiah). For a thorough discussion of this passage,
see Brooke, *Exegesis*, 178-92.

[51]While lines 10-13 are usually treated separately from lines 1-9, these lines
form a literary unity based on the writer's interpretation of 2 Sam 7:10-14 and his
sustained interest in "house" (lines 2, 3, 10). Brooke (*Exegesis*, 178) rightly
observes that "[t]he intention of 4QFlor...is to say that God has established both
houses, the sanctuary and the shoot of David." Nonetheless, Brooke treats lines
10-13 apart from lines 1-9. Dimant ("Sectarian Literature," 521) notes that lines
10-13 "should be seen as a continuation of the first part." The vacant at the end
of line 13 also suggests that this is a cohesive block of material.

[52]Although the priestly messiah ("the Interpreter of the Law") is not dealt with
in this essay, throughout the scrolls, the priest(s), when mentioned, assumes an
equal or superior position. See George J. Brooke, "The Messiah of Aaron in the
Damascus Document," *Revue de Qumran* 15 (1991): 215-30; Collins, *The Scepter*, 74-115.

[53]See lines 2-3; 2 Sam 7:10-11; Exod 15:17-18.

[54]Although the writer does not press the point, the royal figure is identified as
a "son" of God in *4QFlorilegium*. This relationship is already in 2 Samuel 7
(between God and David), but 4Q174 provides firm evidence that in the pre-
Christian period, this title was associated by some Jews with a future, royal,
Davidic figure.

[55]See Jer 33:15; 4Q252.

[56]Cf. the *Damascus Document* (CD-A 7.14-21), where "the tabernacle of David"
is interpreted to be the "books of the Law."

the elimination of Israel's enemies and other unrighteous peoples from Zion and the temple vicinity.

4QIsaiah Pesher[a] (4Q161) frags. 8-10, 3.1-25 provides an interpretive account of Isa 10:33 to 34-11:1-5. The Spirit-endowed figure from Jesse (lines 11-16; Isa 11:1-4) is understood by the writer of 4Q161 to be the [" Branch] of David[57] who will arise in the en[d of days"] (line 17).[58] Apparently the various attributes of the Spirit in Isaiah 11 (lines 11-13) are understood by the writer to be God's empowerment or "support" of the messiah (ואל יסומכנו).[59] The messiah is depicted as a warrior who conquers and judges all of Israel's enemies (lines 18,20).[60] The royal messiah will be "enthroned," "crowned," and dressed in royal "vestments" (lines 19). He will rule (ימשול) over Israel and the nations; however, he will do so in consultation with the priests of the Community (lines 22-24).

A similar but much more fragmented account of a Davidic ruler is given in 4Q285 (*4QWar Scroll*[g]).[61] The messianic king is identified once more as the "Branch of David" (frag. 5.1-2) as well as the "Prince of the Congregation" (frag. 4.1,6; frag. 5.4). As in the *Isaiah Pesher*, he is the leader of an eschatological battle against the "Kittim" (= Rome) (frag. 4.1-9). In fact, 4Q285, frag. 5.1-6 draws explicitly from Isa 10:34-11:1(-4?), which, as shown above, influences the conception of the messiah elsewhere in early Jewish literature. In the conclusion of the war in 4Q285, the messiah is depicted as killing an important figure (cf. Isa 11:4), probably

---

[57]In *4QIsaiah Pesher*[a] (frags. 2-6, 2.15) he is also referred to as the "Prince of the Congregation" (see 4Q285 below).

[58]Translation based on Allegro, *Cave 4*, 14.

[59]Line 11 reads "God will strengthen him by ורה[...]," possibly a reference to the Torah (Allegro, *Cave 4*, 14).

[60]In line 20 the enemy is called Magog. Earlier in 4Q161 (lines 3-9), the opponent is identified as the Kittim (= Rome); in 4Q162 the writer also speaks of "the Congregation of the men of Scoffing who are in Jerusalem" (Allegro, *Cave 4*, 16.)

[61]In 1QM (*War Scroll*) very little is said about the role of the Prince of the Congregation. He is mentioned only in col. 5, where it is said that upon his sh[ield], "they shall write his name [and] the name of Israel and Levi and Aaron and the names of the twelve tribes of Israel according to their generations (2) and the names of the twelve commanders ("princes") of their tribes. "War Scroll," trans. Jean Duhaime, in *The Dead Sea Scrolls,* vol. 2, ed. J. Charlesworth (Louisville: Westminster John Know, 1995). Cf. 1QM 3.12, where the banner of the whole congregation contains the names of Israel and Aaron and the twelve tribes. The literary relationship of 4QM and 1QM remains unclear, although they share many textual correspondences with one another. See Martin Abegg, "Messianic Hope and 4Q285: A Reassessment," *Journal of Biblical Literature* 113 (1994): 81-91.

the enemy leader, and destroying the "Kittim" (frag. 5.4-5).[62] Line 5 also indicates that the Davidic figure will be accompanied by a priest, as noted also in 4Q174 and the 4Q161.

The connection of the "Branch of David" with the "Prince of the Congregation" (נשיא העדה)[63] in 4Q161 and 4Q285 leads to yet more DS texts that bear on the study of a Davidic messiah.[64] In *1QRule of Blessings* (1Q28b), the writer records the "blessing of the Instructor" (משכיל), a priestly figure,[65] over the "Prince of the Congregation" (נשיא העדה) (col. 5.20-29).[66] While the end of the first line of the blessing is unreadable, the Prince is situated within "the covenant of the Community." The Instructor prays that God will use the Prince "to establish (להקים)[67] the kingdom (מלכות) of his people for eve[r...]" (line 21). The technical language[68] contained in these two lines suggests that the Community understands itself to be the recipients of "the kingdom." Israel and the Community are bound up together in the group's theology.

Once again Isaiah 11:1-4[69] exercises a profound influence on the de-

---

[62]This text first gained notoriety as the "Slain/Pierced Messiah text." While it is possible in Hebrew to understand the messiah as the subject or the object of the killing, the grammar favors a reading the messiah as the subject. Moreover, since Isaiah speaks of a descendant of Jesse killing (enemies) with his breath (4Q161, frag. 5.3-5), it is likely the messiah is the envisaged one who is killing the opposing ruler. For further information on the argument, see Collins, *Scepter*, 58-60.

[63]Cf. Ezek 34:24; 37:25.

[64]It is important to note, however, that thus far in this study of the DSS, "messiah" has explicitly appeared only once in conjunction with a Davidic figure (4Q252).

[65]As noted earlier, the royal figure is often accompanied by (a) priestly one(s); the ruler is usually cast in a subordinate position, as here. This subordination is usually more prominent in cultic matters of Torah interpretation or purity requirements (etc.). The Instructor is probably to be equated with the Interpreter of the Law (and the messiah of Aaron), although it is possible there may have been multiple priestly figures of high authority among the Community's hierarchy.

[66]In 1Q28b, col. 1.1, "the Instructor" blesses the whole Congregation. In 3.33 "the blessing of the Instructor" is for the Sons of Zadok.

[67]See line 23: "establish a covenant" ("Blessings (1QSb)," trans. James J. Charlesworth and Loren T. Stuckenbruck, in *Dead Sea Scrolls,* ed. Charlesworth and Stuckenbruck, [Louisville: Westminster John Knox, 1994], 129, ns. 33, 35).

[68]As noted from 4Q252, the "Community" is a technical term for the group at Qumran; furthermore, "covenant" is this context also is technical language and probably refers to the formal membership agreement as contained in such documents as 1QS (*the Community Rule*). 4Q252 refers to "the covenant of the kingdom."

[69]The importance of Isaiah 11 for the messianic conception(s) in early Jewish literature cannot be overestimated. In the study thus far of the Davidic messiah in early Jewish literature, Isaiah 11 has been influential in the *Psalms of Solomon,* 4Q161, 4Q285, and 1Q28b.

piction of the messiah (lines 24-25(28)). Armed only with the "scepter of his mouth" and "breath of his lips," the Prince "destroys the "land" (or "earth") and "kills the wicked" (lines 24-25; Isa 11:4). His attributes of "eternal strength," "the Spirit [...] of knowledge" and the "fear of God" (line 25; Isa 11:2-3) demonstrate that he is the divinely, sanctioned agent of restoration; it is God who establishes him as a world power over other rulers (מושלים) and subjugates the nations to him: ["and all the na]tions shall serve you" (lines 27-28). Therefore, the primary locus of attention in 1Q28b, col. 5 is the messianic, Prince of the Congregation. [70] He is cast as a figure of Israel's, or the kingdom's, re-establishment. Enabled by the Spirit and strength of God, the messiah's reconstitution of the kingdom is portrayed singularly as the defeat and subjugation of foreign powers. His victory is assured through the Community's covenant with God (lines 21).

In the *Damascus Document* (CD-A 7.14-21; CD-B 19.5-14), [71] the writer reflects on the fate of his group and those ("the princes of Judah") [72] who have set themselves outside the covenant, by disavowing his group's interpretation of the Torah (CD-A 7.18-21):

> And the star is the Intepreter of the Law (דורש התורה), who
> will come (or has come) [73] to Damascus, as it is written: (Num

----

[70]The exaltation of the messianic king is alluded to in line 23; he "will be raised to an everlasting height" and made like a "mighty tower."

[71]Two recensions of this text are preserved in the *Damascus Document*. However, only fragments that agree with CD-A 7 are attested at Qumran (4Q267, frag. 3, col. 4; 4Q271, frag. 5). The rescensions of A and B have many correspondences but differ, inter alia, in the OT texts that are cited, as well as the appellations given to the expected figure(s). Thus rather than the Prince of the Congregation and the Interpreter of the Law, CD-B 19.10 refers to the Messiah of Aaron and Israel who will judge those "who did not remain faithful to the covenant" (13-14). As in CD-A, the disobedient ones are called the "princes of Judah" (19.15). Michael A. Knibb ("The Interpretation of Damascus Document VII, 9b-VIII, 2a and XIX, 5b-14," *Revue de Qumran* 15 [1991]: 243-51) argues for the priority of CD-B; Jerome Murphy-O'Conner ("The Original Text of CD 7:9-8:2 = 19:5-14," *Harvard Theological Review* 64 [1971]: 379-86) posits that portions of both A and B were contained in an early version of the document; Sidnie A. White ("A Comparison of the 'A' and 'B' Manuscripts of the Damascus Document," *Revue de Qumran* 48 [1987]: 537-53) argues that both A and B were in the original and a scribal error led to the omission of B in A; Collins (*Scepter*, 80-82) maintains that the textual evidence from the scrolls, which supports A, must be given priority, but he finds White's argument persuasive that both A and B were present in an earlier writing of QD. In this present study priority is given to CD-A in light of corresponding fragments from Qumran. However, if CD-B 19 is early, this would provide a definite link between the Prince of the Congregation and the Messiah of Aaron and Levi.

[72]CD-A 8.3; CD-B 19.15.

[73]The text refers to the "Interpreter" who הבא to Damascus. CD-A 6.8 appar-

24:17) 'A star will go out from Jacob and a scepter will arise from Israel.[74] The "scepter" is the Prince of all of the Congregation, and when he arises, he will destroy all the Sons of Seth. These escaped at the first visitation.

The implications of the division over the interpretation and disobedience of the Torah is central to this passage in CD-A (and CD-B). According to the writer, Israel's disobedience in the past led to the previous division and destruction of Israel and Judah (CD-A 7.7-13). In constructing this historical backdrop, the writer provides an important interpretative context for the expected figure(s). As in 4Q174 (*Florilegium*), the messianic figure is accompanied by the "Interpreter of the Law." The duties of the two figures are closely related but cast in very different terms. The priestly figure will *maintain* Israel's holiness through his instruction of the Torah,[75] while the Prince of the Congregation *eradicates* the unrighteous ones from Israel.[76] Strikingly, in this text, the messiah's destruction is an intra-Jewish activity; the gentiles are not mentioned.[77]

These passages (above) from the DSS contain the most assured references to a future Davidic figure, who may be called a messiah, although as noted, only rarely is he explicitly identified as a משיח. There are, however, several other explicit occurrences of "messiah," which may relate to a future, Davidic figure, although firm terminological grounds are lacking. These passages, therefore, are only briefly identified and discussed.

The first line of 1QSa (*Rule of the Congregation*) establishes the purpose of the document as: "[T]he rule for all the Congregation (היחד) in the

---

ently indicates the Interpreter has already come. Scholars are uncertain whether different figures, past and future, are identified by the same epithet or whether this refers to only one (future or past) figure.

[74]Numbers 24:17 is also argued to have been important for the messianic conception in the scrolls (Collins, *Scepter*, 63-64). While this may be true for other passages in early Jewish literature, its influence has been greatly overestimated in the scrolls. As demonstrated here, Isaiah 11:1-4 (cf. 4Q175 and 1QM 11:6-7) occurs much more often.

[75]Whereas Amos 9:11 ("the raising of the fallen tabernacle of David") is used in *Florilegium* to identify the Davidic messiah, in CD-A 7.15-16 it refers to "the Law," which the Congregation has preserved in their flight to Damascus (CD-A 7.13-14; cf. Amos 5:27).

[76]He mediates God's second visitation (judgment); cf. line 21.

[77]While the text does not explicitly refer to Israel's restoration or a messianic reign, the appellation, "Prince of the Congregation," has royal implications and elsewhere in the scrolls is explicitly connected to kingship (4Q174; 4Q161; *11QTemple Scroll*). Also, the eradication of the "princes of Judah" (CD-A 8.3) probably implies that the Prince of the Congregation will assume power in their stead. Moreover, the writer has set the coming of the Prince within the literary and historical context of Israel's destruction by foreign powers. This time God's own Prince will carry out the judgment duty.

end of days" (1QSa, col.1.1). The subsequent lines provide detailed stipu-
lations for the Congregation to follow, especially in matters of order and
protocol for the various levels of membership and the hierarchy in this
eschatological period. Col. 2.11-22 concerns "the feast[78] for the Council of
the Community when [God] leads forth[79] the messiah (to be) with them"
(lines 11-12). While the text implies a certain importance to the arrival of
the messiah—[80] the meeting is qualified in light of his advent (line 12)—
apparently his entry and seating at the meeting/dining table is preceded
by the chief priest and other priestly figures (lines 12b-14). It is significant, however, that after his entry, the leaders of the twelve tribes of Israel
are seated before him (lines 14-15). There are lacunae at key junctures in
the text, but after the prayer of a priestly figure, the messiah himself
"stretches out his hand" (to bless) and partake of the bread (lines 18-20).
Afterwards the other members of the Congregation participate in order of
importance (lines 21-22). It is difficult to assess the messiah in this text
since the writer provides few details. It is noteworthy that this is the only
place (line12) where משיח occurs in the absolute without any qualifiers
whatsoever; he is simply "the messiah"(המשיח).[81] Although the opening
line of 1QSa places the gathering of the group and the messiah in an
eschatological context ("the end of days"), this period is not elucidated.
The messiah is clearly an important figure; this is demonstrated in his
order in the Congregation, a crucial matter for the DS group. But nonetheless, he is subordinate to the priest(s), at least in certain matters. The
messiah himself exhibits some priestly characteristics in "stretching of the
hand toward the bread."

Other places in the scrolls refer to the messiah(s) of Aaron and Israel
(1QS 9.9; CD-A 12.23-13.1; 14.18-19; CD-B 19.10-11; 19.33-20.1).[82] In the
Community Rule (1QS 9.9), they are expected to be accompanied by a
future prophet as well:

> (10) They shall be judged by the first judgments in which the
> men of the Community began to be instructed, (11) until the

---

[78]מועד probably should be translated "assembly," although the gathering includes a feast.

[79]Geza Vermes (*The Complete Dead Sea Scrolls in English*, 5th ed. [London:
Penguin, 1997], 159) says that יוליד ("begets") "seems to be confirmed by
computer image enhancement." The translation in this study follows Charlesworth
and Stuckenbruck's reconstruction of יוליך. "Rule of the Congregation," in *Dead
Sea Scrolls*, trans. James H. Charlesworth and Loren T. Struckenbruck, ed.
Charlesworth, vol. 1, (Louisville: Westminster John Knox), 115-16.

[80]He is not mentioned in 1QSa, except at the meal.

[81]In lines 14 and 20 he is the "Messiah of Israel."

[82]Charlesworth rightly observes that these references to the messiah(s) in the
important documents of 1QS and CD provide little information regarding the
function of the messiah of Aaron and Levi ("From Messianology," 27.)

coming of the prophet and the Messiahs of Aaron and Levi
(1QS 9.10-11).[83]

This is the only undisputed incident of the phrase "messiahs of Aaron
and Israel" (משיחי אהרון וישראל) in the plural, although most scholars
understand the other instances of the "messiah of Aaron and Israel" to be
a distributive singular construct form, and therefore also plural.[84] In 1QS
9.9, CD-A 12:23-13:1, and 14.18-19, the arrival of the messiah(s) is expected
to signal a change in the Community's government and keeping of their
covenantal laws. The messiah(s) will assume leadership and oversee the
code of righteousness. Thus in CD-A 14.18-19, the writer maintains that
certain requirements be kept by the Community until the messiah of Aaron
and Israel comes; then "he shall atone for their sins."[85] Line 20 is fragmented but refers to punishments as well. The messiah is anticipated to
be a priestly personage who will impose either penalty or forgiveness, as
the case may warrant. The author of CD-B 19.10-11 and 19.33-20.1 expects,
however, the messiah(s) to procure judgment on the Community's enemies and apostates.

C. 4 Ezra

In the pseudepigraphical document of *4 Ezra*,[86] the Davidic messiah
appears in a series of episodic visions that Ezra has regarding the future
age.[87] Ostensibly, the occasion for the visions is the sixth-century BC
destruction of Jerusalem (3:1-3), but in fact, it is the first century AD
destruction of the city and temple to which the author, in the guise of Ezra,
responds. In 7:26-30, Ezra envisages the coming of the messiah with his
(angelic?) cohort, a new Jerusalem, and a hidden land. He is twice identified in the passage by God as "my son" (7:28,29). Although the messiah
lives an extraordinarily long life (four hundred years) the author provides
no details of his purpose or duties.[88] Strikingly, his death is predicted
along with all others on the earth (7:29). The most important aspect of the
messiah in this passage is that his appearance and death are the *last
events* of the old era, or the first age. His death inaugurates a kind of new

---

[83]Charlesworth's translation, "The Rule of the Congregation," *DSS*, vol. 1, 41.
    [84]Martin Abegg, ("The Messiah at Qumran: Are We Still Seeing Double?,"
Dead Sea Discoveries 2 [1995]: 125-44, esp. 129-31) disputes this claim.
    [85]It is noteworthy to point out here that the messiah is explicitly a single figure.
    [86]All references to *4 Ezra* are from the translation of B. M. Metzger, in *OTP*,
vol. 1, 517-59.
    [87]The book of *4 Ezra* (chaps. 3-14) dates to the late first century CE. A later
Christian editor attached chaps. 1-2 and 15 to the Jewish book.
    [88]James H. Charlesworth, "The Concept of the Messiah in the Pseudepigrapha,"
in *Aufstieg und Niedergang der römischen Welt* 11.19.1, eds. Hildergard Temporini
and Wolfgang Haase (Berlin: Walter de Gruyter, 1979), 188-218, esp. 202-05.

creation. The writer says that "the word shall be turned back to primeval silence for seven days, as it was from the first beginnings; so that no one shall be left" (7:30). The primary emphasis in the passage is on the judgment and rewards and punishments in the final portion of the pericope (7:33-44). However, the messiah does not appear in this section.

In the next occurrence of the messiah in Ezra's visions (11-12:1-9), he is explicitly identified as a Davidic figure:

> (12:31) And as for the lion that you saw rousing up out of the forest and roaring and speaking to the eagle and reproving him for his unrighteousness, and as for all his words that you have heard, (32) this is the Messiah whom the Most High has kept until the end of days, who will arise from the posterity of David, and will come and speak to them; he will denounce them for their ungodliness and for their wickedness, and will cast up before them their contemptuous dealings. (33) For first he will set them living before his judgment seat, and when he has reproved them, then he will destroy them. (34) But he will deliver in mercy the remnant of my people, those who have been saved throughout my borders, and he will make them joyful until the end comes, the day of judgment, of which I spoke to you at the beginning.

The messiah is identified as a much anticipated personage of the last days "whom the Most High has kept" (12:32). Whether this implies a pre-existence of the messiah or simply his election is not clear. The figure is primarily portrayed as a warrior who defeats the (foreign) powers over Israel (11-12:1-3). In particular the righteousness of the messiah is contrasted with those of his wicked enemy (12:32-33). From his throne or "judgment seat" he sentences the opposition to death and rules over Israel (the righteous remnant) (12:34). Although there are traces of a cosmic messiah in his long life and the ushering in of the new age, he is very much a figure of this world who brings in the new age by means of political power and war. As Michael E. Stone notes, "[t]he prime features are still military, the overthrowing of the great Roman Empire and the description of this activity in legal terms . . . ."[89] His reign will last until the "day of judgment" (12:34), at which point the new or hidden land and city will be revealed.

One more vision and interpretation of the messiah occurs in 13-14:1-9. Although the future figure is identified as "my Son" (13:32,37,52; 14:9), rather than as messiah, from *4 Ezra* 7:28-29 (above) it is clear that the messiah and God's son are one and the same.[90] In 13-14:1-9, the anticipated

---

[89]Michael Edward Stone, *Features of the Eschatology of IV Ezra,* Harvard Semitic Series 35 (Atlanta: Scholars, 1989), 118.

[90]Charlesworth, "The Concept of the Messiah," 205.

figure is portrayed as a warrior who defeats the nations. The writer's depiction of his destructive activities are dependent upon Isaiah 11:4 and show a strong similarity to *Psalms of Solomon* 17. The writer notes that the messiah uses no weaponry to defeat the enemy, but only "fire" from his "mouth" and "flaming breath" from his "lips" (13:9-10). In the interpretation, the Most High explains that the messiah destroyed the nations with "the law" (13:39). Perhaps the most striking function is his regathering of the ten lost tribes back into the land (13:40,46-50). According to the writer, the tribes had not become dispersed but had escaped Assyria (13:40-41), made a miraculous crossing of the Euphrates, and had been living righteously in Arzareth ("another land") (13:44-45). Therefore his destruction of the nations occurs in conjunction with his gathering and reigning over Israel (13:37-38, 46-50).

III. Conclusion

Although in early Jewish literature a number of messianic and other redeemer type figures are mentioned, this study has demonstrated that some writers and their communities attached great significance to the hope for a messiah from the lineage of David. These passages from early Jewish literature manifests considerable variety in their portrayal of their respective Davidic figures. Some texts (such as *Psalms of Solomon*; *4 Ezra* 13-14:1-9) provide detailed accounts of the person and duties of the messiah from David, emphasizing his role as the warrior who ascends to the throne and regathers Israel, although even here there is much variety. The promise to David (as in 2 Samuel 7) is seen as the guarantee of his coming. Strikingly, the majority of texts are sparse in their descriptions of the royal messiah. Most simply stress that his appearance will mark a decisive shift in the ages and rise of Israel as the supreme power. The few details that are given occasionally emphasize the messiah's kingship (*Psalms of Solomon*; 4Q252; *4QFlorilegium*) and his inauguration of the Davidic line of kings. By far, the most recurring feature of the Davidic messiah is the forceful eradication of Israel's enemies. In the history of scholarship, these enemies have usually been defined as the nations, but as demonstrated here, both gentiles and Jews (variously specified) are the anticipated targets of his attack. In the presentation of the Davidic messiah, it is remarkable that Isaiah 11:1-4 emerges as the most important OT text that informs the description of the expected ruler in early Jewish literature. It is striking that in five of the eight passages referring to a Davidic messiah, Isaiah 11:1-4 exercises a profound influence. Why this OT passage had such an impact on the conception of the Davidic ruler is not altogether clear. Although a synthetic treatment of the texts is avoided in this study, and the use of Isaiah 11 is certainly variegated, it might be surmised that the early Jewish writers' appeal to this Isaianic text was partly based on the Davidic figure's complete reliance on God or his Spirit. This passage might have been attractive in light of the understanding that Israel's enemies ruled unjustly and sinfully by their own power or the power of Satan (Belial). As God's appointee, the Davidic messiah was expected to be empowered by the Spirit to destroy all Israel's enemies, despite overwhelming odds, and to rule as God's regent. Finally, the expectation of a Davidic ruler must be viewed as an important but minority idea in the restoration tradition. Within the wider matrix of Early Judaism, Israel's hopes for restoration could be placed in God alone or a number of other messianic or eschatological figures.

The Spirit in the Fourth Gospel: Narrative Explorations

John Christopher Thomas[*]

In the Spring semester of 1974, I began my academic study of the Fourth Gospel (FG) with a course taught by Don Bowdle at Lee College. At the time, it would have been impossible for me to have guessed that I would devote much of my life to the study of the Johannine literature and eventually write a Ph.D. thesis on the FG. Thus, it seemed fitting that when I was asked to contribute an essay to a volume in Don's honor that it be something on the FG.

The pneumatology of the FG has been of more than passing interest to a variety of NT scholars over the years, with a great deal of attention devoted to John's use of the somewhat enigmatic term παράκλητος.[1]

*John Christopher Thomas (Ph.D., University of Sheffield, England). Professor of New Testament, Church of God Theological Seminary.

[1]Cf. for example the work of H. Windisch, *The Spirit-Paraclete in the Fourth Gospel* (trans. J.W. Cox; Philadelphia: Fortress, 1968); F. Mussner, "Die johanneische Parakletsprüche und die apostolische Tradition," *Biblische Zeitschrift* 5 (1961): 56-70; O. Betz, *Der Paraklet: Fürsprecher im häretischen Spätjudentum, im Johannes-Evangelium und in neu gefundenen gnostischen Schriften,* AGSU 2 (Leiden: Brill, 1963); R.E. Brown, "The Paraclete in the Fourth Gospel," *New Testament Studies* 13 (1966-67): 113-32; G. W. Locher, "Der Geist als Paraklet: Eine exegetisch-dogmatische Besinnung," *Evangelische Theologie* 26 (1966): 565-79; G. Johnston, *The Spirit-Paraclete in the Gospel of John* (Cambridge: Cambridge University Press, 1970); U. B. Müller, "Die Parakleten-vostellung im Johannesevangelium," *Zeitschrift für Theologie und Kirche* 71 (1974): 31-77; F. Porsch, *Pneuma und Wort: Ein exegetischer Beitrag zur Pneumatologie des Johannesevangeliums* (Frankfort: J. Knecht, 1974); R. Schnackenburg, *The Gospel according to St John,* 3 vols., trans. D. Smith and G. A. Kon (New York: Crossroad, 1982), 138-54; E. Frank, *Revelation Taught: The Paraclete in the Gospel of John,* ConBNT 14 (Lund: Gleerup, 1985); G. M. Burge, *The Anointed Community: The Holy Spirit in the Johannine Tradition*

Several things have encouraged my own interest in this topic. First, for nearly two decades now, it has been my happy privilege to teach a course on the FG at least once a year. One of the results of this extensive and regular engagement with the text has been a general dissatisfaction with a number of approaches to this topic from a purely historical-critical perspective. My own thoughts about the Spirit in the FG have taken shape in part as a result of these times of dialogue with a variety of graduate students from all around the world. Second, the kind invitation from Southeastern College in Lakeland, FL to deliver the Staley Lectures in 1997 afforded me an opportunity to formalize some of my ideas about the Holy Spirit/Paraclete in the Farewell Materials of the FG.[2] Third, a recent dialogue with Max Turner and his new book on the Spirit[3] has served to prod me further along in my reflection about the pneumatology of the FG. Fourth, as a Pentecostal I am continually amazed at how differently any number of biblical and theological topics appear when approached afresh from more distinctively Pentecostal approaches.[4] My own conviction is that there is much to learn about the Spirit's role in the FG from a Pentecostal perspective.[5]

For the most part, previous investigations devoted to the pneumatology of the FG have focused upon the topic from the methodological perspective of historical criticism. While such attempts have contributed a great deal to an understanding of the Spirit's role in the FG, these enquiries have usually not paid sufficient attention to the story of the Holy Spirit as it unfolds within the narrative of the FG itself. Unfortunately, this lack of attention to the narrative has resulted in a number of false turns in seeking clarity on the role of the Holy Spirit in the FG. What has been missing is a reading of the FG which informs the reader of the Spirit's

---

(Grand Rapids: Eerdmans, 1987); and J. Breck, *Spirit of Truth: The Origins of Johannine Pneumatology* (Crestwood, NY: St Vladimir's Seminary Press, 1991).

[2]Cf. J. C. Thomas, "He Loved Them until the End: The Farewell Materials in the Gospel according to John," The Staley Lectures, Southeastern College of the Assemblies of God, Lakeland, FL, 20-21 March 1997.

[3]Cf. J. C. Thomas, "Max Turner's *The Holy Spirit and Spiritual Gifts: Then and Now* (Carlisle: Paternoster Press, 1996): An Appreciation and Critique," *Journal of Pentecostal Theology* 12 (1998): 3-22; and Max Turner, "Readings and Paradigms: A Response to John Christopher Thomas," *JPT* 12 (1998): 23-38.

[4]Cf. J. C. Thomas, "Pentecostal Theology in the Twenty-First Century," *PNEUMA: The Journal of the Society for Pentecostal Studies* 20 (1998): 3-19, esp. 13-19.

[5]For an overview of an earlier dialogue on the pneumatology of the FG from a Pentecostal perspective cf. W. G. MacDonald, "Exegetical Circles: An Innovation at the Charlotte Meeting," *PNEUMA* 4 (1982): 19-31.

role as the narrative unfolds.[6] In what follows, I shall seek to offer some reflections on the shape of the pneumatology of the FG from the perspective of narrative analysis. Rather than being a summary of extensive published research, this essay is offered as an initial exploration of this pneumatological territory. Limitations of space necessitate that what follows be no more than a survey of the relevant texts.

I. John 1:32-33

The very first mention of the Spirit's activity in the FG comes in the testimony of John the Baptist with regard to Jesus' identity. Here John testifies that he saw the Spirit come down as a dove and remain upon Jesus, who has previously been identified as the Lamb of God in 1:29. Not only is this descent of the Spirit God's way of revealing Jesus' identity to John, who in turn reveals it to others, but it is also the means by which it is revealed that the one upon whom the Spirit remains is the one who will baptize with the Holy Spirit. At least two things are important about this text for the unfolding of the FG's pneumatological story. First, it is truly remarkable that Jesus, who earlier in the narrative is clearly identified as the pre-existent Logos, should be described as being anointed by the Spirit. Given the Logos' identification with and as God (1:1, 18), his role in the creation of all things (1:2), and his description as the unique Son of God (1:14, 18), the reader is tempted to wonder why such a one would need an anointing by the Spirit. In point of fact, many readers of the FG appear to be so overwhelmed by the Logos Christology of the FG that they scarcely even notice the Christological implications of 1:32-33.[7] Yet, standing alongside the rather obvious Logos Christology is an equally obvious Spirit Christology. Such a narrative placement indicates that for John, these Christological understandings are

---

[6]Cf. the helpful studies of R. A. Culpepper, *The Anatomy of the Fourth Gospel* (Philadelphia: Fortress, 1983); J. L. Staley *The Print's First Kiss: A Rhetorical Investigation of the Implied Reader in the Fourth Gospel,* SBLDS 82 (Atlanta: Scholars Press, 1988); and esp. J. Becker, "Das Geist—und Gemeindeverständnis des vierten Evangelisten," *Zeitschrift für neutestamentliche Wissenschaft* 89 (1998): 217-34. For the application of this approach to two specific pneumatological texts in the FG cf. P. Létourneau, "Le double don de l'Esprit et la Christologie du quatrième évangile," *Science et Esprit* 44 (1992): 281-306.

[7]Cf. R. Bultmann, *The Gospel of John,* trans. G. R. Beasley-Murray, R. W. N. Hoare, and J. K. Riches (Philadelphia: Westminster, 1971), 92, n. 4 and E. Schweizer, "πνεῦμα," *Theological Dictionary of the New Testament,* vol. 6, ed. G. Kittel and G. Friedrich, trans. G. W. Bromiley (Grand Rapids: Eerdmans, 1968), 438.

complementary rather than contradictory.[8] Second, it is only natural
that the one upon whom the Spirit remains is the one who will baptize
with the Holy Spirit. In the FG, it is only after the descent of the Spirit
upon Jesus is described that John the Baptist identifies Jesus as the Holy
Spirit Baptizer. Whether or not Jesus will baptize individuals with the
Holy Spirit within the confines of the narrative of the FG (something
which none of the Synoptics appear to describe despite the citation of
this same prophecy), it is clear from this point that Jesus is connected
with the Spirit in a unique way.

II. John 3

In the passage devoted to Jesus' dialogue with Nicodemus, Jesus dis-
closes (3:3) that in order to see the kingdom of God it is necessary to be
born "from above" (ἄνωθεν). This statement rather obviously is to be
taken as clarification of the words of the FG's Prologue. In 1:12, the
reader learns that all who received him (that is "believed in his name")
were given the authority to become children of God. John goes on to
make clear that this birth is not the result of physical, sexual, or human
means but comes from God himself (1:13).[9] Thus, John 3:3 begins to
reveal how one becomes a child of God.[10] This birth, appropriately
enough, comes "from above." As Jesus continues this explanation he
indicates that one must be born of water and Spirit in order to enter the
Kingdom of God. The debate which surrounds the meaning of water in
this verse is well-known, with a variety of interpretive options offered.[11]
While uncertainty with regard to the meaning of water in 3:5 exists,
there appears to be little uncertainty as to the meaning of Spirit. The
following verses (3:6-8) continue to emphasize, by means of appeal to

---

[8]Cf. the very perceptive comments of C. H. Pinnock, *Flame of Love: A Theology of the Holy Spirit* (Downers Grove, IL: IVP, 1996), 80-111.

[9]For a history of the interpretation of John 1:12-13 see M. Vellanickal, *The
Divine Sonship of Christians in the Johannine Writings* (Rome: Biblical Institute Press, 1977), 105-12.

[10]Vellanickal, *The Divine Sonship of Christians in the Johannine Writings*,
163.

[11]For some of the options see Z. C. Hodges, "Water and Spirit—John 3:5,"
Bibliotheca Sacra 35 (1978): 206-20. Cf. esp. the intriguing suggestion that
water has at least a secondary reference to baptism as a boundary marker by D.
Rensgberger, *Johannine Faith and Liberating Community* (Philadelphia:
Westminster, 1988), 66-70. For a history of interpretation of this passage cf. I.
de la Potterie and S. Lyonnet, *The Christian Lives by the Spirit,* trans. J. Morriss
(Staten Island, NY: Alba House, 1970), 1-12 and Vellanickal, *The Divine Sonship
of Christians in the Johannine Writings*, 179-86.

the Spirit, that birth from above is a necessity (v. 7). The Spirit (πνεῦμα), like the wind (πνεῦμα), blows where it will, it comes from another world—the world of God. There can be little question that this text serves to define for the reader the way in which being born of God is accomplished. Therefore, the reader learns that all who become children of God in the FG, all who believe in his name, are born of the Spirit. Despite the intricate connection with Jesus' exaltation on the cross (3:14-15), such a spiritual experience is already available to those who hear Jesus. In the verses that follow it becomes apparent that this spiritual birth, which comes from God not humankind, brings eternal life (3:16-21). Jesus, who is sent by God (from the realm of God!), is the agent of such a work of the Spirit, for he has received the Spirit without measure (3:34), a clever allusion both to Jesus' place of origin (from above, which is the place of the Spirit) and to his anointing by the Spirit in 1:32-33. The fact that Jesus' role as Spirit Baptizer is not emphasized at this point may suggest that perhaps his function as Spirit agent is multi-dimensional.

III. John 4

The emphasis on the Spirit continues in Jesus' dialogue with the Samaritan woman in John 4. Using double meaning, a favorite Johannine literary technique, Jesus speaks of ὕδωρ ζῶν (v. 10), a Greek phrase that can mean "running water," the running water of a stream as opposed to the still water of a cistern, as well as "living water." The "living water" of which Jesus speaks is not the stream of running water at the bottom of Jacob's well, as the woman supposes. Rather, this water can quench thirst forever, becoming in the one who drinks "a well of water leaping up into eternal life" (v. 14). Just as there is a connection between "birth from above" (by means of the Spirit) and eternal life in chapter three, so here there is a connection between drinking of the "living water" and eternal life (v. 14). The reader of the FG is not surprised by such an association, given the earlier significant occurrences of water to this point in the narrative.[12]

Sensing that Jesus is more than a weary pilgrim, the woman poses a question, which according to Samaritan expectations would be answered by the prophet like Moses (the Taheb): where is the true place of worship? Jesus' surprising response both rejects Jerusalem and this mountain (Mt.

---

[12]J. C. Thomas, *Footwashing in John 13 and the Johannine Community,* JSNTS 61 (Sheffield: JSOT Press, 1991), 88-89. Cf. now the comprehensive study by L. P. Jones, *The Symbol of Water in the Gospel of John,* JSNTS 145 (Sheffield: Sheffield Academic Press, 1998).

Gerizim) as the true place of worship (v. 21) and reveals that by cutting themselves off from important parts of redemptive history, the Samaritans find themselves in an inferior position to the Jews with regard to salvation (v. 22). At this point Jesus reveals that ". . . an hour comes and now is when true worshippers will worship the Father in Spirit and Truth" (v. 23). Here the reader learns that the Spirit is not only the means by which one is "born from above," but the Spirit makes true worship possible. One implication of this statement is that true worship of the Father is possible only for those who are children of God, those born from above by means of the Spirit. It is not surprising that true worship of the Father is also "in Truth." For the reader of the FG, mention of "Truth" is a subtle reference to Jesus,[13] for he is the one who is full of grace and truth (1:14), out of whose fullness all have received one grace after another (1:16), and the one who has given grace and truth (1:17). It naturally follows that "the one who does the truth comes to the Light" (3:21). Such an interpretation of "Truth" in 4:23 is not only appropriate in the light of these previous associations of truth with Jesus in the narrative, but is also in keeping with the later explicit claim of Jesus in 14:6, "I am the Way, the Truth, and the Life." Thus, it would not appear to be going too far to suggest that true worship in this text has a trinitarian dimension (at least in embryonic form)—an understanding not unlike that found in Rev 1:4-5.

From the beginning of the FG, the reader has known of the unique relationship which exists and the unique nature of the identity between God (the Father) and the Word (Jesus). Now in 4:24, the reader learns of the special identity that is shared by God and the Spirit when Jesus says, "God is Spirit." Such a statement reveals that not only is the Spirit essential to true worship, owing to the Spirit's role in the believer's birth from above, but the Spirit is also essential to true worship owing to the Spirit's shared identity with God.

Unlike Nicodemus, who disappears from the narrative in chapter three without believing, many (πολλοί) of the Samaritans believe in Jesus (4:39-42). Given the earlier clues in the narrative, the Samaritans' belief means that they become children of God, they experience eternal life by drinking of the living water, and are able now to worship the Father in Spirit and Truth.

---

[13]I am indebted to my colleague R. H. Gause, for drawing my attention to this interpretive possibility. Cf. the discussion in Burge, *The Anointed Community*, 193-95.

IV. John 6:63

The next reference to the Spirit in the FG is found in 6:63 just after the bread of life discourse. On this occasion, a connection is made between Jesus' scandalous words and the Spirit. Earlier in the passage Jesus speaks of the necessity of eating his flesh and drinking his blood in order to have eternal life (6:53). In 6:63, the reader learns that there is a very tight interplay between eating the flesh and drinking the blood on the one hand and the work of the Spirit on the other. Just as drinking of the living water brings eternal life, so eating his flesh and drinking his blood is tied to eternal life. Jesus' statement that his words are Spirit and life are consistent with the fact that from the beginning of the FG Jesus (the Word) is closely identified with life (1:3-4), and in 14:6 he will make this identification explicit. Neither is it surprising that the one upon whom the Spirit descends and remains (1:32), the one who will baptize with the Holy Spirit (1:33), and the who has been given the Spirit without measure (3:34) should speak words that bring life.[14] Such a statement reinforces the idea of the close relationship that exists between the Spirit and the Truth suggested earlier in 4:23. In contrast to the many disciples who depart and no longer walk with Jesus, Peter, as spokesman for the Twelve, reveals that he and they have paid careful attention to Jesus' teaching at this point and believed in him (6:68).

V. John 7:37-39

Another clear reference to the Holy Spirit found in the Book of Signs (John 1-12) occurs in 7:39, a text filled with interpretive challenges. The narrative context of the verse is the last great day of the feast of Tabernacles. Jesus stands and cries out inviting all who are thirsty to come and drink. But at this point in the passage there arises a host of questions, all of which have some bearing upon the meaning of the text. The major questions concern the punctuation of the text, the location of the Scripture quotation in v. 38, the antecedent of the pronoun 'his' in the phrase "out of *his* belly," and the nature of the Spirit's work mentioned in v. 39. While limitations of space naturally preclude a full discussion of these questions, the following observations may be offered.

With regard to the punctuation of the text, the main question is, does the phrase "the one who believes in me," which in the Greek text is grammatically independent, stand with that which precedes it in 7:37 or

---

[14]Porsch (*Pneuma und Wort*, 210-12) argues that Jesus conveys the Spirit through his words.

with that which follows it in v. 38? If the former, the sentence would read:

> Jesus stood and cried saying, "If anyone thirsts let that one come to me and drink, the one who believes in me. Just as the Scripture said, 'Out of his belly will flow rivers of living water.'"

If the latter, the sentence would read:

> Jesus stood and cried saying, "If anyone thirsts let that one come to me and drink. The one who believes in me, just as the Scripture said, 'Out of his belly will flow rivers of living water.'"

Although certainty on this issue may very well be beyond the reach of the interpreter, it appears that on balance the former option is to be preferred—if only slightly—owing to the punctuation found in the earliest papyri,[15] this preference among a number of the earliest patristic writers, and certain grammatical considerations with regard to the phrase "the one who believes."[16]

The second question focuses on the identity of the person to whom the pronoun αὐτοῦ has reference in the phrase "out of his belly." From whom will the rivers of living water flow, from the one who believes in him or from Jesus? If "the rivers of living water" are promised to gush forth from the one who believes in Jesus, this experience seems to be somewhat different from the "well of water leaping up into eternal life" promised to the Samaritan woman.[17] If the rivers gush forth from Jesus, this would be in accord with some of Jesus' previous promises as Spirit agent. Although it is often assumed that a decision in favor of the former punctuation option necessitates that αὐτοῦ in v. 38 must have reference to the believer,[18] this conclusion does not necessarily follow. Given the wilderness imagery of the FG, the fact that later in the narrative blood

---

[15]Cf. the punctuation of these verses in P66 P75 in *The Complete Text of the Earliest New Testament Manuscripts*, ed. P. W. Comfort and D. P. Barrett (Grand Rapids: Baker, 1999), 405 and 578-79.

[16]On this whole question, compare the very helpful discussion in M. J. J. Menken, *Old Testament Quotations in the Fourth Gospel: Studies in Textual Form* (Kampen: Pharos, 1996), 189-92. For an opposing view, see Burge, *The Anointed Community*, 88-93.

[17]Cf. the comments of H. M. Ervin, *Spirit Baptism: A Biblical Investigation* (Peabody, MA: Hendrickson, 1987), 171-73. The recepient of this *Festschrift* also appears to take this interpretive approach. Cf. D. N. Bowdle, *Redemption Accomplished and Applied* (Cleveland: TN; Pathway Press, 1972), 83.

[18]R. E. Brown, *The Gospel according to John I-XII* (Garden City, NY: Doubleday, 1966), 320-23 and Porsch, *Pneuma und Wort*, 58.

and water do indeed flow from Jesus' side (19:34), and the fact that the believers are to receive the Spirit after Jesus is glorified, it would appear safe to assume that the rivers of living water will flow from Jesus' belly.[19] However, given the FG's love of double meaning and the ambiguity of the text, it should not be thought impossible that the reader would see a reference both to Jesus and the one who believes in him in this verse.

As to the location of the Scripture to which v. 38 refers, it is important to remember that John does not always make clear the exact location of a reference to Scripture (cf. 20:9). Thus the exact location may not be as important as is sometimes thought. Nor is it always the case that a single text serves as the referent of the Scripture citation. Rather, "Scripture may be found to ground *the entire matrix of thought* found in vv. 37-38."[20] Despite a host of other texts proposed as the Scripture to which v. 38 refers, Deut 8:15-16 may merit serious consideration as a viable candidate, given the way its content matches so remarkably the content of the FG:[21]

> He led you through the vast and dreadful desert, that thirsty and waterless land, with its venomous snakes and scorpions. He brought you water out of hard rock. He gave you manna to eat in the desert, something your fathers had never known, to humble and test you so that in the end it might go well with you.

It is significant that this text makes reference to three events in Israel's history to which the FG also makes reference: the serpent in the wilderness (3:14), manna from heaven (6:22-59), and water from the rock (7:38). However, given the general uncertainties surrounding this text, it might be best to leave open the question of the identity of the Scripture.

But even with these tentative answers, the question of the meaning of the words found in v. 39 remains:

> He said this concerning the Spirit which those who believed in him were about to receive. For the Spirit was not yet, because Jesus had not yet been glorified.

What do the words "the Spirit was not yet" (οὔπω γὰρ ἦν πνεῦμα) mean in this verse? Clearly, they cannot be taken literally to mean that

---

[19]Again, Menken's discussion (*Old Testament Quotations in the Fourth Gospel*, 192-94) is a model of clarity. For the view that the rivers of living water come from the disciples see Johnston, *The Spirit-Paraclete in the Gospel of John*, 7-9.

[20]As pointed out by D. A. Carson, *The Gospel according to John* (Leicester: IVP, 1991), 325-26.

[21]Cf. A. D. Palma, "Out of *whose* innermost being?" *Advance* 12 (August 1976): 23.

the Spirit was not yet in existence.[22] Nor does the reader understand them to mean that the Spirit can only work apart from Jesus—after his glorification—for the FG has gone to great lengths to indicate that the Spirit is extraordinarily active in Jesus and his ministry.[23] Nor does it appear that the reader would be inclined to take this statement to mean that the Spirit was not yet active in the lives of those who already believe in Jesus. It has been made very clear that those who believe in Jesus are given the authority to become children of God (1:12), a birth that takes place only by means of the Spirit (3:5); that those who drink of the living water which Jesus gives will have "a well of water leaping up into eternal life" (4:14); and that those who so experience the Spirit ("an hour is coming and now is") are true worshippers who worship the Father in Spirit and Truth (4:23-24). The unequivocal belief of the Samaritans and the disciples in Jesus, as revealed within the narrative world of the FG, strongly suggests that the Spirit is already active to some extent in their lives, a reality that will be reaffirmed later (14:17).

A reading of 7:39 that does not take into account the text's narrative context can result in a one-dimensional understanding of the Spirit's activity in John, an interpretation that the narrative itself tends to subvert. What, then, does the phrase "the Spirit was not yet" mean? It is interesting to note that if Jesus is the source of the rivers of living water, this imagery fits rather well with the imagery found in Jesus' dialogue with the Samaritan woman. There the reader learns that those who drink of the living water will have in themselves "a well of water leaping up to eternal life." As is revealed from the dialogue in John 4, it is clear that a well is not a source of water but rather a channel by which one gains access to a source of water. Just as Jacob's well tapped into a stream or river of subterranean running water, so the one who drinks of the living water that Jesus provides has within him/herself a well that taps into the living water, which has its origin in Jesus. It comes as little surprise, then, when the reader learns in 7:38-39 that rivers of living water come from Jesus. On this reading, this passage is in continuity with that which has come before it in the narrative. At the same time, there also appears to be some degree of discontinuity with what precedes, for the reader would not expect from the imagery of "a well of water leaping up into eternal life" to find "rivers of living water" as the source but a river of living water. Therefore, the imagery found in 7:38-39 is pregnant with meaning. While the rivers of living water certainly

---

[22]However, cf. the attempt to take the phrase literally by H. Boer, *Pentecost and Missions* (Grand Rapids: Eerdmans, 1975), 77-87.

[23]Despite his acknowlegement of this fact, D. Holwerda (*Holy Spirit and Eschatology in the Gospel of John* [Kampen: Kok, 1959], 1-2) still regards the Holy Spirit as "primarily a post-ascension figure in the Gospel of John."

includes the idea of salvation (and that in Jesus there is an abundant
supply—as stated in 3:34), it suggests that there is more in store for
those who believe in him than they have previously understood. This
dimension of the Spirit's work (which at this point in the narrative is not
explained) will only be experienced after Jesus' glorification. With this,
the reader detects a rather subtle shift in emphasis on the Spirit's work
in the FG. The tension created by the statement in v. 39 that "the Spirit
was not yet" despite the Spirit's activity earlier in the narrative, prepares
the reader for the extensive teaching about the future role of the Paraclete
that awaits in John 14-16 and may be a way of reminding the reader that
Jesus is the one who will baptize in the Holy Spirit (1:33).

VI. John 11:33 and 13:21

The Greek term πνεῦμα occurs in both John 11:33 and 13:21, but in
neither of these texts is there a reference to the Holy Spirit. Rather they
refer to Jesus' (human) spirit, which is part of his life as a human being.
With both uses one is not far from a description of the inward emotions
of Jesus. The significance of this use of πνεῦμα is seen later in the FG.

VII. John 14:15-31

The story of the Spirit in the FG continues in the Farewell Materials.
In fact, the bulk of the FG's teaching about the Spirit is found in chapters 14-16, where Jesus' farewell discourse includes two major sections
and one minor one devoted to this subject. The first Paraclete passage is
found in 14:15-31.[24] Throughout this passage there is an emphasis upon
Jesus' departure, the relationship between loving Jesus and keeping his
words, and the work of the Paraclete during Jesus' absence. In point of
fact, the work of the Paraclete in this section is linked both to Jesus'
departure and the keeping of his words. Several aspects of the Spirit's
nature and identity are revealed in this section.

First, the Paraclete comes from the Father as a result of Jesus' own
request. Jesus, who had earlier encouraged the disciples to ask the Father for anything in his name (14:13-14), states in v. 16 that "Even I
(κἀγώ) will ask . . . ," a statement that serves to encourage the disciples
to ask. At first glance, it might be surprising that the one who is anointed

---

[24]The origin of the term παράκλητος has been much debated. For an intriguing proposal with regard to the word's etymology cf. G. E. Ladd, *A Theology of the New Testament* (Grand Rapids: Eerdmans, 1974), 293. Cf. also those
works cited in note 1 of this essay.

by the Spirit, who has been given the Spirit without measure, and who will baptize with the Spirit would have to ask that the Father send the Paraclete. However, it should be remembered that in the FG Jesus does nothing on his own but only those things which the Father desires that he do.

Second, the Paraclete is called "another Paraclete" in v. 16 implying that Jesus himself functions as a Paraclete, a point made explicit in 1 John 2:1. Not only does this statement point to the intimate relationship of Jesus and the Paraclete, but it also serves to underscore the fact that the Spirit is to function in a way analogous to Jesus in the lives of the disciples. While Jesus is soon to depart, the Paraclete will be with them forever.

Third, it comes as no surprise to the reader that the Paraclete is called the Spirit of Truth, for earlier in the FG Jesus is said to be "full of truth" (1:14) and identifies himself as "the Truth" in 14:6. This title or name underscores the intimate connection between Jesus and the Spirit, indicates the trustworthiness of the Spirit, and reminds the reader of the relationship between Spirit and Truth found in 4:23.

Fourth, like Jesus (cf. 1:10-11), the Paraclete is not received by the world, for he is not seen or known by it (v. 17). In contrast, the believers know the Spirit, for he remains among them and *is* in them (v. 17).[25] Picking up on the hints in 7:37-39, this statement at once affirms the basic continuity between the Spirit's work with the disciples to this point in the narrative, while pointing to the discontinuity of his future work. Not only has the Paraclete been present among the disciples through the ministry of the Spirit-anointed Jesus, but he is in those (mainly the disciples, but others as well) who, believing in his name, have become children of God through birth by the Spirit, who have drunk of the living water and have *in* them "a well of living water leaping up into eternal life."[26]

Fifth, in the latter part of the text (v. 26) the Spirit is called the Paraclete, the Holy Spirit, and is identified as coming from the Father.

---

[25]Following the textual tradition that supports the present tense verb ἐστιν rather than the future tense ἔσται. The manuscript support for ἐστιν is slightly better and in this context ἔσται would not only be the more difficult reading, but also the reading that best explains the origin of the other reading since a scribe would be more likely to change the present to the future to conform to the future context of the promise of the coming Paraclete.

[26]For an interpretation that builds on the future tense ἔσται and sees the presence of the Spirit among the disciples as confined to the ministry of Jesus see I. de la Potterie, "Parole et esprit dans S. Jean," *L'Évangile de Jean: Sources, Rédaction, Théologie,* ed. M. de Jonge et. al. (Leuven: Leuven University Press, 1987), 192-93.

In this section, which gives pride of place to the disciples' relationship to the words of Jesus, the Spirit will do two things. First, he will teach the disciples all things. The reader of the FG knows that one of Jesus' primary roles is that of teacher (1:38; 3:2; 6:59; 7:14, 28, 35; 8:20; 11:28; 13:13, 14. cf also 18:20; 20:16). Thus the Paraclete, the Spirit of Truth, the one who is sent by the Father, will do precisely what Jesus has done––teach! This function is necessitated by Jesus' departure. Second, the Paraclete will remind the disciples of the things which Jesus said to them. Although the disciples believe throughout the FG, they do not always fully understand what Jesus has done or said. The first time the reader learns this is after Jesus has cleansed the Temple (2:22). It also occurs in 12:16 and is implied in 13:7. In 14:26, Jesus promises that the Paraclete will play an active role in the disciples' memory and understanding. It is significant that both in 2:22 and 12:16 the disciples remember after the resurrection/glorification of Jesus. In retrospect, the reader is able to understand that it is the Paraclete who is responsible for the disciples remembering the things which Jesus said and did.

VIII. John 15:26

In Jesus' words about the world's hatred of him and the disciples, the Paraclete is mentioned again. Here the reader learns that while the Paraclete comes from the Father, Jesus himself has a role in his sending. Identified again as the Spirit of Truth, emphasizing the intimacy between the Spirit and the Truth, it is now revealed that the Paraclete will be active in his witness to Jesus. Although the text does not explicitly state that the Spirit will inspire the witness of the disciples, the following verses (15:27-16:4a) strongly suggest that the disciples will not experience the persecution of a hating world passively, but will offer witness to Jesus who is anointed by the Spirit.[27]

IX. John 16:4b-15

The second major passage devoted to the role of the Paraclete in the Farewell Discourse (16:4b-15) follows those words about the witness of the Paraclete and the disciples. This passage, also set in the context of Jesus' departure—an event which brings grief to the disciples (vv. 5-6)––for the first time reveals that Jesus must depart in order for the Paraclete to come (v. 7). Although unexpected, this revelation coincides with the

---

[27]Cf. Holwerda, *Holy Spirit and Eschatology in the Gospel of John*, 51-52.

fact that the Paraclete will in many ways be to the disciples what Jesus has been. While the promise of the Paraclete in the first passage focused primarily upon his work within the circle of believers, this passage focuses primarily upon his role in relation to the world, a theme introduced in 15:26.

The FG consistently presents the story of Jesus as a trial, with terms like testimony, interrogation, belief, and judgment appearing frequently. Continuing this motif, v. 8 reveals that the Paraclete will serve as a legal representative. However, instead of being an advocate, as the term Paraclete is sometimes translated, he will serve as a prosecuting attorney, convicting the world on three counts: sin, righteousness, and judgment. On more than one occasion in the FG, Jesus' Jewish opponents confront him about the matter of sin, even accusing him of being a sinner (cf. esp. 9:24). The Paraclete will convict the world of sin because they did not believe in Jesus. Not only will the world be proven wrong about its accusations, it will also discover that its refusal to believe Jesus is itself sin (16:9)!

Righteousness (δικαιοσύνη) is not used here as in Paul's writings, where the term conveys the idea of being judged as righteous. The emphasis in 16:10 is clearly connected to the validity of Jesus' claims that he is going to the Father: "And concerning righteousness because I am going to the Father and you will see me no longer." The reader has been prepared for this idea as early as 5:30, where Jesus in speaking of his authority says, "I am not able to do anything of myself; just as I hear I judge, and my judgment is righteous (δικαία), because I do not seek my will but the will of the one who sent me." This language, no doubt, includes the vindication of Jesus' frequent claims that he is going to the one who sent him and the Jews will be able to see him no longer (7:33; 8:14, 21; 13:3, 33; 14:4, 28; 16:5). As such, the language of 16:10 includes the vindication of his claims with regard to origin as well.

The world will also be convicted of judgment because the ruler of this world stands judged already. Such a statement about judgment has already been signaled in 12:31, where in connection with the lifting up of the Son of Man the time has come for the world's judgment and its leader to be driven out. Clearly, the ultimate vindication of Jesus' person and work are envisaged here.

In addition to his work as prosecuting attorney, this section returns to the idea of the Paraclete's work among the disciples. Owing to the sorrow in the disciples' hearts, Jesus is unable to tell them all that he desires. Thus, much of the additional teaching they need must be conveyed by the Paraclete who may be trusted, for he is again identified as the Spirit of Truth (v. 13). Specifically, the Paraclete will guide into all truth. While such teaching will not be at variance with what Jesus has

earlier taught, owing to the fact that the Paraclete's teaching will come
from Jesus, it does not appear that Jesus anticipates this additional teaching by the Paraclete be identical to what precedes it.   Not only is Jesus
the origin of the teaching, but the Paraclete's teaching will also glorify
Jesus. Verse 15 underscores the essential unity of the Father, Son, and
Spirit.

X. John 19:30

Another reference to πνεῦμα occurs in a text devoted to the death of
Jesus. Immediately following Jesus' final words on the cross ("It is completed!"), bowing his head παρέδωκεν τὸ πνεῦμα ("he gave [up] the
Spirit"). It is quite certain that, at one level, the reader would take these
words as describing Jesus' expiration, his giving up his life, an idea
which goes back to 10:17-18 where Jesus speaks of laying down his life
voluntarily. This use of πνεῦμα is also in accord with its use in 11:33
and 13:21. However, it is just possible that this phrase would convey a
bit more to the reader as the phrase παρέδωκεν τὸ πνεῦμα apparently is never used in antiquity in a strict sense for "to die."[28] What more
than Jesus' death might be present in this phrase? Owing to the fact that
παραδίδωμι rather properly means "to hand over, give, or deliver,"[29] it
is possible to take the phrase as having reference to the bestowal of the
Spirit by Jesus at the moment of his exaltation/glorification on the cross.
Attempts to see here, in the light of 19:26-27, a bestowal of the Spirit
that constitutes the foundation of the community of believers appear to
go beyond the evidence of the text.[30] Based on the distinctive formula
used to describe Jesus' death, the connections between water and Spirit
in 7:37-39 and (apparently) in 19:34, as well as the numerous promises
of the coming of the Paraclete, it may very well be that this phrase points
to the future bestowal of the Spirit in a symbolic or proleptic way.[31]

---

[28]Létourneau, "Le double don de l'Esprit et la Christologie du quatrième
évangile," 283. Cf also Porsch, *Pneuma und Wort*, 328.
[29]W. Bauer, W. Arndt, F. W. Gingrich and F. W. Danker, *A Greek-English
Lexicon of the New Testament and Other Early Christian Literature*, 2nd ed.
(Chicago: University of Chicago Press, 1958), 619.
[30]Cf. esp. M. A. Chevallier, *Souffle de Dieu: Le Saint-Esprit dans le Nouveau
Testament* 2 (Paris: Beauchesne, 1990), 409-564; J.P. Heil, *Blood and Water:
The Death and Resurrection of Jesus in John 18-21*, CBQMS 27 (Washington,
D.C.: Catholic Biblical Quaterly, 1995), 102-09; and Létourneau, "Le double
don de l'Esprit et la Christologie du quatrième évangile," 281-306.
[31]For this general idea cf. Brown, *The Gospel according to John XIII-XXI*,
951 and Burge, *The Anointed Comunity*, 34-35. *Contra* Porsch, *Pneuma und
Wort*, 332-39.

XI. John 20:22

The FG's pneumatological story concludes in 20:22, the meaning of which has been widely debated. The location of this final pneumatological text occurs very near the narrative's conclusion. The broader context (20:19-23) describes an encounter between the risen Jesus and his disciples who are behind locked doors on account of the "fear of the Jews." Given its previous connotations in the narrative, mention of the "fear of the Jews" suggests to the reader that the disciples are in danger of not remaining in Jesus and his word (cf. 8:31). After speaking peace to the disciples, he shows them his side and hands, thereby prompting great rejoicing, and again he speaks peace to them. Jesus then commissions the disciples to be sent just as the Father had sent him. At this point "he breathes" (on them?) and says to them, 'Λάβετε πνεῦμα ἅγιονα,' and authorizes them to forgive and retain sins.

The primary question facing the interpreter at this point is how would the reader understand the phrase "Receive the Holy Spirit"? If the aorist imperative Λάβετε is taken to signify an " . . . immediate and forthright reception of the Holy Spirit,"[32] the phrase "Receive the Holy Spirit" might be interpreted in one of several ways. On this interpretation of Λάβετε the phrase could be taken as having reference to 1) the disciples' regeneration or birth by the Spirit,[33] 2) an equipping of the disciples for ministry, especially with regard to the forgiving of sins,[34] 3) a special measure of the Spirit given to the disciples before Pentecost owing to their unique situation in salvation history,[35] 4) a gift of the Spirit, which

---

[32]So F. L. Arrington, "The Indwelling, Baptism, and Infilling with the Holy Spirit: A Differentiation of Terms," *PNEUMA* 3 (1981): 5.

[33]H. M. Ervin, *Spirit Baptism* (Peabody, MA: Hendrickson, 1987), 14-21 and B. Aker, "'Breathed": A Study on the Biblical Distinction Between Regeneration and Spirit-Baptism,' *Paraclete* 17 (Summer, 1983): 13-16. This suggestion is also made by J. D. G. Dunn, *Baptism in the Holy Spirit* (Philadelphia: Westminster, 1970), 180 and appears to be followed by H. D. Hunter, *Spirit-Baptism: A Pentecostal Alternative* (Lanham, MD: University Press of America, 1983), 110. Cf. also a modified version of this view in M. Turner, *The Holy Spirit and Spiritual Gifts*, 97-102.

[34]Windisch, *The Spirit-Paraclete in the Fourth Gospel*, 33-34. Cf. also Chevallier, *Souffle de Dieu*, 430-38; Létourneau, "Le double don de l'Esprit et la Christologie du quatrième évangile," 281-306; and apparently B. Aker, "Gospel of John," *Dictionary of the Pentecostal and Charismatic Movements*, ed. S. M. Burgess and G. B. McGee (Grand Rapids: Zondervan, 1988), 510. Holwerda (*Holy Spirit and Eschatology in the Gospel of John*, 24) views 20:22 as describing the ordination of the apostles for their future ministry.

[35]S. M. Horton, *What the Bible Says about the Holy Spirit* (Springfield, MO: Gospel Publishing House, 1976), 130-33.

enables them to have Easter faith,[36] 5) a gift of the Spirit, which later assumes the functions of the Paraclete,[37] or 6) the Johannine Pentecost.[38]

However, most of these views fail to convince, owing to textual indicators in the narrative of the FG which are at odds with taking Λάβετε to demand an immediate and forthright reception of the Spirit. One of the more significant textual indicators is the fact that earlier in the narrative Jesus reveals the Paraclete cannot come unless he departs. It is only after Jesus' departure that he will send the Paraclete (16:7), which may suggest that Jesus' glorification of which the FG speaks in 7:37-39 includes more than his exaltation on the cross. In point of fact, John 17:5 seems to state just this point.[39] Therefore, while the grammar might be taken to imply that the Spirit was received at this time (in 20:22), there are indications in the narrative that the Paraclete will not come until Jesus' departure.

Another aspect of the narrative can be seen to subvert such an understanding of Λάβετε. Despite the fact that Jesus commands the disciples to "Receive the Holy Spirit," their later conduct and behavior do not reveal any perceptible change. Most notably, instead of bearing Paraclete-inspired witness to Jesus, something implicitly anticipated in 15:26-16:4, the disciples are still hiding behind locked doors in the very next pericope (20:26) after they have received the command to receive the Spirit. This is a clear indication that their "fear of the Jews" had not diminished. Thus, despite Jesus' commissioning of the disciples to be sent as he was sent by the Father and to forgive sins (20:21-23), the disciples remain inactive in this regard. This is the case despite Jesus' command to "Receive the Holy Spirit." Furthermore there are no other anticipated activities of the Paraclete described after and as a result of Jesus' command in 20:22.[40]

In addition to these narrative indicators, the way in which 20:22 resembles 7:39 and 14:17 should also be noted. In contrast to the texts which speak of drinking from the living water (Spirit) or being born of the Spirit, these texts use the terminology of receiving to describe this Spirit experience. The fact that "receiving" vocabulary is reserved for a post-resurrection experience of the Spirit suggests that the reader is to discern a difference in the work of the Spirit here described and the

---

[36]de la Potterie, "Parole et esprit dans S. Jean," 196-201.

[37]Porsch, *Pneuma und Wort*, 375-76.

[38]Cf. among others Raymond Edward Brown, *Gospel According to John XIII-XXI*, Anchor Bible, vol. 29B (n.p.: Doubleday, 1970), 1038-39; Dunn, *Baptism in the Holy Spirit*, 173-82; Burge, *The Anointed Community*, 123-31; and R. Schnackenburg, *The Gospel according to St John* 3, 324-25.

[39]Cf. Max Turner, *The Holy Spirit and Spiritual Gifts: In the New Testament Church and Today* (n.p.: Hendrickson Publishers, 1998), 95.

[40]Ibid., 96-97.

Spirit's work as described earlier in the narrative. Thus it appears that the FG makes room for distinct works of the Spirit.

If the narrative of the FG itself subverts an interpretation of 20:22 that calls for an immediate and forthright reception of the Spirit, what does the phrase "Receive the Holy Spirit" mean to the reader? Given the fact that the Paraclete will come only after Jesus' departure, that there are no signs of the Paraclete's activity after the command to receive the Spirit in 20:22, and that the FG not only allows for but appears to expect distinct works of the Spirit, it appears that Jesus' action of breathing and utterance of the phrase "Receive the Holy Spirit" should be taken as a symbolic, parabolic, and/or proleptic action that points beyond itself to a reception of the Spirit that is not described in the narrative.[41] Such a reading coincides with Jesus' anticipated work as Spirit Baptizer (1:33), the coming of the Paraclete after Jesus' departure (16:7), and the antici-pated activities of the disciples after the Paraclete arrives (14-16; 20:21-23).[42] From the standpoint of narrative analysis, such an understanding of John 20:22 is less problematic than views which see an immediate and forthright reception of the Spirit in this verse.[43]

Concluding Remarks

This study has sought to contribute to a better understanding of the pneumatology of the FG from the perspective of narrative analysis. These reflections are offered not as the final word but as initial explorations from this perspective. No doubt, numerous interpreters will disagree at various points with the analysis offered here, but perhaps these reflec-tions will serve to generate additional constructive reflection and dia-logue on this important topic and at the same time contribute toward honoring a colleague.

---

[41]An interpretive position that goes back at least as far as Theodore of Mopsuestia. Cf. G. E. Ladd, *A Theology of the New Testament*, 297; D. Guthrie, *New Testament Theology* (Downers Grove: IVP, 1981), 534; Carson, *The Gospel according to John*, vol. 3, 651-55; D. Petts, *The Holy Spirit: An Introduction* (Mattersey: Mattersey Hall, 1998), 47-48; and apparently R. H. Gause, *Living in the Spirit: The Way of Salvation* (Cleveland, TN: Pathway Press, 1980), 66.

[42]In this, the FG is not unlike the synoptics, which also leave the promise that Jesus will baptize with the Holy Spirit unfulfilled within their respective narra-tives.

[43]However, cf. Turner (*The Holy Spirit and Spiritual Gifts*, 97-102), who understands the Spirit's work in John 20:22 as an eschatological new creation, which later will include the work attributed by Jesus to the Paraclete.

Justification by Faith in Romans

French L. Arrington[*]

Justification by faith has been traditionally seen as the conceptual center for Paul's thought. In modern times some scholars have challenged the idea that justification of the ungodly has an irrevocable place in Paul's theology. Among notable advocates of the new appraisal of the centrality of justification to Paul's gospel include William Wrede[1] and Albert Schweitzer.[2] Both deny that justifying grace is the generating center of Paul's thinking. Schweitzer claims, however, that it is merely a polemical doctrine aimed at neutralizing the theological threat posed by legalistic Judaism. Schweitzer, basing his argument on the phrase "in Christ" that appears in Paul's writing, insists that mysticism is the key to the apostle's gospel and that justification by faith is a mere "subsidiary crater" to Paul's theology. In recent times other scholars have also chosen a different organizational framework to understand Paul's thought and have advocated that the heart of Paul's gospel lies elsewhere than in the doctrine of justification. Among them are Adolf Deissmann,[3] Krister Stendahl,[4] W. D. Davies,[5] R. P. Martin,[6] and E. P. Sanders.[7]

On the other hand, Martin Luther, as it is well known, understood justification to be no mere weapon of controversy, but central to Paul's

*French L. Arrington (Ph. D., St. Louis University). Professor of New Testament Greek and Exegesis, Church of God Theological Seminary.
[1]*Paul* (London: Philip Green, 1907), 147, 177-78.
[2]*The Mysticism of Paul the Apostle* (London: Adams and Charles Black, 1967), 220-26.
[3]*Paul: A Study in Social and Religious History* (New York: Harper and Row, 1957), 147-57, 295 ff.
[4]"The Apostle and the Introspective Conscience of the West," Harvard Theological Review 56 (1963): 199-215.
[5]*Paul and Rabbinic Judaism* (New York: Harper and Row, 1948), 221-23.
[6]*Reconciliation: A Study of Paul's Theology* (Atlanta: John Knox, 1981), 46-47.
[7]*Paul and Palestinian Judaism* (Philadephia: Fortress Press, 1977).

understanding of the gospel. A number of biblical scholars have endorsed his judgment, including J. G. Machen,[8] J. I. Packer,[9] Leon Morris,[10] Hans Conzelmann,[11] Gunther Bornkamm,[12] and Ernst Kasemann.[13] Furthermore, F. F. Bruce adds his voice to support that justification by faith has a fundamental place in Paul's theology when he says, "The doctrine was implicit in the logic of Paul's conversion, which revealed to him in a flash the inadequacy of the law."[14]

Though God's act in justifying the sinner played a basic part in Paul's preaching, Bruce observes that it fails to exhaust the apostle's understanding of the great redemption in Christ. Paul's doctrine of justification together with other doctrines is set forth in the context of the new creation that has come into being with and in Christ.[15] Similarly Herman Ridderbos understands that the scope of salvation is wider than that of justification and that it encompasses the whole of creation, "all things," in its vision.[16] Therefore, because of the panorama of theological themes in Paul's thought, it is a mistake to bring everything under the doctrine of justification:

> There are also other concepts, ideas, trains of thought, all of which have the same point of departure—the saving activity of God in the death and resurrection of Christ—and all of which have their essential foundation in this revelation of the righteousness of God, but which nevertheless give expression to the content of the gospel in other ways.[17]

Even though for Ridderbos justification by faith is just one aspect of Christ's redemption, he still considers it to be a central aspect of Pauline thought.

In the last few years some of the more important scholars on this continent have objected strongly to the centrality of justification by faith.

[8]*The Origin of Paul's Religion* (New York: Macmillan Company, 1921), 277-79.

[9]*God's Word* (Downers Grove, IL: InterVarsity Press, 1981), 139-47.

[10]*The Epistle to the Romans* (Grand Rapids: Eerdmans Publishing Company, 1988), 172-242.

[11]"Current Problems in Pauline Research," *Interpretation* 22 (1968): 171-86.

[12]*Paul* (New York: Harper and Row, 1971), 83, 95, 115-19, 135-56.

[13]"Righteousness of God in Paul," in *New Testament Questions of Today* (Philadelphia: Fortress Press, 1969), 168-82; *Commentary on Romans* (Grand Rapids: Eerdmanns Publishing Company, 1980), 21-32, 91-101.

[14]*Paul, Apostle of the Heart Set Free* (Grand Rapids: Eerdmans Publishing House, 1977), 326, cf. 188.

[15]*The Letter of Paul to the Romans* (Grand Rapids: Eerdmans Publishing Company, 1985).

[16]*Paul: An Outline of His Theology* (Grand Rapids: Eerdmans Publishing Company, 1975), 161.

[17]Ibid., 181.

For example, E. P. Sanders, a student of Davies, advocates—as did Schweitzer—that "being in Christ" is the center of Paul's theology rather than righteousness by faith,[18] but this interpretation expresses only one side of the salvific reality—the believer's subjective appropriation. Still missing is the objective side of salvation, God's saving deed in Christ, which is the ground of the believer's participation in Christ.

For J.C. Beker the center of Paul's thought is neither union with Christ nor justification by faith. Rather the "coherent center" lies in

> a symbolic structure in which a primordial experience (Paul's call) is brought into language in a particular way. The symbolic structure comprises the language in which Paul expresses the Christ-event. That language is, for Paul, the apocalyptic language of Judaism, in which he lived and thought.[19]

Adopting an apocalyptic framework, Beker makes a distinction between the "primordial experience" and "symbolic" language. The primordial experience is Paul's encounter with Christ on the Damascus road, where he received his message and commission. The symbolic structure Beker identifies as Christian apocalyptic that points to the triumph of God. On the "deep" level the symbolic structure refers to the significance that the Christ-event has for the consummation of history. But a secondary language is also used by Paul such as justification, reconciliation and adoption to apply the gospel "to the contingent needs of a particular situation."[20] "Thus righteousness must be viewed as one symbol among others and not as the center of Paul's thought."[21]

Likewise Gordon Fee sees justification as only one of a number of Pauline metaphors for salvation. Anyone who reads Paul's letters, Fee contends, should recognize the inadaquacey of the view that justification by faith is the key to Paul's theology. His conviction is that no single theme is broad enough to capture all of Paul's theological concerns. So he is satisfied to describe as "elusive" the search for the center of Paul's theology.[22]

The debate continues as to whether justification by faith has a fundamental place in Paul's theology or is merely a doctrine in the polemics of Paul against legalistic Judaism.[23] Justification by faith is set forth in detail

---

[18]*Paul and Palestinian Judaism,* 434.

[19]*Paul The Apostle* (Philadelphia: Fortress Press, 1980), 15-16.

[20]Ibid.

[21]Ibid., 17.

[22]*God's Empowering Presence* (Peabody, MA: Hendrickson Publishers, 1994), 11-12.

[23]Some scholars have proposed a new understanding of Judaism that Paul confronted and against which he formulated much of his theology. In his mono-

only in Galatians and Romans. Both of these letters grow out of Paul's missionary situation, a situation that makes it natural for him to expound the gospel that has been entrusted to him by the Lord. In the book of Romans, Paul deals with issues confronting the Roman Christians; however, this book is less tied to the circumstances of the first century than any other book in the New Testament. Romans is the longest and theologically the most comprehensive of Paul's letters. The gospel that Paul presents in Romans is the same as his other letters; because it is more orderly and detailed, we will examine the message of Romans to determine the conceptual focus of Paul's theology.

I. Romans 1-8

The first seventeen verses of Romans 1 introduce terms and concepts that are developed throughout the epistle. Such terms as "gospel" (vv. 3,9,15) and "grace" (vv. 5,7), various concepts such as the saving work of Christ (vv. 3-6), and the link between the gospel and the prophetic word of the Old Testament (v. 2) foreshadow a prominent theme in the epistle, justification by faith, which is a righteous status before God given by him. Furthermore, the terms "Gentiles," (vv. 5,13), and "Jew" (vv. 16-17) imply the universality of salvation made available by God's justifying grace. The Roman believers have received the gospel by faith, and likewise Paul has "received grace and apostleship to bring about the obedience of faith among all the Gentiles" (v. 5).[24] Paul's distinct ministry to the Gentiles underscores the fundamental importance of justification in Romans. That is, the nature of God's justifying work supports the Gentile mission. Paul's

---

graph, *Paul and Palestinian Judaism*, E. P. Sanders argues that Palestinian Judaism in the first century was a non-legalistic religion and that the Judaism that Paul knew was not a religion in which works were the means of salvation. According to Sanders, first-century Jews embraced what he calls "covenantal nomism" and believed that they were saved by corporate election as a covenant people. Works were seen as the proper response of God's people for maintaining their status in the covenant. J. D. G. Dunn has become a leading advocate of this reconstruction. See his article, "The New Perspective of Paul," *Bulletin of John Ryland's University Library of Manchester* 65 (1983): 95-122. Sander's and Dunn's views have influenced recent studies of Paul, but there must have been in Paul's day Jews who were more legalistic than nomistic and who believed that justification was by the works of the law rather than by faith. It seems that is the most natural way to read the relevant passages in the Pauline letters. In this regard, see Stephen Westerholm, *Israel's Law and The Church's Faith* (Grand Rapids: Eerdmans Publishing House, 1989).

[24]All quotations are from the New American Standard Version unless otherwise specified.

commitment to this mission does, therefore, emphasize his understanding that God's flow of salvation is universal and impartial and sets the stage for his exposition of justification by faith that takes place throughout the body of this epistle.[25]

In verses 16-17, which recapitulate the message of Romans, Paul teaches that justification by faith plays a central role in the new way by which both Jews and Gentiles can enter into fellowship with God. These verses set forth four truths that are integral to the doctrine of justification: (1) the universality of God's salvation, (2) the fundamental equality of Jew and Gentile in the plan of salvation, (3) the gospel as God's saving power, and (4) faith as the means by which all alike participate in salvation. To both Jews and Gentiles "the righteousness of God"—meaning His saving action—acquits, conferring a status of righteousness upon us, has been made available through faith. Therefore, justification by faith provides the basis for the universality and impartiality of salvation.

Having given an overview of his understanding of salvation, Paul shows humankind's need for justification, that no one can be righteous before God except by faith (1:18-3:20). Paul centers his view of humankind in Psalm 14:3: "There is none righteous, no not even one" (3:10). Every person, Jew and Gentile, stands guilty and worthy of condemnation because of human sinfulness. For example, God made plain in creation "His eternal power and divine nature" (1:20), yet the Gentiles did not honor God evident in creation nor "give thanks" to him. The Jews thought of themselves as morally superior, but were no better than the Gentiles. Although the Jews knew the law, they had failed to abide by it (2:17-23). Their guilt and need for justification were just as great as that of the Gentiles. The Jews' pride and disobedience and the Gentiles' immorality disclosed that both groups "have sinned and fall short of the glory of God" (3:23). As a result both stand under God's wrath and condemnation. God's wrath is universal and impartial and is revealed in the preaching of the gospel (cf. 1:17-18). The proclamation of the gospel reveals the status of righteousness before God and his wrath against human sin. Consequently the revelation of righteousness and wrath are really two aspects of the same process.[26] God's righteousness harmonizes with God's wrath and reminds us of God's kindness, patience and forbearance in trying to lead Jew and Gentile to repentance (2:4). Such an understanding of God's righteousness fits well with justification by faith and demonstrates the need of justification to set sinners free from the wrath and condemnation that they deserve.

---

[25]Cf. Luke T. Johnson, *The Writings of The New Testament* (Philadelphia: Fortress Press, 1986), 318.

[26]C. E. B. Cranfield, *Romans: A Shorter Commentary* (Grand Rapids: Eerdmans Publishing Company, 1985), 30.

The antidote to the guilt and condemnation under which everybody stands is God's saving work in Christ (3:21-4:25). Occupying a central place in this epistle, 3:21-26 contains the essential truths of the gospel. Christ takes center stage in Paul's understanding of God's justifying sinners. The provision of Christ as a "propitiatory sacrifice" (v.25) satisfies God's condemnation of the sinner. God's forgiveness of the sinner through faith "demonstrates His righteousness because in the forbearance of God He passed over the sins previously committed" (v.25). God wills to forgive the sinner, being himself truly merciful and forgiving him without in any way condoning sin. Justification by faith displays God's righteousness in that his wrath is satisfied through Christ's death and his mercy is satisfied through justifying sinners who have faith in Christ.[27]

The law of works does not offer a way of justification, only the law of faith does (3:27-31). Faith universalizes God's justifying grace, affirming that he is the God of both Jew and Gentile. The law (Gen 15:6; see Rom 4:3) and prophets (Hab 2:4) point to the disclosure of God's righteousness through faith in Christ (3:21-22). Paul offers Abraham as an Old Testament example of justification by faith (4:1-25). Since Abraham's justification preceded the institution of both the law and circumcision, he was justified by neither. Abraham's salvation exposed the Jews' misunderstanding that he was the supreme example of justification by works. He did not boast in his works or depend on his works. Rather, as Paul quotes Genesis 15:6, "Abraham believed God, and it was reckoned to him as righteousness" (4:3). He entered into a right relationship with God solely on the basis of his faith or trust in God. At the time of Abraham's justification, he was neither a Jew nor was he circumcised, showing that such faith crosses racial, cultural, and religious boundaries. Abraham is a marvelous example in his initial faith in God's promise, but also in that he did not weaken in faith, continually believing the promises of God (4:19-21). Just as Abraham's faith was reckoned for righteousness, so will all those who believe in Christ. God does justify "those who believe in Him who raised Jesus our Lord from the dead, He who was delivered up because of our transgressions, and was raised because of our justification" (4:24-25).

Beginning with chapter 5, Paul moves beyond the proof and explanation of justification by faith to the benefits and doctrines that build upon it (5:1-8:39). Similar to the Exodus, justification marks movement from one place in life to a new status or position.[28] This new status or position brings the believer into a new life, indicating what justification by faith means for Christians. Their new life in Christ means being reconciled to

---

[27]Cf. Robert H. Mounce, *Romans* (Nashville, TN: Broadman & Holman Publishers, 1995), 116-18.

[28]Cf. Gerhard Forde, "The Exodus from Virtue of Grace: Justification by Faith Today," *Interpretation* 34 (January 1980): 32-34, especially 36-37.

God, being sanctified, being free of the law of condemnation, being indwelt by the Holy Spirit, and being placed in God's family through adoption.

Justification is not merely forensic but dynamic and effective, opening the door for the believer to relate to God in a new way and issuing into obedience of faith (1:5; 16:26). For example, the justified are at "peace with God" (5:1). Since God's wrath has been satisfied by the death of Christ, those justified have a new relationship with God based on peace instead of wrath and enmity. Or as Paul puts it later, "while we were enemies, we were reconciled to God..." (5:10). Justification involves reconciliation and the two are inseparable because when God justifies us he gives himself to us in friendship and establishes peace between himself and us.[29] Further-more, we accept the fires of tribulation due to our faith in Christ as part of God's discipline that teaches us to wait patiently for his deliverance (5:3-5). Perseverance and character are tied to hope in God and the fulfillment of his promises. Such hope depends on trusting in God's love and in his eventual deliverance of us from tribulations.

Indeed justification by faith is more than mental assent to a set of truths. It involves a radical change of life. This change includes not only a new relationship to God but also a new relationship to sin. Paul uses three metaphors—baptism, slavery, and marriage—to illustrate that what happens in justification makes clear that sin no longer has dominion over the justified. The first metaphor is the symbolism of baptism (6:3-11). Being baptized with Christ and being raised by God with him show that we have died to sin and been raised to a new life in Christ. The second metaphor, slavery, presents two alternatives: slavery to sin and slavery to obedience (6:15-23). Being set free from sin because of obedience to the gospel leads to becoming "slaves of righteousness" (v.18). The issue here is the dominion of sin. Before justification, sin controls people's lives, presenting them "as slaves of impurity and lawlessness" (v.19). But presenting themselves to God they become "instruments of righteous-ness" (v.18). In summary, the benefits of justification by faith in relation to sin: their slavery to God results in sanctification[30] and they will obtain eternal life (v.22). The third metaphor comes from marriage and shows that through faith in Christ sin has been conquered (7:1-4). As a husband and wife are bound together until the death of the spouse, so a person is bound to sin by the law until death sets him free. When he becomes a believer, death does occur, thereby liberating him from captivity to sin so

---

[29]Cranfield, 101-02.

[30]Justification and sanctification are normally discussed as separate theological ideas. Paul, however, demonstrates that they are not far apart and that justifica-tion is integral to sanctification. Justification necessarily precedes sanctification so that one is in a right relationship with God before he or she enters a new life and bears fruit to God.

that he is free to take another partner, namely Christ. Through justifying grace, the believer is dead in relation to the law of works, and therefore, no longer bound to a sin-dominated life, but is free to bear fruit to God.

In addition to being the key to freedom from sin, justification by faith liberates believers from the condemnation of the law (7:1-8:1). The strength of condemnation of the law is due to the law's revealing sin and the need for holiness and purity. By exposing a person's sin, the law pronounces condemnation, but justification gives victory over such condemnation. On the assumption that 7:14-25 has in view a Christian, a believer—despite freedom from condemnation—may understand the law legalistically and may try to keep it through his or her own strength. The believer may remain bound to the works of the law and may be unable to keep the law because of indwelling sin (7:17-23). God does provide the believer a remedy to this problem through the ministry of the Holy Spirit. Because of justification by faith, at the end of chapter 7 Paul declares thanks to God, knowing that God will surely deliver the believer in the future. Paul states in 8:1 that the one in Christ is no longer under the condemnation pronounced by the law.

Finally, justification by faith frees the believer from the authority and power of death (8:2-39). "The law of sin and death" exercises authority over unbelievers, but for those righteous by faith it is replaced with "the law of the Spirit of life in Christ" (8:2). This replacement is possible because God sent his Son in the flesh as an offering for sin. In Christ's earthly life the full weight of what the law required for human sin—condemnation and death—fell on him (8:3-4). Only by faith can we appropriate the salvific work Christ did for us. Once justified, no longer must we live according to the flesh since "the Spirit of God dwells" in us (8:9). Death is characteristic of life controlled by the flesh, but life and peace are characteristic of life in the Spirit (8:6, 10-11). The defeat of death is therefore evident in a Spirit-led life here and now, but it also has eternal or eschatological implications (8:14-17). Life in the Spirit now reflects the hope of resurrection and "the redemption of our body" (8:23). Such hope is based in the fact that God causes all things to work together for good to those who love God (8:28) because those "whom He justifies these He also glorified" (8:30).

Justification not only provides the believer the opportunity for living a Spirit-led life in the present and for eschatological hope for the future, but it also gives assurance of God's protection: "If God is for us who is against us?" (8:31). Paul concludes chapter 8 with the most sweeping language—all time, all adversaries, all worlds—to speak about how God protects those who are righteous by faith (vv. 31-39). None of these powers separate them from God's love.

II. Romans 9-11

Romans 9-11 shows how the gospel brought a new era of salvation history and how justification by faith fits into that history.[31] God's justification of the ungodly can be detected as the key means by which he deals with the Jews and the Gentiles.[32]

God's election and seeming rejection of Israel stem from common elements of justification by faith, such as God's mercy, patience, and wrath. These elements are a reoccurring emphasis in 9:1-29. God chose Israel not because of their works but because of his mercy. Divine election depending on mercy but not on human will and effort (v. 16) supports the doctrine of justification by faith since faith relies on God's mercy. God's wrath shows the need for justification in order to be delivered from it. His patience shows his intent to justify the ungodly (v.22). God's mercy, wrath, and patience always figure prominently in the doctrine of justification. These characteristics show that God's will to justify demands the satisfaction of his character. His mercy and patience must be satisfied as well as his wrath. Moreover, it shows that justification by his grace has always been God's *modus operandi*.

Dealing with a perplexing problem, Paul raises the whole issue of salvation and the nation of Israel. He describes Israel as a covenant people fully blessed by God (9:4-5), who failed to keep their side of the covenant. God had kept his promise to the Jews by sending his Son into the world. By rejecting him, they continued to seek righteousness through the law. They lost sight of the nature of their election because the covenant God made with their father Abraham was based on a faith relationship. Abraham believed God's promises and God considered him righteous (vv. 7-9; cf.

---

[31]Since Paul uses the Old Testament in his exposition of justification, he must show how the place given to the Jews in the Old Testament can agree with such a "system of salvation." See Morris, *The Epistle to the Romans*, 343.

[32]Romans 9-11 has been seen as not cohering with chapters 1-8 and 12-15 and, therefore, frequently viewed as either an appendix or a separate treatise. Some interpreters have a distaste for this section because of the specificity of Paul's historical view of Israel and salvation history. In Romans Paul deals with a church consisting of both Jewish and Gentile Christians, and their relation to one another is central to salvation history. His emphasis on the gospel for Jews and Gentiles is sounded both in the initial thematic statement (1:16) and in the climax of Romans (15:7-12). Although the gospel draws large numbers of Gentiles, it remains the gospel for the Jews. The Jews must understand that they can only be Israel by faith in Jesus Christ. Futhermore, Jewish and Gentile Christians must understand the priority of Israel in salvation history and Israel's distinct place in the future of God's plan. Thus 9-11 express the essential theological perspective of the entire letter and reflect a high degree of coherence and integration. Cf. Beker, 63-64, 70-71, 77-78, 90-91.

Gen 15:6). Trusting in the law and their heritage for righteousness they had a perverted understanding of God's plan of salvation.

The way God deals with humankind, including the Jews, reveals their misunderstanding of God's sovereign freedom as well as their misunderstanding of the nature of salvation. Paul uncovers this misunderstanding in his reference to Abraham and Sarah, Jacob and Esau, Moses and Pharoah, and the potter and the clay (9:6-24). Two observations are in order here: the first observation is that the Jews failed to realize that their election did not depend on biological descent but the promise of the sovereign God (9:8). God did not pass down indiscriminately his promise to all of Abraham's descendants or to all of Isaac's descendants (9:9-13), but he chose Isaac and Jacob through whom to transmit the promise to whomsoever believes. God's choice did not depend on the human will but on his mercy (9:16), thereby supporting justification by faith in an indirect fashion. Salvation is neither by heredity or works, for justification rests only on God's mercy. The second observation is that the Jews had failed to recognize God's sovereign freedom. Despite the question of theodicy (9:14), Paul confronts the Jews' belief that God is obligated to save everyone of them because of their national identity. As Paul shows, God is free to have mercy on whom he wills—including, of course, the Gentiles (9:18). God is not bound to save only or all the Jews. Therefore, his mercy is not limited to any ethnic group. He is free and acts according to his righteousness, which finds expression in justification by faith (cf. 1:16-17; 3:21-26).

In 9:30-10:21, Paul describes Israel's rejection of the gospel, which stems from an attempt to attain righteousness based upon law as opposed to righteousness by faith. Israel's unsuccessful attempt to achieve righteousness by specific acts of obedience to the law such as circumcision, Sabbath observance, and ritual purity proves the necessity of justification by faith (9:32). Paul's use of Abraham shows that faith had always been the means to appropriating justification, but Christ is "the end of the law" in the sense that he is both the termination of the period dominated by the law, and his life is the true fulfillment of the law. Christ's work transcends national and ritual boundaries[33] and makes more readily available the gift of righteousness to "everyone who believes" in him. Although continuity existed between the Old and New Covenants, especially in view of Abraham's faith, Christ did terminate the previous epoch of salvation history. He makes justification by faith characteristic of God's plan of salvation, replacing the covenant situation in which Israel appears to be God's main concern. Now we need only to believe in the One who came to earth and was raised from the dead (10:6-7) because "there is no distinction between the Jew and Greek" (v. 12). Faith has always been the way, from Abraham to the present, of God's accepting people as righteous in his

[33]James D. G. Dunn, *Romans* 1-8; 9-16 (Dallas: Word Books, 1988), 613.

sight. We are now offered a new way of faith, that is, justification through faith in Jesus Christ.

In his discussion of the people of Israel, Paul speaks about the salvation of the remnant and urges Gentile Christians to be humble (11:1-36). Rather than being justified (or chosen) according to their meritorious achievements, the Jews or the remnant, who had believed in Christ, had been chosen by grace. Again salvation rests upon the power of faith and not the power of works. Likewise, the Gentiles who were "grafted" into the Kingdom of God had been saved in the same way. Paul reminds them, "you stand by your faith" and admonishes them not to become proud (11:20). God's mercy had brought them into the kingdom: "For God has shut up all in disobedience that He might show mercy to all" (v. 32). In summary, justification never is granted to Jew or Gentile by the works of the law, but is by faith so that it may be according to God's grace and mercy.

III. Romans 12-15

In chapters 1-11 Paul has laid out his doctrine of justification by faith and has given the historical basis for both Jews' and Gentiles' reception of salvation through faith. Now Paul turns from doctrine to more practical and ethical issues. To try to make a distinction between the doctrinal and practical issues would be erroneous, for the whole epistle has practical implications for life.

Justification by faith marks the entry of the believer into the community of faith. Chapters 12-15 develop the norms and values by which life is built on the solid foundation of Christ. These chapters stand in literary and theological continuity with the rest of the epistle and demonstrate the fundamental connection between exhortations and justification by faith.[34]

This section clearly demonstrates theological continuity pertinent to the doctrine of justification by faith. Important to Paul is the ethical

---

[34]The shift in topical emphasis between 11:36 and 12:1 should be noted, but there are good reasons to understand the literary unity of the epistle. Since the whole epistle is both doctrinal and practical with a shift of emphasis, it is better to see the shift as from "indicative" to "imperative" or from "instructional" to "exhortation." See Douglas J. Moo, *The Epistle to the Romans* (Grand Rapids: Eerdmans Publishing Company, 1959), 704. In 12:1, the transitional marker "therefore" draws the whole epistle together and makes a connection not merely between the preceding chapters (9-11) but between the first eleven chapters and the ensuing exhortations. Chapters 1-11 are concerned with the saving action of the merciful God, so it is fair to say that justification by faith is on Paul's mind when he says "therefore."

response of those who have received justifying grace. Therefore, "Let love be without hypocrisy" (12:9). Also, "let us not judge one another anymore, but rather determine this—not to put an obstacle or stumbling block in a brother's way" (14:13). Finally, "accept one another, just as Christ also accepted us to the glory of God" (15:7). Such admonitions flow out of justification by faith and serve as a reminder that salvation is only through the mercies of God.

Moreover, the exhortations of believers to be obedient to the state stand in continuity with God's sovereignty that is basic to justification by faith (13:1-7). Paul calls for believers to submit to the governing authorities (v. 1).[35] Submission to authority is the heart of justification. "Jesus is Lord" (10:9) and his lordship is universal, extending beyond the church and including civil authorities. By faith we submit to his lordship. A corollary to this submission is to submit to other systems that are subject to divine control (13:1,3). Therefore, submitting to God by faith entails that we submit to governing authorities and rulers.

Another demonstration of theological continuity of chapters 12-15 with justification by faith is God's missionary nature. According to chapters 9-11, God's sovereign plan includes people from all racial groups (cf. 5:8). Convinced of that, Paul urges the believers to live honorably before those on the outside (13:13) and to put no stumbling blocks in the way of those who are members of the church (14:15). By their lifestyles they are to support God in his plan of salvation instead of hindering him.

Finally, chapters 12-15 provide guidelines by which the community of faith should live. Hence justification by faith does not merely provide the

---

Furthermore, the use of cultic language in 12:1-2 alludes to Paul's discussion of Judaism and the works of the law (Dunn, *Romans*, 717). Paul redefines the language according to the law of faith. As in Judaism, Christianity demands sacrifice, the appropriate response to justification. The offering is not animals but ourselves, the only kind acceptable to God, and the place of worship is no longer at the altar, but in all relationships. Justification by faith makes salvation available to all, but it also universalizes the realm of the practice of faith. Believers are to live the faith at all times and with all people. Transformed in their character, they are enabled by the power of the Spirit to present themselves "as instruments of righteousness" (6:13) and can overcome evil with good (12:21). The final chapters, which provide a detailed description of what it means to do so, expound the new life in Christ, the life justified by faith, in terms of what it looks like and how it should function in relation to the body of Christ and the community at large.

[35]Paul may be speaking about obedience to a system rather than to an individual ruler. He states that the sovereign God has appointed governing authorities and their appointed task is to govern well and maintain order. God wills government, but this fact should not be taken to mean that Christians must obey every command of godless leaders (Acts 5:29).

way of salvation, but also introduces people to a community based upon different rules and has different goals. Love is the norm for the community of faith.

Summary and Conclusion

The end of the debate about what underlies all that Paul wrote is nowhere in sight, but on the basis of the foregoing study of Romans we offer the following observations:

(1) Justification is the basis for understanding that God's plan of salvation is impartial and universal. From the initial thematic statement (1:16) to the climax of 15:7-12 Paul has repeatedly emphasized that the gospel is for all people—"it is the power of God for everyone who believes" (1:16). God is the God of the Gentiles as well as the God of the Jews (3:29). This universalism and impartiality show that the gospel reaches beyond Israel to all humankind. Through the preaching of the gospel God reveals that his purpose is to offer mercy to all and to call all to accept by faith Jesus Christ as Savior.

(2) Christ's saving work takes center stage in Paul's understanding of justifying grace. Justification occurs by faith in Christ alone and rests solely on his atoning death (3:21-29; 5:6-8). God's wrath and mercy express his righteousness. This righteousness has been fully manifested in that God's wrath is satisfied in Christ's death, and God's mercy is satisfied through justifying the sinner who relies on Christ's work for salvation.

(3) Justification is indispensable to the rest of God's works of grace—sanctification, reconciliation, redemption, adoption, and glorification. It stands at the beginning of the Christian life and is fundamental to our union with Christ and our life in him. Since justification brings us from death to life, from darkness to light, and from the old order of the flesh to the new order of the Spirit, it introduces us into God's all-embracing eschatological salvation. It leads us into the kingdom of grace and the age of everlasting life. The justified one is inserted into the process of salvation and into a new position of service. Therefore, justification is the starting place from which the other saving works of God can begin.

(4) Paul does employ the doctrine of justification in a legalistic context, but it must not be seen merely as a doctrine used for polemical purposes against Jews and Christian legalists. The doctrine of justification addresses the fundamental concern of how sinful humans can be accepted as righteous in God's sight and is fundamental to God's unfolding of his revelation in both the Old and New Testaments. The truth of justifying grace does function as a polemic against error, but Paul's intent was more than merely neutralizing the threat posed by legalism. His intent

includes showing how sinful human beings can find acceptance in the sight of the righteous God.

(5) Studies of Paul have focused on a number of major themes, each of which deserves careful attention; but though there are thematic shifts in Romans, justification by faith can be traced throughout this epistle and throughout Paul's theology. This conclusion does not represent an attempt to reduce his thought to a bear minimum. Justification is not the whole message of the gospel, but this great theme underpins all that Paul wrote and stands at the center of the gospel.

Divine Sovereignty and Existential Anxiety in Paul: Soliloquy and Self-Disclosure in Philippians

William A. Simmons[*]

Phil 1:

> 19 For I know that this shall turn to my salvation through your prayer, and the supply of the Spirit of Jesus Christ, 20 according to my earnest expectation and *my* hope, that in nothing I shall be ashamed, but *that* with all boldness, as always, *so* now also Christ shall be magnified in my body, whether *it be* by life, or by death. 21 For to me to live *is* Christ, and to die *is* gain. 22 But if I live in the flesh, this *is* the fruit of my labour: yet what I shall choose I wot not. 23 For I am in a strait betwixt two, having a desire to depart, and to be with Christ; which is far better. 24 Nevertheless to abide in the flesh *is* more needful for you. 25 And having this confidence, I know that I shall abide and continue with you all for your furtherance and joy of faith; 26 That your rejoicing may be more abundant in Jesus Christ for me by my coming to you again (KJV).

Introduction

It can be argued that Philippians is the most "personal" of all the Pauline epistles. In this brief letter Paul uses the pronoun "I" no fewer than sixty-five times. The apostle clearly has a very close relationship

[*]William A. Simmons (Ph.D., University of St. Andrews, Scotland). Associate Professor of New Testament, Lee University.

with this congregation, which permits him to be more transparent in Philippians than in some of his other epistles.[1] He can afford to be more vulnerable with this beloved church and take the risks associated with self-disclosure. Consequently he is able to share some of the inner turmoil he is experiencing as one imprisoned for the sake of Christ. His motive for doing so is both didactic and pastoral. The apostle desires to teach the Philippians from the context of his personal suffering and to let them know that he understands their pain as well. Thus Paul's life becomes a paradigm for theological insight. This essay will examine how Paul uses his own life context to address the tension that exists between the immutability of God's sovereign will and the ever changing nature of one's personal experience.

Paradigmatic Correlates: Personal Anxiety and Supreme Confidence

Paul's personality was not characterized by ambivalence and indecisiveness. When confronted by Christ on the Damascus road, Luke says that Paul immediately (εὐθέως) began to preach Christ in the synagogues. Similarly, in response to the "Macedonian vision," there is no hint of confusion or timidity. He and his cohorts immediately (εὐθέως) forge westward into Europe with the gospel (Acts 16:10). Paul openly rebukes a fellow apostle because he did not walk rightly in accordance with the gospel (Gal 2:11 ff). He is willing to lose Barnabas as a missionary partner over concerns about the suitability of John Mark (Acts 15:37-39). In many instances Paul appears as the paragon of decisiveness and control. Therefore when we see the apostle grappling with weighty alternatives in Phil 1:19-26, expressing both anxiety and uncertainty about the future, it commands our attention. Upon closer scrutiny of Paul's existential turmoil, we discover an intriguing admixture of personal ambivalence and supreme confidence in God's sovereign hand. That is, in the very place where Paul reveals his personal limitations and lack of prescience, he also conveys an unshakable trust in divine providence. It becomes clear that the interplay between these antithetical realities generates an extraordinary degree of existential anxiety in the mind and heart of the Apostle Paul.[2] It will be

---

[1]As Richard B. Hays comments, ". . . the generally cordial tone of this letter assumes a theological and hermeneutical harmony between Paul and his readers," *Echoes of the Scripture in the Letters of Paul* (New Haven: Yale University Press, 1989), 21. Gordon Fee notes that Paul views the Philippians as his "dearest friends" (*God's Empowering Presence: The Holy Spirit in the Letters of Paul* [Peabody, MA: Hendrickson, 1994], 734).

[2]Rodney R. Reeves, "To Be or Not to Be? That is not the Question: Paul's Choice in Philippians 1:22," *Perspectives in Religious Studies* 19 (1992): 273. Reeves questions whether Paul is actually entertaining two real alternatives or is

discovered that the resolution of this kind of spiritual tension is found in *2*
a dynamic synergism consisting of intercessory prayer, the supply of the
Holy Spirit, and reliance on the sovereign will of the Father.

Paul has expressed confidence in the work of God in the lives of the
Philippians (1:6). He is even confident that God is able to use unworthy
vessels to further his purposes in the world (1:15-18; cf. also Rom 9:6-29).
In 1:19, Paul evidences that same confidence with regard to God's work in
his own life. In particular, he trusts that in a providential way, what has
happened to him will result in his salvation.[3] As a ship guided safely to
port, Paul trusts that as a result of their prayers and the ample supply of
the Holy Spirit,[4] he will arrive at his ultimate destination, that is, "salvation."[5] In this context, "salvation" probably does not refer to the redemption of Paul's soul. In several instances in the New Testament "salvation"
(σωτηρία) means deliverance from harm, destruction, or captivity (cf. *3*
Luke 1:71; Acts 16:30; 27:31, 34; 2 Cor 1:6). This is surely what Paul has in
mind in 1:19. He is persuaded that the spiritual interaction of their prayers
and the supply of the Holy Spirit will eventually result in his deliverance
from captivity. However Paul is ambiguous concerning the exact nature of
his deliverance. We naturally think of his future release from prison,
anticipating another visit to the Philippians. Paul seems to anticipate just
such an acquittal, and indicates that he will see the Philippians again (1:26-
27). On the other hand, he also contemplates the real possibility of being
martyred for Christ (1:20-24). As will be shown below, the meaning of
"deliverance" is sufficiently ambiguous to encompass both prospects.
He may well be delivered from the executioner's sword, and thus be able to
minister among the Philippians again. Yet, his defense before the Roman
tribunal may not go well, and he may be martyred for his faith. If this be the
case, he then will be "delivered" from the trials of this life, and be ushered
into the very presence of Christ (1:21, 23).

Once again intercessory prayer plays a significant role in Paul's relationship with the Philippians. He prays for them (1:9f.), and trusts in the
power of their prayers for him. This kind of "synergism," or dynamic

---

he simply "thinking out loud" about theoretical issues (275).

[3]Hays, *Echoes of Scripture*, 21-22. Hays notes that the phrase τοῦτό μοι
ἀποβήσεται in 1:19 is a verbatim quote of Job 13:16 in the *LXX*. He postulates
that this parallel constitutes a literary "echo" whereby Paul identifies with the
"righteous sufferer" so dramatically set forth in the book of Job.

[4]For a discussion on the meaning of the phrase "the Spirit of Christ," see below.

[5]The word for "turn out" or "result in" (ἀποβήσεται) often describes disem-
barking from a boat (Luke 5:2; John 21:9). Walter Bauer, William F. Arndt and F.
Wilbur Gingrich, *A Greek-English Lexicon of the New Testament and other Early
Christian Literature*, (Chicago: The University of Chicago Press, 1957), 88.

[6]Gordon Fee, *Paul's Letter to the Philippians*, (Grand Rapids: Eerdmans, 1995),
134.

working together of his trust in God, the Philippians' prayers, and the supply of the Holy Spirit, reveals much about Paul's understanding of the sovereign work of God in his life. He did not view the believer as a passive automaton that is arbitrarily moved hither and yon on the chessboard of life. Rather, his deliverance will result from the interplay of personal faith, corporate intercession, and the work of the Holy Spirit.

Paul's reliance on the intercession of others is common in his epistles (cf. Rom 15:30-31; 2 Cor 1:9-11; 1 Thess 5:25; 2 Thess 3:1). Also, Spirit-anointed prayer was a hallmark of Paul's life, and of the early church (1 Cor 14:13ff; Eph 6:18; 1 Thess 5:17-19). All of this is in perfect compliance with the Spirit, who also intercedes for the believer (Rom 8:23, 26-27). It is this kind of spiritual nexus that grants Paul the confidence that God's perfect will shall prevail in his own circumstances, even though he expresses some doubt about the final resolution of his affairs.

The grammatical construction of the phrase "the supply of the Spirit" allows for several interpretations. Is Paul saying that it is the Holy Spirit that is being supplied (an objective genitive), or is he saying that the Holy Spirit will supply what is necessary for his deliverance (a subjective genitive)? Similarly, do the words, "the Spirit of Jesus Christ" mean that Jesus is the Spirit (objective genitive), or that Jesus sends or grants the Holy Spirit (subjective genitive)?[6] While either of these interpretations is possible, we must keep in mind that Paul is speaking of what the prayers of the Philippians will accomplish with regard to his circumstances.[7] Similarly, it seems likely that he is also referring to what the Holy Spirit will supply or bring to bear on his circumstances. Furthermore, Paul does not seem to be referring to the impartation of the Holy Spirit by Christ. More than likely, "the Spirit of Jesus Christ" is just another way of speaking of the Holy Spirit (cf. Rom 8:9; 1 Cor 15:15; Gal 4:6).[8]

Once again, an eschatological note is struck in 1:20 (recall 1:5, 6, 10). The words, "eager expectation and hope" are the exact same expression that Paul uses in Rom 8:19-20. Here he describes the end time deliverance of the entire creation. The word translated "eager expectation" (ἀποκαραδοκίαν) is an interesting one, expressing intense anticipation. The image is one of standing on tip toes, straining forward while waiting for the faintest glimpse of a long awaited event or visit.[9] Paul anxiously expects that whether he survives his upcoming trial or experiences his

---

[7] Fee, *God's Empowering Presence,* 740-42. Fee argues that it is the Spirit that is being supplied so that Paul may be able to magnify Christ. Therefore the Spirit is the object in the phrase, "Spirit of Christ."

[8] Ibid., 741. Fee notes that, "Paul has none of our hang-ups over whether a Spirit person can 'receive the Spirit.'"

[9] I-Jin Loh and Eugene Nida, *A Translator's Handbook on Paul's Letter to the Philippians,* (Stuttgart: United Bible Societies, 1977), 29.

personal eschaton at the hands of the Roman Empire, he will not be "ashamed" of his witness for Christ. The word for "ashamed" is only used here and in 2 Cor 10:8. However it frequently appears in the *LXX*, especially in the Psalms. A constant refrain of the psalmist is that the righteous will never be disgraced by the enemies of God (Pss 24:3; 34:26-27; 39:15-17).[10] Paul shares the same sentiment in the light of his upcoming trial (Rom 1:16; 1 Cor 1:18-25). His confidence has nothing to do with his personal ability or character. Rather, Paul is totally dependent upon the faithfulness of God in Christ. Also, Paul is not worried about his own reputation, as if he fears personal embarrassment during this critical phase of his trial. Rather, Paul's concerns relate to giving a strong testimony for Christ in the midst of trying circumstances. As he notes, "now as always" the Lord has granted him the necessary courage to exalt Christ in the face of opposition (1:20). Again these words would have been especially significant to the Philippians, for it was in their own presence that Paul boldly magnified Christ and was savagely beaten for his testimony. Yet without fear, Silas and he continued to praise the Lord while imprisoned in Philippi (Acts 16:16-25). Paul's determined commitment to Christ has not changed. His own life is of no consequence to him. His present motive and future goal are entirely christocentric. The crucial point for Paul is that whether in life or death, the totality of his earthly existence ("in my body") is dedicated to the exaltation of Christ.[11] Again, Paul serves as a living paradigm modeling total consecration to the cause of Christ. He is not only telling them how to witness, but is living out that kind of radical testimony the Philippians should give in the presence of their tormentors (1:28-30; 2:15).

This extraordinary focus on Christ means that in any eventuality, the gospel will be proclaimed through Paul. Whether he is acquitted or put to death for his faith, Christ will be magnified in his body. The word "magnified" (μεγαλυνθήσεται) is the same word used to describe the broadening or enlarging of the fringes on prayer garments (cf. Matt 23:5). Paul also uses the word in 2 Cor 10:15, expressing confidence that the Corinthians will afford him the proper respect due an apostle. Thus the word speaks of drawing special attention to a thing or person for the purpose of ascribing glory, honor, and praise. Similarly, Paul will bring glory and honor to Christ through his body, whether it be a living testimony or a martyr's corpse. Indeed the graphic expression "in my body" strikes a somber, yet significant note here. For Paul human existence is bodily existence, and God speaks through the body, whether it be through verbal proclamation or the silent testimony of those who died for the faith (cf. Heb 11: 32-40).

---

[10]Gerald F. Hawthorne, *Philippians* (Waco, TX: Word Books, 1983), 43.
[11]Fee, *Philippians*, 136.

The total claim of Christ on Paul can be seen in his own words, "To live is Christ, and to die is gain" (1:21). If he is acquitted and released, he will continue to live in this world as one totally absorbed in the person and work of Christ. In fact, in order to capture more accurately the sentiment of Paul in this instance, the phrase might be better translated, "For me, life is Christ."[12] If he should be killed for the cause of Christ, then this will be "gain" (1:21).

Paul uses a number of literary techniques to convey the unusual power of these words. He employs alliteration, the rhyming of syllables, a quality impossible to perceive in the English.[13] He also arranges this terse statement in the form of a Greek "X," following the A-B-A-B pattern that may well form the structure of the entire epistle. A schematic representation of Paul's words would be as follows:

$$
\begin{array}{ll}
\text{``to live''} & \text{``is gain''} \\
(A) & (B') \\
(A') & (B) \\
\text{``to die''} & \text{``is Christ''}
\end{array}
$$

This chiasmic construction was used in 1:16-17, and will be seen again in 1:23-24. It is clearly one of Paul's favorite ways of intertwining ideas in his letter to the Philippians.[14]

Again the grand theology of Rom 8:28 comes forth in Paul's words to the Philippians. Although Paul is not able to discern the exact contours of God's plan for him, as one supremely called according to God's purpose, all that he experiences within the great parameters of earthly existence (i.e., life or death) will be for the furtherance of the Kingdom and the glory of Christ.[15] Thus to die "is gain" because in death Paul finally arrives at his lifelong goal (3:10). The executioner's sword cannot extinguish his witness. It can only transport him into the very presence of God in Christ. However, we must not interpret "gain" as a subtle disparaging of this

---

[12]Peter T. O'Brien, *Commentary on Philippians* (Grand Rapids: Eerdmans, 1991), 120.

[13]Fee, *Philippians,* 140.

[14]For an extensive treatment of Paul's use of chiasmus in Philippians, see A. Boyd Luter and Michelle V. Lee, "Philippians as Chiasmus: Key to the Structure, Unity and Theme Questions," *NTS* 41 (1995): 89-101.

[15]As Dailey notes, "life" and "death" are not viewed by Paul as antithetical alternatives, but represent the extremes of earthly existence that are completely encompassed by Christ (cf. Rom 14:8). Thomas F. Dailey, "To Live or Die: Paul's Eschatological Dilemma in Philippians 1:19-26," *Interpretation* 44 (1990): 25-270.

present life.[16] As Paul clearly indicates, his life *is Christ*. And at any rate, continuance in this world only affords Paul the opportunity to produce additional "fruit" for Christ (cf. 1:22 below). This labor of love is Paul's joy and the sole *raison d' etre* of his entire existence (3:7-14).

Paul's words in 1:22-26 are difficult to interpret. In addition to the very clipped style (the omission of verbs in some clauses), he appears to express conflicting ideas. In an effort to make sense of this section, it has been argued that Paul is contemplating a purely hypothetical situation. *If* he actually had a choice of staying in this world or going on to be with Christ, he does not know what he would choose. The operative word here is *if*. Since Paul has totally committed his fate to God, then his personal wishes would be of no real consequence. Nevertheless, it can be argued, *if* it were left to him, he would indeed be confronted with a thorny dilemma.

While this kind of interpretation certainly has merit and does much to exonerate Paul from apparently contradictory statements, it strikes one as *too* theoretical to address the Philippian context. Is Paul really fabricating a purely abstract theoretical soliloquy in 1:22-26? Granted, Paul is not conveying genuine personal choice with regard to his fate. Yet he is expressing an authentic personal struggle in the face of real possibilities. It is this kind of struggle that the Philippians are facing on a daily basis. For these reasons it is concluded that Paul is purposely allowing the Philippians to look into the anguish of his soul so that they too might learn to cope with the vicissitudes of life in Christ.

Paul certainly can see the value of continuing ἐν σαρκί, that is, "in flesh." Of the many ways that Paul uses the term "flesh," the context of 1:22 indicates that "in flesh" (ἐν σαρκί) be interpreted as referring to life in this world. [17] Thus, the phrase does not contain any of the negative moral connotations so often found in other Pauline passages (cf. Phil 3:3-4; Rom 8:8-9; 2 Cor 10:3). What he means here is the same as in Gal 2:20 where he states, "... and the life that I now live *in the flesh* I live by the faith of the Son of God who loved me and gave himself for me." In this way

---

[16]Fee, *Philippians*, 140-43.

[17]The great number of ways that "flesh" is used in the Scriptures merits some attention. First, the word for "flesh" is clearly a Pauline term. Of the thirty-nine times σάρξ appears in the New Testament, Paul uses it thirty-two times. He masterfully renders a wide variety of meanings from the word, the sense of which must be determined from the context. For example, σάρξ can refer to the blood relation or human descent of an individual (Rom 4:1) or the ethnic identity of an entire race (Rom 11:14). Also, "flesh" may simply mean human corporeality or physical existence in this world (1 Cor 7:28). And finally, in a negative sense, σάρξ may signify the fallen human nature. In this case it represents that thoroughgoing egocentricity of fallen humanity that continually seeks to disobey God. A. R. G. Deasley, "Flesh," in the *Evangelical Dictionary of Biblical Theology* (Grand Rapids: Baker Books, 1996), 260.

Paul contrasts the reality of living in this world with the possibility of
going on to be with Christ in heaven.

As noted above, abiding "in flesh" affords the opportunity for additional "fruit of labor" (καρπός ἔργου). Again, Paul uses an agricultural
motif in describing effective missionary service. Therefore when contemplating the choice of continued service for Christ in this world or enjoying
complete fellowship with God in heaven, Paul experiences considerable
ambivalence. On a personal level, it would be a difficult decision for him to
make.

The rendering of the phrase οὐ γνωρίζω ("I do not know") is again
difficult to interpret. Paul certainly has knowledge of the alternatives
facing him. Once again, Paul is probably expressing the personal ambivalence born of human limitation and divine providence. In something akin
to metaphor, Paul is using the image of personal choice to address the
intersection of his individual fate and the sovereign plan of God for the
ministry. In any case, both alternatives, continuing to serve Christ in this
world or going to be with him in heaven, are desirable.

In 1:23-24, Paul once again arranges his thoughts in the form of a
chiasmus.[18]

A	B
Life in this world is fruitful labor	**I can not choose**

B'	A'
My choice is death	*God's choice is fruitful labor*

By arranging his thoughts in this way, Paul graphically expresses the
eschatological tension of living in this world, yet longing for the age to
come.[19] "Already" he is a child of the Kingdom; however, the Kingdom is
"not yet" fully realized (1 Cor 4:8-13; 5:9-10). Thus he is literally "held
together" or "hemmed in" (συνέρχομαι) by two powerful alternatives.

It should be noted that Paul is not actually struggling with whether he
is to live or die. He is certainly not seeking to escape the misery of this life
so that he might go to heaven. Rather he is wrestling with two competing
loyalties. He feels a burden of love to remain in this world so that he might
benefit the church. At the same time he longs "to depart" and be with
Christ. Again, Paul resorts to maritime imagery to describe his journey to
God in Christ (cf. 1:19). "Depart" (ἀναλῦσαι) was used to describe the
casting off of ships or the breaking of camp.[20] The word clearly describes
a movement from one place to the next, perhaps indicative of a pilgrim's

---

[18]Fee, *Philippians,* 145.
[19]Dailey, "To Live or Die," 20-21.
[20]Fee, *Philippians,* 148.

journey. For Paul this life is only a temporary stop on the way to the Lord. It serves as a transition paving the way for complete communion with Christ.

We must be careful to avoid the notion that Paul is devaluing life in this world when compared to existence in heaven. Paul understands the totality of his existence as being "in Christ." Nevertheless, he does recognize different aspects of Christian life. One aspect he describes as "remaining in the body," and is synonymous with living for Christ in this world. Another aspect is spoken of as "being with Christ," which means being ushered into the very presence of God upon death. Thus, for Paul there is never a time when the believer is not in communion with Christ. He certainly does not envision any period of "soul sleep" in which the consciousness of the believer is suspended awaiting the last day.[21] As he states in 2 Cor 5:8, "We are confident, I say, and willing rather to be absent from the body, and to be present with the Lord." The same consciousness and sense of personal identity that he experienced in this life as a Christian will also be experienced if he should be martyred, yet on a more intense level.[22] The executioner's sword will actually facilitate his journey to heaven.

This is not to say that 1:23-24 contains the whole of Paul's views on personal eschatology. He certainly does not anticipate eternally existing in a disembodied state. Such a condition would fall short of complete redemption. God's salvation encompasses not only the totality of humanity, including our physicality, but the restoration of the entire universe (1 Thess 4:13-18; 1 Cor 15:3-57; 2 Cor 5:1-5; Rom 8:19-23). For Paul, human existence is bodily existence, whether it be in this world or the world to come. Only when he experiences the power of Christ's resurrection will he have arrived at complete redemption (Phil 3:10-11).

The mutually exclusive fates introduced in 1:22, and the tremendous tension contained therein, find their resolution in 1:25. All sense of personal turmoil is swept away when Paul states that he is "convinced" (πεποιθώς, cf. 1:6) of "this." The "this" must refer to God's perspective

---

[21]The portrayal of death as "sleep" was employed by the ancient Greek writers and used repeatedly throughout the Bible and the apochrypha (Homer, *Iliad*, 11.241; Sophocles, *Electra*, 509; 2 Macc 12:45; Gen 47:30; Job 14:12; John 11:11-13; Acts 13:36; 1 Cor 11:30; 1 Thess 4:13); see Charles A. Wanamaker, *Commentary on 1 & 2 Thessalonians* (Grand Rapids: Eerdmans, 1990) 166-67. To interpret "sleep" as referring to an extended period of stasis between death and the final state is to press the metaphor beyond Paul's intention in Phil 1:19 ff. The Bible never speaks of the soul as falling asleep. Yet the Scriptures do describe the fellowship of believers with God and with Jesus as occurring immediately after death (cf. Luke 16:19-31; Acts 7:59; Rev 6:9, 7:9). Louis Berkhof, *Systematic Theology*, (Grand Rapids: Eerdmans, 1939), 689.

[22]Dailey, "To Live or Die," 22-25.

on the issues he had previously expressed. Paul is convinced that God desires him to remain in the world and serve the church. The phrase "remain and continue" (μενῶ καὶ παραμενῶ) is very emphatic, indicating an ongoing presence in a specific place or staying with a particular people.[23] *Through the eyes of faith*, Paul can envision an extended ministry among the Philippians.

Even when contemplating a favorable verdict in his upcoming trial, Paul's thoughts are focused on the Philippians. His release will be for their "progress and joy" of the faith. Again, the word for "progress" (προκοπὴν) was previously used in 1:12 to describe the progress of the gospel. So just as God is able to use his imprisonment to promote the gospel, Paul is equally convinced that his release will result in the strengthening of the church. In either eventuality, the Kingdom will be advanced.

The complete selflessness of Paul is again seen in 1:26. The purpose of his release has nothing to do with escaping death. Rather, he realizes that his personal fate is bound up with God's sovereign plan for the church. He will remain with the Philippians *so that* their "joyous exaltation" (καύχημα, frequently translated "boasting") in Christ might increase. The absolute basis for their sense of triumph is Christ Jesus. However, Paul will serve as the instrument through whom God will increase their joy in Christ. Hence, with regard to their progress and joy, Paul says their joy will be "by me (ἐν ἐμοὶ) and through my presence again to you all."[24]

What then is the immediate purpose of Paul's words comparing the benefits of earthly life with those of heavenly existence? No doubt he intended his own deliberations to serve as a teaching model or paradigm for the saints in Philippi. Particularly, the Philippians are to perceive the apostle as one completely sold out to the cause of Christ, regardless of personal difficulties that he might be experiencing. Similarly, they are to emulate this kind of dedication, especially when confronted by their oppressors.

Paul's emphasis on spiritual formation is continued in 1:27ff.[25] By presenting himself as one committed to Christ regardless of suffering and pain, Paul has established a theme that will continue through the end of the second chapter.[26] For example, he first focuses full attention on the

---

[23]Moses J. Silva, *Philippians* (Chicago: Moody Press, 1988), 85.

[24]Ibid.

[25]Paul's use of "worthy" in 1:27 indicates that the gospel contains ethical and moral principles that must be actualized in the life of every Christian (Fee, *Philippians*, 162). In other words, to take pride in the joyous victory of salvation (1:26), one must practice sanctification. Indeed Silva entitles 1:27 to 2:39 "A Call to Sanctification," thereby stressing the need for holy living (*Philippians*, viii, 89).

[26]Fee notes that Paul constructs a perfect chiasm in 1:26-27, thus constituting another example of the "X" pattern found throughout Philippians (Fee, *Philippians*, 157; cf. note 14).

present situation of the Philippians (1:27-30). He will then follow with the supreme example of Christ (2:1-11). And finally, Paul will drive his message home by pointing to the extraordinary dedication of one of their own, Epaphroditus (2:25-30).

Conclusion

In the "reflective soliloquy" set forth in Phil 1:19-26, Paul acknowledges two competing eventualities.[27] His upcoming trial may not go well, and he will be executed. In this instance, he will be present with the Lord. On the other hand, the court may rule in his favor, and he will be able to continue his ministry among the Philippians. Trusting the sovereign hand of God, Paul conveys his confidence that either eventuality will be beneficial. At the same time, one detects some degree of anxiety born of human limitations. He does not know, from his perspective, what would be the best outcome. Nevertheless, through the eyes of faith, he rests in the delivering hand of the Lord and trusts that he will soon join the Philippians again. Ultimately the purpose of this extraordinary self-disclosure is not to resolve his own inner struggles. Rather, Paul's intent was to express supreme confidence in the sovereign will of God, in the midst of his personal weakness and ambivalence. As a living message to the Philippians, he hoped to advance them on their spiritual journey.

---

[27]Fee, *God's Empowering Presence*, 739.

II. Historical &
Theological Studies

Tertullian on Women and Women's Ministry Roles in the Church[*]

Daniel Hoffman[**]

When the North African church apologist and theologian Tertullian (c. AD 165-220), in a short essay directed to Christian women in the early third century, blamed Eve for the introduction of sin into the world and wrote that women through Eve were "the devil's gateway,"[1] he provided apparently clear evidence of an inherent hostility toward women in at least one early Christian leader now honored as a "Church father."[2] Indeed, Tertullian's words in this infamous passage, and in some other frequently cited sections from his many writings such as *Virg. Vel.* 9 (*On the Veiling of Virgins*), *Bapt.* 1 and 17 (*On Baptism*), and *Prae. Haer.* 41 (*Prescription Against the Heretics*), are often used today to prove that early orthodox Christian authorities increasingly kept women from high status positions

---

[*]Previously published portions of this essay have been used with the permission of the Edwin Mellen Press from Daniel Hoffman, *The Status of Women and Gnosticism In Irenaeus and Tertullian.* Studies in Women in Religion 36 (Lewiston: Edwin Mellen, 1995).

[**]Daniel Hoffman (Ph.D., Miami University, Ohio). Assistant Professor of History, Lee University.

[1]*Cult. Fem.* 1.1. (*On the Apparel of Women*), cited from *The Ante-Nicene Fathers,* 10 vols., ed. A. Roberts and J. Donaldson; American edition, ed. A. C. Coxe (Grand Rapids: Eerdmans, 1950), 4:14. See also *Fathers of the Church,* 69+ vols., L. Schopp, gen. ed. (Washington: Catholic U. of America, 1947—), 40:118. Unless otherwise noted, Latin citations for Tertullian will come from the *Corpus Christianorum, Series Latina,* 176 vols. (Turnholti: Editores Pontificii, 1954—). This phrase is *diaboli ianua*; *CCSL,* 1:343.

[2]Patricia Gundry, "Why We're Here," in *Women, Authority, and the Bible,* ed. A. Mickelsen (Downers Grove: Intervarsity, 1986), 21; and R. W. Pierce, "Evangelicals and Gender Roles in the 1990s: 1 Tim 2:8-15: A Test Case," *Journal of the Evangelical Theological Society* 36/3 (September 1993): 345.

and leadership roles in the church, and that the "patriarchal" church disliked and feared women in general.[3] However, Tertullian's views about women, especially toward women in ministry roles in the church, are much more positive than they appear from the dramatic, "misogynistic," excerpts usually quoted.[4] The following essay will attempt to show that even Tertullian's harshest criticism of some women, when considered in detail and balanced with some other favorable expressions toward women, should not be considered evidence of a general misogyny on his part or within the early church. Moreover, Tertullian's use of some much debated New Testament passages relating to women including 1 Cor 11:2-16; 14:34-35; and 1 Tim 2:8-15 will show an interpretation that supports orthodox women ministering in various positions of authority, for example as teachers, and prophetesses. His commendations of Christian women in these and other vital church roles, and the biblical interpretations on which they are based, are both worth reexamining today as charges and challenges over ministry roles for women still abound among Christians committed to the inspiration and authority of Scripture.

I. Background

Before any specific passages about women from Tertullian are presented, some details about his life and work should be covered. Unfortunately, few facts about Tertullian are known apart from the brief allusions that he provides himself in his writings. Nevertheless, one common misconception, perhaps derived from his arguments that women wear modest clothes and that virgins remain veiled in church, is that he was an archconservative and an advocate of the status quo. Nothing could be

---

[3]See for example, Simone de Beauvoir, *The Second Sex* (New York: Vintage Books, 1974), 110, 189; Vern Bullough, *The Subordinate Sex: A History of Attitudes Toward Women* (Urbana: U. of Illinois, 1973), 114; Elisabeth Schussler-Fiorenza, *In Memory of Her: A Feminist Theological Reconstruction of Early Christian Origins* (New York: Crossroads, 1983), 55; Marie-Henry Keane, "Women in the Theological Anthropology of the Early Fathers," *Journal of Theology for Southern Africa* 62 (March 1988): 4-5; and Elaine Pagels, *The Gnostic Gospels* (New York: Random House, 1979), 60-61, 69.

[4]Some scholars qualify their charges saying that Tertullian was "no ordinary misogynist" (George Tavard, *Women in Christian Tradition* [Notre Dame: U. of Notre Dame, 1973], 59), or not a "simple misogynist" since he did not always have a "hostile and forbidding tone" (Jo Ann McNamara, "A New Song: Celibate Women in the First Three Christian Centuries," *Women and History* 6/7 [1983]: 110). A few others give a relatively positive interpretation of Tertullian's view of women, e.g., Elizabeth Carnelley ("Tertullian and Feminism," *Theology* 42 [1989]:31-34), F. F. Church ("Sex and Salvation in Tertullian," *Harvard Theological Review* 68 [1975]:83-100), and Hoffman (*Women and Gnosticism*, 145-207).

further from the truth![5] For although he seems to have come from a wealthy family,[6] he is a sharp critic of most aspects of the polytheistic and pagan society of Carthage.[7] For example, in *Ad Martyras* (*To the Martyrs*) he tells those arrested not to worry about the loss of "the world's enjoyments" or "life's sweets" because "if we reflect that the world is more really the prison, we shall see that you have gone out of a prison rather than into one."[8] In *Ad Nationes* 2.1 (*To the Nations*) he makes it clear that he is against the dominate pagan culture of his day:

> It is therefore against these things that our contest lies—
> against the institutions of our ancestors, against the authority
> of tradition, the laws of our governors, and the reasonings of
> the wise; against antiquity, custom, submission; against pre-
> cedents, prodigies, miracles,—all which things have their part
> in consolidating that spurious (*adulterinam*) system of your
> gods.[9]

This revolutionary attitude can also be seen in his discussions about women. For example, even in *Cult. Fem.*, where he argues that women should not wear ornaments or jewelry and so give the appearance of immodesty, he bases his views on the belief that those things are part of the evil world system. He believes that system should be rejected along with its trapping by every true Christian as he writes: "Let us cast away earthly ornaments if we desire heavenly."[10] In seldom noted passages in this same work he calls Christian women "handmaids of the living God" and "fellow-servants and sisters,"[11] and then urges them to "love not gold" but instead to "hate what ruined your fathers."[12]

Tertullian's rejection of the political and social status quo is not surprising in the light of the persecutions experienced by Christians in North Africa at the hands of various Roman authorities during the years of his literary career (c. 196-212).[13] His famous *Apology* and *Ad Martyras* (both

---

[5]Susanne Heine, *Women and Early Christianity* (Minneapolis: Augsburg, 1988), 31.

[6]In *Test. An.* 4 (*ANF*, 3:178), he mentions that men try to perpetuate their name and memory after their death by building lavish tombs and composing literature. Such means would only be open to men of relative wealth. See also *Prae. Haer.* 39 and *Ux.* 2.4.

[7]W. H. C. Frend (*The Early Church* [Philadelphia: Fortress, 1984], 80) says that Tertullian was "one of the born rebels of history."

[8]*Mart.*2; *ANF*, 3:693-94.

[9]*ANF*, 3:129. See also *Pall.* 5.

[10]*Cult. Fem.* 2.13; *ANF*, 4:25.

[11]*Cult. Fem.* 2.1; *ANF*, 4:18.

[12]*Cult. Fem.* 2.13; *ANF*, 4:25. See also Heine, *Women*, 30-32.

[13]W. H. C. Frend, *Rise of Christianity* (n.p.: Fortress Press, 1986), 349-51, and Robert D. Sider, "Tertullian," in *Encyclopedia of Early Christianity*, gen. ed. E.

written c. 197) were certainly motivated by such persecutions. In 202, under the emperor Severus, the catechumens Perpetua, Felicitas, and some others were killed in Carthage.[14] Tertullian's *De Fuga in Persecutione* (*On Flight from Persecution*) written c. 209 takes a hard line against Christians who would flee to escape harm. From these references and other information in Tertullian's works, it is clear that persecution continued to shape North African Christianity.[15]

The frequent persecutions in and around Carthage may account for some of Tertullian's ambivalent views toward Christians entering into marriages and having children. He notices, for example, that children can be an unnecessary tie with the world and that they may especially hinder women from following God and renouncing the corrupt society.[16] Some of his theological ideas, such as his expectation that the end of time was near, also influence his views of women. Scholars often mention that his eschatological faith leads him to discourage people from marrying, especially in those writings after 206 that show Montanist leanings.[17] However, it is less frequently recognized that this same faith prompts his acceptance of women in prophetic ministries. In other words, it also accounts in part for the esteem he gives to the Montanist women like Prisca (or Priscilla) and Maximilla, and others whose revelations urged moral purity in light of the soon return of Christ.[18]

Some additional important aspects of Tertullian's life should be considered before we examine his words relating to women in church ministries. First, he was married and seemingly had a good relationship with a Christian woman whom he calls "my best beloved fellow-servant in the Lord."[19] This fact in itself might be surprising for some who see him as an extreme misogynist,[20] but it could certainly help explain why he does not renounce marriage in principle, even in his late, Montanist works. Next, he apparently spent most of his life in Carthage, writing and teaching, and he seems to have gained a position of some responsibility in the North African church based on the fact that he addressed some of his works to

---

Ferguson (New York: Garland, 1990), 884. Frend and Sider essentially assume the dates and order for Tertullian's writings set out by T. D. Barnes (*Tertullian: A Historical and Literary Study* [Oxford: Oxford UP, 1971]), and Barnes' dates will also be followed in this essay.

[14]Frend, *Rise of Christianity*, 291. See also section III below.

[15]Ibid., 290-94, 350-51.

[16]*Ux.* 1.5; *ANF*, 4:41-42.

[17]Robert D. Sider, "Approaches to Tertullian: A Study of Recent Scholarship," *Second Century* 2 (1982): 256-57.

[18]E.g., *Ex. Cast.* 11; *ANF*, 4:56.

[19]*Ux.* 1.1, 2.1; *ANF*, 4:39, 4:44.

[20]Clarence L. Lee, "The Search for Mrs. Tertullian," *Africa Theological Journal* 14 (1985): 46.

catechumens.[21] On the other hand, he was not a priest and did not hold any ecclesiastical office as he numbered himself among the laity on two occasions in his later writings.[22] This lack of ecclesiastical position along with his apparently secure financial situation could have given him more literary freedom. He was certainly not at all reluctant to attack men or women whose views differed from his own. Nevertheless, his works in some measure represented those of the official church in Carthage as many were copied and used by later North African church leaders.[23] Cyprian, the bishop of Carthage from c. AD 248-58, is a prominent example of such a leader. He derived many of his theological and ethical ideas from Tertullian and was even thought to have called him "his master."[24] Finally, T. D. Barnes suggests that Tertullian was widowed later in his life and that the loss of his wife prompted his shift toward Montanism with its stress on continence.[25] The date of his death cannot now be fixed with any certainty.[26]

II. Ontological Views About Women

Let us turn next to Tertullian's expressions relating to the general status of women and see what they reveal. First, there are several statements that support the idea that he considered women ontologically equal with men. However, as with most aspects of Tertullian's ideas about women, this issue is complicated since there are some expressions that seem to indicate that he did not think women were created in the "image" of God. The infamous "devil's gateway" passage in equating women with Eve might give this impression:

---

[21]E.g., *De Spectaculis* and *De Oratione*. See also Johannes Quasten, *Patrology* (Westminster: Newman, 1952), 2:293, 296.

[22]*Mon.* 12.2 and *Ex. Cast.* 7.3 according to Barnes (*Tertullian*, 11).

[23]For example, Tertullian's views on sex, marriage, and women were cited by Cyprian in *De Habitu Virginum* 2, 5, 12, 14 (*FOC*, 36:32-43); by Prudentius (a Christian provincial Roman governor in the fourth century) in *Psychoachia*, line 183 (*FOC*, 52:87); by Novatian in *In Praise of Purity*, 3, 12 (*FOC*, 67:167, 175); and by Ambrose, *Letter to the Church at Vercelli* (*FOC*, 26:344).

[24]According to Jerome, *De Viris Illustribus*, 53. Although Barnes has convincingly attacked the accuracy of Jerome's account in many areas, there is little doubt about the great influence of Tertullian on Cyprian. The influence of Tertullian on Cyprian's view of penance and several related doctrines, for example, has been systematically explored by Cahal Daly, *Tertullian the Puritan and his Influence* (Dublin: Four Courts, 1992). For a survey of Tertullian's influence in other areas see Frend, *Rise of Christianity*, 348-52.

[25]Barnes, *Tertullian*, 136-37.

[26]Ibid., 59.

> And do you not know that you are (each) an Eve? The sen-
> tence of God on this sex of yours lives in this age: the guilt
> must of necessity live too. You are the devil's gateway: you
> are the unsealer of that (forbidden) tree: you are the first
> deserter of the divine law: you are she who persuaded him
> whom the devil was not valiant enough to attack. You de-
> stroyed so easily God's image, man. On account of your
> desert—that is, death—even the Son of God had to die.[27]

This dramatic passage certainly seems to offer decisive proof of a terrible
view of women in general on the part of Tertullian.[28] The key phrase,
which could be interpreted as denying that women are created in the
image of God, is: "You destroyed so easily God's image, man" (*tu
imaginemdei, hominem, tam facile elisiste*).[29] However, the Latin text
reading preferred by the editors of the *Corpus Christianorum, Series
Latina* has "*tu imaginem dei, hominem Adam, facile elisisti*":[30] "You destroyed easily God's image, the man Adam." By limiting the reference to
Adam, the negative corollary about women not being created in the image
of God possibly inferred from the more general expression of the other
reading would seem to be avoided. Of course, neither the divine image in
Eve or women, nor anything else favorable toward women would be affirmed in either case in this particular section, but given the rhetorical
pattern of the argument (discussed below), such an affirmation would be
unlikely at that point.

On the other hand, a few chapters later in *Cult. Fem.* 1, Tertullian
assumes that women have the same nature as men since they have the
same future, which will include judging the evil angels:

---

[27]*ANF*, 4:14. ". . . *et Evam te esse nescis? Vivit et reatus necesse est. Tu es
diaboli ianua, tu es arboris illius resignatrix, tu es divinae legis prima desertrix; tu
es quae eum suasisti, quem diabolus aggredi non valuit; tu imaginem dei, hominem Adam, facile elisisti; propter tuum meritum, id est mortem, etiam filius dei
mori habuit: et adornari tibi in mente est super pelliceas tuas tunicas?*" *CCSL*,
1:343. The *ANF* translation is based on a slightly different Latin text than that
given above from *CCSL*.

[28]In addition to those authors cited in note 3 above, others that find evidence
for Tertullian's misogyny in this passage include W. E. Phipps (*Was Jesus Married?: The Distortion of Sexuality in the Christian Tradition* [New York: Harper &
Row, 1979], 145) and Rosemary Ruether ("Misogynism and Virginal Feminism in
the Fathers of the Church," in *Religion and Sexism: Images of Women in the Jewish
and Christian Tradition*, ed. R. Ruether [New York: Simon & Schuster, 1974],
157).

[29]*Cult. Fem.* 1.1; *ANF*, 4:14. See, e.g., Gen 3:12 and 1 Tim 2:14 for the biblical
basis of Tertullian's charge against Eve (considered in more detail below). Also,
for a short survey of Jewish and Apocalyptic literature and other writings of the
Church fathers which blame the fall on Eve, see Heine, *Women*, 14-18.

[30]*CCSL*, 1:343 and text note on 1.1 line 19.

> You realize, of course, that the same angelic nature is prom-
> ised to you, women, the selfsame sex is promised to you as to
> men, and the selfsame dignity of being a judge. Therefore,
> unless here in this life we begin to practice being judges by
> condemning their works which we are destined to condemn in
> them some day, then they will rather judge us and condemn
> us.[31]

The idea that women will have the same sex as men mentioned in this passage is *not* equivalent with a Gnostic idea current at about the same time that women should be made into men.[32] Instead, Tertullian thinks that women and men will share a common, *non-sexual*, unimpaired, human nature in the future based on his understanding of the angels in heaven.[33]

The ontological equality of men and women from creation (and before heaven) also seems to be indicated in *De Spectaculis* (*On the Shows*), probably Tertullian's earliest work. Here he makes an important statement regarding the nature of fallen humanity (*homo*): "Man himself, guilty as he is of every iniquity, is not only a work of God—he is His image, and yet both in soul and body he has severed himself from his Maker."[34] Al-though the text says nothing specifically about women, it is reasonable to conclude that it refers to all human beings as works of God made in the divine image. If not, it would still be quite remarkable for a different rea-son. It would be saying that men (males) are guilty of every iniquity and that they severed themselves from God. That idea would certainly con-trast with a surface reading of *Cult. Fem.* 1.1 where Eve (and women) seem guilty of everything.

Next, Tertullian's description of the *original* spiritual character of Eve set in the context of her relation to Adam given in a later work, *De Anima* (*On the Soul*), may help to dispel the notion that he believed there was any inherent inequity in Eve (or women) stemming from creation. Of course, merely defining the creation of woman in terms of man might prejudice some modern readers against Tertullian, but his literal understanding of Genesis 2, rather than some inherent antipathy toward women, is probably responsible for his description.[35] Gen 2:7, for example, does say that God

---

[31]*Cult. Fem.* 1.2; *ANF*, 4:15. "*Nam et uobis eadem tunc substantia angelica repromissa; idem sexus quit et viris eandem iudicandi degnationem pollicetur....*" *CCSL*, 1:346.

[32]See especially *The Gospel of Thomas* logion 114 (51,18-26), *The Gospel of Philip* 68,22-26, and *The (First) Apocalypse of James* 41,15-19. For an analysis of these and other related Gnostic texts, see Hoffman, *Women and Gnosticism*, 23-77.

[33]See *Ad. Val.* 32 (where Matt 22:30 may be cited) and *Res. Mort.* 62. See also Church, "Sex and Salvation in Tertullian," 99-100.

[34]*Spect.* 2; *ANF*, 3:80.

[35]Church, "Sex and Salvation in Tertullian," 91.

breathed into Adam the breath of life so that he became a living being. Later in the Genesis 2 account, Eve is said to be taken from Adam, and there is no specific mention of her receiving the breath of God. Within those parameters, Tertullian seems willing enough to speculate:

> Adam was the first formed . . . Eve was the later formed. So that her flesh was for a long time without specific form . . . ; but she was even then herself a living being, because I should regard her at that time in soul as even a portion of Adam. Besides, God's breath (*afflatus*) would have animated her too, if there had not been in the woman a transmission from Adam of his soul also as well as his flesh.[36]

This understanding is enough for Tertullian. He does not think that Eve needed a specific breath of God to share in the divine nature or to become a "living being" even though this had been necessary for Adam. If there had been a need for this to insure that Eve also had both soul and flesh, God would have met it.

Tertullian elsewhere implies that Adam needed the direct breath of God because the material used to form him, that is "clay," was actually inferior to the flesh used to form Eve. His views on this appear in an essay arguing for the future resurrection of the flesh against various Gnostic theories. The text, *De Resurrectione Mortuorum* (*On the Resurrection of the Flesh*), was written in his Montanist phase about the same time as *De Anima* cited above. In it he reasons that the clay from which Adam had been formed "was obliterated and absorbed into flesh . . . at the time that man became a living soul by the inbreathing of God."[37] Then this flesh, by God's action, "not only laid aside its clayey [sic] rudiments, but also took on itself the ornaments of the soul."[38] This indeed is the part of creation that was most important for Tertullian as the soul is considered "more proximate in character to God."[39] Eve not only shares equally in the soulish "likeness" of God as implied in *De Anima*, but her flesh shares the same substance with Adam's.[40] This belief is evident in a passage where

---

[36]*An.* 36; *ANF*, 3:217. Tertullian's traducianism (*An.* 27, 36) also shows no spiritual differentiation between men and women.

[37]*Res. Mort.* 7; *ANF*, 3:550

[38]Ibid.

[39]Ibid., 3:550-51. However, Tertullian was not formulating a dualist position with the flesh and soul sharply separated. Both flesh and soul would be regenerated in Christ. See *Res. Mort.* 8 and *Pud.* 6. See also Church, "Sex and Salvation in Tertullian," 89.

[40]*Res. Mort.* 7; *ANF*, 3:550. In equating the "image" and "likeness" with the flesh and the soul/spirit, Tertullian differed from Origen and such later fathers as Augustine who identified the image exclusively with the soul. See Maryanne Horowitz, "The Image of God in Man—Is Woman Included?," *Harvard*

Tertullian attempts to refute an erroneous view that held that Adam and Eve were not "flesh out of clay" until they put on the "coats of skin" of Gen. 3:31.[41] Tertullian says:

> Long before that Adam had already recognized the flesh which was in the woman as the propagation of his own substance ("This is now bone of my bone, and flesh of my flesh"), and the very taking of the woman out of the man was supplemented with flesh; but it ought, I suppose, to have been made good with clay, if Adam was still clay.[42]

Tertullian's argument assumes that Eve's substance was the same in character or nature as Adam's. However, since Adam had already been made flesh at the time of the creation of Eve, her creation out of that flesh did not require the same touch of God that his creation from clay had required.

Finally, there are two passages in Tertullian's late work on chastity, *De Exhortatione Castitatis*, which affirm the belief that Adam and Eve were ontologically equal, and that all those created in God's "image" could (and should) be restored to the divine "likeness" by leading a holy and sanctified life. In the first case, Adam and Eve are presented as an authoritative example of a monogamous marriage:

> There were more ribs in Adam, and hands that knew no weariness in God; but not more wives in the eye of God. And accordingly the man of God, Adam, and the woman of God, Eve, discharging mutually (the duties of) one marriage, sanctioned for mankind a type by (the consideration of) the authoritative precedent of their origin and the primal will of God.[43]

The second important passage in this book appears near the beginning as part of Tertullian's exhortation to a friend whose wife has died. This man is encouraged to avoid the temptation of remarrying since God has called all believers to be holy: "Now, 'the will of God is our sanctification.' For He desires that we who are his 'image' should also become His 'likeness,' in order that we may be holy as He Himself is holy."[44] Altogether, the evidence from Tertullian in this area shows that Eve was assumed to be made in the outward divine image and in the spiritual likeness of God,

---

Theological Review 72 (1979):175-206.

[41]*Res. Mort.* 7; *ANF*, 3:550.

[42]Ibid.

[43]*Ex. Cast.* 5; *ANF*, 4:53.

[44]*Ex. Cast.* 1; *FOC*, 13:42. The pertinent biblical references within this passage are 1 Thess 4:3, Gen. 1:26, and 1 Pet 1:16 according to *FOC*, 13:134-35 (notes 3-5). Again, for Tertullian the outward "image" is of little importance except as a rhetorical device to encourage or motivate people toward the vital "likeness."

albeit through a somewhat different creation process than Adam. Moreover, that process did not convey a higher status to Adam than to Eve,
and did not imply that males were somehow better positioned than fe-
males to be restored in Christ to the likeness of God.

Tertullian uses Adam in many texts beyond those cited above, and
contrary to the unique presentation of Eve in *Cult. Fem.* 1.1, it is usually
Adam who is blamed for the first sin.[45] An examination of the rhetorical
character of *Cult. Fem.* 1.1, when compared with other arguments that
utilize a fall motif, should make it clear that Tertullian did not particularly
blame Eve or women for the first sin, or consider all women inferior because of Eve's action. Such an examination may also promote a more
balanced understanding of Tertullian's obviously harsh and extreme arguments in *Cult. Fem.* 1.1. *Cult. Fem.* 1 and 2 are themselves only two
essays among several that deal with rather limited moral and ethical subjects relating to Christian discipline. Tertullian also wrote treatises on
prayer, patience, modesty, monogamy, fasting, and other similar subjects.
Nor is *Cult. Fem.* 1.1 the only one to employ somewhat strange and exces-
sive arguments relating to the Fall. For example, in another late, Montanist
work, *On Fasting (De Jejunio),* Tertullian writes:

> Adam had received from God the law of not tasting "of the
> tree of recognition of good and evil," with the doom of death
> to ensue upon tasting. However, even (Adam) himself at that
> time, . . . yielded more readily to his belly than to God, heeded
> meat rather than the mandate, and sold salvation for his gullet!
> He ate, in short, and perished; saved (as he would) else (have
> been), if he had preferred to fast from one little tree.[46]

Tertullian goes on to argue that since "the murderous gullet" was the
"source whence Adam was slain," Tertullian himself should account "food
as poison" and take "the antidote, hunger" even if there were no specific
commands to do so. Moreover, he argues that fasting would even "purge
the primordial cause of death—a cause transmitted to me also, concur-
rently with my generation" and that through fasting "man may make God
satisfaction through the self-same causative material through which he
had offended, that is, through the interdiction of food."[47]

It is important to note that this whole section of *Jej.* 3 employs the
same type of rhetorical form apparent in *Cult. Fem.* 1.1-2, but since it

[45]Church ("Sex and Salvation in Tertullian," 86) notes: "The 'gateway passage'
is the only place in all Tertullian where the exclusive culpability of Eve is spelled
out." There are other sections where they are mutually guilty and some where
Satan is blamed. See, for example, *Ad. Jud.* 2, *Pat.* 5, and *Ad. Marc.* 2.2.
[46]*Jej.* 3; *ANF,* 4:103-4.
[47]Ibid.

places the fall on Adam's appetite rather than on Eve and women, it does not receive much attention or concern today. Yet if Tertullian's words in this section were handled in the same way as some do with those of *Cult. Fem.* 1.1., then the message being conveyed would be that Adam alone was guilty, that his calamitous appetite had been passed down to all men (males), and that males should therefore starve themselves in order to be saved. In all probability, even though Tertullian certainly favored both fasting for men and modest adornment for women, it is unlikely that he meant to relate either exclusively to one sex.[48] Similarly, it is very unlikely that he believed the fall was exclusively due either to Eve's desertion "of the divine law" or to Adam's seeking the "pablum rather than the precept."[49] In fact, in both *Cult. Fem.* and *Jej.* the *ad feminam* and *ad hominem* arguments serve as the *exordium* for the rest of the discourse.[50] According to Robert Sider, the rhetorical purpose of the *exordium* was to "set the audience in a receptive mood by an immediate appeal to considerations of an ethical and emotional character."[51] There can be no doubt that the "devil's gateway" passage is highly emotional: "replete with *ethos* and *pathos*, which were the favored means of proof for an introduction," according to F. Forrester Church.[52] Tertullian obviously believed that the words, which are so provocative today, would favorably incline his audience for the rest of his presentation.[53]

Furthermore, none of the specific negatives attributed to Eve and women in *Cult. Fem.* 1.1 are presented elsewhere as exclusively or especially true for them.[54] Instead, Adam and men share equally in the first sin, in the loss

[48]For example, on the issue of ostentatious dress and the attempt to attract the opposite sex through outward deceptions, Tertullian thinks men can be as guilty as women: "If it is true, (as it is,) that in men, for the sake of women (just as in women for the sake of men), there is implanted by a defect of nature, the will to please; and if this sex of ours acknowledges to itself deceptive trickeries of form peculiarly its own,—(such as) to cut the beard too sharply; to pluck it out here and there; to shave round about (the mouth); to arrange the hair, and disguise its hoariness by dyes; to remove the incipient down all over the body, . . . to take every opportunity for consulting the mirror; to gaze anxiously into it; . . . all these things are rejected as frivolous, as hostile to modesty" (*Cult. Fem.* 2.8; *ANF*, 4:22).
[49]This phrase is from the section of *Jej.* 3 cited above as translated by Church, "Sex and Salvation in Tertullian," 86.
[50]Ibid.
[51]*Ancient Rhetoric and the Art of Tertullian* (Oxford: Oxford University Press, 1971), 21.
[52]Church, "Sex and Salvation in Tertullian," 86 (n. 14).
[53]Ibid. Church notes that "in Tertullian a given problem, such as the fall, may be adapted freely to the requirements both of subject and audience." See also, Peter Brown, *The Body and Society: Men, Women, and Sexual Renunciation in Early Christianity* (New York: Columbia UP, 1988), 76.
[54]Heine, *Women*, 28-32.

of the image and likeness of God, in the death of the Son of God, and so forth. In fact, Tertullian usually finds Adam, not Eve, especially guilty.

In other texts written later in his life, Tertullian presents Adam as especially guilty for the first sin because he did it willfully, that is with full knowledge that it was wrong: "the originator of our race and our sin, Adam, willed the sin that he committed. For the devil did not impose upon him the volition to sin, but subministered material to the volition."[55] In another interesting passage echoing Montanist themes, Tertullian finds all "flesh . . . as being in Adam, with its own vicious nature, easily indulging concupiscence after whatever it had seen to be 'attractive to the sight.'"[56] This section is especially noteworthy since in Gen 3:6 Eve recognizes the visual attractiveness of the forbidden fruit. Yet here Tertullian (in contrast to *Cult. Fem.* 1.1) attributes this and other similar sins that result from the lustful flesh to Adam. He goes on to point out that "whatever flesh (is) 'in Christ' has lost its pristine soils" and is "no longer (generated) of the slime of natural seed, nor of the grime of concupiscence."[57] In this regard, Tertullian clearly differed from Gnostic theories of his day that viewed the flesh as evil even for those who had acquired true *gnosis*.[58] Altogether in Tertullian's discussions of the first sin and its effects, *Cult. Fem.* 1.1 is alone in assigning blame to Eve. Everywhere else it is Adam who is guilty for that sin and for the transmission to humanity of a sinful nature full of lust or concupiscence.[59]

III. Women in Christian Service

Tertullian's ontological views supporting the spiritual equality of men and women are reflected in several of his works that discuss roles for women in Christian service. One of the most important of these is his clear recognition of both the theoretical and practical equality of the wife in the marriage relationship in the two late, Montanist tracts he addressed *To His Wife* (*Ux.* 1 & 2). In the process of urging his beloved wife, in the event of

---

[55]*Ex. Cast.* 2; *ANF*, 4:51. See also Church, "Sex and Salvation in Tertullian," 87.
[56]*Pud.* 6; *ANF*, 4:79.
[57]Ibid.
[58]Pheme Perkins, "Gnosticism," in *EEC*, 374-75, and Hoffman, *Women and Gnosticism*, 23-77.
[59]M. Turcan, *De Cultu in Tertullien: La Toilette de Femmes Sources Chretiennes* 173 [Paris: Les Editions du Cerf, 1971], 37) says that except for *Cult. Fem.* 1.1, "*C'est toujours Adam qui est sur la sellette.*" ("It's always Adam who is on the culprits' seat").

his death, to remarry only a believer,[60] or not remarry at all,[61] Tertullian also gives what one modern writer has called "as moving a tribute to matrimony itself as is to be found anywhere in early Christian literature":[62]

> How beautiful, then, the marriage of two Christians, two who are one in hope, one in desire, one in the way of life they follow, one in the religion they practice. . . . They pray together, they worship together, they fast together; instructing one another, encouraging one another, strengthening one another. Side by side they face difficulties and persecution, share their consolations. They have no secrets from one another; they never shun each other's company; they never bring sorrow to each other's heart. Unembarrassed they visit the sick and assist the needy. They give alms without difficulty; . . . Psalms and hymns they sing to one another, striving to see which of them will chant more beautifully the praises of their Lord. Hearing and seeing this, Christ rejoices.[63]

This apparently ideal marriage assumes an ontological equality between the husband and wife, and contains many remarkable roles for the wife. When Tertullian's description in *Ux.* 2.4-5 about the hypothetical problems of a Christian wife with an unbelieving husband are taken together with the roles mentioned in the text above, it seems clear that Tertullian

---

[60]*Ux.* 2.1; *ANF*, 4:44. It is interesting to note that he argues strongly against his wife remarrying if he should die, but leaves the choice up to her. His only command to her, based on his understanding of 1 Cor 7, is that she remarry "in the Lord." Elsewhere in his Montanist writings he is less charitable to others seeking second marriages. See Church, "Sex and Salvation in Tertullian," 94-95; Heine, *Women*, 28-29; and Tavard, *Women in Christian Tradition*, 59-62.

[61]*Ux.* 1.1-7; *ANF*, 4:39-43. Tertullian offers many reasons against remarriage. The two most important are based on his eschatological beliefs (as noted previously) and his concern that remarriage will foster sinful lust and endanger salvation. These motives carry over into his discussion about women's apparel as he writes in *Cult. Fem.* 2.1 to the "handmaids of the living God, my fellow servants and sisters" that "salvation—and not (the salvation) of women only, but likewise of men—consists in the exhibition principally of modesty." Church ("Sex and Salvation in Tertullian," 83-101) argues persuasively that Tertullian's primary concern in all his exhortations involving women, remarriage, continence, etc., was the salvation of men and women. Church's interpretation precludes the view that Tertullian was against women in any general sense. For example, his advocacy of continence did not involve a rejection of women: *both* widows and widowers were encouraged not to remarry. Sexuality was a danger to *both* sexes and both should be disciplined according to *Mon.* 10 and other texts.

[62]Church, "Sex and Salvation in Tertullian," 95. Similar positive descriptions are offered by Barnes (*Tertullian*, 137), and Tavard (*Women in Christian Tradition*, 60).

[63]*Ux.* 2.8; *Ancient Christian Writers,* 48+ vols., ed. J. Quasten (London: Newman, 1946), 13:35.

favored Christian wives praying, teaching, singing, witnessing, ministering to the poor and sick, providing hospitality in their homes for Christian
travelers, encouraging the martyrs in prison, and engaging in various
other acts of Christian service either with or without their husbands.[64]

Moreover, Tertullian not only assumes that married Christian women
will have an active ministry at home and in the community, but he also
supports various ministry roles for other women in the church. This is
evident, first, in his discussion of widows. His comments about this
special group of Christian women all occur in his late works, and his words
recognize and endorse the high status that had already been present for
these women in the early church. For example, he recognizes indirectly
that widows formed a recognized order (*ordo*) in the church in Carthage as
he complains about a virgin "of less that twenty years of age" that had
been "placed in the order of widows!" (*Virg. Vel.* 9).[65] On the other hand,
Tertullian notes that properly qualified women (based on 1 Tim 5:3-15)
were elected to the order of widows and had special seating in church
meetings with the clergy in Carthage.[66] In one case at least, they sat in
front with the elders and witnessed the prostrate repentance of an adulter-
ous man (*On Modesty; Pud,* 13).[67] By giving them special seating with
clergy, the North African church appears to have initiated a practice that
continued for several centuries.[68] This practice, endorsed by Tertullian,
recognized that these widows were involved in important ministries. They
were not mere charity recipients.

Next, in various passages Tertullian praises female virgins for their
continence, notes their special devotion to God, and assumes they too
have a special ministry of prayer. He probably meant to include them in his
praise for the women in "ecclesiastical orders" who "owe their position to
continence and have preferred to be wedded to God."[69] Still, some critics
charge that Tertullian's support only for *veiled* virgins (and veiled widows)

---

[64]*ANF,* 4:46-47.

[65]*Virg. Vel.* 9; *ANF,* 4:33. "*Pane scio alicubi virginem in viduatu ab annis
nondum viginti collocatam*" (*CCSL,* 2:1219). Also, in *Mon.* 11 (*On Monogamy*)
he sarcastically asks a hypothetical opponent considering remarriage whether the
"monogamist bishop," the presbyters, the deacons, or the "widows whose Order
you have in your own person refused" should be expected to approve or solem-
nize a remarriage (*ANF,* 4:67).

[66]*Virg. Vel.* 9; *ANF,* 4:33. On the special seating for the order of widows, see
Roger Gryson (*The Ministry of Women in the Early Church* [Collegeville: Liturgical Press, 1976], 21), and Bonnie Thurston (*The Widows—A Women's Ministry in
theEarly Church* [Philadelphia: Fortress Press, 1989], 81-85).

[67]*ANF,* 4:86. See also Thurston, *Widows,* 82-85, 89-91.

[68]Ibid., 82-83.

[69]*Ex. Cast.* 13; *ANF,* 4:58. See also *Ex. Cast.* 1, *Virg. Vel.* 14 and 17, and *Res.
Mort.* 8.

shows that he thought the veil "symbolized a woman's inferiority."[70] Tertullian's arguments in favor of virgins remaining veiled do indirectly testify to a somewhat novel practice of the church in Carthage, that is attempting to grant a special distinction or honor to virgins by having them dispense their traditional veils in the church service.[71] However, his attempt to reverse this practice was not motivated by a desire to denigrate women, but was instead based on his understanding of 1 Cor. 11, and his strong desire to maintain modesty and chastity among all Christians.

These assertions can be demonstrated from Tertullian's many other arguments about the veil. First, rather than a symbol of subjection or inferiority, he saw the veil as allowing church roles for women that would otherwise may have been prohibited to them based on various New Testament passages. The clearest reflection of this idea is in Tertullian's work against Marcion (*Ad. Marc.* 5.8) where he recognizes that veiled women may pray and prophesy in the church even if 1 Tim 2:11-12 and 1 Cor 14:34-35 might otherwise seem to prohibit that.[72] In fact, viewing the veil as a "symbol of authority" based specifically on 1 Cor 11:10 seems most closely to match Tertullian's views in this context.[73] Next, he sees the veil as a

---

[70]E.g., Dennis R. MacDonald, "Corinthian Veils and Gnostic Androgynes," in *Images of the Feminine in Gnosticism*, ed. Karen King (Philadelphia: Fortress, 1988), 281-82, 287. MacDonald not only believes that for Tertullian the veil symbolized a women's inferiority, but also that it was the appropriate "sign of mourning for Eve's sin" for women. MacDonald quotes a portion of *Virg. Vel.* 16 and *Cult. Fem.* 1.1 to attempt to prove his contentions. However, the former does not mention "inferiority" but rather "modesty" as the reason for the veil, and the latter (in a highly rhetorical way as we have already noted) argues for "humble garb," not a veil, as a way for women to emulate the mourning of Eve.

[71]Barnes, *Tertullian*, 140; McNamara, "A New Song," 110-12; and Thurston, *Widows*, 79-80.

[72]David Rankin, *Tertullian and the Church* (Cambridge: Cambridge UP, 1995), 175, 179-80, 184-85.

[73]Tertullian does cite 1 Cor 11:10 in *Ad. Marc.* 5.8 (*ANF*, 3:445): "But wherefore 'ought the woman to have power over her head, because of the angels?'" "*Sed et quare mulier potestatem super caput habere debebit?*" (Latin from E. Evans, ed. and trans. *Tertullian: Adversus Marcionem*, 2 vols. [Oxford: Clarendon, 1972], 2:556.) Tertullian, unfortunately, does not say why or how the veil gives the woman "power" (*potestatem*), instead he goes on to discuss the angels. Later in *Ad. Marc.* 5.8, however, it is clear that he thinks the veil allows women to pray and prophesy in church. For some studies on 1 Cor 11:10 (and 1 Cor 11 in general) that provide more details on the view that the veil is a symbol of authority or power (Greek *exousia*), see Samuele Bacchiocchi, *Women in the Church* (Berrien Springs: Biblical Perspectives, 1987), 131-37; James Hurley, *Man and Woman in Biblical Perspective* (Grand Rapids: Zondervan, 1981), 175-78; Jerome Murphy-O'Connor, "Sex and Logic in 1 Corinthians 11:2-16," *Catholic Biblical Quarterly* 42 (1980):496; Alan Padgett, "Paul on Women in the Church: The Contradictions of Coiffure in 1 Corinthians 11:2-16," *Journal for the Study of the New Testament*

safeguard for women and helpful in the maintenance of modesty and propriety in the church. He believes that the "very excellence of women, natural beauty" may lead men (and angels) to lust after them if they are not veiled.[74] Therefore, uncovered women in the church could imperil the salvation of both men and women and lead to all sorts of improprieties.[75] These concerns about the veil are clear in another dramatic exclamation: "Every public exposure of an honorable virgin is (to her) a suffering of rape."[76] Even Tertullian's argument against the young virgin who had been placed in the order of widows (but had not been wearing a veil) that "nothing in the way of public honor is permitted to a virgin"[77] actually reflects his ideas that purity, decency, and humility be maintained in church. He clearly recognizes that the *veiled* women in the order of widows had a prominent, public position in the church. Moreover, he accepts virgins (when veiled) engaging in special prayer and possibly other ministries in church. Thus, it seems obvious that he is not against visible honors and important roles for women in the church or community.[78]

Next, Tertullian, in an early essay addressed to some of the valiant Christians arrested for their faith in Carthage, offers high praise for the endurance and testimony of Christian women martyrs then in prison as he calls them "blessed martyrs designate" and "blessed ones."[79] He attempts

---

20 (1984):71-73; James Sigountos and Myron Shank, "Public Roles For Women in the Pauline Church: A Reappraisal of the Evidence," *JETS* 26/3 (September 1983):284-85; and Cynthia Thompson, "Hairstyles, Head-coverings, and St. Paul: Portraits from Roman Corinth," *Biblical Archaeologist* 51 (1988):99-115.

[74]*Cult. Fem.* 1.1; *ANF*, 4:15. See also *Orat.* 22.

[75]*Virg. Vel.* 13-14; *ANF*, 4:35-36. See also Eric Osborn, *Tertullian, First Theologian of the West* (Cambridge: Cambridge UP, 1997), 235.

[76]*Virg. Vel.* 3; *ANF*, 4:29. In *Virg. Vel.* 13 (*ANF*, 4:36) he writes: "The very concupiscence of non-concealment is not modest; . . . she must necessarily be imperiled by the public exhibitions of herself, while she is penetrated by the gaze of untrustworthy and multitudinous eyes . . ." Modesty, chastity, and the sanctity necessary for salvation are the concerns evident in Tertullian's discussion of appropriate clothing for women in general. For example, Christian women are encouraged to minister in the church and world as "modesty's priestesses" (*sacerdotes pudicitiae*) according to *Cult. Fem.* 2.12 (*ANF*, 4:24).

[77]*Virg. Vel.* 9; *ANF*, 4:33. In *Virg. Vel.* 10 Tertullian also reasons that male virgins also should not have any visible physical distinctions from the norm (e.g., no wearing feathers or exhibiting tattoo marks!).

[78]Karen Torjesen (*When Women Were Priests* [San Francisco: HarperCollins, 1993], 155-176) argues that Tertullian's standards of "public" modesty for women were based on the stricter standards of earlier days in Roman history. In his own day, those strict standards were only maintained by the Roman Vestal Virgins. Somewhat "paradoxically" she notes that Tertullian accepted "women prophesying in church" and says that Tertullian was instrumental in forming a new theory that the church was now in the "public" sphere.

[79]*Mart.* 1 and 3; *ANF*, 3:693-94.

to encourage them not to give in to any weakness of the flesh in one particularly interesting passage:

> Perhaps the flesh will dread the heavy sword, . . . the capital punishment of the flames, and all the executioner's talent for torture. But let the spirit respond to itself and to the flesh that these things, while very painful, have, even so, been received with equanimity and with acute desire for the sake of fame and glory, not only by men, but also by women, that you, *O blessed ones*, too may be worthy of your sex.[80]

Here Tertullian indirectly shows a high estimation of women martyrs of the past, demonstrates a high regard for the women currently imprisoned, and encourages these women to live up to the high character of the female sex. Unlike others of his time that equated women with weakness and men with strength,[81] Tertullian does not see these as gendered qualities but as attributes of the flesh and spirit respectively.[82] Elsewhere, he assumes that women can and will persevere in their Christian walk no matter what physical or emotional difficulties they may face:

> Wherefore, blessed (sisters), let us meditate on hardships, and we shall not feel them; let us abandon luxuries, and we shall not regret them. Let us stand ready to endure every violence, having nothing which we fear to leave behind.[83] Seek not to die on bridal beds, nor in miscarriages, nor in soft fevers, but to die the martyr's death, that He may be glorified who has suffered for you.[84]

This last passage, which was a Montanist saying,[85] alludes to one of the perceived benefits of martyrdom, but there were several others according to Tertullian. He apparently thought that martyrdom was like a more perfect baptism, which washed away sins. He may even have thought that it allowed the martyrs to go directly into paradise without a delay in Hades (which other Christians would apparently face as they awaited the day of the Lord).[86] Clearly, male and female martyrs were assumed to be

---

[80]*Mart.* 4.2-3 quoted in Church ("Sex and Salvation in Tertullian," 97 [italics added]). The "blessed ones" were the women according to the *ANF* translators (3:695) and R. Arbesmann (trans., *To the Martyrs, FOC*, 24).

[81]E.g. the Valentinians who produced or accepted *Gos. Phil.* See especially *Gos. Phil.* 76,6-9. See also Hoffman, *Women and Gnosticism*, 41-43.

[82]Church, "Sex and Salvation in Tertullian," 97.

[83]*Cult. Fem.* 2.13; *ANF*, 4:25.

[84]*Fug.* 9; *ANF*, 4:121.

[85]See Church, "Sex and Salvation in Tertullian," 98 (n. 63). The dictum of *Fug.* 9 is also cited in *An.* 55 (*ANF*, 3:231).

[86]*An.* 55 (*ANF*, 3:231) argues that "the sole key to unlock Paradise is your own

able to grant special peace to those who had otherwise been unable to find it.[87] Proof that for Tertullian female martyrs had a special authority can best be seen in the later work *De Anima*, produced after the persecution of 202. Here he writes that "the most heroic martyr Perpetua on the day of her passion saw only her fellow martyrs there, in the revelation she received of Paradise."[88] The reference to Perpetua is quite important since we know much more about her revelations and her martyrdom from the extant *Passion of Perpetua and Felicitas,* which many believe Tertullian edited.[89] Whether he did or not, it seems clear that he greatly admired and respected her, and accepted her revelation as accurate teaching that increased the strength of his own contention that martyrs went directly to heaven. In short, her teaching—at least on this subject—was authoritative.[90]

Finally, in his Montanist phase Tertullian also admired, respected, and encouraged women directed by the Spirit who were engaged in various prophetic roles in church and in the larger community. While Tertullian's relationship to the Montanist movement is a complex and unresolved question that cannot be covered in detail here, it is increasingly recognized that the movement was theologically orthodox. However, it was somewhat unreasonably condemned as "heretical" by the early catholic church for reasons that had little to do with its basic doctrines.[91] In

---

life's blood." Tertullian then refers the reader to a work now lost, *De Paradiso*, to point out that he has already "established the position that every soul is detained in safe keeping in Hades until the day of the Lord." In context, and based on the revelation of Perpetua, Tertullian probably believed that the martyrs went directly to paradise. See also, Brown, *Body and Society,* 77-78.

[87]*Mart.* 1; *ANF*, 3:693. However, in arguing against adultery (defined very broadly), Tertullian is not willing to give martyrs any special ability or power to bestow grace or forgiveness on others. See *Pud.* 22; *ANF*, 4:100.

[88]*An.* 55; *ANF*, 3:231.

[89]The editor of the *Passion* in the introduction cites Joel 2:28-29 as Tertullian does in *Ad. Marc.* 5.8; the conclusion has high praise for martyrs as does Tertullian; and the style is somewhat similar to Tertullian's according to R. E. Wallis (*ANF*, 3:697). The identification of Tertullian as the editor is accepted by Tavard (*Women in Christian Tradition*, 56), but he refers the reader back to the 1920 work of LaBriolle. More recent works usually do not accept Tertullian as the editor (although the editor is thought to have been a Montanist). See, for example, David Scholer, "Perpetua and Felicitas," in *EEC*, 712.

[90]Church ("Sex and Salvation in Tertullian," 98 [n. 63]) says that Tertullian "derives both personal inspiration and matter for his teachings from such individuals as Perpetua."

[91]See, for example, the excellent recent study of Montanism by Christine Trevett (*Montanism: Gender, Authority and the New Prophecy* [Cambridge: Cambridge UP, 1996]). Trevett concludes (146) that, "there was little to separate the Prophets from their catholic co-religionists. Differences were mostly differences of degree . . . orthodoxy was not at stake . . . *Authority* was at stake."

addition, it is quite clear that women were extremely prominent in this group as founders, leaders, and members.[92] It is often noted that in this group there was a "complete religious equality of men and women."[93] Epiphanius, the late fourth century bishop of Salamis (the capital city of Cyprus), for example, comments that some women in Montanist groups had been "ordained to the episcopacy and presbyterate."[94] Of course, Epiphanius may not be a reliable source, and even if his information can be trusted, it is not certain that the Montanists known to Tertullian ordained women.   Nevertheless, it is reasonable to suppose that a high status equivalent with those leadership positions did exist for the Montanist women mentioned by Tertullian.[95] If so, Tertullian reacted very differently than Epiphanius to it. For example, when Tertullian discusses Prisca and Maximilla, he does *not* use Gen 3:16, 1 Cor 11:8, or 1 Tim 2:12-14 as proof-texts to argue against Eve or against women speaking in church, as Epiphanius does. In fact, Tertullian never seeks to limit the authority or lower the status of these women at all.

So what does he show in his Montanist writings about the status of women as prophetesses? Clearly he accepts these women on an equal or even preferred basis compared with men. This fact is evident in his specific references to Prisca and Maximilla and their teachings and his use of their revelations to increase the strength of his own arguments. First, in the famous work *Adversus Praxeam (Against Praxeas),* in which Tertullian explains the Trinity to refute Praxeas' belief that the Father became the

---

[92]E. S. Fiorenza, "Word, Spirit, and Power," in *Women of Spirit: Female Leadership in Jewish and Christian Traditions*, ed. R. Ruether and E. McLaughlin (New York: Simon and Schuster, 1979), 41-42; Frederick Klawiter, "The Role of Martyrdom and Persecution in Developing the Priestly Authority of Women in Early Christianity: A Case Study of Montanism," *Church History* 29 (1980):251-61; and D. Williams, "The Origins of the Montanist Movement: A Sociological Analysis," *Religion* 19 (1989):339-43.

[93]L. Harris, *Woman in the Christian Church* (Brighton: Green Oak, 1988), 13.

[94]Epiphanius, *Pan.* 49.2-3; R. S. Kraemer, ed. *Maenads, Martyrs, Matrons, Monastics* (Philadelphia, Fortress, 1988), 227. See also Klawiter, "Women: Case Study of Montanism," 251 (n. 20), 261 (n. 35). *Pan.* 49 also says that these sects appealed to Gal 3:28 to justify having female "bishops, presbyters, and the rest."

[95]Klawiter ("Women: Case Study of Montanism," 251-61) argues that the very high status of women in the Quintillian, Cataphrygian, Priscillian, and related sects discussed by Epiphanius was also present in the earliest days of the Montanist movement. He suggests that as women in Asia minor (like Prisca, Maximilla, and Quintilla) made confession of their faith in Christ, were imprisoned, and released (or martyred), they gained as "confessors" the status of presbyters and obtained thereby the "power of the keys." This meant they could "bind and loose" as could male "confessors" and martyrs (according to a letter of the churches of Vienne and Lyons to the churches of Asia and Phrygia excerpted by Eusebius [*Hist. Ecc.* 5.2.1-2]).

Son and died on the cross, there is an important reference to these
Montanist women. Tertullian notes that Bishop Victor of Rome originally
"had acknowledged the prophetic gifts of Montanus, Prisca, and Maximilla,"
but later Praxeas got Victor to change his mind by "urging false accusations against the prophets themselves and their churches."[96] Thus, Praxeas
did two terrible services for victor, "the devil at Rome," in Tertullian's
estimation: "he drove away prophecy, and he brought in heresy; he put to
flight the Paraclete, and he crucified the Father."[97]

Next, in his essay urging Christians to fast, Tertullian writes that the
reason the Montanists have not been accepted is unrelated to their doctrines since "Montanus, Priscilla, and Maximilla" do not "*preach* another
God" or "overturn any particular rule of faith or hope." Instead, their
prophecies have been rejected because "they plainly *teach* more frequent
fasting than marrying."[98] It seems reasonable to assume from these comments that Tertullian recognized and agreed with the common view of his
day regarding the work of prophets or prophetesses: a prophetic ministry
involved more than making predictions of the future but also included
preaching and teaching.[99] Moreover, Tertullian obviously accepted women

---

[96]*Ad. Prax.* 1; *ANF*, 3:597.

[97]Ibid. The "Paraclete" refers to the promised "Helper" or "Comforter" of John
14:16; 15:26; and 16:7 who is usually identified as the Holy Spirit. Montanists
believed that the Paraclete was the one who brought their ecstatic revelations. It
is possible that Montanus thought he was the Paraclete himself, but this may have
been an unfounded charge of later detractors. See D. F. Wright, "Why were the
Montanists Condemned?" *Themelios* 2 (September 1976):19.

[98]*Jej.* 1; *ANF*, 4:102.

[99]Frend, *Rise of Christianity*, 139-40, 253-56, and Cecil Robeck, Jr., *Prophecy in
Carthage: Perpetua, Tertullian, and Cyprian* (Cleveland: Pilgrim Press, 1992),
100-01, 260. In earlier years, true prophets would also celebrate the Eucharist,
but Tertullian does not indicate that this practice occurred in Carthage. Wayne
Grudem ("Prophecy—Yes, but Teaching—No: Paul's Consistent Advocacy of
Women's Participation Without Governing Authority," *JETS* 30/1 [March 1987],
11-23) argues that NT prophecy carried a separate and lesser authority than
teaching since it "did not consist of the interpretation and application of Scriptures"
(17). Nevertheless, for Tertullian (at least in his Montanist phase) prophets and
prophetesses, and their prophecies in my opinion did provide the kind of "doctrinal
and ethical guidance for the Church" that was characteristic of NT teaching according
to Grudem (18). In fact, the reliance of the Montanists on prophecy for determining
correct church doctrine and practice is one big complaint that later Church fathers
had against them. For example, Hippolytus (*Ref.* 8.12; Kraemer, trans., *Maenads*,
225) says: "These have been rendered victims of error from being previously
captivated by [two] wretched women, called Priscilla and Maximilla, whom they
supposed [to be] prophetesses . . . And they allege that they have learned something
more through these, than from law, and prophets, and the Gospels . . . . They
introduce . . . the novelties of fasts, and feasts, and meals of parched food, and
repast of radishes, alleging that they have been instructed by women."

exercising such leadership functions and considered their words authoritative. In his work against those heretics who denied the resurrection of the flesh, Tertullian also cites a "shrewd saying which the Paraclete utters" specifically through "the prophetess Prisca: 'They are carnal and yet they hate the flesh.'"[100] This oracle agrees with Tertullian's view that these heretics live licentiously, and he uses it to bolster that contention.

Finally, Tertullian cites Prisca alone again in his essay on chastity:

> Through the holy prophetess Prisca the Gospel is thus preached: that "the holy minister knows how to minister sanctity." "For purity," says she, "is harmonious, and they see visions; and, turning their face downward they even hear manifest voices, as salutary as they are withal secret."[101]

This last oracle reveals something of the workings of Montanist worship services that seem to have been conducted at times by women like Prisca, and to have included lay participation by men and women.[102] To a limited degree, Tertullian also accepts some roles for the laity in church. For example, he acknowledges that in an unavoidable necessity (perhaps when the bishops and priests are absent) a layman could baptize.[103]

Tertullian also shows appreciation and esteem for an otherwise unknown prophetess at Carthage. Tertullian and many other Christians in Carthage frequently saw this woman in church and heard her prophesy after the Eucharistic service had concluded:

> We have now amongst us a sister . . . favored with sundry gifts of revelation, which she experiences in the Spirit by ecstatic vision amidst the sacred rites of the Lord's day in the church: she converses with angels and sometimes even with the Lord; she both sees and hears mysterious communications; some men's hearts she understands, and to them who are in need she distributes remedies. . . . After the people are dismissed at the conclusion of the sacred services, she is in the regular habit of reporting to us whatever things she may have seen in vision.[104]

Tertullian also notes that her revelations are checked, presumably by Scripture and the rule of faith, to see if they are true.[105] But it is clear that

---

[100]*Res. Mort.* 11; *ANF*, 3:552.

[101]*Ex. Cast.* 12; *ANF*, 4:56.

[102]Williams, "Origins of the Montanist Movement," 340.

[103]*Bapt.* 17; *ANF*, 3:677. See also *Ex. Cast.* 7.

[104]*An.* 9; *ANF*, 3:188.

[105]Just as 1 Cor 14:29 commanded for NT prophecy. It should be pointed out that both Tertullian and the church community at Carthage obviously did not think that prophecy had ceased at the end of the first century or with the closing

Tertullian accepts her communications wholeheartedly as he goes on to cite her vision of the "soul in bodily shape" to prove his own point on this subject. In fact, he clinches his argument by saying that God bears witness for this woman and that Paul's prediction of spiritual gifts coming to the church has been fulfilled in her.[106] The information that she "distributes remedies" to those in need may imply that in addition to her ministry as a prophetess, she might also have been a deaconess.[107]

Conclusion

Tertullian's own views toward women can be summarized in one final text, briefly mentioned above, where he is arguing against the notorious heretic Marcion. It might be expected that Tertullian, in reacting against the heretical women conspicuously present in Marcion's sect, would be prompted to make some negative comments about women in general—for example, how easily they went astray and how they could not be trusted. This might also be expected from someone who wrote that women were the "devil's gateway" and who is frequently presented as a pathological misogynist. Yet Tertullian actually argues that the spiritual activity *of the women* of his community proves that his group is superior to Marcion's:

> The facts themselves will be called upon to prove which of us is making rash claims . . . . Let Marcion . . . produce some psalm, some vision, some prayer, so long as it is a spiritual one, in ecstasy, . . . let him also prove to me that in his presence some women prophesied, some great speaker from among those more saintly females of his. If all such proofs are more readily put in evidence by me, and are in full accord with the rule and ordinances and regulations of the Creator, without doubt both Christ and the Spirit and the apostle will belong to my God. Anyone who cares to demand it has here the statement of my case.[108]

---

of the NT canon. See especially John Penney, "The Testing of New Testament Prophecy," *Journal of Pentecostal Theology* 10 (1997):59-64, 72-82.
    [106]*An.* 9; *ANF*, 3:188.
    [107]Torjesen, *When Women Were Priests*, 29-30. The suggestion that she was a deaconess is my own. Although Tertullian does not directly refer to deaconesses, the women in "ecclesiastical orders" (*Ex. Cast.* 13) could have included them.
    [108]*Ad. Marc.* 5.8, from *Tertullian: Adversus Marcion*, trans. Evans, 2:560-63. The Latin from "let him also prove . . ." is: *"probet etiam mihi mulierem apud se prophetasse ex illis suis sanctioribus feminis magnidicam: si haec omnia facilius a me proferuntur, et utique conspirantia regulis et dispositionibus et disciplinis creatoris, sine dubio dei mei erit et Christus et spiritus et apostolus. Habet*

Thus, Tertullian uses the ecstatic prophetic utterances of the women on his side of the doctrinal and ethical dispute with Marcion as the final confirmation of his argument: his side had women prophetesses whose activities and words both proved the existence of the Creator and honored that deity's rules for a disciplined life.

For Tertullian, any person who was filled with the Spirit and lived in conformity with a strict interpretation of biblical and ecclesiastical morals would be honored. He was deeply concerned with modesty and purity among Christians in light of the impending end of the age: Christian men and women must live a disciplined life to insure their own salvation and to witness properly to the surrounding pagan world. When such motivations are considered, his obviously intolerant expressions directed toward women in some texts take on a different meaning. Although Tertullian does not seem to have allowed for full role interchangeability between genders in church ministry positions,[109] his affirmation of women, created in the eternal likeness of God, ministering in the community and church in many ways, should prove to be a worthwhile example for Christians today. Certainly his recognition that in heaven, "No one then will make a thing of me, in which they will discover masculinity"[110] is worth remembering during the continuing debate on women's ministry roles in the church as we pray for God's will to be done "on earth as it is in heaven."

---

professionem meam qui voluerit eam exigere." The future indicative conditional sentence translated above, "If all such proofs are . . . put in evidence by me (*proferuntur*) . . . the apostle will (*erit*) belong to my God," and the context indicate that Tertullian is certain that his church group has the spiritual women (and the rest of the signs). Thus, *ANF* (3:447) has: "Now all these signs are forthcoming from my side without any difficulty . . ." See also Ronald Kydd, *Charismatic Gifts in the Early Church* (Peabody: Hendrickson, 1984), 66-67.

[109]See Hoffman, *Women and Gnosticism*, 167-68, 175-81.

[110]*Ad. Val.* 32 quoted from Church, "Sex and Salvation in Tertullian," 100. See also note 33 above.

The Yoke of Necessity:[1]
The Use of the Terms *Necessitas* and
Coactio In the Thought of John Calvin

Terry L. Cross[*]

> The decisive point for the understanding of man is the under-
> standing of human freedom. It is no accident that it is at this
> point that conflicts break out, which have never yet come to
> an end; some, indeed, are still going on at the present time.
> Those who do not understand human freedom, do not under-
> stand man. Those who do not understand the 'unfreedom' of
> man, do not understand sin.[2]   *Emil Brunner*

Introduction

The history of Christian doctrine reveals that theological concepts
often are hammered out on the anvil of opponents' arguments. The shape
of the resulting theological construct is usually forged by the questions
and concerns of the opponent. One need only consider Augustine's
treatise, *De libero arbitrio (On Free Choice)*, which was leveled against
the Manichees in his early career. Arguing against their determinism, he
wrote in glowing terms about the freedom of the will. Some twenty years

---

*Terry L. Cross (Ph.D., Princeton Theological Seminary). Associate Professor
of Theology and Philosophy; Assistant Dean, School of Religion, Lee University.
[1]Calvin often uses the term, "yoke," to describe the bondage of the will. As will
be noted below, he speaks of a yoke of necessity, a yoke of sin, and the devil's
yoke, as being the same. This metaphor best pictures the essence of Calvin's
thought on this issue.
[2]Brunner, *The Christian Doctrine of Creation and Redemption*, in *Dogmatics:
Volume II*, trans. Olive Wyon (Philadelphia: The Westminster Press, n.d.), 121.

later, Pelagius, an ardent opponent, noted how close Augustine was to his own position in that tract. Augustine spent the next fifteen years arguing against Pelagius and perhaps even his earlier views on free will (even though Augustine would not admit any inconsistency). The opponents' anvils shaped the structure of his doctrinal argument.

John Calvin's doctrine concerning free will was also forged by opponents' anvils. Against Catholics and Protestants alike, he hammered out his understanding of providence and election, which appeared to eliminate freedom of the will in order to elevate the grace of God. Humans could do nothing that would merit grace; it was all from God. Roman Catholic opponents charged him with Stoic determinism. In response, Calvin carefully chiseled the finer points of his doctrine of the will, of which the most important feature was his distinction between *necessitas* (necessity) and *coactio* (coercion). Human will is bound by sin, but clearly humans have freedom to choose—in some sense. It is this fine distinction of language that defines Calvin's doctrine of the human will. As Brunner has noted, many conflicts arise at the point of human freedom. Calvin's understanding of free will is no exception.

On account of original sin, humans now sin out of necessity, but not out of some external compulsion. For Calvin's opponents, this sounded too deterministic—too fatalistic. Who could be blamed for sin? If it were necessary that descendants of Adam sin, then were they not compelled in some sense? How can there be freedom of the will when it is so bound? Calvin chose to cut this knot by a technical distinction between a *necessity* for sinning and a *compulsion* to sin. Opponents could still not see that this distinction made any difference; they charged Calvin with eliminating human responsibility for sin since a power outside of them made them fall. Taken to its extreme, God would then be the author of sin. However, if challengers still wished to call him a fatalist, it was because they confused this distinction.

This essay will trace the development of the concept of necessity for sinning through several Church Fathers. It will then examine Calvin's use of the distinction between *necessitas* and *coactio* and its significance for averting Calvin's doctrine from strict determinism and for shaping Calvin's own thought on freedom and determinism.

I. A Historical Development of the Concept of the Necessity of Sinning

Augustine

The problem of free will and determinism with which Calvin was contending in the sixteenth century had already been discussed for many centuries. In the fifth century, Augustine contended with the Pelagian conception of free will and sin. His anti-Pelagian writings provide much of the substance for Calvin's subsequent debates with Catholic opponents who appeared Pelagian to him. Therefore, it is important to consider them and their setting.

Pelagius, a British monk, stressed the freedom of the will to the apparent exclusion of a need for the grace of God. The human will has been endowed by its creator with the ability to choose good as well as evil. Humans are able to do all that God's law requires for righteousness. Augustine quotes Pelagius as saying, "Inasmuch as not to sin is ours, we are able to sin and to avoid sin."[3]

The offensive that Augustine launched against Pelagius and his followers lasted about sixteen years (AD 412-428).[4] He approached Pelagius' teaching as heretical primarily because it denied original sin, mitigated the importance of grace, and falsely elevated the freedom of the will. While Calvin extensively used Augustine's argumentation for all of these issues, his use of Augustine's understanding of the will is important for our consideration.

Before the Pelagian controversy, Augustine wrote a treatise on free will against the dualistic and deterministic tendencies of Manichaeism. This work, *De libero arbitrio,* spoke more directly to the origin of evil than to the use of the will for righteousness. It was completed soon after Augustine's ordination in AD 391.[5] As Luchesius Smits comments, "It is evident that he insists here on the freedom of the will without scarcely being concerned to place an emphasis on the necessity of grace."[6] Later, this led Pelagius to quote Augustine as supporting his own views. Augustine contended that these passages were "*media*" or neutral.[7] Pelagius had wrongly lifted words from the context that centered on grace, not the

---

[3]Augustine, *On Nature and Grace* 49.57, in *Nicene and Post-Nicene Fathers,* vol. 5, ed. Philip Schaff (Grand Rapids: Wm. B. Eerdmans Publishing Co., 1956), 140. Hereafter, this volume will be abbreviated NPNF; cf. *De natura et gratia,* 49.57, *Patrologia Cursus Completus Latina,* vol. 44, ed. J.P. Migne (Paris: 1865): 274. Hereafter, this collection will be abbreviated MPL. The Latin reads, "*Quia non peccare, inquit, nostrum est, possumus peccare et non peccare.*"

[4]Benjamin B. Warfield, "Introductory Essay on Augustine and the Pelagian Controversy," NPNF, xvii-xxi.

[5]W. M. Green, "Preface," *De libero arbitrio* by Augustine, in *Corpus Christianorum: Series Latina,* vol. 29 (Turnholt: Brepols Editores Pontificii, 1970): 207.

[6]Luchesius Smits, *Saint Augustin dans l'oeuvre de Jean Calvin,* vol. 1, *Étude de Critique Littéraire* (Assen: Van Gorcum & Co., 1957): 153. "*Il est évident qu'il insiste ici sur la liberté de la volonté sans guère se soucier de mettre en relief la nécessité de la grâce.*" All translations throughout the essay are my own unless otherwise noted. Dale Coulter, a colleague at Lee University, has helped clarify several Latin passages and has assisted in finding other sources.

[7]Augustine, *De natura et gratia,* LXI, MPL, 44:282.

impossibility of righteousness.[8] According to Augustine, Adam and Eve were created with free choice and chose to sin.[9] Thus, the entire human race became corrupt and unable to please God.[10] The decision-making process of humans had been affected in this fall; the will itself remained an indifferent faculty, ready to turn wherever the human nature wished. It is this nature that has been corrupted by the fall and so it can never turn the will toward good on its own.[11] Free will was not eliminated by the fall, but the freedom that existed in paradise has perished.[12] For this reason, humans need grace to live righteously. Free will, however, remains in humanity and by it all sin; consequently, they become servants of sin. Only the grace of the Savior can free humanity to do what is good: "Therefore, they are not free by righteousness, unless by choice of the will; however, they do not become free from sin, unless by the grace of the Savior." [13] Only when the Savior frees a person for righteousness is he or she truly free. For the will is free to do evil, but not free to do good.[14]

Therefore, Augustine can speak of a "certain necessity for sinning" (*quaedam peccandi necessitas*).[15] Pelagius, on the other hand, argued that if there is such a necessity, how can humans be held responsible for sinning and how can there be *free* will at all?[16] Augustine replied that

---

[8] *"De gratia . . . non de impossibilitate iustitiae,"* De natura et gratia, LXVII (80): MPL, 44:286. Augustine later adds: *"de qua re cum istis tota vertitur quaestio, ne gratiam Dei quae est in Christo Jesu Domino nostro, perversa naturae defensione frustremur,"* MPL, 44:288.

[9] Augustine, *De correptione et gratia,* 10.28. He states, *"Sic et hominem fecit cum libero arbitrio et quamvis sui futuri casus ignarum, tamen ideo beatum, quia et non mori et miserum non fieri in sua potestate esse sentiebat,"* MPL 44:933.

[10] Augustine, *Contra Iulianum,* iv.3, 25, in *The Fathers of the Church,* vol. 35, trans. Matthew Schumacher (New York: Fathers of the Church, Inc., 1957): 189-190; cf. MPL 44:750-751.

[11] Benjamin B. Warfield, "Introductory Essay," xvii. Cf. also, Augustine, *De spiritu et littera,* 33.58; MPL 44:237-239. See also *De peccatorum meritis et remissione,* 2.30i MPL 44:180-181. Warfield likens the will in this narrower sense to a weathercock; in the broader sense (of heart), he likens it to the wind. Because the wind always blows toward evil, the weathercock (the will) is directed toward evil.

[12] Augustine, *Contra duas epistolas Pelagianorum,* 1.2.5. MPL, 44:552. He describes this freedom as *"habendi plenam cum immoralitate iustitiam,"* (". . . having a full righteousness with immorality").

[13] Ibid. *"Liberi ergo a iustitia non sunt, nisi arbitrio voluntatis: liberi autem a peccato non fiunt, nisi gratia Salvatoris."*

[14] Ibid., 1.3.7. Augustine states: *"Haec voluntas quae libera est in malis . . . ideo libera in bonis non est, quia liberata non est."* ("This will that is free for evil... the same is not free for good, since it has not been freed"); cf. MPL 44:553-554.

[15] Augustine, *De natura et gratia,* LXVI; MPL, 44:286; NPNF, 149.

[16] Augustine quotes Pelagius' question in *De natura et gratia,* XLVI: *"Voluntatis enim arbitrio ac deliberatione privatur, quidquid naturali necessitate constringitur?"*

imperfections (*vitiis)* of the fallen human nature, not the condition of human nature itself, caused this necessity to sin.[17] Originally, humans used free will to sin and there followed a *"poenalis vitiositas"* (penal corruption), in which liberty brought about necessity.[18] Only God's grace can raise one from this wretched condition. Humans should listen to exhortations to do good and then pray the psalmist's prayer: "Bring Thou me out of my necessities" (Psalms 25:17).[19] It is freedom from this necessity to sin that Christ offers and can lead to happiness—a "happy necessity" of living rightly.[20]

Calvin recognized that his confrontation over this issue with Albert Pighius and the theologians of the Sorbonne was similar to Augustine's work against Pelagius. Calvin called his opponents, "Pelagians of our own age."[21] He frequently appealed to Augustine as supporting his own view—and indeed, the 'orthodox' view of the will.[22] While Augustine did

---

("For by choice or deliberation of the will is withheld whatever by natural necessity is restrained)."

[17]Ibid., LXVI. *"Quod autem ex vitiis naturae, non ex conditione naturae sit quaedam peccandi necessitas . . ."* ("However, that which out of the imperfections of nature, not from the condition of nature, may be a certain necessity for sinning . . ."); cf. MPL 44:286.

[18]Augustine, *De perfectione iustitiae hominis,* iv 9. *"Per arbitrii libertatem factum ut esset homo cum peccato; sed iam poenalis vitiositas subsecuta, ex liberatate fecit necessitatem."* ("Through freedom of choice, it has come about that humanity is with sin; but now the subsequent penal corruption has made a necessity from freedom").

[19]Ibid. Also in *De natura et gratia,* LXVI. The Latin Scripture which Augustine uses reads, *"De necessitatibus meis educ me."*

[20]Augustine, *De perfectione iustitiae hominis,* iv 9. He says, *"ita ut sit etiam bene vivendi et nunquam peccandi voluntaria felixque necessitas."* Cf. also, *De spiritu et littera,* xxx.52 in which Augustine contends that free choice is not voided by grace, but rather established: *"ita liberum arbitrium non evacuatur per gratiam, sed statuitur, quia gratia sanat voluntatem qua institia libere diligatur."* (". . . thus free choice is not emptied through grace, but it is established, since grace makes whole the will by which goodness is freely chosen"); cf. MPL 44:233.

[21]John Calvin, *Institutes of the Christian Religion,* II. 3, 13, ed. John McNeill and trans. Ford Lewis Battles, *Library of Christian Classics,* vols. 20, 21 (Philadelphia: The Westminister Press, 1960), vol. 20, 307. Hereafter, this work will be cited in this manner: *Institutes,* LCC, 20:307. Calvin calls Pelagius the father of these theologians. Cf. also, *Defensio sanae et orthodoxae doctrinae de servitute et liberatione humani arbitrii adversus calumnias Alberti Pighii Campensis,* 5, in *Calvini Opera quae supersunt omnia,* VI (Brunsvigae: C.A. Schwetschke & Sons, 1867): 364; *The Bondage and Liberation of the Will: A Defense of the Orthodox Doctrine of Human Choice against Pighius,* ed. A.N.S. Lane; trans. G.I. Davies (Grand Rapids, MI: Baker Books, 1996), p. 190. It should be noted that Pighius returned the favor by calling Calvin a "Manichee" and a "Stoic."

[22]Doede Nauta, "Augustine and the Reformation," *Free University Quarterly* 3 (1954-1955): 244.

not hold the level of authority for Calvin equal to that of Scripture, he did hold substantial weight against some Catholic writers and those who argued as Pelagius had. On some points Calvin disagreed with Augustine. However, on the issue of original sin and free will, Calvin saw himself in agreement with Augustine.[23] In some places he cites him word for word. Luchesius Smits records 1051 references or allusions by Calvin from Augustine's anti-Pelagian writings.[24] This constitutes about one-quarter of all his Augustinian references, exceeding the other areas of writing by far.[25]

On the matter of original sin, Calvin followed Augustine closely. The discussion of free will and necessity raised some apparent differences. Georges Bavaud believes that Calvin did not follow Augustine when he spoke of sinning necessarily in an "ontological" sense.[26] Augustine, Bavaud claims, "speaks often of the bondage of freedom, but it is always in reference to the evil end of humans."[27] However, it seems Bavaud's comments do not fully consider Augustine's concept of "necessary sinning." While Calvin admittedly differs from Augustine on whether God willed or permitted Adam to sin, there is not so great a difference between them on the issue of the necessity of sinning, as Bavaud would lead us to

---

[23]Luchesius Smits, "L'autorité de Saint Augustin dans 'L'institution Chrétienne' de Jean Calvin," *Revue d'Histoire Ecclésiastique* 45 (1950): 687. Smits comments: *"Sur les questions essentielles, Calvin se sent pleinement d'accord avec son maître . . . ensuite le fait qu'il a découvert lui-même dans les écrits augustiniens le principe fondamental de la Réforme, c'est-à-dire la corruption foncière du coeur humain."* "On the essential questions, Calvin places himself fully in line with his master . . . following the fact that he had discovered himself in these Augustinean writings the fundamental principle of the Reformation, that is to say, the deep-seated corruption of the human heart."

[24]Luchesius Smits, *Saint Augustin dans l'oeuvre de Jean Calvin*, vol. 1, 168. He speaks of Calvin "abandonly using" Augustine's treatise, *De gratia et libero arbitrio*, against Pighius (167). In addition, Smits notes that an important work of Augustine's, *Contra Julianum opus imperfectum*, was not published until 1654 and so *"Calvin n'eut pas l'occasion de le consulter,"* (166). This is significant since there is similarity of discussion on necessity in this work and Calvin's writings that apparently remained unknown to Calvin. Cf. *Institutes*, LCC, 20:317.

[25]Ibid., 182. Smits lists 289 references from the anti-Manichaean writings, 161 references from the anti-Donatist writings, and 32 from the anti-Arian.

[26]Georges Bavaud, "Predestination et Réprobation chez Augustin et Calvin," *Revue des Études Augustiniennes* 5-6 (1959-1960): 437. He states that according to Calvin, one sins of necessity, *"non seulement morale mais encore ontologique, enracinée dans leur être,"* ("not only a moral but even moreso an ontological rootedness in their being"). Bavaud also sees nominalistic influence in Calvin's contradiction in sacrificing free will and yet affirming responsibility.

[27]Ibid. *"...parle souvent de la servitude de la liberte, mais c'est toujours en reference a la fin mauvaise de l'homme."*

believe. This is not to say that Calvin found all his thoughts on this topic in Augustine. Hermann Barnikol notes that Calvin wanted to find the distinction between *necessitas* and *coactio* in Augustine's writings, but actually did not.[28] There is a *voluntaria necessitas* and *felix necessitas,* but these belong to the convert.[29] Barnikol believes Calvin broadened this linguistic distinction through the help of Bernard to include necessity in the acts of sinful humanity.[30] It is to Bernard that we now turn to examine what he offered toward Calvin's distinction.

Bernard of Clairvaux

Calvin appealed not only to Augustine for support, but also to other scholars of the Church who handled this subject similarly. Since Calvin considered Bernard of Clairvaux to be a "guardian of the spirit" of Augustine, he cited him several times as supporting Augustine's and his own views on *"necessitas."*[31] Bernard's treatise, *De gratia et libero arbitrio,*

---

[28]Hermann Barnikol, *Die Lehre Calvins vom unfreien Willen und ihr Verhältnis zur Lehre der übrigen Reformatoren und Augustins* (Neuwied: J. Meincke, 1927), 98.

[29]Cf. Augustine, *De perfectione iusticiae hominis,* iv. It should be noted here that Augustine is largely responsible for centering the discussion of human freedom around the freedom of choice (*liberum arbitrium*) rather than freedom of the will (*libera voluntas*). The focus in *arbitrium* is human choice or freedom of human acts; in *voluntas* there is something fuller in the discussion. Bernard McGinn has described the difference well: "Thus it is around the fundamental problems involved in the term *liberum arbitrium* rather than around the systematic concern to elucidate the notion of will that the patristic and medieval approach to the problem developed," Bernard McGinn, "Introduction," *On Grace and Free Choice by Bernard of Clairvaux,* trans. Daniel O'Donovan (Kalamazoo, MI: Cistercian Publications Inc., 1988), 8.

[30]Barnikol, 99. It may be that Barnikol has not adequately considered the force of Augustine's *peccandi necessitas.* Consider, for example, Augustine, *De natura et gratia,* LXVI. Even the passage, which Barnikol cites, speaks of a necessity to sin. Cf. also, *De perfectione iusticiae hominis, iv.* Perhaps it would be better to say that Calvin found *necessitas* (both to sin and to do good) in Augustine, but not the specific distinction that he needed with *coactio.* This distinction would come much later, beginning incipiently with Bernard until it blossomed fully with Luther. See Martin Luther, *The Bondage of the Will,* trans. Henry Cole (Grand Rapids: Eerdmans Publishing Co., 1931), 72. More of Luther's contribution will be examined below. Thomas Aquinas offers a distinction between *necessitas coactionis* and *necessitas praecepti* in *Summa Theologica,* II, q. 58, art. 3, but this was not precisely fitting for Calvin's needs. See George Fonsegrive, *Essai sur le libre arbitre: sa theorie et son histoire* (Paris: Felix Alcan, 1986), 112. Fonsegrive states that, *"...une contrainte venue du dehors, une violence extérieure et contre nature, que saint Thomas appelle coactio."* ("...a coercion coming from outside, an exterior violence, and against nature, is what St. Thomas calls *coactio*").

[31]Georges Bavaud, *"Les rapports de la grace et du libre arbitre: Un dialogue*

was an especially rich source for Calvin's thought. For Bernard, in order
for there to be human willing, there must be freedom. If the will is compelled or violently forced upon, it is no longer voluntary.[32] "For surely
where there is necessity, already there is not willing."[33] If one acts under
compulsion, then he or she cannot be responsible.

Bernard distinguished three freedoms, which Calvin himself noted:
freedom from necessity, freedom from sin, and freedom from misery. Only
grace can make one free from sin; only heaven will deliver one from misery.
However, one is innately free from necessity.[34] Bernard's discussion makes
it clear that freedom from necessity means freedom from compulsion (to
place Calvin's distinction more clearly on Bernard's thought). It is this
liberty that is required for the will to be called free at all. This is not to say
there is complete freedom from sin, but rather freedom to choose. This
freedom is marred by its captivity to sin. Therefore, humans by nature
possess freedom from necessity, but because the other two freedoms are
lost, humans cannot will "the good."[35]

Sin causes a captivity (*captivitas*) of the free will.[36] In his sermon on
the Song of Songs, Bernard speaks similarly of a "yoke of voluntary servitude" under which one is oppressed because the will consents to sin and
thereby becomes a slave to sin.[37] Therefore the soul is both enslaved and

---

entre saint Bernard, saint Thomas d'Aquin et Calvin," Verbum caro 14 (1960):
328. Bavaud states Calvin felt Bernard, *"a garde l'esprit de saint Augustin,"*
unlike some of the later scholastics.

[32]Bernard, *De gratia et libero arbitrio*, 1.2; MPL, 182: 1002. Bernard states,
"Alioquin si compelli valet invitus, violentus est, non voluntarius." Cf. also, *On
Grace and Free Choice*, trans. D. O'Donovan (Spencer, MA: Cistercian Publica-
tions, 1988), 55.

[33]Ibid, 11.4; col. 1003. *"Ubi quippe necessitas, iam non voluntas."*

[34]Ibid., III. 6,7; col. 1004-1005. Cf. Calvin, *Institutes*, II. 2.5; LCC, 20: 262.

[35]As Bernard McGinn notes, Bernard uses linguistic distinctions of *liberum* to
make his theological point. While he does not use Augustine's precise terms,
"peccandi necessitas," or Calvin's distinction between *necessitas* and *coactio*, he
does have conceptual similarity with these terms. Coordinated with the three
freedoms, Bernard speaks of a *liberum arbitrium*, a *liberum consilium* [free coun-
sel], and a *liberum complacitum* [freedom to please or a free pleasing]. These
linguistic terms are analogous to those Calvin will use in this respect: they attempt
to create a theological point by semantic differentiation. See Bernard McGinn,
"Introduction," *On Grace and Free Choice by Bernard of Clairvaux*, (Spencer,
MA: Cistercian Publications, 1988), 22.

[36]Bernard, *De gratia et libero arbitrio*, IV. 12; col. 1008.

[37]Bernard, *On the Song of Songs*, vol. 4, Sermon 81. 7, trans. Irene Edmonds
(Kalamazoo, MI: Cistercian Publications, 1980): 164. Cf. also *Sermones super
Cantica Canticorum*, 36-86, in *S. Bernardi Opera*, vol. 2 (Rome: Editiones
Cistercienses, 1958): 288. Bernard speaks of *voluntariae servitutis*, which be-
cause it is voluntary, is inexcusable. Calvin often uses the metaphor of "yoke" in
a similar way. Cf. *Institutes*, II. 3.5; 4.1.

free—"a handmaid on account of necessity, free on account of the will."[38] While willing freely is innate, willing good is not. Humans do not possess the power or the wisdom to do well.[39] Bernard says that it is one thing to fear, it is entirely another thing to fear God; in the same way, it is one thing to will freely and entirely another thing to will *the good*.[40] Grace is needed for this ability. The result of Adam's fall into the pit of sin by his free choice is that humanity cannot will themselves out of this pit—they must be raised. Hence, a person is not able not to sin (*non possit non peccare*).[41] This is Bernard's 'necessity for sinning' that Calvin appreciated, even if there was no precise distinction between *necessitas* and *coactio*.[42] As A. N. S. Lane comments:

> But Bernard's 'freedom from necessity' is substantially
> Calvin's 'freedom from coercion' while Calvin's 'necessity'

---

[38]Bernard, *Sermo* 81. 9; *Super Cantica*, 289. The Latin reads, ". . . *ancilla propter necessitatem, libera propter voluntatem.*"

[39]Bernard, *De gratia et libero arbitrio*, IV. 16; VIII. 26.

[40]Ibid., VI.16. He states, "Free choice, accordingly, constitutes us willers; grace, willers of the good. . . Just as, simply to fear is one thing, and to fear God, another; to love, one, and to love God, another . . . so also will is one thing, and to will the good, another," *On Grace and Free Choice*, 6.16; p. 72; trans. D. O'Donovan.

[41]Ibid., VII. 23; MPL, 182: 1014.

[42]See Calvin, *Institutes*, II.3.5; II.5.1; LCC, 20: 295-296; 317). It should be noted that Calvin chides Peter Lombard for not seeing this distinction (*Institutes*, II.3.5; LCC, 20:296). There is no such reprimand for Bernard, even though Lombard speaks almost word for word some of Bernard's thoughts. For example, Lombard discusses the three freedoms (*Sent.* II. Dist. 25.8), and suggests that free will was not totally lost in the fall, *sed libertatem a miseria et a peccato* (but freedom from misery and from sin) However, Lombard also uses *necessitas* and *coactio* side by side without distinction when he describes the inability of humans in heaven to commit sin. He states: ". . . *'liberum' videtur dici arbitrium quia sine coactione et necessitate valet appetere vel eligere quod ex ratione decreverit*" (". . . 'free' seems to speak of choice since without coercion and necessity, one is able to reach for or to choose out of reason that which will have decreased"), (*Sent.* II. Dist. 25.4.2). And yet even Bernard speaks of compelling and necessity in the same context without distinction (*De grat.* I.2). Calvin does disagree with Bernard's understanding of free choice in two respects--he says Bernard obscures free choice by calling it "consent," and that Bernard grants too much power to the captive will so that it appears to be able to do good. See Dennis E. Tamburello, *Union with Christ: John Calvin and the Mysticism of St. Bernard* (Louisville, KY: Westminster John Knox Press, 1994), 30-31. Calvin clearly misread Bernard's intentions because Calvin preferred to eliminate the use of "free choice" entirely and Bernard did not. Lombard and Bernard, then, are seen as co-conspirators in this lapse. Perhaps Lombard did not stress the bondage of the will in sinning as much as Bernard and so received more of Calvin's disapproval because such an emphasis would lead to an illusion of power. For the references to the *Sentences*, see Lombard, *Sententiae in IV libris, Liber I et II*, (Rome: Collegeii S. Bonaventurae ad

is substantially Bernard's 'bondage to sin.' The verbal
disctinction between necessity and coercion is not found in
Bernard and Calvin learnt it elsewhere . . . . Calvin and Bernard agree in affirming an intrinsic bondage of the will to sin
and in denying any external constraint. Although they differ
in terminology there is a broad agreement in substance.[43]

Luther and Erasmus

The sixteenth century was the setting for more debate on the issue of
free will. The controversy between Erasmus and Luther helped to prepare
the way for Calvin's approach to the theological discussion and the linguistic differentiation.[44] Among other charges, Erasmus rebuked Luther
for following John Wycliffe by teaching that things occur out of *mera
necessitas* and not free will.[45] If this is so, what is to become of merits,
responsibility, or admonitions?

Luther responded in part with the distinction between *necessitas* and
coactio. A person without God's Spirit performs evil deeds not by violent
coercion, "as if he were taken by the neck and forced to it," but spontaneously with an eager will.[46] By necessity, Luther means *necessitas
immutabilitatis.*[47] This means that the will cannot change or turn itself
around and so is not free. If the will were forced, it would not be a will. In
this sense, *"coactio potius est (ut sic dicam) Noluntas,"* ("rather, coercion is no will [if I may say it this way]").[48]

As to Erasmus' charge that necessity eliminates merits, Luther responded that this is true only of the *necessitas coactionis,* not of the
necessitas immutabilitatis. Since people will to do good or evil, rewards
or punishments naturally follow.[49] Luther's words here are crucial:

Doesn't it clearly follow, then, while God is not present in us
by his own work, that everything which we do is evil and that

---

Claras Aquas, 1971): 452-453; also, MPL 192: 707-08.

[43]A.N.S. Lane, *Calvin and Bernard of Clairvaux,* in Studies in Reformed Theology and History (Princeton: Princeton Theological Seminary, 1996), 42-43.

[44]For an excellent survey of this relationship, see A. N. S. Lane,
"Introduction,"*The Bondage and Liberation of the Will: A Defence of the Orthodox
Doctrine of Human Choice against Pighius,* ed. A. N. S. Lane; trans. G. I. Davies
(Grand Rapids, MI: Baker Books, 1996), xxvii-xxviii.

[45]Erasmus, *De libero arbitrio διατριβη sive collatio,* ed. J. Walter (Leipzig:
Georg Böhme, 1910): 10, 79. He asks: *"Verum unde sumes initium meritorum,
numquam fuit libera voluntas?"* ("Truly how may you be the initiator of merits if
the will was never free?"), 50.

[46]Martin Luther, *The Bondage of the Will,* 72.

[47]Luther, *De servo arbitrio,* in *Martin Luthers Werke: kritische Gesamtausgabe,*
vol. 18 (Weimar: 1908): 634.

[48]Ibid., 635.

[49]Luther, *On the Bondage of the Will,* 189.

> we necessarily produce nothing which makes us worthy of salvation?. . . Now I say 'necessarily,' not 'coerced,' but, as they say, an immutable necessity, not a coerced one, that is, a person without the Spirit of God does not do evil unwillingly, not to be sure by violent force—as if a thief, pulled up by the collar, but does evil spontaneously and freely by the will.[50]

While the discussion of Luther is not necessary to prove the "genetic" development of Calvin's thought, it is important for the debate that would ensue with Albert Pighius, the Roman Catholic opponent on the question of free choice. Pighius lumped Calvin and Luther together, so Calvin found it necessary to defend Luther point by point as well as to distance himself (in a much later treatise *after* Luther had died) from some of Luther's more deterministic tones (namely, God is the cause of everything). It appears that Calvin knew Luther's treatise and debate with Erasmus quite well; it is also evident that Calvin may have borrowed the linguistic distinction between *necessitas* and *coactio* from Luther, nonetheless filling it with his own precise meaning. Luther was not too concerned with the support of the Fathers for his thesis—the Scriptures should supply him with enough shot for the cannon. However, Pighius' main charge was that Calvin misread the Fathers; therefore, Calvin found it necessary to support his thought with 'historic Christianity.' In this endeavor, Bernard and Augustine were most useful because of their ideas; Luther may have been useful because of his technical distinctions in the language of necessity and coercion.[51]

This distinction made by Luther was largely followed by Calvin, with his own style and with a greater sense of the teachings of the Fathers on this point than Luther.[52] It now remains for us to examine Calvin's usage of this distinction.

---

[50]Luther, *De servo arbitrio*, 18:634. The Latin reads, "*Nonne clare sequitur, dum Deus opere suo in nobis non adest, omnia esse mala quae facimus, et nos necessario operari quae nihil ad salutem valent?. . . Necessario vero dico, non coacte, sed ut illi dicunt, necessitate immutabilitatis, non coactionis, hoc est, homo cum vacat spiritu Dei, non quidem violentia, velut raptor, obtorto collo, nolens facit malum. . . sed sponte et libente voluntate facit.*"

[51]The linguistic distinction may have begun with Anselm (*Cur Deus Homo*, 2.17). A. N. S. Lane correctly suggests, however, that the medieval theologians did not use this distinction consistently nor with the same meaning as Calvin. Lane concludes, as do I, that Luther's response to Erasmus shaped Calvin's use of this distinction. See Lane, *Calvin and Bernard*, 43, fn. 284. Lane also suggests Martin Bucer as a possible source.

[52]François Wendel, *Calvin: Origins and Development of His Religious Thought*, trans. Philip Mairet (Grand Rapids: Baker Books, 1997),190. It seems clear that Calvin did not thumb through a dictionary to find the distinction between *necessitas* and *coactio*. The history of the Latin language seems to have viewed these terms as synonyms. Following Luther, Calvin proposes this word usage as something

II. Calvin's Doctrine of the "Freedom" and Necessity of Humanity

Calvin's "Determinism"

The usage of *necessitas* and *coactio* is better understood against the background of Calvin's "determinism." Calvin was not a fatalist, even though he has been so accused. He was especially careful to distinguish his view of providence from Stoic fatalism.[53] He posited that God is the ruler and governor of everything; nothing is left to chance. This is what caused some to call him fatalistic. He defended himself from this charge by pointing out that the Stoics saw *necessitas* contained in nature, "out of the perpetual connection and intimately related series of causes."[54] In contradistinction to this, Calvin saw providence contained in God's counsel.[55] This understanding of providence removed fatalism from Calvin's doctrine (he believed) and emphasized instead the fatherly care of God.[56]

---

that the Fathers would have used, had they thought of it. Johannes Altensteig published a compendium of theological definitions in 1517; it was very popular for over a century, undergoing numerous publications. It is possible that this compendium was known by Calvin. Under the term *necessitas*, Altensteig recites several medieval scholars' opinions to elucidate its meaning. Several pages describe the rather obscure medieval distinction between *necessitas absoluta* and *necessitas consequentia*. His section on *coactio* rehearses Richard of St. Victor's discussion of coercion, but has nothing regarding Calvin's distinction between the two terms. From this we may surmise that Calvin relied on the concepts of the Fathers he had studied more than on the technical vocabulary of the dictionaries. This also gives further weight to our assumption that he borrowed the distinction from Luther. See Johannes Altensteig and Johannes Tytz, *Lexicon Theologicum quo tanquam clave theologiae fores aperiuntur* (Hildesheim: Georg Olms Verlag, 1974; reprint of 1619 edition), 147-48, 582-85.
[53]Calvin, *Institutes*, I.16.8; LCC, 20: 207.
[54]Ibid. This is from the 1539 edition, as is most of his material on necessity.
[55]P.H. Reardon, "Calvin on Providence: The Development of an Insight," *Scottish Journal of Theology* 28 (1975): 525. Reardon details Calvin's writings on Stoicism. Cf. also, *De aeterna Dei praedestinatione*, in *Opera Quae Supersunt Omnia*, vol. VIII, 353, where Calvin sees the Stoics being imitated by the astrologers of his day: "*quibus fatalis ex stellarum positu dependet rerum necessitas.*" Although an old source, August Lecerf is also helpful in this area. See *Le Déterminisme et la Responsabilité dans le Système de Calvin* (Paris: Henri Jouve, 1895), 26-30.
[56]Emil Brunner suggests that Calvin attempts to distance himself from the Stoics and from the extreme version of Zwingli's view of providence. In both of these views, the responsibility of humanity is negligible. Zwingli even suggests that a robber is "forced to do it," and since God is the author of all, God is responsible. But it is done so that the robber "may be executed," *De providentia*, 2 (cited in Brunner, op cit., 171). Calvin retreats from such language, but Brunner believes he fails. "Zwingli accepts the Stoic *necessitas*, Calvin rejects it in theory, but introduces it again without calling it by its right name" (Brunner, 174). Brunner's

In 1545, Calvin wrote a treatise against a religious sect called the Libertines. In this treatise, he distinguished his view on providence from their brand of determinism. The Libertines believed that God (*seul esprit*) does all things and so everything that is done in the world, "must be reputed directly to his work."[57] Therefore, nothing can be called evil, "*entant que Dieu en est autheur*" ("to the extent that God is its author").[58]

Calvin cites three detestable consequences of this determinism: 1) there would be no difference between God and the devil; 2) people would have no conscience in order to avoid evil; and, 3) people would not dare to judge anything because everything must be good.[59] The alternative Calvin offers to Libertine determinism is God's providence. He does not deny that all things are done through the will of God, but this does not mean God does everything. God has given humans a choice and will by nature and so they are responsible for their actions.[60] Nonetheless, God governs the universe through three means: 1) the order of nature (*l'ordre de nature*), 2) the work in his creatures whereby they serve his will, and 3) the governance of believers through the indwelling Spirit.[61] The alternative to Libertine determinism is this providential care of God and the fact that humans have a will. God's power is not divorced from his goodness, as

---

understanding of Calvin here rests entirely on his words on providence; if the discussion on freedom of the will had been included, the final pronouncement might not have been as severe. In addition, Calvin responded to Pighius' charge that he agreed with Luther's view of absolute necessity whereby God was the author of all happenings. In response, Calvin used a scholastic distinction between relative and absolute necessity. A. N. S. Lane suggests that this difference is crucial for understanding Calvin. Why would Calvin, who usually abhorred scholastic sophistry, take up this distinction? Lane suggests, "It was in order to rescue the simple from Luther's conclusions that Calvin resorted to the uncharacteristic use of scholastic distinction." See Lane, "Did Calvin Believe in Free Will?" *Vox Evangelica* 12 (1981):75. To be sure, Calvin makes it sound like humans have no responsibility, but to be fair, he shades his meanings more closely than most interpreters are willing to observe. While a linguistic distinction, which we are positing in this essay, does not alleviate Calvin from all of the charges of determinism, it should remind us that his views are too complex to be judged from any and every part of the *Institutes* that we choose.

[57]Calvin, *Contre la Secte Phantastique et Furieuse des Libertines qui se nomment spirituelz,* chapter 13, in *Calvini Opera Quae Supersunt Omnia,* vol. 7, 183.

[58]Ibid. Calvin also says the Libertines "*n'attribuent a l'homme nulle volunté non plus que s'il estoit une pierre,*" (". . . do not attribute to humans any more will than if they might be stones").

[59]Ibid., 13; VII: 186.

[60]Ibid., 14; VII: 191: "*il nous faut noter que de nature nous avons en nous election et volunté.*" (". . . it is necessary for us to note that we have in us choice and will by nature").

[61]Ibid. This is the subject of chapter 14, VII: 186-92.

the Libertines would have it; neither does God violate the nature of people, as if they were stones.[62]

In what sense, then, is Calvin deterministic? How does he view the freedom and responsibility of God and humanity? Calvin seems to posit a certain freedom, but not free will.[63] As God's omnipotence was not "neutral" (that is, without relation to God's goodness) in the above discussion on providence, so human freedom is not neutral—it is bound necessarily by a corrupt, depraved nature. Allen Verhey describes this "freedom" as an ability "to establish one's self on certain ends and purposes."[64] Its source is in God, and by it humans know they are responsible.

This seems to imply a contradiction—humans are free and yet not free. It is here that Calvin's distinction of *necessitas* and *coactio* becomes important. Calvin uses this distinction to point out that humans are spontaneous in that they have a will (and so "free" in the sense of not coerced), *yet* this will is bound by sin and a corrupt nature and so sins of necessity.

Calvin's Usage of necessitas *and* coactio

Calvin primarily discusses these terms in two places: the *Institutes* (II.2.5-7; II.3.5f), and in his *Defensio adversus calumnias Pighii.*[65] The passages from the *Institutes* will be discussed later; since Calvin's treatise offers a more definitive introduction to his thought on free will, it will be considered first.

Albertus Pighius was a scholar who served the Roman Catholic cause, writing much anti-Reformation literature. Pighius was aware of Calvin's

---

[62]Allen Verhey, "Calvin's Treatise 'Against the Libertines,'" *Calvin Theological Journal* 15 (November 1980): 200-01. Verhey offers a fine introduction to several chapters of this little recognized treatise. His comment is helpful: "That we have always to do with God must be said against the position that things happen through chance. But that we have always to do with the goodness and justice of God must be said against the Libertines," 201.

[63]*Institutes,* II.2.7; LCC. 20:264.

[64]Verhey, "Against the Libertines," 205. Verhey admits that this is a "subtle alternative" on which Calvin's argument hinges, yet it is valid because it allows for both God's providence and human responsibility. God's freedom does not destroy human freedom and human freedom does not limit God's freedom. Cf. Charles Partee, "Calvin and Determinism," *Christian Scholar's Review* 5 (1975). Partee also sees Calvin affirming his own type of freedom.

[65]These passages from the *Institutes* were primarily in the 1539 edition. The complete title of Calvin's treatise is, *Defensio sanae et orthodoxae doctrinae de servitute et liberatione humani arbitrii adversus calumnias Alberti Pighii Campensis,* in *Calvini Opera Quae Supersunt Omnia,* vol. VI, 233-404. Of specific import are pages 279-80; 333-34; and 358f. Albert Pighius wrote a response to the 1539 *Institutes* in 1542 (cited in note 66) and Calvin responded with this treatise in 1543 as well as another treatise (*De aeterna Praedestinatione Dei*) in 1552.

view of free will and his distinction between *necessitas* and *coactio*.[66] In 1542, Pighius' treatise on free will was published, charging that Calvin did not have the Church Fathers on his side (especially Augustine), and further that Calvin was deterministic, notwithstanding his proposed distinction. By no means could Pighius admit to Calvin's view of necessity.[67] If one agrees to this necessity, what becomes of freedom, merit, or responsibility?[68] It was clear to Pighius that free will was this: "that (a person) might do nothing, wish nothing, will nothing necessarily, but accordingly, he or she is able to cease from an action of this kind, just as he or she was able not to do it from the beginning."[69]

Calvin responded in 1543 with his treatise in defense of a sound and "orthodox" doctrine, citing the Fathers in his support—especially Augustine and Bernard.[70] However, it was the distinction between *necessitas* and *coactio,* "on which the greater part of this question rests."[71] It was this essential distinction that Pighius "constantly confused."[72]

For Calvin, humans are not coerced to sin; they do so spontaneously through their wills. When they are "arranged to do good by the Spirit of God," their wills are still not excluded. Grace inclines their wills to pleasing God and desiring good. Calvin sees that the will might "become good by grace alone, and become righteous, so that it might necessarily value and follow that which it previously abhorred."[73]

---

[66]Albertus Pighius, *De libero hominis arbitrio et divina gratia,* (Cologne: Melchioris Noue, 1542), folio xii. Pighius reviews Calvin's doctrine of necessity and notes that Calvin believes he may offend those who "*inter necessitatem et coactionem distinguere nesciant,*" ("may not know to distinguish between necessity and compulsion"). Pighius places himself in the "offended" camp.

[67]Ibid., fol. xli. "*Quod dicit voluntatem qua beati esse volumus, ea libertate non esse nobis liberam, sed necessariam neutiquam illi admisero.*" ("Although he says that the will by which we wish to be blessed, by this freedom is not for us free, but I shall admit to him no necessity at all").

[68]Ibid., fol. xlv. Also, Pighius reiterates a familiar formula: "*si liberum non est, non est voluntas,*" fol. xliv. ("If it is not free, it is not a will").

[69]Pighius, fol. xli. The Latin reads, "*ut nihil agat, nihil velit, nihil nolit necessario, sed quodque ita, ut possit cessare ab actione eiusmodi, sicut potuit ab initio non agere.*"

[70]Calvin, *Defensio,* 333. "*Sic ante nos Augustinus, sic Bernardus loquuti sunt.*" ("Thus before us Augustine, thus Bernard, have spoken").

[71]Ibid. The Latin reads, "*unde pendet maiori ex parte haec questio.*"

[72]Ibid., 280. "*perpetuo confundit.*" Calvin's logic brought him to this conclusion: "There can be no such thing as a coerced will, since the two ideas are contradictory," *Defensio,* 280; trans. A. N. S. Lane, *The Bondage and Liberation of the Will,* 69.

[73]Ibid., 359. Calvin illustrates the distinction between necessity and compulsion through the examples of God and Satan. God is unavoidably, necessarily good because of his good nature; Satan is necessarily evil (333-334). Hermann Barnikol notes that for Calvin God does good with his will and yet necessarily of

However, because of Adam's fall, the "yoke of necessity . . . has been imposed on us."[74] This is a necessity to sin—a bondage of the will. Calvin comments on this:

> Finally, the will is enslaved, which on account of corruption is held captive under the command of evil desires, so that it is able to choose nothing except that which is evil—even if it does so spontaneously and freely without impulse from external motion.[75]

One sins necessarily, but not by compulsion.

Calvin's definition of *coactio* in this treatise is clear: that which is "not inclined this way or that spontaneously of itself nor moved by inward movement of choice, but is forcibly carried along by external motion."[76] Spontaneity, on the other hand, is that which "directs itself of its own accord . . . and is not snatched nor hauled away against the will."[77] The problem seems to lie in a human's *internal* depraved nature that bends one always toward sin, not in an *external* force that manipulates a human by compulsion. Thus, Calvin's terminology may be clarified, but what of his unique concept of freedom? He answers forcibly in this treatise as well:

> However, we deny freedom because of the innate depravity of humanity, a person is necessarily driven to evil—he or she is unable to desire anything except evil. And so it is allowed for us to deduce this: there is a great difference between necessity and compulsion. For we do not speak of humans being hauled away to sin against their will. But since their will is corrupt, it is held captive under the yoke of sin *(sub peccati iugo)*, and thus necessarily *(necessario)* wills evil. For where there is servitude, there is necessity *(ubi enim servitus, illic*

---

his nature; "likewise, Satan can do nothing other than evil, so he sins with his will," *Die Lehre Calvins vom unfreien Willen,* 135-136. Barnikol feels these examples are important: "With these examples of the necessary and yet free acts of God and the devil, we are able to grasp the thought of Calvin about the peculiarity *(die Eigenart)* and essence of this profound necessity *(dieser Notwendigkeit tiefer)."*

[74]Calvin, *Defensio,* 334-335. The Latin reads, *"necessitas iugum . . . nobis impositum."* Calvin says that Bernard and Prosper said this *une ore,* (with one mouth).

[75]Ibid., 280. The Latin reads, *"Serva postremo voluntas est quae propter corruptionem sub malarum cupiditatum imperio captiva tenetur, ut nihil quam malum eligere possit, etiam si id sponte et libenter, non externo motu impulsa, faciat."*

[76]Ibid. *"Eam ergo sic vocamus, quae non sponte sua, nec interiore electionis motu, inclinatur huc vel illuc sed externo motu violenter fertur."*

[77]Ibid. *"Spontaneam dicimus, quae ultro se flectit, quocunque ducitur, non autem rapitur aut trahitur invita."*

necessitas). But there is a great difference as to whether the servitude is voluntary or coerced.[78]

This is perhaps Calvin's most succinct statement of the issue. Freedom is denied by him, but not the spontaneous freedom of choice [*arbitrium*]. To deny this latter freedom would be to say the same thing as the Libertines—that humans are stones without wills. Humans are "free" to choose, that is, without compulsion, yet because sin has yoked them, they are not free.[79] Having considered Calvin's treatise, let us examine his *Institutes*. The majority of the material on the distinction between *necessitas* and *coactio* was written four years before the treatise against Pighius. In the 1539 edition of the *Institutes,* Calvin was establishing his doctrine of necessity, not responding to one person's challenge against it. He set his distinction between necessity and compulsion within the larger discussion of freedom of the will. Calvin realized that many philosophers and Church Fathers asserted that the will is free, but he still saw humanity "hedged about on all sides by most miserable necessity."[80] In attempting to define free will, most of the Fathers seem confused, Calvin says. However, Peter Lombard offers a clearer understanding: humans have free will because they are free from compulsion, not because they are able to do good or evil; yet this freedom is unhindered by slavery to sin.[81] Calvin responds that this is well-said, but to say that one is free because he or she acts wickedly by his or her will and not by compulsion, is to give such slight

---

[78]Calvin, *Defensio,* 280.
[79]John Leith makes an astute observation on this point: "While Calvin speaks of the loss of freedom of will in the sense of contrary choice, a close reading indicates that he only denies freedom of the will as the power of choice in certain particular situations in which the self is deeply involved and in particular in the self's relationship to God." See Leith, "The Doctrine of the Will in the *Institutes of the Christian Religion,*" in *Reformatio Perennis: Essays on Calvin and the Reformation in honor of Ford Lewis Battles,* ed. B. A. Gerrish (Pittsburgh: The Pickwick Press, 1981), 53. Leith has pointed to a "soteriological will" in Calvin's argument. The natural will is free to choose spontaneously one way or another, but never free to choose for God. Richard Muller echoes a similar refrain when he suggests, "Like Augustine and like Luther, Calvin does not deny the basic freedom of will: the faculty is free from external compulsion, albeit that it operates under certain necessities belonging to its nature under God or under sin. He therefore argues the restriction of choice to sinful choice. We find here...not a philosophical but a soteriological voluntarism...." See Richard Muller, "*Fides* and *Cognitio* in Relation to the Problem of Intellect and Will in the Theology of John Calvin," *Calvin Theological Journal* 25 (November 1990): 215.
[80]Calvin, *Institutes,* II.2.1; LCC, 20: 255.
[81]Ibid., II.2.6; LCC, 20:264.

"freedom" a "proud name."[82] Why should we even call such bondage to sin free? Calvin concedes he does not like to quarrel over words, but when people hear the word "free," they immediately consider themselves their own masters; this use of freedom leads to a "ruinous self-assurance."[83]

Calvin does admit there is some kind of freedom here, but he refuses to call it freedom; he does not offer a substitute (perhaps "spontaneity" is a suitable term?). Indeed, if a person could use the word "freedom" with full understanding of its poorer sense, then Calvin would allow it. However, he quickly added to this concession that its usage offers a "great peril" for the church and therefore should be eliminated. "I prefer not to use it myself, and I should like others, if they seek my advice, to avoid it."[84] The danger of this term lies in attributing to humans too much power. Thus, the "precept of the Christian religion" is humility arising out of an awareness of the condition of humanity.[85]

The will has become bound because of the fall of Adam—this is the human condition. The will did not perish in the Fall, but became enslaved by "wicked desires," and is "restrained by the stoutest bonds."[86] However, humanity did not begin in this condition of slavery: "it is not from creation but from corruption of nature that men are bound to sin and can will nothing but evil."[87] Adam and Eve sinned voluntarily, bringing about this necessity to their posterity.[88]

---

[82]*Institutes,* II.2.7; LCC, 20: 264. *"superbo titulo insignire."* A. N. S. Lane makes an understated observation: "Calvin was certainly not keen on the term," in "Did Calvin Believe in Free Will?" 79.

[83]Ibid.

[84]Ibid., II.2.8; LCC, 20: 266. In this context, Calvin was discussing Augustine's approach to free will; in II.3.14, he again discusses Augustine and says, "Thus there is left to man such free will, if we please so to call it . . ." It seems that Calvin personally abhors the phrase free will but has to use something to speak of Augustine's terms since Calvin himself does not offer an alternative. However, away from an Augustinean context, Calvin rules out the usage of "freedom" in relation to the will. This is apparent in his *Defensio adversus calumnias Pighii* which we noted above: "we deny freedom . . ." (280). Yet, Calvin's reason for not using this term is clear in both cases—to use it is to give humanity an illusion of power or ability which they do not possess.

[85]Ibid., II.2.11; LCC, 20:269.

[86]Calvin states the idea of bondage often: *Institutes,* II.2.12; 27; II.5.1; LCC, 20: 271, 288, 317.

[87]Ibid, II.5.1; LCC, 20: 317.

[88]A recent study on Calvin's view of the will by Dewey Hoitenga makes a strong case for Calvin's inconsistency on freedom of the will. Posing a key question, Hoitenga asks that if Calvin can assert the total ineffectuality of the will toward good after the fall, then what does that say of God's creation of the will? In other words, Calvin's view that the fallen will is totally deficient for good misunderstands the created will before the fall. In arguing this case, Hoitenga is

However, to say one sins necessarily now does not remove the voluntary aspect. This is the crux of the issue—one willingly (in fact, eagerly) sins out of necessity, but not through compulsion or external coercion.[89] People live as captives under the yoke of sin and the devil. Calvin explains:

> Nonetheless the will remains, with the most eager inclination disposed and hastening to sin. For man, when he gave himself over to this necessity, was not deprived of will, but of soundness of will.[90]

Calvin admits that unless the distinction between necessity and compulsion is kept clear, people will be confused and offended. The example of God and Satan should illustrate the distinction well enough. God does

---

convincing. However, he understands Calvin as viewing the fallen will devoid of its supernatural gifts, but only partially deficient in its remaining natural gifts. The loss of supernatural gifts clearly makes a soteriological point against the Pelagians—humans cannot do anything that turns them toward God. However, when Calvin says that human nature is "utterly lost," or "utterly devoid of all good" (*Inst.* II, 3.2.), Hoitenga believes he has moved the discussion beyond a soteriological point and has eliminated the natural goodness of the will. Augustine understood the will had lost supernatural gifts and that the will was so bent to evil that it could not do good (i.e., save itself). To this Calvin heartily assented. Yet Hoitenga notes that Augustine had a third aspect of the will to which Calvin did not adhere—a freedom of choice not entirely lost in the fall. Hoitenga states, "Calvin simply ignores a third alternative. . . that something of the will's own created inclination to goodness might persist into the fallen state, *without* being wholly lost in the way that the supernatural gifts were lost" (Hoitenga, 84). Thus, Hoitenga suggests Calvin cannot truly have a freedom of the will in terms of choice, since there are no legitimate options. Further, Calvin's position denegrates any natural accomplishments of the fallen will that we might label as "good." It is clear that Hoitenga has demonstrated several problems in Calvin's thought, but has missed the emphasis Calvin placed upon *necessitas* and *coactio*. While it is true that Calvin may be "deficient" (85) in a full-orbed discussion of the will, there are several passages that seem to suggest Calvin really meant to downplay the good achieved by a fallen will so as to deny salvation by any human effort. Yet in the *Institutes*, he sees humans as striving after good things such as mathematics, science, and the arts (II, 2. 14-18). Again, we see that in response to an opponent, Calvin hammers out a construct less than complete. Hoitenga, then, is in error when he says that on an issue of substance (namely, free will), ". . . Calvin turns it into a merely verbal matter," (107). The verbal distinctions we have analyzed in this essay are *substantive* for Calvin's argument, not mere semantical ping-pong. See Dewey Hoitenga, *John Calvin and the Will: A Critique and Corrective* (Grand Rapids, MI: Baker Book House, 1997).

[89]The crucial section for the development of the distinction is found in *Institutes,* II.3.5. However, more explicit definition of the terms themselves is found in his later treatise against Pighius, as discussed above.

[90]Ibid., II.3.5; LCC, 20: 294.

good necessarily out of the goodness of his nature, not by "violent impulsion."[91] However, this does not violate God's free will. Satan sins with his will, yet he can only do evil. Likewise, humans sin willingly even though they are subject to necessity.[92]

The "chief point" (*summa*) of the distinction between *necessitas* and *coactio* is that humans sin willingly, not by compulsion. A person sins,

> by the most eager inclination of his heart, not by forced compulsion; by the prompting of his own lust, not by compulsion from without.[93]

The will is so corrupt that a person can only move toward evil. Without this distinction, however, many are led into a "pernicious error."

Conclusion

Calvin's understanding of the will was hammered out on the anvil of Pelagian opponents. As such, his case is overstated to such a degree that questions arise as to whether he really intended to vacate the will of freedom so severely. In contrast to a Pelagian focus on human freedom (and therefore responsibility), Calvin insisted on the freedom of God and the yoke of bondage for the human will in things pertaining to salvation. Of course, Calvin insisted that humans possess some spontaneous freedom of choice, but not with regard to choosing good. In this respect, humans are always bound to do evil; their wills are emptied of anything good. This overstatement (along with comments that deny free will altogether) opens Calvin to the charge that even in things natural, humans can never choose or do good. The opponents' anvil has caused a vicious overstrike.

In order to compensate for this, Calvin reminds his opponents that the chief sum of the matter is his linguistic distinction between *necessitas* and *coactio*. We necessarily sin, yet are never coerced. Since we sin because of corrupt *internal* inclinations, *external* force is not involved. Therefore, we sin voluntarily yet also of necessity—and this is never a contradiction

---

[91]Calvin frequently uses "impulsion" as a synonym for *coactio*, but almost always with a preceding modifier, such as "violent," or "external," (in *Defensio*, 280). However, without a modifier, it can mean a motivating force with good intent, such as in this phrase: *"ad quem tamen nemo nisi Spiritus impulsu aspirat,"* ("...to which, however, no one draws near unless by the impulse of the Spirit,"), *Institutes*, II.2.26.

[92]Ibid.

[93]*Institutes*, II.3.5; LCC, 20: 296. The Latin reads: *"affectione animi propensissima, non violenta coactione; propriae libidinis motu, non extraria coactione."* This "chief point" is grasped by Leith: "Central to his case is the distinction between necessity and coercion (*coactio*)," Leith, 78.

for Calvin. For his opponents, it was mere linguistical subterfuge. The reality was obvious—Calvin was an absolute determinist.

Attempting to be fair to Calvin's argument, it seems more reasonable to see him as a "soft determinist," or a "providential determinist" who attempts to be faithful to the tenet of justification by *faith alone* than as a philosophical fatalist. His linguistic distinction offers an avenue for him to do this while not surrendering any ground on the soteriological point. God is in control, but humans are still responsible for their actions. Calvin believed that predestination and free will [of a very limited sort] can go together in the mystery of salvation. To say otherwise ignores the experience of every human who understands freedom as an essential component of human life. To offer the will anything more than token freedom in terms of its choosing the good is to open the door to Catholicism and a works righteousness. For Calvin, predestination and determinism are not synonyms; his linguistic distinction between *necessitas* and *coactio* sufficed to show this.[94] His opponents pass over this too quickly, missing his main point. Therefore, just like Pighius, they are ". . . always craftily confusing coercion with necessity, when it is of the greatest importance for the issue under discussion that the distinction between them be maintained and carefully remembered."[95]

There is another yoke of which Calvin speaks—not one of sin, but of salvation. The yoke of necessity for sinning can only be overcome by the grace of God; necessity for sinning then turns into a *felix necessitas* of obedience—and that yoke is "easy" by comparison.

---

[94]Willem Balke reminds us of this distinction in Calvin between predestination and determinism: "It is a serious misunderstanding to identify predestination more or less with determinism. In itself, the statement that Calvin believed in unchanging laws, and that this faith was strengthened by the doctrine of God's providence, appears to bear every mark of truth. Predestination and determinism do of course share the implication that nothing can take place by accident. Yet predestination has to do with God's free will and desire and lays its entire weight on the Lord's governance in heaven, while determinism is a form of necessitarianism and is a matter of fate and exigency," in "Revelation and Experience in Calvin's Theology," *Toward the Future of Reformed Theology: Tasks, Topics, Traditions*, ed. David Willis and Michael Welker (Grand Rapids, MI: William B. Eerdmans Publishing Co., 1999), 347-48.
[95]*Bondage and Liberation of the Will*, 280; trans. G. I. Davies, 69.

Theological Truth and Poetic Practice in Herbert's *The Temple*

Sabord Woods*

According to Izaak Walton, George Herbert, shortly before his death, spoke to his friend Duncon about disposition of his collection of religious poems called upon publication *The Temple*:[1]

> Sir, I pray deliver this little book to my dear brother Ferrar,
> and tell him he shall find in it a picture of the many spiritual
> conflicts that have passed betwixt God and my soul, before I
> could subject mine to the will of Jesus my Master, in whose
> service I have now found perfect freedom; desire him to read
> it: and then, if he can think it may turn to the advantage of any
> dejected poor soul, let it be made public; if not, let him burn it,
> for I and it are less than the least of God's mercies.[2]

*Sabord Woods (Ph.D., University of Tennessee). Professor of English, Lee University.
[1]George Herbert, *The Temple: Sacred Poems and Private Ejaculations*, in *The Complete English Poems,* by George Herbert, ed. John Tobin (New York: Penguin Books, 1991), 1-187. This study employs the above-named edition throughout for all references to Herbert's poems, citing page numbers of this edition within the text of the study.
[2]Izaak Walton, *The Life of Mr. George Herbert*, in *The Complete English Poems*, by George Herbert, ed. John Tobin (New York: Penguin Books, 1991), 310-11. Current scholars, while not totally discounting the data of Walton's *Life*, consider the biography "hagiography" and apply critical judgment both to Walton's account of the biographical data and to his own judgments regarding Herbert. Note, for instance, Amy Charles's statement on the first page of the "Preface" of her *Life of George Herbert* (Ithaca: Cornell University Press, 1977): "Walton's life of Herbert, although it has been made to serve for more than three centuries, is neither accurate nor dependable." She later on the page refers to it as "this essay in hagiography." There is little reason, however, to doubt the approximate accuracy

Here one sees Herbert's *conscious intention* regarding this book of devotional poems at the end of his years-long work on it—his description of its contents and his spiritual purpose for its readership. When one looks at the poems themselves, one sees not a contradiction of Herbert's statement above but a complexity of content and motive, which nearly four hundred years of reading and commentary has not nearly untangled. These poems are both highly experiential and deeply theological—to suggest the complexity and to echo Herbert's own description; they also are often ambiguous and ambivalent in tone, image, and idea. In many of the poems of *The Temple*, Herbert presents theology realized in miniature dramas or embodied in metaphor or mediated through formal devices or in a combination of the above. In any case, seldom does one find purely discursive presentation of theological propositions.[3] Often one finds rendered in concrete experience the agony of waiting endlessly in God's presence for an answer, or the abject sorrow over sins for which one yet cannot truly repent, or, conversely, intimate dialogue with God, or sheer delight in the divine presence—always conveyed sparely and usually by means of trenchant allegory, powerful metaphor, or ingeniously crafted elements of form.

The theology of *The Temple* is that of the Thirty-Nine Articles of the Church of England. Having said that, however, one has not solved the complex issue of Herbert's placement in the spectrum of religious thought of his age, for the Thirty-Nine Articles lend themselves to various interpretation. Seasoned Herbert scholars have, in fact, found the poetry to support contradictory positions.[4] Careful study of *The Temple,*

---

of the above statement by Herbert regarding his conscious poetic intention, though the intention itself may have evolved over a period of several years. Sharon Cadmon Seelig, in *The Shadow of Eternity: Belief and Structure in Herbert, Vaughan, and Traherne* (Lexington: The University Press of Kentucky, 1981), in fact, traces such an evolution, "a movement from a rigid or fruitless adherence to patterns, to a violation and questioning of them, to a final yielding and embracing of the divine form."

[3] A major exception is "Perirrhanterium," a long poem replete with observations on practical theology and ethics, which, together with the short poem which follows it, "Superliminare," constitutes "The Church Porch," the first major section of *The Temple.*

[4] See, for example, Christopher Hodgkins' *Authority, Church, and Society in George Herbert: Return to the Middle Way* (Columbia: University of Missouri Press, 1993), which views Herbert as "closer to the heart of Calvin's 'Calvinism' than were many of the reformer's most ardent English and Continental devotees"; or Ilona Bell's "'Setting Foot into Divinity': George Herbert and the English Reformation," in *Essential Articles for the Study of George Herbert's Poetry*, ed. John R. Roberts (Hamden, CN: Archon Books, 1979), 63-83, which views Herbert as gradually moving "away from a traditional Catholic vision to create a more Protestant poetic voice and style"; or Bruce A. Johnson's "Theological Inconsistency and Its Uses in George Herbert's Poetry," *George Herbert Journal* 15.2

nonetheless, can plausibly lead to the conclusion that the theology of the poems is broadly Protestant, rooted in the Reformation with its emphasis on *sola Scriptura* and justification by faith through grace—and this without a strongly predestinarian emphasis (which is not to say *non-belief* in predestination).[5] The Christian thought behind (and very often on the surface of) Herbert's poems is that closely related to the practical devotional life—such topics as the Trinity, the Incarnation, redemption, the Church, the relationship of the Christian to members of the Godhead, the nature and practice of prayer, and the means of combating sin and doubt and achieving spiritual peace. The attitudes conveyed in the process of given poems are multiplex as Herbert treats doctrines central to Christian formation variously in verse always highly affective and remarkably capable of tempting readers into complicity with its aims—despite such readers' own particular religious dispositions.

Herbert employed a wealth of poetic strategies in these poems that embodied theology. His conscious purpose in *The Temple* might be primarily spiritual, but his meters, rhythms, sub-genres, poetic devices, and rhetorical strategies adhere to no narrow sacred regimen for poetry, but rather astound the astute reader who looks and listens sensitively rather than grasping mainly for the intellectual content through their amazing

---

(1992): 1-18, which, along with such major Herbert scholars as Louis Martz, sees a "'generous ambiguity' (Martz's words) in Herbert's theology." But note as well John Bienz's statement in "Images and Ceremonial in *The Temple*: Herbert's Solution to a Reformation Controversy," *Studies in English Literature* 26 (1986): 87-88: "Readers of Herbert can no longer either overlook or take for granted the profound impact of key Reformation doctrines on him. However, a recognition of Herbert's Protestantism should not overshadow his receptivity to techniques and styles of worship not typically associated with the Reformers. For Herbert the problem posed by images and ceremonial to a biblical faith was less a doctrinal than a pedagogical or a rhetorical one."

[5]Herbert's poem "The Water-Course," *The Temple*, 160, appears to support double predestination:

> That so in pureness thou mayst him adore,
> 　　　　　　　　　　　　　　　　Salvation.
> Who gives to man, as he sees fit 　{
> 　　　　　　　　　　　　　　　　Damnation.

Bruce Johnson, 5, however, points out that "'as he sees fit' need not necessarily mean 'arbitrarily.'" Arminius himself believed in predestination. According to Henry Betterton, ed., *Documents of the Christian Church*, 2nd ed. (London: Oxford University Press, 1963), 268, "though he [Arminius] did not deny election he based it not on a divine arbitrary decree, but upon God's foreknowledge of man's merit." It was the implications of divine election for Christian life and destiny that were at issue.

range and complex relatedness to poetic meaning.[6] For example, a number of the poems are English sonnets—that is, "Love (I)" and "Love (II)" (48). The first addresses "Immortal Love," equated with deity, and the second employs a metaphor, "Immortal Heat," for the same divine entity. Both sonnets end in a worshipful stance:

> Who sings thy praise? Only a scarf or glove
> Doth warm our hands, and make them write of love.
> . . . .
> All knees shall bow to thee; all wits shall rise,
> And praise him who did make and mend our eyes.

Other poems in *The Temple* employ a variety of stanzaic patterns. "The Temper (I)" (49), for instance, consists of seven four-line stanzas with a simple *abab* rhyme scheme for each but with the first line of each stanza iambic pentameter, the second and third lines iambic tetrameter, and the fourth line iambic trimeter. The diminishing line length in each stanza parallels falling or contracting in the thought. "Man's Medley" (122-23), the title itself a pun, is composed of six six-line stanzas of various line lengths, with frequent irregularity in metre within a given line in tension with a settled pattern for each line:

Hark, how the birds do sing.	a	iambic trimeter
And woods do ring.	a	iambic dimeter
All creatures have their joy: and man hath his.	b	iambic pentameter
Yet if we rightly measure,	c	iambic trimeter
Man's joy and pleasure	c	iambic dimeter
Rather hereafter, than in present, is.	b	iambic pentameter

Medley refers to motley cloth as well as to a type of musical composition characterized by diversity or incongruity,[7] and "man," Herbert's generic

---

[6]See Joseph H. Summers, "The Poem as Hieroglyph," *George Herbert: His Religion and Art* (Cambridge, MA, 1954); *George Herbert and the Seventeenth-Century Religious Poets*, ed. Mario A. Di Cesare, A Norton Critical Edition (New York: W. W. Norton, 1978), 255-69, for a succinct treatment of Herbert's use of technical resources to achieve poetic meaning. Jonathan F. S. Post, in "Substance and Style: An Introduction to *The Temple*," *George Herbert Journal* 18.1 & 2 (Fall 1994, Spring 1995): 1-28, very effectively illustrates the fecundity of form and matter in Herbert's religious poetry. Also, in a somewhat analogous conclusion regarding Gerard Manley Hopkins' relatedness of form and meaning which offers some insight into Herbert's earlier achievement, Thomas Merton, in *A Thomas Merton Reader*, ed. Thomas P. McDonnell (New York: Doubleday, 1974), 250, states: "Hopkins' spiritual struggles fought their way out in problems of rhythm. He made his asceticism bearable by thrusting it over the line into the order of art where he could handle it more objectively."

[7]Herbert, *The Complete English Poems*, 389.

name for humankind, too is a medley of flesh and spirit, a diversity of parts reflected generally in the very stanzaic pattern employed in the poem, which exhibits diversity and incongruity rather than simple harmony or regimentation.

Herbert is known for the creation of "shaped verse," particularly in "The Altar" (23) and "Easter Wings" (38), and Dryden, later in the seventeenth century, following the ascendant critical stance of his age, would satirize this characteristic of these very poems in his brilliant lampoon "Mac Flecknoe," when the unfortunate Shadwell was advised ironically to write acrostic verse in which "thou maist wings display and Altars raise" (1. 207).[8] But Herbert was no superficial versifier; rather, he does here very evidently what he sought to accomplish typically. He marshals all resources available to the poet in the crafting of a work of art, which with high originality and profundity examines aspects of authentic spiritual experience, the external reflecting the internal, even as Pope's "*Sound must seem an Eccho to the Sense*" (1. 365).[9] Herbert's "broken altar," his imperfect heart, contrasts with the crafted altar of the poem's shape, which emblematically draws the reader into the poem's theological depth— Christ's redemptive power applied to the hardened human heart.[10] "Easter Wings" works similarly. The wings of the poem's shape, formed by varying line lengths, are grasped instantaneously when the poem is printed sidewize according to Herbert's intention, affording the reader an immediate entrance into the core of the poem's meaning—soaring spiritual flight achieved through Christ's victory over sin epitomized in his resurrection, flight communicated metaphorically through the magnificent lark image. Apparent in examples considered already is Herbert's complex fusion of disparate elements in his typical poetry,[11] reflective of the complexity of spiritual experience the poet would have his reader enter into with entirety rather than merely apprehend intellectually.

Herbert employs ingenious rhetorical strategies in his transmutation of theology into verse. Given the plausibility of his own deathbed statement, his intention was to share with receptive individuals his private

[8]John Dryden, *Mac Flecknoe*, in *Eighteenth-Century English Literature,* ed. Geoffrey Tillotson et al. (New York: Harcourt, Brace & World, 1969), 150.

[9]Alexander Pope, *An Essay on Criticism*, in *Eighteenth-Century English Literature,* ed. Geoffrey Tillotson et al., 559.

[10]See Bienz, "Images and Ceremonial," 82, for evocation of rich theological associations with Herbert's "altar."

[11]See Dr. Samuel Johnson's famous disparagement of metaphysical poetry in "From *Cowley,*" in *Eighteenth-Century English Literature*, ed. Geoffrey Tillotson et al., 1077: "a kind of *discordia concors*; a combination of occult resemblances in things apparently unlike . . . . The most heterogeneous ideas . . . yoked by violence together." Dr. Johnson most astutely pinpoints the typical effect, though students of Herbert would not agree that the effect is bad.

184 The Spirit and the Mind

devotional experience with God—"sacred poems and private ejaculations," in the words of his own title. Rhetorical critics, however, find rather naive the assumption that Herbert's actual experience forms the content of these poems.[12] Rather, the poet is a craftsman who constructs tiny fictive worlds as he applies formal strategies to the raw material of his experience. As Wordsworth's universally known Romantic description of his own poetic process would suggest,[13] the ultimate artistic result is a mediation of actual experience, or a transmutation. But it would be as implausible to see little or no experiential basis for the poems as to postulate naively the poet's communication of raw, untransformed experience, though the degree of relatedness to the poet's own experience varies from poem to poem. Herbert's religious poetry is typically his subjective but transformed private spiritual reality artistically rendered for an audience, or for three possible audiences—himself, God, and others, as one commentator suggests.[14]

Herbert's devotional experience is quite often formed into a tiny drama in which a theological reality translates into a personal encounter (for example, "The Collar," 144; "Affliction I," 41; or "The Pilgrimage," 133-34) with dialogue ("Dialogue," 106-07) or without it ("The Collar"). Instead, however, a mere narrative setting may be created as the basis for analysis of inner states without *dramatized* conflict (i.e. "Artillery," 130-31, or "The Pulley," 150); or a poem may be constructed around a single central metaphor ("The Flower," 156-57) or a series of metaphors ("Prayer I," 45-46).

---

[12]Note Richard E. Hughes' "George Herbert's Rhetorical World," *Essential Articles for the Study of George Herbert's Poetry*, ed. John R. Roberts (Hamden, CN: Archon Books, 1979), 105-13, in which the poet's mode of rhetoric is explored and some of his rhetorical stances are laid out.

[13]In his "Preface to the Second Edition of *Lyrical Ballads*," in *English Romantic Writers,* ed. David Perkins (New York: Harcourt, Brace World, 1967), 328, Wordsworth states, "I have said that poetry is the spontaneous overflow of powerful feelings; it takes its origin from emotion recollected in tranquillity: the emotion is contemplated till, by a species of re-action, the tranquillity gradually disappears, and an emotion, kindred to that which was before the subject of contemplation, is gradually produced, and does itself actually exist in the mind. In this mood successful composition generally begins, and in a mood similar to this it is carried on. . . ." One need not buy into Wordsworth's Romantic definition of a poem as primarily emotive to see value for understanding of Herbert in Wordsworth's account of the creative process.

[14]Bruce A. Johnson, "The Audience Shift in George Herbert's Poetry," *Studies in English Literature* 35 (1995): 87. Martin Elskey's "Herbert's 'The Church' and Spiritual Autobiography," *Journal of English and Germanic Philology* 83.3 (July 1984): 317-18, explores the relation of autobiography to the poems; and Nicholas R. Jones' "Texts and Contexts: Two Languages in George Herbert's Poetry," *Studies in Philology* 79.2 (Spring 1982): 162-76, distinguishes "texts" from multiple contexts in the poems.

Quite often the traditional device of apostrophe controls poetic structure (i.e., "Peace," 116-17, "Vanity II," 116, or "Avarice," 70). Also, poems may assume traditional forms from the liturgy such as *prayer* ("Misery," 92-94, "Trinity Sunday," 61, or "Prayer II," 95), an *antiphon* ("Antiphon I," 47, "Antiphon II,' 86-87), a *psalm* ("The Twenty-third Psalm, 162-63), or a *hymn* ("A True Hymn," 158-59). Regardless of the mode, however, immediacy of relationship or urgency of communicated truth or intensity of emotional encounter or quiet realization of spiritual reality is invariably transmitted to the expectant souls among Herbert's readership.

Herbert dramatizes the central doctrine of Christian faith—redemption, or the atonement—in his English sonnet "Redemption" (35-36), which in narrative form communicates succinctly the replacing of the Old Testament covenant of works with the covenant of grace. The first-person narrator has long served as a tenant under a "rich Lord" without thriving but now seeks cancellation of the old lease and its replacement by a new one. The "I" seeks the Lord at his manor in heaven, where he is told that the Lord has gone to earth to take possession of newly acquired land. On earth again, the "I" seeks his Lord in various centers of cultivated life, only to find him in the company of "thieves and murderers." States the narrator: "There I him espied, / Who straight, *Your suit is granted*, said, and died" (ll. 13-14). Here central theological truth becomes intimate spiritual experience, accentuated by the concluding direct response, in a simple allegorical narrative that in terms of Reformation theology conveys the essence of Christian redemption. The "rich Lord" of Herbert's sonnet is, as the Second of the Thirty-Nine Articles has it, that "one Christ, very God, and very Man; who truly suffered, was crucified, dead, and buried, to reconcile his Father to us, and to be a sacrifice, not only for original guilt, but also for actual sins of man."[15] The Mosaic covenant of the Old Testament constitutes the old lease; the Christian Gospel of the New Testament is the "new small-rented lease"; for, according to Heb 9:15-16, Christ the Lord "is the mediator of the new testament, that by means of death, for the redemption of the transgressions that were under the first testament, they which are called might receive the promise of eternal inheritance. For where a testament is, there must also of necessity be the death of the testator."[16] "Redemption" denotes "buying, purchasing and, by extension, ransoming,"[17] Christ's climactic death at the end of the sonnet being the redemptive act. Thus in this rich sonnet Herbert presents not his oft-recurring technical subtlety, but, instead, the power of simple story, which

---

[15]*The Book of Common Prayer* (New York: The Church Pension Fund, 1945), 603.

[16]Tobin, ed., *George Herbert: The Complete English Poems*, 340-41. Tobin quotes Heb 9:15-16 in a note to line 4.

[17]Ibid., 340. Tobin defines "redemption" so in a note to the title.

—aided by the built-in discipline of the sonnet form itself—conveys with total sufficiency the essence of this central Christian truth.

The final lyric of that large middle section of *The Temple* called "The Church" is "Love (3)" (178), based on the Johannine equation "God is love" (1 John 4:16). It too is a straight-forward narrative with two characters—Love (here God the Son) and the "I"—who engage in dialogue which develops experientially a timeless theological truth: The narrator is welcomed by Love, but his soul hesitates because of guilt due to sin. Love immediately senses the hesitation and inquires if the narrator "lacks anything." The answer is, "A guest . . . worthy to be here" (l. 7). Love assures him that he shall be a worthy guest, upon which he confesses his lack of kindness and gratefulness and his resulting inability to "look on" Love. Love takes the narrator's hand and replies with a question, "Who made the eyes but I?" (l. 12). The narrator feels that he has "marred" his eyes and insists that his shame "Go where it doth deserve." (l. 14). Love responds, "Who bore the blame?" (l. 15). The narrator insists then that *he* will serve, but Love says, "You must sit down . . . and taste my meat." The narrator concludes, "So I did sit and eat" (ll. 17-18). Through simple dialogue, step by step, the poet unfolds the idea of *grace*—spiritual salvation as a free gift from God—whose very essence is selfless Love. A banquet of spiritual delights awaits the responding soul, who can plead no merit but need only sit and partake. Article X of the Thirty-Nine Articles is most germane: "The condition of Man after the fall of Adam is such, that he cannot turn and prepare himself, by his own natural strength and good works, to faith, and calling upon God. Wherefore we have no power to do good works pleasant and acceptable to God, without the grace of God by Christ preventing us, that we may have a good will, and working with us, when we have that good will."[18] We can do nothing, but we need do nothing other than respond positively and partake of the joyous result of grace. One notes how much more effective Herbert's poetic dialogue is in conveying the timeless truth than is any commentator's paraphrase. One apprehends through the emotions and senses immediately, while the intellect lags behind, catching up only gradually. The alternating iambic pentameter and iambic trimeter lines reinforce the conversational quality of the verse, lightening the tone and slowing the pace through the necessary pauses introduced. The *ababcc* rhyme scheme of each of the three stanzas Herbert manipulates so as to emphasize important ideas (I—*back, sin, slack, in, questioning, anything;* II—*here, he, dear, thee, reply, I;* III—*shame, deserve, blame, serve, meat, eat*). The result is a tiny, highly concrete narrative, paced so as to induce meditation which, in turn, yields insight into basic Christian truth.[19]

---

[18]*The Book of Common Prayer*, 604-05.

[19]Terry G. Sherwood's commentary in *Herbert's Prayerful Art* (Toronto:

In "The Pulley" (150), Herbert creates a little myth as means to insight regarding human nature. The slight narrative occupies only two of four stanzas: God, having just created man, holds a glass of blessings which he pours on him profusely—strength, beauty, wisdom, honor, pleasure. But the last blessing God withholds—*rest*. A typical "metaphysical" image expresses the verbally indescribable divine gift: "Let the world's riches, which dispersed lie, / Contract into a span" (ll. 4-5). The idea is of an immense quantity *contracted* so as to be pour-able on a single head. The withheld blessing, rest, is the "pulley," the "jewel" which is to prevent resting in "Nature" instead of the God of Nature. "Repining restlessness," if "goodness" be insufficient, "may toss him to my breast." Herbert introduces a pun by his double use of "rest" as both *absence of activity* (l. 10) and *the remainder* (l. 16), and he reenforces his central idea by using "rest" as a verb denoting *false, or insufficient, rest* (l. 14). "Restlessness" as a pulley becomes an illustration of prevenient grace—the Holy Spirit employing such restlessness as a means to further grace at God's "breast," or in intimacy of relationship with the Divine. Also, in the middle of each stanza there is a restlessness of movement in the three long lines which subsides in the final line of each stanza, the meter thereby being employed to reinforce Herbert's main idea.

John Tobin sees "The Rose" (167-68) as having the Church as the ultimate referent for its central metaphor.[20] Article XIX of the Thirty-Nine Articles says of the Church, "The visible Church of Christ is a congregation of faithful men, in the which the pure Word of God is preached, and the Sacraments be duly ministered according to Christ's ordinance, in all those things that of necessity are requisite to the same."[21] If indeed Herbert refers to the Church in his controlling metaphor for this poem of renunciation of "worldly" *deceits*, or *delights* (ll. 9-10), he must have in mind the Church primarily as means of sustenance and growth and as agent of God's discipline for his "faithful" ones. Discipline in the Church would come through the Word of God itself, through the proper performance of the regular offices recumbent on that body, and through the interaction with and among the congregation itself, means to renunciation of the pseudo-delights and joys of stanzas one through three. In stanza four the "I" offers "this gentle rose" as the essence of those worldly joys

University of Toronto Press, 1989), 49-50, provides interesting context but also illustrates thereby that, even with Herbert, recourse to secular analogues does not always produce highly germane results.
[20]Tobin, *George Herbert: The Complete English Poems,* 411. In a note to the title, Tobin states, "The rose is to be understood as the Church, following the traditional allegory of the Song of Solomon 2:1, 'I am the rose of Sharon, and the lily of the valleys.'"
[21]*The Book of Common Prayer,* 606.

he himself has renounced, a rose offered as a purgative. In stanza six "all
that worldlings prize" is "contracted to a rose" with a bite at the end (ll. 21-
24), a means of inducement to repentance. But the "I" then turns to the
ultimate inner meaning of the rose when in the last stanza he presents his
choice of "health" as opposed to "physic." He opposes to the life of
pleasure of the worldlings the answer inherent in the ultimate meaning of
the rose. The image, then, could not at the end of the poem be the exterior
meaning of stanza six but, rather, must encompass all the sweetness and
pain inherent in the traditional associations of rose with *Church*—a life of
discipline, of acceptance of limitations, of joy in *koinonia*, that Christian
fellowship with the faithful ones of Christ's Church who experience growth
and pain and joy together in Christ. Hence, Herbert offers first a superficial meaning for the rose of the title with appeal to "worldlings," connotation finally contradicted by the inner meaning of this controlling image of
the poem.[22]

Often Herbert structures a poem around the traditional device of poetic apostrophe, in which one addresses a dead or absent person or an
abstraction as if such were present and able to respond. For instance, in
"Justice (2)" (123-33) the abstraction of the title is addressed, personified,
and characterized. Behind the abstraction is the traditional image of the
justice of God as balances for weighing held in the divine hand. The
terrifying image of justice with glowing hand conveyed in stanza one is
equivalent to an engine of torture when the unremitted "sin and error" (l.
3) of the narrator form a distorting glass through which to view it. Under
the condemnation of the Old Testament law, moreover, even to raise the
head would be evidence of pride and boldness. In stanza three, however,
the narrator sees the scales of justice as transformed through Christ's
"pure veil":

> Thy hand is white,
> Thy scales like buckets, which attend
> And interchangeably descend
> Lifting to heaven from this well of tears.

The scales of justice have become a well with balanced twin buckets as a
means of access, and the tears of repentance the visible evidence of contact with heaven and availing oneself of heaven's promises. Hence, Justice now stands in the narrator's favor rather than against him. Here, then,
Herbert transforms a forbidding traditional image into a favorable image of

---

[22]But note also Hans Biedermann's statement in his *Dictionary of Symbolism*,
trans. James Hulbert (1989; New York: Facts on File, 1992), 289: "In Christian
symbolism the red rose stood for the blood shed by Jesus on the Cross, and thus
for God's love." Certainly, a plausible reading could result from Biedermann's
identification.

cleansing and sustenance, and "Justice" is not untypical of Herbert in its mode of structure.

In a number of poems in *The Temple*, Herbert follows forms familiar from their employment in the Anglican liturgy. *The Book of Common Prayer,* of course, contains *The Psalter,* and Herbert, like many of his contemporaries, created paraphrases of various psalms. His most noteworthy, used as a hymn, is certainly "The Twenty-third Psalm" (162-63),[23] characterized by simplicity, succinctness, and dignity:

> The God of love my shepherd is,
> And he that doth me feed:
> While he is mine, and I am his,
> What can I want or need?

Herbert's only innovation in idea occurs in line one, where he calls "the Lord" (*Yahweh* in the Hebrew)[24] "the God of love," interpretive but appropriate, since the rest of the psalm illustrates the divine covenant love inherent in the Hebrew designation for deity. An original creation among Herbert's psalms is "Praise (2)" (137-38), according to Tobin, "made out of lines from a number of the Psalms of praise."[25] Herbert brings his expected skill in rhyme and metrics to the creation of this hymn composed of seven quatrains:

> King of Glory, King of Peace,   a   trochaic tetrameter
> I will love thee;   b   trochaic dimeter
> And that love may never cease,   a   trochaic tetrameter
> I will move thee.   b   trochaic dimeter

The second and fourth lines of successive stanzas conclude with rhyming groups (such as *love thee... move thee; heard me... spared me; sing thee ... bring thee; clear me... hear me; praise thee... raise thee; relentedst ... dissentedst; enrol thee ... extol thee*) which accentuate the forward movement of the verse toward its triumphant conclusion: "Ev'n eternity is too short / To extol thee." Thus does Herbert ever employ technique so as to harmonize with poetic intention as he translates Christian truth into celebratory art.

---

[23]Readers of the Penguin Classics edition are invited by Tobin (405-08) to compare Herbert's rendering with several others, including that of the *Book of Common Prayer,* the Authorized (or King James) Version, two by Sternhold and Hopkins, and that by Sir Philip Sydney.

[24]Holy Bible, New International Version (Grand Rapids: Zondervan Publishing House, 1984), x, 392.

[25]Tobin, *George Herbert: The Complete English Poems,* 395. The quoted lines appear in a note to the title.

Herbert's accomplishment in *The Temple* is noted by such diversity and richness, and this consideration of his modes of transformation of theology into poetry only begins to suggest the wealth and depth of meaning inherent in his work. Herbert demonstrates that orthodoxy in thought need not produce stultification of intellect or creativity. Indeed, readers who do not content themselves with surface readings should expect to find multiplicity of meaning, multiplex tonalities, and multivalence in appeal in all the aspects of Herbert's religious poetry; for this poet poured forth his devotion to God through consecrated intellect fused with high artistry and ingenious craftsmanship, a combination deserving of equally committed reader response.

Women, Culture, and Post-World War Two Pentecostalism

David G. Roebuck and Karen Carroll Mundy*

ARE YOU A QUEEN?

You may not be clothed in ermine,
Or bedecked in jewels rare;
Your feet not shod in golden slippers,
No chains of pearls entwine your hair;
A gaudy throne is not your place
Of ease, nor yet a mansion fair.

But these, my dear, make not a queen;
You see, they are but the outward scene.
If within, a heart of love and service true
Rules your every thought, so that you seem
To live for others, giving all to God and them—
Lift up your head, you're chief of that team.
And of a surety all want to crown you
A queen, in your home supreme.

Introduction

The poem "Are You A Queen?" introduced a new column to the readers of the *Church of God Evangel* in 1952. In this inaugural installment, the homemaker was encouraged to battle the temptation to become impatient with the repetitive tasks that kept her from the world her husband

*David G. Roebuck (Ph.D., Vanderbilt University). Assistant Professor of Religion and Director of the Hal Bernard Dixon, Jr. Pentecostal Research Center, Lee University. Karen Carroll Mundy (Ph.D., University of Tennessee). Professor of Sociology, Lee University.

entered every day. She was told that God created her to influence the destiny of the world through the training of her children. She was reminded that home, husband, and children were "God-given trusts." Accordingly, she was encouraged, "Take your rightful place as the queen of your home— –the loved, trusted and needed one!"[1] Of course, as the poem noted, her acclamation as queen was based on influence and service rather than fashion and position.

Published from 1952 through 1956, "The Homemaker's Chapel" attempted to speak to the needs of the mother who was keeping her home. There were no similar columns for working men or women, youth, or any other constituency—not even a regular column for ministers. Yet the Church of God considered support for the homemaker so vital that "The Homemaker's Chapel" appeared in almost every issue of the *Church of God Evangel* during this period of time.

While the World War may have ended in 1945, the Church of God found itself embattled in a new war—a war for the home and family and against the influence of the world. As in many wars throughout human history, leadership in this war marshaled troops and rallied supporters with vivid presentations of their enemy—presentations that elicited fear of the future and called for a return to a former ideal. The Church of God and the broader Pentecostal movement were not alone in this war, however. Indeed, a movement that prided itself on opposing American culture found itself marching lockstep with the culture in this war to save family.

Women were central in this war. In an effort to protect the home and family, the denomination circumscribed the roles of women and fortified the home. The results were greater restrictions on women than had previously existed. Because the Church of God saw women's fashions as revealing the downward spiral of worldliness in American culture, it increasingly spoke out against women's dress and decoration; because the Church of God perceived the very fabric of American society being threatened by communism from without[2] and the decay of law and order from within, the denomination proclaimed the importance of God's order as established in creation, particularly the submission of women in this order; and because the Church of God observed that the American home was in crisis, leadership cried out against women in the workplace and accentuated the role of homemaker.[3] By elevating certain roles for women,

---

[1]Avis Swiger, "The Homemaker's Chapel," *Church of God Evangel*, 20 September 1952, 11.

[2]For example, James A. Cross wrote, "If our government endures the insidious attacks made upon it by the communistic forces of today, the direct contributing factor must be the family and the home." J. A. Cross, "The Family," *Church of God Evangel*, 31 October 1953, 11.

[3]For a discussion of fashions and law and order see David G. Roebuck, "Limit-

particularly those related to home and family, women were conscripted into an "army" to save the family; and by denigrating alternative views, women were constricted into a safe, ordered existence. Indeed, women in ministry were casualties of that war.

The Pentecostal movement has been known for its openness to women ministers. The Church of God licensed women from a very early time. However, the period following World War II saw a significant change in the roles of women in the denomination. From a high of 18.2 percent in 1950, the percentage of ministers who were women declined to 7.7 percent by 1990.[4] This diminishing role of women in the Church of God during the post-war period is especially noteworthy when considered in the context of the cultural changes in American society. The "problem that has no name," described by Betty Friedan in her book in the early 1960s,[5] was in fact the idealized role of women promoted in the denomination. This circumscribing of the roles of women reflected the rhetoric of American culture immediately following the war. But such rhetoric belied the changing realities of women pouring into the workplace, and as the larger culture began to reconsider the work of women in the 1960s, the Church of God's voice was increasingly distant from the lives of women members.

Although there is some debate about the extent of the freedom and limitations Church of God women have experienced, our understanding of changes in the roles of women continues to advance. Carolyn Dirksen's "Let Your Women Keep Silence" described a past where women were respected and encouraged to exercise their many "gifts." Her thesis was that the decline of women leaders came with the exclusion of women from ordination and the rapidly growing bureaucracy.[6] The suggestion of a "golden age" for women in the early years of the denomination is consistent with the theory that religious movements often begin as sects. Sects appeal to the disadvantaged who "reject the rejectors," standing against a culture that excludes them. Women and other minorities find a home in sectarian movements, which provide an avenue for leadership that is precluded by conventional society. Such movements rarely offer complete

---

ing Liberty: The Church of God and Women Ministers, 1886-1996" (Ph.D. diss., Vanderbilt University, 1997), 213-26.

[4]This differs from Carolyn Rowland Dirksen's suggestion that a high of 29 percent of Church of God ministers were women in 1913. Dirksen's statistics were higher than those suggested here because they specifically excluded the office of deacon—an ordained order of ministry from which women were specifically excluded. See Roebuck, "Limiting Liberty," 57-60; and Carolyn Rowland Dirksen, "Let Your Women Keep Silence" in *The Promise and the Power: Essays on the Motivations, Developments, and Practices of the Church of God*, ed. Donald N. Bowdle (Cleveland, TN: Pathway Press, 1980), 177.

[5]Betty Freidan, *The Feminine Mystique* (New York: Dell, 1963).

[6]Dirksen, "Let Your Women Keep Silence," 165-96.

equality, however, and women in the Church of God have always experienced freedom within limits.[7]

Religious movements carry ideas that may change society. Classical Pentecostalism, as an expressive movement of the working class, often appealed to disenfranchised groups.[8] Its very hallmark of glossolalia made it appear suspect in respectable society. So it was not strange to have women preachers or daughters prophesying, because cultural rejection was a badge of honor. The implicit values of Pentecostalism facilitated upward mobility for believers. Thus, Benton Johnson asked in 1961, "Do Holiness Sects Socialize into Dominant Values?" His answer was "yes," and followed an essentially Weberian argument.[9]

Liston Pope considered the premise that religious beliefs foster upward mobility in his classic study of millhands and preachers in the mining towns of Appalachia.[10] The upward mobility of Pentecostal churches and the institutionalization of the movement narrowed the opportunities for ministry of laity and women. In their related study, "Prophetic vs. Priestly Religion: The Changing Role of Women Clergy in Classical Pentecostal Churches," Charles H. Barfoot and Gerald T. Sheppard suggested that the Pentecostal movement moved from ministry based on charisma and calling to routinization and regimentation, from the prophetic to the priestly.[11] Within the Church of God, ministry based on the priesthood of all believers became a priesthood of ordained men. As charisma and the charismatic leader declined in favor of the ordained minister in terms of

---

[7]Elsewhere Roebuck has suggested that although women had limited speech within early Pentecostalism, their boundaries prohibited egalitarianism and preclude identifying the early movement as a "golden age." See Roebuck, "Limiting Liberty," 21-65.

[8]Two studies that discuss the social origins of classical Pentecostalism include Thomas Hood and Karen Carroll Mundy, "Social Trends, Institutional Context, and Social Movement Organizations: Rationality and Emotional Expression in the Twentieth Century" (paper presented at the Southern Sociological Society, 1980); and Murl Dirksen and Karen Carroll Mundy, "Social Justice and Evangelization: A Pentecostal Perspective" (paper presented at the International Roman-Catholic Pentecostal Dialogue, Paris, France, 1993).

[9]Benton Johnson, "Do Holiness Sects Socialize into Dominant Values," *Social Forces* 34 (1955-1956): 309-16. The Weberian argument is that religious ideas can transform the material conditions of society. This is the thesis of Max Weber's book, *The Protestant Ethic and the Spirit of Capitalism* (New York: Scribner and Sons, 1958).

[10]Liston Pope, *Millhands and Preachers* (New Haven: Yale University Press, 1942).

[11]Charles H. Barfoot and Gerald T. Sheppard, "Prophetic vs. Priestly Religion: The Changing Role of Women Clergy in Classical Pentecostal Churches," *Review*

institutional importance, the ministry of women was moved to the margins of the denomination.[12]

It is not our purpose to dwell on the role of women in the early days of the Church of God, except as a reference point for more contemporary analysis. Mickey Crews, in his *The Church of God: A Social History*, surveyed the ministries of women and suggested that Victorian ideals concerning the place of women influenced attitudes toward women in the early years of the Church of God. After World War II, the Church of God encouraged traditional roles for women and looked askance at the Women's Rights Movement and the Equal Rights Amendment.[13] If the sect-church model can be applied to the Church of God, it seems logical that the role of women in the early years of the denomination should challenge the dominant culture rather than reflect Victorian ideals. However, it is possible, although not consistent, to hold to the ideals of a culture while also rejecting them. Early Pentecostals could then embrace a faith that encouraged women and minorities and the poor to find service in the church, while also professing a Victorian worldview inconsistent with these very actions.

David G. Roebuck further explored the changes in attitudes of the Church of God as an institution in his 1997 dissertation, "Limiting Liberty: The Church of God and Women Ministers, 1886-1996." According to Roebuck, the decline of women in ministry in the Church of God must be understood within the context of the denomination's interaction with changes in gender roles in American culture. Although the Church of God was at the forefront of allowing women to preach, the denomination has had a narrow understanding of women's place. Often the Church of God responded negatively to the enlarging of roles for women in American culture. Changes in the roles of women were perceived as compromise with the world. The women who adapted to these changes were "worldly." Following World War II, the intensity of the rhetoric increased, battle lines were clearly delineated, and women were challenged to choose immediately between the church and the world.

Surprisingly, for the period immediately following World War II, this negative reaction to changes in women's roles was in actuality an

---

of Religious Research 22/1 (September 1980): 2-17.
[12]Understanding the roles of women in a denomination requires an institutional context. For example, Mark Chaves, in his book, *Ordaining Women: Culture and Conflict in Religious Organizations* (Cambridge, MA: Harvard University Press, 1977), considers the internal environment of the denomination, as well as the way denominations negotiate with external environments. The woman question, in this case the ordination of women, is decided both internally and with an eye to external constraints and influences.
[13]Mickey Crews, *The Church of God: A Social History* (Knoxville: University

adaptation to the culture rather than a clear separation from American culture.[14] As women quickly moved into the workplace, the dominant American culture reacted in fear toward these changes that were taking place—perhaps as a futile attempt to restore a dying ideal. By the 1960s, a new reality was emerging for American women—a reality that soon placed Church of God rhetoric out of step with the majority of women.

I. A Culture of Fear and Containment

The roles of women in American culture have changed dramatically during this century. The first two decades witnessed the emergence of the New Woman. Two decades later, the 1940s and 1950s saw radical shifts in the numbers of working mothers. An emphasis on women's liberation followed in the 1960s. Public debate about women's proper place accompanied each of these changes. Such shifts in women's roles in American society frightened many Pentecostals. Even those who traditionally were the most supportive of women ministers, such as the International Church of the Foursquare Gospel founded by Aimee Semple McPherson, began to question that support.[15]

Pentecostals were not alone in their fear of societal changes, however. Such fear was common among Americans. Brett Harvey emphasized the magnitude of this fear that gripped American society following World War II in her book, *The Fifties: A Women's Oral History*. According to Harvey, fear was the "engine" that drove the rules. Two world wars and a depression had given Americans something about which to be afraid. Although the Allies had won the war, the nation continued to experience "a sense of vulnerability." The world continued to be a dangerous place. Leaders

of Tennessee Press, 1990), 98, 105.

[14]Edith Blumhofer has suggested that Evangelicals and Pentecostals have "simply reacted to social changes related to the role of women rather than searching for a response faithful to their own inheritance. She noted the "yearning for order" in the face of cultural disorder and a hardening of views regarding biblical authority. For women, this resulted in an increasing focus on family and the subordinate role of women within the family. Edith L. Blumhofer, "Women in Evangelicalism and Pentecostalism," in *Women and Church: The Challenge of Ecumenical Solidarity in an Age of Alienation*, ed. Melanie A. May (Grand Rapids: William B. Eerdmans, 1991), 3.

[15]According to General Supervisor Eugene Kurtz, Foursquare Gospel congregations became increasingly reluctant to accept women pastors during the 1940s. Kurtz believed that because of society's concerns about proper place, the women who were most successful as pastors were those who had been at their churches for a long time or those who were able to validate their ministries with "signs and wonders." Eugene Kurtz, Interview by David G. Roebuck, March 13, 1991, personal notes in possession of author, Cleveland, Tennessee. Kurtz was the

warned that the single goal of the "Red tide" was to destroy the American way of life. Demagogues such as Senator Joe McCarthy created an atmosphere of suspicion.[16]

Consequently, "containment" became the political policy and a social obsession for the nation. According to Harvey, "The response of government, aided by the social scientists and the media, was a massive effort to channel all these disturbing energies into one safe harbor: the family."[17] Joseph Gusfield, in his book, *Symbolic Crusade: Status Politics and the American Temperance Movement*, noted that fear of change is a catalyst for moral crusades. Status groups who see their way of life threatened will support moral reform as a solution to culture conflict.[18] Thus, the nation experienced a "headlong rush into domesticity" in which a woman's entire world was ideally contained within her marriage and family. American society came to view those who looked outside the family for satisfaction as "unwomanly."[19] Glenna Matthews concurred that the home of the 1950s became a haven for women as it had been in the antebellum years. This time society expected women to keep silent, however. The domesticity of the nineteenth century had empowered women as moral agents of change,[20] but the domesticity of the 1950s combined with the pervading fear of the time made it difficult for women to think of themselves as able to influence society.

Society, and the Church of God, viewed the career woman as a threat. According to Matthews, "In an age of anxiety engendered by the Cold War and the nuclear threat, the chief quality desired of women was that they be soothing . . . . The woman who was reluctant to cater to the whims of another adult was unfeminine, according to the best wisdom of the day."[21] The social and political policies of the day made this lifestyle possible for many women. Financing of inexpensive homes in suburbia,

---

supervisor of all churches in the United States at the time of the interview.
   [16]Brett Harvey, *The Fifties: A Women's Oral History* (New York: HarperColliins Publishers, 1993), xii-xiii.
   [17]Ibid., xiv.
   [18]Joseph Gusfield, *Symbolic Crusade: Status Politics and the American Temperance Movement* (Urbana: University of Illinois Press, 1993).
   [19]Harvey, *The Fifties*, 70-72. Harvey cited a 1959 *Life* magazine cover story that reflected the intertwined themes of fear, family, and a growing consumerism. The magazine pictured "a newlywed couple spending their honeymoon in their own bomb shelter, surrounded by canned goods, water supplies, and generators: a perfect metaphor for marriage as a self-contained world—secure, private, surrounded by consumer goods."
   [20]Glenna Matthews, *"Just A Housewife": The Rise and Fall of Domesticity in America* (New York: Oxford University Press, 1987), 64-65.
   [21]Ibid., 210. Matthews suggested that the best known housewife of the 1950s was Lucy Ricardo of the television show, "I Love Lucy." When she attempted to get into her husband's show, he stopped her because her place was at home. When

almost universal car ownership, the highway system, and an abundance of consumer goods made it possible for women to be servants of the family.[22]

Perhaps the other side of the cultural icon of woman as family servant was the greedy family, so aptly described by Arlie Hochschild and Anne Machung.[23] Greedy families would not be considered, however, until the backlash against the superwoman in the 1980s. Hochschild would take her argument a step further in the late 1990s, asserting that women were under such pressure at home that work was becoming their refuge.[24]

II. Fortifying the Ideal

In the 1950s, the Church of God engaged in the battle against the changing roles of women in American culture with a reassertion and some-times exaggeration of earlier ideals. This concern manifested itself in a renewed call for women to take their proper biblical roles in the home[25] and was part of a new attitude toward women working that had been develop-ing since World War II. The denomination quickly marshaled its efforts to protect the family. James A. Cross blamed the breakdown of the family on war jobs:

> In the mass migration that has been on for the past few years, there has been much family disorganization. Much of the delinquency among both the juvenile and the adult is the di-rect result of mass migration to the war works where jobs are plentiful and many members of the family can be employed.[26]

Clearly women belonged in the home in this battle for home and family. Both the editor of the *Church of God Evangel*, J. D. Bright, and his wife emphasized the importance of the mother in the home. She wrote, "By far the greatest sphere of the wife's work for the kingdom of God is in the home. The true wife is the helpmeet of her husband."[27] He deplored the

---

she did perform, her performance was ridiculous.

[22]Ibid., *"Just A Housewife,"* 212.

[23]Arlie Hochschild and Anne Machung, *The Second Shift: Working Parents and the Revolution at Home* (New York: Viking Press, 1989).

[24]Arlie Hochschild, *The Time Bind: When Work Becomes Home and Home Becomes Work* (New York: Henry Holt & Company, 1997).

[25]As examples, see Nettie M. Hanvey, "A Mother's Debt to Her Home and Her Church," *Church of God Evangel*, 7 May 1949, 5, 15; Mrs. Doyle Stanfield, "The Woman's Page: A Woman in the House," *Church of God Evangel*, 21 January 1963, 15; and Dora P. Myers, "The Woman's Page: A Woman's Place in Prayer," *Church of God Evangel*, 4 March 1963, 14.

[26]Cross, "The Family," 9.

rise of babysitters and pondered, "I wonder what will become of that grand old domestic statement honoring motherhood, 'the hand that rocks the cradle rules the world.'"[28] Another article, lamenting the changes that were taking place in American society, praised the American heritage that had produced a "virtuous womanhood that made early American home a little heaven instead of just a place to eat, sleep, and quarrel."[29]

In an article entitled, "A Helpmeet for Man," James L. Slay commented on the fact that despite modern advancements, "there is more trouble in the home than ever before."[30] According to Slay, the primary reason for such difficulty was the abandoning of biblical principles. Advising young men, Slay suggested, "Better to have a wife that knows how to keep house than to have a girl who knows how to dance or jitterbug." Slay continued, "The wife more than anyone else, makes the home something other than a house with walls . . . . We feel that God made woman to be in the home, and it was a sad day for us when the mothers left home and went to work."[31] At a later date, the *Church of God Evangel* included an article on the "Editorials" page entitled, "Half Working Women in Nation Are Married."[32] One writer tried to reassure women, who felt as youth that they should be serving God on a full-time basis, that they should abandon their guilt and serve God exactly where they were. After all, the division between secular and sacred occupations was a false division. Yet after assuring her readers that their present roles were a place of service to God, the author only spoke of two possibilities: the "mother and housewife" and the "unmarried woman serving in the business world or chosen career."[33]

Despite the concerns regarding women working, by the 1960s the denomination reluctantly admitted that women were a permanent part of the workforce. If a woman did enter the workplace, she was encouraged to find opportunities to be a Christian example.[34] Although there are no

---

[27]Mrs. J. D. Bright, "The Pastor's Wife," *Church of God Evangel*, 7 May 1949, 4.

[28]J. D. Bright, "Bonded Baby Sitter," *Church of God Evangel*, 13 May 1950, 3.

[29]George L. Britt, "Our American Heritage," *The Lighted Pathway*, July 1949, 13.

[30]James L. Slay, "A Helpmeet for Man," *Church of God Evangel*, 1 October 1949, 8.

[31]Ibid., 15.

[32]Although this reprint of an Associated Press article did not comment on the value of this point, the very fact that it was reprinted was a negative signal regarding the situation. Reprinted articles on the editorial page frequently informed the readership of problems around the world. "Half Working Women in Nation Are Married," *Church of God Evangel*, 23 July 1949, 3.

[33]Mrs. Paul S. Cook, "The Woman's Page: Secular or Sacred," *Church of God Evangel,* 15 April 1963, 9, 17.

[34]Barbara Moore Page, "The Woman's Page: Christian Women in the Business World," *Church of God Evangel*, 9 December 1963, 10; Lucy Harris Bennett, "A

statistics available about the number of Church of God women entering the work force, there is no reason to believe that they were different from other American women—35 percent of whom were in the workforce by 1965.[35] Many Church of God families came from working-class backgrounds where the outside employment of the wife was essential to the family. Whatever the actual numbers, the denomination continued to speak out against the trend of working mothers. This was especially insensitive to working women,who were often the backbone of the local church and struggling to support their families.

Regarding women in ministry, it can be surmised that if more Church of God women were both raising a family and working outside the home, then fewer women had the time or energy to be involved in ministry. The rhetoric regarding women's place in the home was potentially discouraging to married women considering a commitment to ministry.[36] Would not the same arguments that a woman should not be in a factory apply to a woman preaching revivals?

Although Church of God women were working outside the home, the denomination continued to call for women's proper place in the home and society as it entered the turbulent 1960s. James A. Cross repeatedly expressed alarm about the disintegration of the home in his general overseer's address in 1962. In addition to the rise of divorce and the elimination of prayer and Bible reading from the public schools, Cross noted that the responsibility of caring for children had been turned over to babysitters—an implied call for the return of the mother to the home.[37] Certainly women carried a special responsibility for these terrible circumstances. Along this theme, Mrs. Charles W. Conn, wife of the general overseer and president of the Ladies Willing Worker Band (now the Department of Women's Ministries), wrote a four-part series in the *Church of God Evangel* entitled, "Woman and the Home." According to Edna Conn, "Woman is divinely ordained and endowed for the responsibilities of a wife, mother, and homemaker."[38]

Christian Businesswoman Witnesses," *Church of God Evangel*, 13 September 1965, 10-11, 19; Mrs. Daniel N. Sikes, "God's Woman in Today's World," *Church of God Evangel*, 13 October 1975, 10, 29; and Faye McBrayer, "God's Woman in Today's Education," *Church of God Evangel*, 13 October 1975, 12, 19.

[35]Alice Kessler-Harris, *Out to Work: A History of Wage-earning Women in the United States* (New York: Oxford University Press, 1982), 301.

[36]Although an emphasis on family and home may not have discouraged single women from entering the ministry, it clearly assumed that the ideal roles for any woman were those of wife and mother. Consequently single women ministers were encouraged to marry.

[37]J. A. Cross, "Let the Church Speak," *Minutes of the 49th General Assembly* (Cleveland, TN: Church of God Publishing House, 1962), 9-11.

[38]Mrs. Charles W. Conn, "Woman and the Home," *Church of God Evangel*, 20

Of course, the Department of Women's Ministries emphasized the family. Articles in their publication, *The Willing Worker* (later called *Unique*), regularly discussed the importance of the family and the roles of women in the family.[39] Advertisements featured books related to the family.[40] The disintegration of family life was lamented, often with an appeal to mothers to keep the family together.[41] Working mothers were devalued and particularly viewed as damaging for children.[42] One executive official writing in *The Willing Worker* attributed a "spiritual dearth" in the church to women working outside the home.[43] Additionally, the department routinely criticized the women's liberation movement. It was condemned because God already had given women sufficient opportunities,[44] because women already had influence without being militant,[45] because it promoted a variety of sinful activities,[46] and because it did not teach the

May 1968, 10.

[39]As examples, see Florence Clawson, "The Christian Home," *The Willing Worker*, Winter 1969-1970, 7; "Do You Have A Family Altar," *The Willing Worker*, Spring 1971, 13; Mrs. H. G. Poiter, "Our Family Altar," *The Willing Worker*, July-August 1972, 8; Mrs. Jim O. McClain, "Rekindling the Fire on Your Family Altar," *The Willing Worker*, November-December 1972, 10-11, 18.

[40]As examples, see "Choice Books," *The Willing Worker*, Winter 1969-1970, 20 and "Book Reviews," *The Willing Worker*, March-April 1984, 15.

[41]Mrs. R. Leonard Carroll, "An Open Letter from the President," *The Willing Worker*, Winter 1970-1971, 4-5; Euverla Hughes, "The National President: More Godly Mothers," *The Willing Worker*, May-June 1979, 3; Mrs. James D. (Rebecca) Jenkins, "E. R. A. Revival," *The Willing Worker*, March-April 1980, 22; Peggy Scarborough, "The Hedge around the Home," *The Willing Worker*, March-April 1982, 16-17; and Helen Elizabeth Taylor, "Family Reflections," *The Willing Worker*, September-October 1982, 18-19.

[42]"A Letter from Mama," *The Willing Worker*, January-February 1979, 17.

[43]Robert White, "Women in Worship and Celebration," *The Willing Worker*, September-October 1984, 4. White lamented the changes in the way women were participating in worship, particularly the fact that they rarely spent long hours in prayer and visitation as they once had. According to White, now that more women were working outside the home and heading single-parent families, there was little time for these activities.

[44]Mrs. S. E. Jennings, "Our Place," *The Willing Worker*, Winter 1970-1971, 8. For Jennings, ministry primarily related to kindness, encouragement, and prayer.

[45]This article began with the story of Sally Olsen, a prison chaplain in Puerto Rico. Darter concluded she and her readers would "likely never be a Sally Olsen" but were needed more to influence persons not to go to prison. Willie Lee Darter, "God's Woman," *The Willing Worker*, Spring 1971, 3, 19.

[46]In addition to destroying marriages and promoting homosexuality, discussed elsewhere, women's liberation was blamed for an increase in smoking among teenage girls. "Family Forum: 20th Century Women Addressing Issues of Our Day," *The Willing Worker*, May-June 1980, 8, reprinted from "Teen Girls Puff Away," *Chicago Tribune*.

proper biblical position about the submission of women to their husbands as well as the importance of homemaking.[47]

As a counter-offensive to the "women's liberation movement," the Department of Ladies Ministries stressed the importance of homemaking. Opposition to women in the workplace and the significance of women in the home was, of course, based on the Church of God's reading of Scripture, especially Titus 2:3-5:

> The aged women likewise, that they be in behavior as becometh holiness, not false accusers, not given to much wine, teachers of good things; That they may teach the young women to be sober, to love their husbands, to love their children, To be discreet, chaste, *keepers at home*, good, obedient to their own husbands, that the word of God be not blasphemed.[48]

One article used this passage to speak to the importance of woman as keeper and queen of her home rather than employee:

> Keepers of the home. Here I'm afraid is where a lot of wives fail . . . but God's Word says we're to be "keepers at home." There are many advantages to keeping houses that are over-looked. It is much better to be at home and be in your own private kingdom than to be out competing in a man's world where the attitude seems to be "dog eat dog." Who wouldn't prefer to be at home surrounded by the love of your children and your husband than to be at the mercy of this evil world. Count your blessings and be glad you're at home.[49]

The author then asked, "Why try to be something God never intended you to be? Be a wife, be a housekeeper, be a mother, and be glad and rejoice because God has seen fit to bless you with a good husband and living children."[50] Thus, the empowerment of women could only come

---

[47]Mrs. A. C. Wheeler, "Women's Lib: Who Needs It?" *The Willing Worker*, Winter 1971-1972, 3, 16; Garnella Covington, "Where Do We Go from Here?," *The Willing Worker*, November-December 1975, 5; Peggy Scarborough, "The World Is Waiting for Us," *The Willing Worker*, July-August 1975, 10-11; and Helen Taylor, "Family Reflections," *The Willing Worker*, January-February 1983, 12.

[48]Quoted in Mrs. James Franklin, "The Woman's Page: The Position of Wives," *Church of God Evangel*, 20 May 1963, 11 (italics added).

[49]Ibid., 11.

[50]Ibid. See also, Mrs. Noelle Midgley, "The Woman's Page: Missionary Housewife," *The Church of God Evangel*, 18 November 1963, 9; Ellen B. French, "Our Heritage," *Church of God Evangel*, 3 May 1965, 5, 19; Mrs. Ernestine McGee, "The Helpmate," *Church of God Evangel*, 3 May 1965, 16, 23; Mrs. Hollis L. Green, "Homemaking: Art Or Job?" *The Willing Worker*, July-August 1972, 9, 18; and Dalpha Parsons, "God's Woman in the Home," *Church of God*

through the relinquishing of power through submission to God and husband. Although the reality was that more and more women were entering the work force, the Department of Ladies Ministries continued to emphasize the importance of the home.

Calls for men to take their rightful place in all areas of life accompanied the call for women to return to the home. One of the best examples of this was an article entitled "God Wants Men." According to the author, who made it clear that he was talking about males rather than "the weaker sex," "God is looking for men. There is much work that needs to be done: God wants men to do it."[51] The author lamented the fact that at a recent missions rally more women than men responded to the call to the mission field. He highlighted "heroic men of God" in the Scriptures, the history of Christianity, world politics, and the business world. Suggesting that "True Christianity is manliness . . . ," he asked, "Brethren, how long will we let the fairer sex put us to shame? Why should there be more women than men going to the mission fields?"[52] The author concluded with an examination of why more men should be responding to the call of God. His first concern was:

> Fulfilling the great commission is a man's job. It was given
> first to men. In the Old Testament the elders appointed to
> assist Moses were men; the great prophets were mostly men;
> and in the New Testament the disciples chosen by Jesus, and
> even the deacons chosen by the early Church, were men. . . .
> At home and abroad, the cry of the hour is, "God wants men."
> . . . The challenge of the hour must be faced; the needs can be
> met—by men of God![53]

In the context of the increased rhetoric regarding women's proper place, articles like this one sent a clear message about the importance of separate spheres for men and women in the home and in ministry.

Conclusion

Following World War II there was a significant emphasis in the United States on the importance of the home and women's place in the home. This emphasis grew out of an attempt to return to an earlier ideal and a fear of rapid social changes. The image of the mother as homemaker was a

---

Evangel, 13 October 1976, 11, 19.
    [51]Leonard S. Stahl, "God Wants Men," *Church of God Evangel*, 18 March 1957, 5.
    [52]Ibid., 6-7.
    [53]Ibid., 7.

powerful image that stood at the center of this rhetoric. Yet, in many ways this was an attempt to reassert an ideology that was becoming less and less possible for many women. For women entering the middle class, however, the ideology was a powerful influence.

This ideology was especially influential in the Church of God, which considered itself to be entering the middle class. Bolstered by the denomination's entrance into the broader Evangelical world, particularly in its relationship with the National Association of Evangelicals, the Church of God included this ideology in its portrait of women and their roles in the home, society, and the church. Although the denomination did not teach explicitly that women did not belong in the pulpit, they did increasingly emphasize the role of women in the home.

Altogether, these conditions created an environment that discouraged young women from entering into "official" ministry. This was in contrast to cultural trends that encouraged women to dream and consider new areas of work and activity. Thus, Church of God women were faced with contradictions of culture and subculture, and a church rhetoric of inclusion into the body of Christ but exclusion from the work of the denomination.

Hans Küng on the Nature of the Church

Faye S. Bodley[*]

Introduction

During the second session of Vatican II (1963), Hans Küng began *Die Kirche* as an explication of the Council's theological activity, not completing his work until 1967, the year after Vatican II concluded. Küng's intention was to create a detailed analysis of those things he considered to be the constituent parts of the 'true Church.' The end result is an ecclesiology that reflects the innovative spirit of Pope John XXIII who, through calling the Council, wished to allow some "fresh air" to blow through Roman Catholicism. In *Die Kirche*, Küng, breaking with traditional idealized and irreproachable views of Roman Catholic ecclesiology, attempts to evaluate and prescribe the vocations for a truly Holy and Catholic Church.[1] Due to his criticisms of Papal infallibility and Church hierarchy, Küng was censured by the Vatican and charged with doctrinal heresy.[2] The purpose of this essay is to explore the foundational theological criterion upon which Küng builds his ecclesiology and to examine how this criterion influences and shapes his prescription for the ordering of the 'true Church.' Küng's prescription will then be evaluated according to his Roman context so as to demonstrate how this prescription places him at odds with his Vatican contemporaries.

---

[*]Faye S. Bodley (M.Div. student, Gordon-Conwell Theological Seminary).
[1]Robert Nowell, *A Passion for Truth: Hans Küng and His Theology* (New York: Crossroads, 1981), 136-37.
[2]David L. Mueller, "Hans Küng—in Limbo?" *Perspectives in Religious Studies* 8 (1981): 12.

I. The Gospel

The foundational theological criterion that molds and shapes Küng's doctrine of revelation and hence influences his entire ecclesiology is the Gospel, the testimony of the first witnesses to the life and works of Jesus of Nazareth. As such, the Gospel is the standard by which the Church through the ages is to examine and reform itself. Küng opens his volume by distinguishing between the essential nature of the Church and its historical form, stressing the interdependence of the two. Out of the context of this distinction he draws his criterion. Küng's starting point for his ecclesiology is rooted in his understanding that the essential nature of the Church, drawn from its permanently decisive historical origins, finds expression in its changing historical forms. This constant factor, the true and permanent nature, can only be discerned when it appears constant, in different particular historical forms, surviving all changes in each form. Essence and form are inseparable, for an essence that has no form is unreal, and is a metaphysical ideal rather than an existential reality amidst continual historical metamorphoses. However, the two are not to be equated, for only by distinguishing between them can a criterion or norm be established by which what is legitimate in any historical manifestation of the Church might be determined.[3]

According to Küng, the New Testament church should not be used as the criterion by which to determine whether a particular historical form conforms to the Church's true nature, for within the New Testament are present different images of the Church from which the different historical forms later developed. The New Testament must be taken as a whole, and through exegesis it must be determined out of the many voices within it what is common in all its images of the church and all its presentations of the life and teachings of Jesus. Such a study reveals that the Gospel message of God's saving act in Jesus Christ (that which frees from the Law and offers the free gift of forgiveness of sins and a new righteousness to all who renounce their own worth before God) is the common point for all testimonies and images.[4] This Gospel is the initial testimony to and understanding of the first witnesses to the life and actions and preaching of Jesus of Nazareth. Jesus of Nazareth, by virtue of his person and work rather than any documents or declarations, demonstrates himself unequivocally as God's revelation. The Gospel, the testimony of the first witnesses, unerringly reflects this revelation—hence this Gospel, this indissoluble reality, is the only infallible norm to which all other personal and written

---

[3]Hans Küng, *The Church* (New York: Sheed and Ward, 1967), 4-6, 28.
[4]Ibid., 15-24.

norms must conform, and by which all historical manifestations of the Church are to be evaluated.[5]
The original testimony to this Gospel is first given to us in the Old Testament and then in the New Testament. For Küng, Scripture is not itself revelation but attests to that revelation of God in Jesus of Nazareth.[6] In critique of the Roman Catholic tradition, Küng declares Scripture is not to be regarded as infallible, for the writings are completely human documents composed by human authors with human gifts and limitations and potentialities for both knowledge and for error. The consequence is that the possibility of errors cannot be totally excluded. Scripture is inspired insofar as God acts with and on the hearer through the human words of Scripture, causing the words to move the hearer to faith, so that the words become instruments of the Spirit. Scripture is infallible in that through human frailty, historical conditioning and limitations of the authors, God's call—as it was finally sounded aloud in Jesus—is truthfully heard, believed, and realized.[7]
The unique place of these kerygmatically-minded fallible human documents lies in their being the only testimonies recognized and acknowledged by the Church as sound, original tradition.[8] The Scripture is (by virtue of its originality) unique, incomparable, and unrepeatable. It is therefore actively obligatory—binding and normative for the Church in all ages.[9] It is normative secondarily, to the degree that it reflects the primary norm, the Gospel. The Gospel is contained within the New Testament as a whole, amid distortions and errors, but this original testimony may be extracted from the New Testament with high probability through the use of the modern historical-critical method.[10] The Church in each of its historical manifestations must take the Gospel as its starting point and "do all it can to make critical evaluations, as a foundation for the reforms and renewal, which the Church will always need."[11]
The New Testament church, by virtue of its closeness in temporal proximity to Jesus Christ, reflects the original design for the Church.[12] Hence Küng argues, in consistency with the historical orientation of his theology, that normative priority must be given to the earliest models of ecclesiology, which the New Testament church presents. In this respect, the Gospel as found in the New Testament through exegesis has primacy

---

[5]Peter Chirico, "Infallibility: Rapprochement Between Küng and the Official Church?" *Theological Studies* 42, no. 4 (1981): 534-36.
[6]Küng, *The Church*, 15-24.
[7]Ibid., 218-19.
[8]Chirico, "Infallibility," 534-36.
[9]Küng, *The Church*, 15-24.
[10]Chirico, "Infallibility," 535-36.
[11]Küng, *The Church*, 28.
[12]Ibid., 24.

over Church tradition, which can at best do no more than circle around this original testimony to interpret, comment, explain, and apply the original Gospel message according to constantly changing historical situations.[13] However, Küng asserts that although an absolute precedent is to be granted Scripture, it can be rightly read only within the Church, so that ultimately Scripture and Church tradition belong together.[14] Nevertheless, "the New Testament message, as the original testimony, is the highest court to which appeal must be made in all the changes of history."[15]

Küng not only redefines the concept of infallibility with respect to Scripture but also with respect to the papacy. At this point he clashes with the Roman understanding of papal infallibility, set forth by Vatican I, which affirms the jurisdictional primacy of the Pope and the infallibility and immutability of the Pope's ex-cathedra pronouncements.[16] Küng argues that one cannot reconcile Rome's claim to essential infallibility with its history of undeniable errors. The attribution of infallibility to the college of bishops, he says, has its roots in the traditional theory of the bishops' direct and exclusive apostolic succession, a theory that he dismisses as unhistorical. Küng questions the concept of infallible pronouncements on the basis that human propositions by nature fall short of perfect reality and can only be translated within definitive human limits. Therefore, a considerable degree of ambiguity is inherent in propositions, which can consequently be understood differently by different people, so that regardless of motivation, misunderstandings and misuse are inevitable.[17] Infallibility must no longer be understood as the Church being free from error, as it has been traditionally understood. Rather, the idea behind this term should be that "the Church is not deceiving or deceived." Despite all error and sin, the Church has not ultimately been corrupted but has remained in the truth. Küng redefines infallibility as "a fundamental remaining in the truth, which is not disturbed by individual errors."[18] The great miracle is not that error never occurred, but rather that by the work of the Holy Spirit, the Church—in spite of all her defection from God—has continued to be sustained by God through the ages. Thus the Church ultimately shares in the truth of the Holy Spirit in the Church, the Spirit who can neither deceive nor be deceived.[19]

---

[13]Ibid., 15-24.

[14]Nowell, *A Passion for Truth,* 72.

[15]Küng, *The Church,* 24.

[16]Jürgen Moltmann, "Hans Küng, Rome and the Gospel," *The Christian Century* 97 (1980): 189; John Jay Hughes, "Hans Küng and the Magisterium," *Theological Studies* 41, no. 2 (1980): 383.

[17]Nowell, *A Passion for Truth,* 191-92.

[18]Küng, *The Church,* 342-43; cf. Nowell, "*A Passion for Truth,* 193-98.

[19]Küng, *The Church,* 342-43.

II. Ecclesiological Structure

Drawing from his principle of "primacy of originality," Küng's critique of Roman Catholic ecclesiology extends beyond the arena of revelation to the governing structure of the visible Church. He finds in Scripture seemingly contradictory images of what the Church structure should be, and to these Scriptural foundations he attributes the divergence of governing models within Protestant and Roman Catholic ecclesiologies. Here, he explains, is found a particular instance in Scripture that exemplifies his principle that changing situations and individuals give rise to diverging views and differing forms of ecclesiology. As the Gospel has been proclaimed throughout the ages, the mode of proclamation has changed. This change compels a constant modification of the original message, and the human and theological individuality of each new person, making the proclamation, plays a considerable role in this. Thus, reasons Küng, mutually opposed differences in the New Testament were bound to come about.[20]

Relying on the historical-critical method, Küng identifies in the Pauline epistles a reflection of what he believes to be the Church's earliest dominant ecclesiological structure. Romans 12, 1 Corinthians 12, Colossians 1, and Ephesians 4 all testify to a prevailing pneumatic or charismatic structure. In these texts, he contends, there is no reference to ordination or to the offices of bishop and elder. Paul speaks simply of the charismatic gifts, bestowed by the Holy Spirit upon each of the members of the body in varying degrees, which lie at the basis of ministry. While Paul does distinguish between apostles, teachers, prophets, and evangelists, the early Pauline churches show no evidence of having produced a ruling class.[21] According to Pauline understanding, the Church is constituted by the Spirit who gives to each member a gift or *charisma*. Küng defines *charisma* as signifying "the call of God, addressed to an individual, to a particular ministry in the community, which brings with it the ability to fulfill that ministry."[22] Charismatic gifts embrace not only leadership and preaching positions, but involve many forms of service on behalf of others. Consequently charisms cannot possibly be limited to those who hold office.[23] The charisms of leadership did not produce a ruling class of those endowed with the Spirit who separated themselves from the community and rose above it to rule over it. On the contrary, the charisms of

---

[20]G. H. Duggan, *Hans Küng and Reunion* (Westminster: Newman, 1964), 30-32.
[21]John Kiwiet, *Hans Küng,* Makers of the Modern Theological Mind, ed. Bob E. Patterson (Peabody: Hendrickson, 1991), 75-6; Küng, *The Church,* 179, 187.
[22]Ibid., 188.
[23]Ibid., 179-84.

leadership are characterized by service in humility.[24] Thus the charismatic structure of the Church includes, but goes far beyond, the hierarchical structure of the Church. It is the Holy Spirit who orders the outworking of these charisms. Any individual who attempts to set themselves above others and to seize control will create disorder rather than order.[25]

This understanding of the pneumatically endowed early Church brings Küng to examine critically the Roman Catholic structure wherein only ecclesiastical officials rather than all members are active and to question whether "the Spirit has not been sacrificed along with the spiritual gifts."[26] His emphasis upon the Church as a community of people endowed for service by the Spirit stands in contrast to the Petrine episcopacy reaffirmed in Vatican II, which understands the Church as a society subsisting in the governing succession of Peter and the bishops in communion with him. Küng criticizes this understanding because it regards the laity as a mere appendage of the Church rather than the true constituency of the Church.[27]

Küng criticizes the Roman Catholic Church for neglecting these earlier New Testament passages and limiting their sources for ecclesiastical structure to the models reflected in the Pastoral Epistles and Acts, which he holds as representative of a later period of canonical literature. The charismatic structure of the early Christian Church was dismissed as obsolete when it should have been given "a primacy of originality" because of its temporal closeness to the Gospel of Jesus. Roman institutionalization, says Küng, arose from the Pastoral letters where the term *charisma* is used only twice and then in connection with ordination (for example, 1 Tim 4:14, 2 Tim 1:6). The book of Acts speaks of the laying on of hands without reference to the charisms. Every evidence of hierarchical structure in the early Church, such as the appointing of elders, Küng insists, should be interpreted against the background of the fundamentally charismatic structure of the Church, that is, those Spirit-endowed dispensations of personal empowering.[28] Küng does not call for the abandoning of the episcopal structure of the Roman Catholic Church, for both the pneumatic and the hierarchical structure have a legitimate Scriptural basis. He calls instead for a reconstruction of the nature of the episcopal office in terms of service (as it was initially intended) rather than as it is presently

---

[24]Ibid., 187.
[25]Ibid., 188-89.
[26]Ibid., 187.
[27]Bernard M. G. Reardon, "Recent Thinking on Christian Beliefs: The Doctrine of the Church in Recent Catholic Theology," *The Expository Times* 88, no. 6 (1977): 165.
[28]Kiwiet, *Hans Küng*, 75-76; Küng, *The Church*, 179-80, 190.

understood in terms of authority, dominion, rule, and subjugation. The office should be seen not so much as a matter of authority as service.[29] Küng wrestles with the question of whether there are legitimate grounds for assuming the primacy of Peter, and if so whether that primacy should continue, specifically through the bishop of Rome.[30] In his discussion of the apostolic dimension of the Church, he overturns the traditional Roman Catholic understanding of apostolic succession as involving those juridical successors of the Roman See; apostolic succession is a matter of obedience and consequently the whole Church is the successor of the apostles.[31] The apostolic office as a whole is thus unique and unrepeatable. The decisive element in the early church for apostolicity, according to Küng, involved a personal and direct meeting with the risen Christ, by which the apostles all—in one form or another—knew Jesus as one who had been dead and was alive again. Apostolicity understood in this sense does not allow successors to the apostles; instead apostolic mission and ministry are inherited. These Küng redefines in terms of obedience to the apostles as original witnesses and messengers of the risen Christ. Apostolic succession is not limited to a few individuals but incorporates the whole Church. The Church is apostolic—a true follower of the apostles' mission and ministry—when it preserves in all its members a continuing agreement with the witness of the apostles and a vital continuity with their mission and ministry.[32]

The emergence of the papacy, Küng argues, is much further removed from the Church's origins than the emergence of the classic three-fold ministry of bishop, priest, and deacon, for rather than being apostolically implemented, the papacy was an evolutionary development.[33] Nevertheless, regardless of what Catholic or Protestant exegetes might conclude regarding Petrine primacy, Küng insists that they cannot deny that the ministerial primacy of a single person is not contradictory to Scripture.[34] Therefore, papal authority is not inherently anti-biblical. What is decisive in the last analysis, Küng relates, is the pragmatic question of functionality. Even if it could be proven that papal ascension derives from Peter and that his successor was directly invested by Peter as his successor with all the rights and duties of the apostolic office, this apostolic succession is of no ultimate use to the Pope or the Church if that Pope does not give proper witness or proper performance of a truly apostolic mission and ministry.

[29]Duggan, *Hans Küng and Reunion*, 29.
[30]Küng, *The Church*, 456, 52; Nowell, *Passion for Truth*, 137; Duggan, *Hans Küng and Reunion*, 149.
[31]Küng, *The Church*, 354-56.
[32]Nowell, *Passion for Truth*, 145; Küng, *The Church*, 354-57.
[33]Nowell, *Passion for Truth*, 149-51.
[34]Küng, *The Church*, 462-63.

What is decisive are not the claims, the rights, and the chain of succession, but the exercise and carrying out of a ministry in service.[35] Küng does not therefore call for the abolition of the episcopal structure or the papacy, but instead for the reform of both according to the Pauline charismatic understanding of servanthood.

III. Evaluation

In the ecclesiology of Cardinal Joseph Ratzinger, the Cardinal Prefect of the Sacred Congregation for the Doctrine of Faith, the official ecclesiastical commission responsible for the preservation and promotion of Roman Catholic orthodoxy, one can survey the essential differences between the pneumatological structure that Küng prefers and that of mainline Roman Catholicism. In Ratzinger's ecclesiology, the nature of the true Church cannot be separated from its episcopal structure. The Church is constituted by the sacraments insofar as believers are incorporated into the Body of Christ through baptism and the Eucharist.[36] The Church is therefore hierarchical by nature in that "hierarchy based on apostolic succession is the indispensable condition to arrive at the strength, the reality of the sacrament."[37] The authority of the episcopate was invested to it by Jesus Christ himself. Ratzinger locates "the principle and foundation of unity" in the Church in its episcopate.[38] The Church is not a body of individual subjects, but is one subject. The Pope is the visible head through whom Christ, the ultimate Head, governs his body. Each bishop over each local church gathers the members of that church into a communion, and that bishop himself represents the unity of that particular community, and represents that community to the whole Church and to Christ. The horizontal network of bishops and their congregations depend on their vertical connection with the Pope. The unity of the Church is based on this cross-connection of bishops to each other, but the Pope is over all of them as the head of the Church who embodies and secures the unity of the Church. He is, then, the visible bond of unity. Only those churches in communion with Rome stand in the one, holy, catholic, apostolic Church.[39] "For a Catholic," Ratzinger explains, "the Church is indeed composed of

---

[35]Nowell, *A Passion for Truth,* 149-51.

[36]Joseph Ratzinger, *The Ratzinger Report: An Exclusive Interview on the State of the Church. Joseph Cardinal Ratzinger with Vittorio Messori* (San Francisco: Ignatius, 1985), 47.

[37]Ibid., 49.

[38]Ibid., 59.

[39]Miroslav Volf, *After Our Likeness: The Church as the Image of the Trinity* (Grand Rapids: Eerdmans, 1998), 55-60.

men who organize her external visage, but behind this, the fundamental structures are willed by God himself, and therefore they are unavoidable."[40]

By contrast, Küng contends for a Church constituted not by the sacraments administered through the hierarchical structure but by the Spirit as he works, not through the hierarchy so much as through the gifts he has endowed to the individuals within the whole community of which the hierarchy is part. The hierarchy of such a church is defined in terms of service to the apostolic mission and ministry. Here his ecclesiology is more in keeping with that of the Free Church model presented by the Protestant evangelical theologian, Miroslav Volf, than that of orthodox Catholicism. Volf argues for a conception of the Church as constituted by the Holy Spirit through the communal confession of faith—expressed through both words and ministerial deeds. The general call of the Spirit to new life becomes specific in the *charismata*, which are spiritual gifts of authority and capacity for ministry, given to each believer upon inception into the faith.[41] "The church arises and lives," Volf states, "insofar as salvation is mediated through mutual service with the pluriform gifts of the Sprirt."[42] Such a model does not allow for the passivity of the laity but requires their active involvement in the church. The task of the leadership, who have their authoritative offices as gifts of the Spirit, is also to encourage and guide the laity to put into service what has been given to them. The authority of leaders, Volf insists, is not absolute but based on their active service in the church.[43] Küng conceives of the church in much the same manner. The church these two theologians portray can only be truly present where the Spirit is actively at work in and through its members.

What lies behind the differences in the ecclesiologies of Ratzinger and Küng is the question of the source of revelation. Both theologians hold the Christ event itself to be divine revelation and find in Scripture the normative testimony to and interpretation of that initial revelation.[44] For Ratzinger, the authoritative interpretation of Scripture can only take place in the Church that lives in the form of apostolic succession, with the Petrine office as its center.[45] Ratzinger keeps interpretive priority within the confines of ecclesial authority and apostolic succession. The Christ event is for him the pivotal interpretive key. The first witnesses to the life

---

[40]Ratzinger, *The Ratzinger Report,* 46.
[41]Volf, *After Our Likeness,* 224-26.
[42]Ibid., 226.
[43]Ibid., 230-31.
[44]Karl Rahner and Joseph Ratzinger, *Revelation and Tradition* (New York: Herder, 1966), 41.
[45]Volf, *After Our Likeness,* 55.

and work of Christ, through the guiding of the Spirit, reinterpreted Scriptures according to the reality they had encountered in Christ.[46] This interpretation of Scripture through the Christ event did not cease with the closing of the canon but continues down through the ages in ecclesial tradition. This "arrested process of the new exposition of scripture with Christ as basis," has, he declares, "no desire to be independent, to be shut in on itself in literal exposition of a text, but can only subsist within the spiritual reality of Jesus Christ, who remains with his own 'always, to the close of the age.'"[47] It is in the Church that Christ's presence, his spiritual reality, continues and therefore within the Church that the authoritative exposition of Scripture must take place.[48] While he defines tradition as interpretation "according to the Scriptures," it is not to be understood as interpretation "in the sense of purely exegetical exposition, but in virtue of the spiritual authority of the Lord operative in the whole existence of the Church."[49]

While Küng holds that Scripture cannot be interpreted apart from the context of the Church and its tradition, his final criterion for theologizing lies in the realm of the Academy rather than the Magisterium. His historical approach leads him to elevate the primitive and earliest texts to the level of theological normativity.[50] He is thus criticized by his Roman Catholic contemporaries as one who seeks a "canon within the canon" that exalts the earliest textual material to the position of normativity and subordinates other textual material to these. Roman Catholic tradition, by contrast, regards the Scripture in its entirety as normative.

Peter Chirico summarizes effectively Küng's gospel, his "canon within the canon," as "the concrete Jesus of Nazareth as reflected in the original message of eyewitnesses and determined for us from the whole of Scripture by modern exegetes using the historical critical method."[51] A significant implication of such a criterion for Roman Catholicism is that with Scripture involving both truth and error and with historical criticism as the tool by which the true Gospel is to be extracted from Scripture, the responsibility of interpreting Scripture and determining what is theologically normative belongs to those trained in the historical-critical method—to the scholars and teachers—and not to those endowed by Christ with apostolic authority, as tradition would have it.[52] On the other hand, Ratzinger, insisting that it is to the Church that the Lord has given the

[46]Rahner and Ratzinger, *Revelation and Tradition,* 37.
[47]Ibid., 39.
[48]Ibid., 41.
[49]Ibid., 47.
[50]George Tavard, "Hans Küng's Church," *Continuum* 6, no. 1 (1968): 109.
[51]Chirico, "Infallibility," 541.
[52]Ibid., 547-48.

Word, asks, "Can the Word be posited as independent without thereby delivering it up to the caprice of exegetes, evacuating it of meaning in the controversies of historians and so robbing it entirely of binding force?"[53] This question, which he directs towards Protestants, may also be directed toward Küng.

A second implication of Küng's ecclesiological criterion is that only with the initiation of the modern historical-critical method is the Church able to determine the full Gospel, since prior to modernity the Church did not have access to these tools. Centuries of pre-Enlightenment Catholic teaching, held traditionally to be infallible, are thrown into the shadow of the modern scholar whose concern is foremost with the initial testimony of the first witnesses to the Gospel. George H. Tavard's objection to this is that the norm of Küng's ecclesiology is in reality "the earliest read by the latest," and that consequently "neither the Fathers nor the later Church councils nor the definitions and theologies of more recent centuries enter into the picture, except to be criticized in the light of the primitive."[54]

Conclusion

Throughout *Die Kirche*, Küng demands that the Roman Catholic Church no longer places confidence in its juridical structure, apostolic succession, and the tradition of the councils as the basis for its authoritative legitimacy. The Second Vatican Council was called for the purpose of bringing the Roman Catholic Church out of centuries of theological malaise. Küng moves in accord with this intention. However, he transgresses boundaries within which Rome wishes to remain. Such divergences between Küng's ecclesiology and that of the Roman See lead his Roman Catholic contemporaries to question the extent to which he may continue to align himself with Rome. Chirico's response is that Küng "in the basic notion upon which all his theologizing rests is too restrictive and particularistic. *He is not catholic enough.*"[55] Frederick Sontag identifies Küng's novelty for Roman Catholics as follows: he "popularizes views on the church, the Bible, and theology long common in Protestant circles."[56] Interestingly enough, Ratzinger locates the true antithesis in the ecclesiologies of Catholics and Protestants not in the Protestant liberation of Word from tradition but in the liberation of Word from office.[57] Thus he states: "This idea that the Word of God is fettered in the Catholic

---

[53]Rahner and Ratzinger, *Revelation and Tradition,* 31.
[54]Tavard, "Hans Küng's Church," 110.
[55]Chirico, "Infallibility," 553.
[56]Frederick Sontag, "Martin Luther Küng?" *Encounter* 45, no. 1 (1984): 234.
[57]Volf, *After Our Likeness,* 55.

Church through its connection with the authority of the ministry is repeatedly expressed in the writings of the Reformers."[58] The liberation of Word from office is precisely what Küng appears to accomplish. Furthermore, in Küng's schema, neither tradition nor the canon as a whole holds the status of primary normativity. The Gospel, as his "canon within the canon," which he holds to be the final criterion, must be extracted from Scripture through modern historical-critical methods. It is therefore little wonder his contemporary, Karl Rahner, publicly denounced Küng as a "liberal Protestant."[59]

Rome eventually took action against these theological divergences. Thirteen years after the publication of *Die Kirche*, the Sacred Congregation for the Doctrine of the Faith publicly declared, "Professor Hans Küng departs from the integral truth of Roman Catholic faith in his writings. For this reason he can neither be regarded as a Catholic theologian nor can he function as such in a teaching role."[60] The particular areas of contention behind the denouncement centered on his views of papal and Scriptural infallibility and apostolic succession.[61]

Within the writings of Küng, Protestants hear a voice of critique resounding within the Roman Catholic ranks that resonates with their own criticisms. Within the context of the contemporary interest in ecumenical dialogue, the critique set forth by Küng and the response of the Roman See demonstrate to Protestantism what Catholics hold to be most sacred and clarify where their theological boundaries are drawn.

In Küng one finds a Catholic theologian, dismissed by the Roman Catholic Church as a liberal Protestant, who sets forth an ecclesiology that understands the nature of the Church as one that has its beginning and end in the working of the Spirit through gifts endowed to all believers—a Church that Pentecostalism can find little to fault. Such a Church requires a leadership, characterized by servitude, which guides the members to use the gifts that have been invested by the Holy Spirit to each of them. It requires members that are open to the movement and ministry of the Spirit through them and are not content to sit passively by, leaving ministry to the leadership alone. Küng, however, demonstrates that the full operation of the Spirit in a church does not necessitate the abandoning of an authoritative hierarchical structure for the purpose of allowing freedom for the moving of the Spirit. Küng therefore offers to Pentecostalism an insightful balance that allows for the spontaneity of the Spirit along with the order and accountability of a strong authoritative governing structure.

---

[58]Rahner and Ratzinger, *Revelation and Tradition,* 28.
[59]Kiwiet, *Hans Küng,* 28.
[60]As quoted in David L. Mueller, "Hans Küng—in Limbo?" 13.
[61]Kiwiet, *Hans Küng,* 89-96.

Exploring Pentecostal Ethics: Reclaiming Our Heritage

John Sims[*]

In 1973, Carl Henry, editor of *Christianity Today*, urged evangelicals to reclaim " . . . the solid substance of the Christian ethical tradition, and to do some new systematic, creative thinking, in order to be able to face the powers of this world not merely with a way of thinking, but also with a consistent and biblically valid way of life."[1]

Evangelicals had recovered biblical authority, Henry noted, but too many were at a loss to provide a consistent biblical ethic to match their theology. As long as they could apply explicit biblical commands, prohibitions, and precepts to the issues of their environment, most evangelicals felt fairly comfortable with their ethical responses. Once off the solid ground of repeating selected biblical texts, however, they tended to capitulate to worldly wisdom and in chameleon-like fashion take on the ethical coloring of their social environment. In the absence of clear biblical answers to issues not exhaustively dealt with in Scripture, confused and frustrated evangelicals too often resorted to paraphrasing worldly opinion. Living under the social influence of modern rationalism and subjectivism, and the attending implications of these impulses, the typical evangelical often thought and behaved in a manner more consistent with a relativist, hedonist, or utilitarian, than a biblically consistent Christian. Henry's plea to evangelicals in the '70s was for an ethic solidly in touch with the Christian tradition and a consistent biblical way of life.

[*]John Sims (Ph.D., Florida State University). President, European Bible Seminary, Rudersberg, Germany; Professor of History and Religion, Lee University (on leave).
[1]Carl F. H. Henry, "Needed: Evangelical Ethics," *Christianity Today* (12 October 1973): 43.

Times, of course, have changed. Since Henry wrote that article, the full-blown advent of the postmodern *Zeitgeist* has given rise to a significant paradigm shift in theological and ethical reflection. The challenge today is not how to live in a society where thinking and behavior are dominated by the influences of Marx, Mill, and Sartre, but one that has been radically influenced by the likes of Michel Foucault, Richard Rorty, and Jacques Derrida. The postmodern paradigm casts a deep suspicion over knowledge/ rationality and embraces a radical relativism, pragmatism, and particularity, which denies that any overarching truth can be "true" or any practice "good" for everyone. Attention has shifted away from claims for universal objective truth to the greater need for lived truth in the particularity of one's church, the marketplace, and the academy.

As a postmodern theologian has noted, one does not have to be a relativist to understand that the truth question in the postmodern era will be settled more by how well Christians live than by how well they make their case for objective truth.[2] It is a timely opportunity, as Stanley Hauerwas argues, for the church to live as a "peculiar people," a "community of character."[3] More than any time in their history, Pentecostal Christians find an openness to their particularity and their claim for an alternative life-view, but in many instances the claim is betrayed by a self-serving therapeutic lifestyle that does not behave or run its institutions any differently from common cultural patterns.

The moral imperative facing contemporary Pentecostals is to rediscover the nature and power of those convictions that have shaped the best of their common life and character, regain their moral vitality, and operationalize the meaning of being the church. Preparing to live as the church in a postmodern and post-Christian world is more challenging than knowing how to apply abstract ethical principles or make difficult choices. It requires more than understanding. It challenges our courage to be the kind of persons, the sort of Christian community, that we ought to be. Reclaiming those stories and traditions that helped to shape our own is a necessary first step and vital part of making sense of our present life and purpose.

---

[2]Philip D. Kenneson, "There's no such thing as objective truth and it's a good thing, too," in *Christian Apologetics in the Postmodern World*, ed. Timothy R. Phillips and Dennis L. Okholm (Downer's Grove, IL: InterVarsity Press, 1995), 156-70.

[3]See, in particular, Stanley Hauerwas, *A Community of Character* (Notre Dame, IN: University of Notre Dame Press, 1988), along with Will Willimon, *Resident Aliens: Life in the Christian Colony* (Nashville, TN: Abingdon Press, 1989).

I. Guidance from the Tradition

Connecting with the solid substance of the Christian ethical tradition, as Henry urged evangelicals to do, is no small matter for Pentecostals. The Bible is the great source book for Christian ethics and certainly its authoritative guide for moral living. But there is much to be gained from the ethical reflection of the Christian community as it has sought to live out the meaning of its faith during the last two millennia. The tradition reveals much about the diversity and the unity of thinking regarding the moral life. Virtually all of the major traditions and paradigms contribute something significant to the ongoing question of what it means for a Christian to live out his/her life in the world, but John Calvin and John Wesley in particular have had a broad and significant influence on the Holiness/Pentecostal movement. Pentecostals have derived solid substance for their own ethical tradition from these predecessors of their faith.

Popular opinion tends to set these two traditions widely apart, but in reality there are major ethical and moral threads running through Calvin and Wesley that point to more unity than diversity in their theologies and life-views. There are, to be sure, significant theological and practical differences with regard to election, the process of sanctification, enthusiasm and revivalist practices, but it is well to remember that Wesley himself said that he was "within a hair's breadth of Calvinism."[4] The common emphases that tie Calvin and Wesley so closely together are many, including a strong theological and practical commitment to the transformed life, a love that obeys, and a theocentric faith.

Medieval Catholic theology, by contrast, tended to place an emphasis on future salvation. This present life was seen as a probation for the life to come. To be a Christian was to belong to another sphere, to focus one's interest on higher things, to live for the rewards of a future life. The transformation of human nature could only be a gradual process completed in another world. Asceticism was the medieval Catholic ideal and purgatory a necessary piece of the logic of salvation. Consequently, there was no expectation of personal or societal transformation in this life on the scale that Calvin or Wesley envisioned.

A. C. McGiffert, prominent church historian, clearly points out that Luther did little, if anything, to improve the church's expectations in this regard. Luther's reaction to Rome was not on moral but religious grounds. His primary concern was God's acceptance of him as a sinner, not moral

---

[4]Waldo Beach and H. Richard Niebuhr, *Christian Ethics* (New York: John Wiley and Sons, 1973), 356. Also, see Robert C. Monk, *John Wesley: His Puritan Heritage* (Nashville, TN: Abingdon Press, 1966).

purity. By making salvation wholly a matter of divine forgiveness rather than a transformation of human character, Luther in essence rejected both the Catholic and the Pauline understanding of salvation. McGiffert writes:

> The significance of Luther's position at this point lies in the fact that he claimed to be already saved, not because already pure and righteous, but on other grounds altogether, and while still continuing to be impure and unrighteous. This constitutes the great difference between him and the Apostle Paul. Paul, too, thought of salvation as a present possession and of the Christian as already saved, but the ground of the salvation was moral transformation, not divine forgiveness. By the indwelling of the Spirit the Christian is not merely in process of sanctification, but is actually changed already into a holy being, or, in other words, is already saved. Paul was moved primarily by moral considerations, as Luther was not. To Paul the one dreadful thing was the corruption of the flesh to which the natural man is subject. To be freed from it by the agency of divine power—this and this alone meant salvation.[5]

Notwithstanding their separation in time and tradition, Calvin and Wesley were nonetheless closer to Paul and to each other in their moral supposition regarding the transformation of life and society. This supposition, perhaps more than any other, turned Calvin and Wesley into the moral parents of the Holiness/Pentecostal tradition. Calvin's supposition was that the elect are not simply predestined to forgiveness but to holiness. Forgiveness anticipates sanctification. A holy and righteous God is benevolent toward the elect and justifies the sinner by his grace, but God's grace continues to work through various stages of a person's life so as to transform his/her character and bring about loving obedience to the will of God. As Waldo Beach explains:

> Calvin understands very clearly what is obscured in some Christian thinkers: that the reconciliation of man to God through the work of Jesus Christ does not result in an automatic, effortless change of man's whole moral and spiritual nature. It is rather the beginning of a new and intense activity. The Christian life, as Calvin sees it, is a continuous and hard struggle to realize in every sphere of existence the consequences of the new beginning.[6]

Wesley's Arminian emphasis upon free will and his own insistence upon the possibility of perfection in love were obviously at odds with Calvin. But what is too often overlooked in emphasizing these differences

---

[5]A. C. McGiffert, *Protestant Thought Before Kant* (Gloucester, MA: Peter Smith, 1971), 25.
[6]Beach, *Christian Ethics,* 272.

is Wesley's and Calvin's mutual agreement that " . . . God has called us to be 'total' Christians, saved by faith in Christ and living now under his tutelage in strict moral group and self discipline."[7] Wesley spoke of this "total commitment" through one of his letters:

> I take religion to be not the bare saying over so many prayers, morning and evening, in public or in private, nor anything superadded now and then to a careless or worldly life; but a constant ruling habit of soul, a renewal of our minds in the image of God, a recovery of the divine likeness, a still-increasing conformity of heart and life to the pattern of our most holy redeemer.[8]

Grace and obligation go together. Calvin's Geneva and Wesley's methodical lifestyle of personal holiness and social involvement demonstrate their common commitment to a love that obeys.[9]

Out of his great fear of legalism, Luther never embraced Melanchton's third use of the law. He followed instead Augustine's view that love does not need the supporting structure of law. "Love God with all your heart," Augustine admonished, "and then do as you please."[10] Calvin, however, regarded the third use of the law as its chief use. That is to say, it serves the Christian as a guide for Christian living. Whereas Luther apprehended law more negatively under the conditions of sin, Calvin apprehended it more positively under the structure of the Creator's love. Law only becomes negative for Calvin when sin intervenes.

For Calvin, covenant history is central and the Abrahamic covenant (Genesis 17) becomes the basis for moral obligation and all covenant

---

[7]Ibid., 357.

[8]Ibid., 358.

[9]Calvin's sense of divine sovereignty turned the world into God's kingdom, subject in all its activities to God's laws. Every believer is to regard his/her work as a post of duty for which he/she is responsible. Government is a necessary restraint against the wicked and sinful tendencies of humanity, but Calvin also assigned a more positive role to civil powers whose responsibility it is to provide the kind of society where free and rational people can live together under God. Calvin is credited with encouraging the development of constitutional and parliamentary government.

Social change, for Wesley, begins through changed individuals. He had no hope of changing society except through people whose hearts had been changed. Politically, Wesley was a conservative Tory, but his message was socially revolutionary. Working from within to effect outward change, Wesley's message resulted in economic improvement for his own followers, changed institutions, and increased social concern. Wesley was particularly involved with prison reform, helping the poor, medical care for the disadvantaged, homes for widows, schools for poor children, and the abolishment of slavery. See Beach, *Christian Ethics*, chaps. 9, 12.

[10]*Enchiridion*, chap. 117.

relations. It is a covenant of grace that is to be responded to in loving and faithful obedience. This covenant is also the historical basis for understanding the doctrine of predestination. Through the covenant we understand that God elects his people who are then enabled to fulfill the obligations of the covenant through love, which is the sum of the law.[11]

The grace of God is always foremost in Wesley's thinking as well. Christ is the great transformer of life who cleanses from all sin so that believers can be delivered from the power of sin in this life. The New Testament does not say, "the blood of Christ will cleanse at the hour of death, or in the day of judgment, but it 'cleanseth,' at the time present, 'us,' living Christians, 'from all sin.'"[12] The obligation to perfect our love, however, has a strong volitional emphasis which can be seen in one of Wesley's descriptions of Christian perfection. He talks in terms of a perfection of desire or intention. He writes:

> In one view, it is a purity of intention, dedicating all the life to God. It is giving God all our heart; it is one desire and design ruling all our tempers. It is the devoting, not a part, but all, our soul, body, and substance to God. In another view, it is all the mind which was in Christ, enabling us to walk as Christ walked. It is the circumcision of the heart from all filthiness, all inward as well as outward pollution. It is a renewal of the heart in the whole image of God, the full likeness of Him that created it. In yet another, it is the loving God with all our heart, and our neighbor as ourselves.[13]

There is no need to argue, as so many have, the question of sanctification as a progressive or instantaneous act. The core issue, for Calvin and Wesley, is that it is meant to be "total" and transforming and is in its very essence a love that obeys. It begins in regeneration and admits to a continual increase, so long as one lives in an unbroken relationship with Christ.[14]

The command to love our neighbor as well as God naturally necessitates a working out of the ethic of love into a right outward ordering of life in relation to others, a horizontal as well as a vertical dimension to our

---

[11] John Calvin, *Institutes of the Christian Religion* II.6-9.

[12] From the sermon "Christian Perfection," in *The Works of John Wesley,* ed. Thomas Jackson, 14 vols. (London: Wesley Conference Office, 1872), 6:5-6.

[13] John Wesley, *A Plain Account of Christian Perfection,* sec. 27.

[14] See Colin Williams, *John Wesley's Theology Today* (Nashville, TN: Abingdon Press, 1979), 182ff. Wesley stressed both the instantaneous gift of perfection, and the gradual nature of this work of grace. This is not a self-contradictory position but a coherent one as Wesley presented it. Wesley did not mean that one can be perfect with regard to the moral law but that one is to live in an unbroken relationship to Christ with a constant desire to do his will.

faith. Calvin and Wesley provide a commendable model for both dimensions by avoiding the tendency either to fall into an individualistic form of mysticism or float the second table of the Law without a proper theocentric grounding in the first commandment. The first error has many examples from the long history of Christian mysticism. The second error can be seen in some forms of the social gospel and liberation theologies. Drawing a horizontal ethic from a theocentric basis has two essential advantages. On one hand, it provides the most fundamental and compelling case for moral obligation. On the other, it provides the basis for the power (that is, grace) to actualize good intentions when the good of others conflicts with the good of the self.

It is only through the vertical relation to God of the believing and acting self that one can find an adequate basis for deriving the "ought" from the "is." Plato's appeal to the rule of reason, Kant's appeal to moral duty, the humanist's appeal to human dignity, the existentialist's appeal to autonomous freedom, and the utilitarian's appeal to social responsibility, all fail to provide an adequate basis for moral obligation. Dostoevsky was right in his conclusion that apart from God there is no real basis for moral obligation: "If God is dead all things are permissible." As Arthur Holmes succinctly put it, "We can never derive an 'ought' from a premised 'is' unless the 'ought' is somehow already contained in the premises."[15] To understand and use the word "God" in the morally significant way that Calvin and Wesley used it, on the other hand, is to make the term morally obligatory. There is then a proper referent of moral language to God's love and justice in relation to his creation.[16] "How and why the neighbor is loved depends on how and why God is loved. Thus, in Jesus' summary of the law, the Second Commandment, to love the neighbor, is described as like or part of the First."[17] The dilemma of the self is that it cannot, apart from grace, do the good that is visualized and intended. The loving relation of the self to others is always betrayed in self-love. One's ethic must

---

[15]Arthur F. Holmes, *Ethics: Approaching Moral Decisions* (Downer's Grove, IL: InterVarsity Press, 1984), 70. The question for many, particularly in the modern world, has been how the "ought" can be legitimately derived from the "is." Many claim that it cannot. Thus the response, "why bother about ethics?" Existentialists like Jean-Paul Sartre contend that there is no real "ought" beyond one's freedom to choose. Others like John Locke, F. H. Bradley, and W. D. Ross argue that moral obligations arise out of contractual relationships in society such as marriage, family, government, etc.

[16]In many modern approaches to ethics, it is held that ethical terms do not convey any truth or meaning that is external to ourselves. Ethical Emotivism, for example, holds that moral judgments are merely emotional expressions while Ethical Egoism and Utilitarianism locate the reference for ethical terms in human experience.

[17]Beach, *Christian Ethics,* 5

start with and depend upon God and his grace or be left with a humanistic
ideal that lacks the power to fulfill itself.[18]
  Calvin's and Wesley's ethical models are persuasive to Pentecostals
because they build on a strong theocentric foundation that calls the church
to a way of life and community in keeping with the character and will of
God.

II. Grounded in Scripture and Christian Experience

  It is indeed important for an Evangelical and Pentecostal ethic to reclaim the solid substance of the Christian ethical tradition, but it is even
more important that it be grounded in Scripture and authentic, biblically-
based experience. A Christian ethic must, in the words of Carl Henry, be
derived from "a consistent and biblically valid way of life."
  The teaching of ethics has traditionally centered on great ethical texts
such as the Decalogue, the prophets, the Sermon on the Mount, and the
Great Commandment. What has been neglected too often has been the
vital and distinct role of the Holy Spirit in the moral life. The need is not
simply to point out the necessity of the ethical dimension in the life of the
Spirit-filled Christian, but to show, from the standpoint of Scripture, the
difference that the Holy Spirit makes in the moral and ethical realm. The
cost for this neglect of the Spirit has been a loss of the distinctiveness of
the Christian ethic and an impoverishment of its meaning.[19]
  Pentecostals have something significant to contribute in this regard,
but there are extremes that must be avoided both by Pentecostals and
their detractors. There is, on the one hand, the spiritual paranoia of the
detractors who identify any suggestion of being "Spirit-filled" or "Spirit-
led" with ecstatic and emotional extremism and consequently restrict their
thinking to more cognitive, empirical considerations of the moral life. The
problem is that those who have not experienced the reality of the Holy
Spirit as a guiding and empowering force in their lives are not likely to
appreciate, as they should, the meaning and moral worth of "life in the
Spirit."
  The other error, so common to Pentecostals, is the emotion-centered
approach to the moral life. Pentecostal theologian, Hollis Gause, describes
some of the common manifestations of this too-heavy dependence on

  [18]Edward John Carnell, *A Philosophy of the Christian Religion* (Grand Rapids,
MI: Eerdmans, 1961), 240-43.
  [19]Henlee H. Barnette, *Introducing Christian Ethics* (Nashville, TN: Broadman,
1961), 87-95.

emotional experience at the expense of a sound Scriptural understanding of moral issues:

> The use of emotional experience as a critique has served to develop a sort of incipient gnostic level of judgment. Morality is decided on the basis of what seems appropriate and this judgment is then translated into the leading of the Holy Spirit. It appears in man-made ordinances which say, 'touch not, taste not' (Colossians 2:20-23). It also appears in the 'imitation of Jesus' motif which judges all things by the question 'What would Jesus do in this situation?' The subjective answer to this has to be taken as the answer of the Holy Spirit. This problem also surfaces in another extreme —libertinism. Here it is assumed that the Holy Spirit (as understood emotionally and experientially) confirms as good whatever one is and whatever one does when he is being 'blesssed.' This is a shallow form of emotional pragmatism that is passed off as the guidance of the Holy Spirit.[20]

Suffice it to say, a proper Christian ethic presupposes both a sound theology and an authentic Christian experience. It will not do to emphasize one at the expense of the other. Throughout his academic career at Lee University, Don Bowdle has led by example in encouraging students, colleagues, and whomever would listen, of the need to make a commitment of will and resources to theological training and discipleship formation.[21] A solid grounding in theological truth, wise application of ethical principles, and sound hermeneutical approaches to ethical texts, are all essential to a balanced and holistic understanding of ethics and morality. Many Pentecostals, for instance, need a better understanding of how to read and interpret texts. A selective and narrow biblicism that over-simplifies complex issues under the guise of "holding to the authority of the Bible" is no more adequate than the more liberal "cultural gap" view that the Bible is outdated and virtually irrelevant to contemporary issues and problems. The church must take the Bible seriously as the measure whereby all other claims for truth are tested but understand as well that we do not honor the Bible by using it inappropriately. An ethic drawn from a partial pneumatological perspective or experience will inevitably lack the holistic perspective of one drawn from a more complete Christian theology. Apart from a fundamental understanding of the controlling themes that tie the

---

[20]Hollis Gause, "Issues in Pentecostalism," *Society for Pentecostal Studies Newsletter* 3:3 (April 1973): 7.

[21]Donald N. Bowdle, "Holiness in the Highlands: A Profile of the Church of God," *Christianity in Appalachia: Profiles in Regional Pluralism,* ed. Bill J. Leonard (Knoxville, TN: University of Tennessee Press, 1999), 251.

whole Christian story together, a proper framework for moral thinking, being, and action will be lacking.

It is important as well to emphasize the moral implications of biblical and theological truths. These are not always evident to readers. The biblical accounts of creation and fall, for example, are fundamental to our understanding of self, our place in the world, and God's purpose for our lives. Through creation, the universe is disclosed to us as having a divine order and purpose. We learn that the meaning of our life is not something we create, or find socially imposed upon us, but a truth revealed through God's purposes for us and the created order. As Christians our values, choices, and actions are to correspond to the value that God gives his creation and the covenental relationships that he intends. We are free to use and enjoy God's gifts, but we must not misuse or abuse them. God's purposes for his ordered world lay certain responsibilities and obligations upon us that are sometimes obscured by sin and abnormality. Consequently, we cannot read the "ought" out of the "is." The meaning of our moral obligations can only be clearly revealed through the character and will of the God we know in Jesus Christ.

If we understand life only in terms of natural forces, we have no other choice but to see ourselves as the mere product of time and chance. All of life stands under the judgment of decay and death, and we are forced to conclude with Shakespeare's Macbeth that life is nothing more than a "tale told by an idiot, full of sound and fury, signifying nothing." But God's image in us means that we have dignity and value by reason of our relation to him. Life is a gift from God. Through the unique rational, artistic, and moral endowments that we have been given, God expects us to live life out to our full potential in ways that honor and glorify him.

We take seriously the fact of sin in ourselves and in society, but we know as well the grace of God that has been manifested through the life, death, and resurrection of Jesus Christ. In Jesus Christ, God has decisively confronted and defeated the power of sin and evil that infects humankind and the created order. A new age in which "righteousness dwells" has already been inaugurated. Those who are "in Christ" and share God's redeeming and healing grace have been called to share in the task of making all things new.

Through the cross, God's self-giving (*agape*) love has been revealed. The commitment to sanctification and growth in grace begins through the disclosure and power of the cross, which shows us the sacrificial love of Christ as the norm for living on both the personal and social level. The cross is not a symbol for sentimentality or passivity. It is God's answer to and protest against the sinful self-interest that permeates all human relationships. It shatters all illusions and pretensions to self-righteous morality and all attempts to excuse oneself from moral obligation. The grace of sanctification, like that of justification, shows us the inadequacy of our own power, but it also bespeaks the necessity of an unrelenting coopera- tion with God on our part to fulfill the law of life that has been revealed in Jesus Christ.

The work of the Holy Spirit must not be relegated to the realm of emotion and experience, for the Spirit's primary work is to reveal and develop the character of Christ in the believer. The Holy Spirit is God in action, the one who establishes God's standard within us, guides us into the truth, and energizes us for the ethical task.

The Spirit is the Spirit of God who is by nature Holy Spirit. Because of his holy character, it is the nature and work of the Holy Spirit to strive against sin and rebellion, to convict and convince the world of sin, righteousness, and judgment (John 16:8). His will is to create a new heart and effect a new birth in the believer (Titus 3:5), to make us "new creatures" in Christ (II Corinthians 5:17), and produce in us the character of his love, joy, peace, patience, kindness, goodness, faithfulness, gentleness, and self-control (Galatians 5:22).

As eschatological gift, the Holy Spirit constitutes the continuing pres- ence of the Kingdom of God. Ethical manifestations of the Kingdom such as repentance, a transformed life, and the repudiation of the old life, are expected and required of all who would participate in the life and work of the Kingdom. Living under the reign of God and in the power of the Spirit entails a commitment to truthfulness, the pursuit of holiness, and a life of love.[22] But it is not our adherence to the law, our personal character, or strength of will, but the Spirit of God that provides the strength of commit- ment from which the Christian life is lived out. The Holy Spirit is the "power for righteousness" that supercedes the law in the life of the be- liever (Romans 7:6). The righteousness that the law requires, but cannot enable us in our weakness to attain, can only be realized through the power of the Holy Spirit. Through the unity of Word and Spirit we are saved from the legalistic and antinomian extremes. The letter, divorced from Spirit, inevitably kills and enslaves because it has no life or power, while an emphasis upon the Spirit, divorced from the truth and guidance of the Word, results in some form of antinomian or fanatical extreme. To- gether, however, they provide guidance and power for the Christian life.

In Jesus and the life of the early church we have the model for how the Holy Spirit wills to work in the community of faith to effect the will of God. The purpose of the Holy Spirit is not to operate solely in the life of the isolated individual but to create and bring us into a new community of faith (*koinonia*) where our individuality becomes a part of Christ's body in its totality. We become the this-worldly form of Christ's existence in the

---

[22]Hollis Gause, *Living in the Spirit* (Cleveland, TN: Pathway Press, 1980), 96- 97.

world. As we discover from the early church, the Holy Spirit works to give our "togetherness" a spiritual dimension that manifests itself in worship, fellowship, a devotion to sound doctrine, and a caring and inclusive community (Acts 2:42ff).

The Spirit, who is the source and bond of fellowship (Ephesians 4:3), inspires brotherly and sisterly love and seeks to break down all inequalities based on sex, race, nationality, or status in society. Love and concern for the poor in their midst prompted early Christians voluntarily to sell their possessions and share everything with those in the church who had need (Acts 2:44,45). The church did not have to attach a social ethic to its religion; it was, by its very nature, a social ethic in action. The Spirit-filled church in Acts proved itself to be an extension of Jesus who had already demonstrated a special concern for the despised, the outcasts, and those discriminated against by society—lepers, tax collectors, Samaritans, women, children, the poor. His gospel was so elevating and transforming that Paul could write, "There is neither Jew nor Greek . . . slave nor free . . . male nor female; for you are all one in Christ Jesus" (Galatians 3:28). Jesus' life and ministry are programmatic for our own, but if we are to minister today as Jesus ministered, the Holy Spirit must be restored intellectually to the physical and social realities of life.

Susana Vaccaro de Petrella, a Pentecostal leader in Argentina, puts the matter in a perspective that all Pentecostals should appreciate:

> We believe there are two elements that are indispensable to any Christian community: spiritual renewal and commitment to freedom, justice, and peace. If we limit ourselves to the first, we reduce the gospel to an other-worldly state of glory. If we limit ourselves to the second, we fall inevitably into the error of attempting to do good for its own sake. But our Spirit-inspired Pentecostal message is charged with the strong desire both for spiritual renewal and for the liberation that every human being needs so as to live in a climate of freedom, justice, and peace.[23]

Unfortunately, many Pentecostals have not understood the Christocentric nature of the Holy Spirit's work as it relates to piety and morality. In critiques of the movement, Pentecostal theologians Hollis Gause and Don Bowdle noted repeated tendencies to elevate secondary benefits of the Spirit-filled life to a primary level. Gause commented that "We do not take seriously enough the fact that the Holy Spirit is the Spirit of Christ . . . . The surest evidence of the Holy Spirit-filled life is the Christ-

---

[23]L. S. Vaccaro de Petrella, "The Tension Between Evangelism and Social Action in the Pentecostal Movement," *International Review of Missions* 75 (January 1986): 36.

filled life. It is a superficial emphasis to talk about the baptism in the Holy Spirit as giving power for witnessing. It is empowerment for godly living. This is evident in the fact that the spiritual graces that identify holy living are called the fruit of the Spirit." [24] Bowdle, moreover, cautioned against an ongoing glossocentric emphasis that confuses many as to the real purpose of the Holy Spirit. He noted that whereas "Baptism in the Holy Spirit remains the divine power whereby to discharge the Great Commission, glossocentrism diverts one's attention from both the balanced spiritual life and the urgent responsibilities of Christian service." [25]

It is the purpose of the "Spirit of truth" to bear witness to the truth, Jesus Christ (John 1:17; 14:6,17). It is the will of the Holy Spirit to establish Christ as Lord and to extend his character and work through Christ's body, the Church. "No one can say 'Jesus is Lord' except by the Holy Spirit," (1 Corinthians 12:3). Christ's life and work are the key to understanding our own. Christians are called to be what Jesus Christ would be if he were on the earth today living under human conditions. The truth of the matter is that Jesus does still live on the earth today, under human conditions, enfleshed in believers. In word and deed Jesus still releases men and women from the idols that enslave them—nation, race, wealth, power—so that they might, in the words of Martin Luther, be a "Christ to their neighbor." The world would see Jesus, but they want to see a Jesus with skin on, a Jesus enfleshed in those who bear his name.

In Jesus Christ, the inbreaking of the Kingdom of God has already occurred. The final victory of Christ has yet to be consummated, but the decisive victory has already taken place. The significance of that victory must not be annulled or obscured by any eschatological interpretation of the future that can be understood to mean that we have been released from the social and moral obligations of the present. God calls on us now to participate with him, through the Spirit, in making all things new.

A degree of tension, frustration, and disappointment will always accompany our efforts to reclaim this world for Christ. But the sheer massiveness and complexity of human needs and problems must not be allowed to overwhelm and paralyze. Our labors always seem small and insignificant when viewed in light of the task. But we do not bear the burden of bringing the process to completion ourselves. God can be trusted to consummate what he has chosen to begin through our participation.

In the power of the Spirit, God calls upon us to live faithfully and productively in the interim between the "already" and the "not yet." Life in the "already" dimension of the Spirit redeems us from paralysis and withdrawal from human need and suffering. The "not yet" dimension, on

---

[24]Gause, "Issues in Pentecostalism," 7.
[25]Bowdle, "Holiness in the Highlands," 252.

the other hand, saves us from utopian thinking. Christ must consummate and finalize that which has already begun. For that reason, the Holy Spirit within us will not cease to groan and long for the day of final redemption. In the tension of the interim in which we live, the Church must not cease to be the Church. Empowered by the Holy Spirit, the church does not have to turn its task over to special interest groups or social agencies. Neither does it look to alien philosophies or ideologies for its motivation and energy. Its life and action flows from its own character and source of strength as a Christian community. It is not a parochial statement or an empty claim to say that the only conditions under which the oppressed can be freed and the world truly liberated are the terms of Christ.

III. The Ethical Agenda

To this point, the guidance of the tradition, the primacy of Scriptural truth, and the importance of living in the Spirit, have all been emphasized as vital resources for the fulfillment of the church's ethical agenda. The role of reason and the application of ethical principles in the ethical decision-making process have not been emphasized. There have been, for example, no references to sticky issues like *in vitro* fertilization, transplant surgery, civil disobedience, abortion, capital punishment, or other ethical problems that require careful, reasoned decisions. Moral and ethical issues relating to medicine, the work place, economic and political life, and social justice require the benefit of competent and reliable technical information, reasoned choices, and the wise application of biblical principles.

Augustine's famous dictum, "I believe in order that I may understand," has moral as well as theological implications. Just as reason can be employed to help one better understand his/her faith (theology), it can also be applied to understand better what it means to love one's neighbor (ethics). Two extremes, however, have to be avoided—both of which, in varying degrees, have had their influence upon Pentecostal Christians. Out of an unwarranted fear and suspicion of the mind and "worldly education," Pentecostals in the past did not always seek out or welcome scientific information or reasoned wisdom. As a consequence, difficult decisions were often made without the benefit of reasoned choices. It is by no means a disparagement of Scripture or the "leading of the Holy Spirit" to say that the Creator intended for his rational creatures to make full use of their rational capacity.

On the other hand, the greater danger today may well be with the other extreme. The rapid rise of educational levels throughout the church frequently has resulted in too naïve an application of "unconverted reason" to moral issues and Christian service. As Carl Henry warned, a denomination or movement can easily capitulate to worldly wisdom and take on the ethical coloring of the social environment. In ethics, no less than theology, the mind as much as the heart and the will must be thoroughly converted. A denomination seeking social acceptance and intellectual responsibility must especially be on guard against various forms of cultural accommodation. It is easy to compromise the integrity of one's thought life and behavior without being fully conscious of the fact that one has done so. The wisdom and culture of natural humanity can lend valuable and sometimes indispensable insight and direction to ethical and moral problems but only after it has been converted and redirected toward God. As Augustine admonished, all wisdom that is the product of human reason must be restored to its true center in God.

All accommodations to culture and society are not related to philosophical or scientific reason. In the pragmatic environment of America, for example, the "success ethic" has driven much of the compromise with culture. Don Bowdle has noted this form of accommodation in his writings:

> A secularization of holiness has become the spiritual "Achilles heel" of the current Pentecostal denominationalism. The compromise with culture which it represents ultimately will prove a liability to those who fail to discern it and lack the will to address it. This condition is manifested by all those who, substituting style for substance, measure effectiveness in Kingdom work in terms of numbers, finances, buildings, and programs. Far from an appeal to "the good old days" when legalism prevailed, this is a call to maturity in worship that denies the "glitz" of much media Pentecostalism, a responsibility in stewardship of resources that is indicative of social concern, and a commitment truly to seek and to save the lost. The urgency of the times, the enormity of the task, and the terror of final accountability require no less.[26]

It is perhaps time to be reminded again that a Christian ideal or action cannot be sanctified by widespread approval, pragmatic results, or the feeling of being "blessed." Pentecostals can profit from some serious reflection and soul searching on the task of again putting priorities into focus as they relate to the moral life and the decision-making process.

In a somewhat different vein, it is worthy of note that Pentecostals have had a rich legacy of story-telling and testimonies in their churches that have had a major role in shaping lives and encouraging moral conduct. But these have been, in many instances, essentially replaced by

---

[26]Ibid.

more formal and abstract approaches to worship, preaching, and training programs. It is somewhat ironic that this is happening at a time when contemporary theologians and ethicists are recognizing the power of story and narrative in character formation.[27] Abstract theologies and principles have their value, but they lack the power to provide the moral guidance that we receive from the narratives of Scripture or the living testimonies of Christians sharing the struggles and victories of the Christian life. Stanley Hauerwas suggests, "Stories help us imagine what sorts of persons we ought to be. They point to the importance of virtue and character in ethics, for these are formed, not in an isolated moral decision, but in the shape of a life. If we see someone who needs help, the story of the Good Samaritan may be more use to us than any abstract principle, and we lose part of the helpfulness of the story if we try to reduce it to an abstract principle."[28]

Emphasizing the development of virtue and Christian character over isolated moral decisions is the greater need in the Pentecostal community. It is imperative that the church encourage and foster the kind of spiritual environment where people can expect and experience transforming experiences, but there must be no misunderstanding as to how true Christian character is formed. It may begin with, but it is not the product of, a crisis experience or an act of deliverance from a bad habit or addiction. Discipleship and Christian formation simply cannot take place this way. Moral development is of necessity a process involving the development of a Christian mind and behavior that disposes one to choose and do the right consistently. It is not enough for the church to emphasize a crisis experience followed by a commitment to "follow the rules." What is needed is "trained habit,"[29] a moral disposition to do what is right that has been formed through one's thought life, spiritual condition, and moral discipline. Like a garden that requires both the resources of nature and the hard, disciplined work of the gardener, virtuous and godly living require the kind of trained habit that only God can produce in us but that we must be willing to practice and nurture.

The question facing Pentecostals at this point in their history is one that relates more to their future than to their past. How will they respond to the ethical and moral challenges of a new millennium? It has been said

---

[27]For example, several Postliberal theologians with roots at Yale including Hans Frei, George Lindbeck, and Stanley Hauerwas—all of whom owe some indebtedness to H. Richard Niebuhr.
[28]As quoted in William C. Placher, "Postliberal Theology," *The Modern Theologians,* vol. 2, ed. David F. Ford (Oxford, UK: Blackwell Press, 1995), 122.
[29]"Trained habit" is a term borrowed from C. S. Lewis. For a more complete view of Lewis' understanding of moral development, see *The Abolition of Man, Mere Christianity,* and *The Four Loves.*

that there are three possible ways that people, institutions, and movements respond to change. Some make it happen, others watch it happen, while a third group wonders what happened. The choice that Pentecostals have to make is whether to engage in critical reflection and intentionalize their commitment to be a community of caring and character or apathetically allow their tradition to become a synonym for moral irresponsibility, moving aimlessly wherever the cultural tide or drift of their own movement takes them.

Conclusion

The size, strength, and acceptance of the Pentecostal movement have increased so significantly that more is now expected than when the movement was considered a mere sect (sociologically and theologically) existing in the backwaters of society. In many parts of the world today, Pentecostals and their constituents comprise high percentages of the population and their economic and political influence is no longer negligible. Determining the kind of moral leadership that the Pentecostal church can and should exert as a mainline movement is itself an important consideration. It should not be left to chance. In those instances where the influence of the movement is able to penetrate the structures of society as a whole, it must take seriously its responsibility to help shape the conscience of society and serve the good of the larger community. Moral leadership in the larger world will undoubtedly require Pentecostal churches to go beyond the bounds of benevolence and philanthropy into social issues and struggles that most have heretofore tended to avoid. It will not be enough to watch it happen, become a comfortable social critic, and react with sentimental feelings to the social and moral problems of the day. More will rightly be expected of the Pentecostal community as a "people of action" and "agents of change." Will the church work to "make it happen" by shaping and working through legal and educational systems, governmental structures, public policy, and the use of its economic resources, or will it at some point in the future simply "wonder what happened," having taken no leadership role in helping to shape the future?

A denomination or movement in the process of upward social mobility, settling comfortably into middle-class life styles, will find it difficult to move beyond a natural preoccupation with itself. But if the church is to be a community of character, engaging the world in the name of Christ, it must move beyond religious narcissism. A church that claims to "live in the Spirit" must, by reason of its own character and mission, be one that is morally sensitive, cares deeply about human need and social justice, and commits itself to being an inclusive community.

234   The Spirit and the Mind

Even in cultures and societies where Pentecostal churches are considered to be sociologically or theologically sectarian, the movement can still effectively exercise its influence as an alien faith. One must not underestimate, as George Lindbeck suggests, the effect that a so-called sectarian society can have, provided it lives as a close-knit, disciplined community that knows and practices what it believes.[30] The early Christian community was itself considered a sect. Throughout history, Christian pacifists, socialists, Quakers, and others too numerous to mention, have shaped the consciences and institutions of society on issues ranging from slavery, the rights and protection of workers, to war and peace.

Involvement for involvement's sake, however, should never dictate the life and work of the church. Pentecostal Christians, like others who have been effective instruments of God's love and justice throughout Christian history, must be a discerning people—knowing when, where, and how God is at work in his world.

---

[30]George A. Lindbeck, "The Sectarian Future of the Church," in *The God Experience,* ed. Joseph P. Whelan (New York, 1971), 226-43. Living and working as a sectarian community is not as much of an issue in America as it is in other parts of the world, particularly in Europe where state churches tend to dominate and in cultures where Christians are a decisive minority (e.g., Muslim).

III. Practical Studies

Partners in Scandal: Wesleyan and Pentecostal Scholarship

Cheryl Bridges Johns[*]

I have in my possession a treasured family picture taken around 1910 of my great-grandparents, John and Sarah McNeely, their children, and grandchildren. The eleven sons and daughters and their spouses and children have on their Sunday best: high-collared shirts, starched dresses, shined shoes, large hair bows for the girls, and knickers for the boys. The picture would be "perfect" except for the presence of one person, my great-uncle, Harvey. As the story goes, he arrived from hunting just as the picture was being snapped and "had to be included." On the left side of the picture stands "Harv," leaning on his gun, wearing overalls, with dead rabbits hanging from a leather belt strapped around his waist. His wife, great-aunt Agnes, stands just behind him, her lips pressed into a resolute grimace. The story of this picture always included an explanation that Uncle Harv was somewhat different. Somehow the shame associated with this day has survived generations. The photo has been copied by numerous cousins of my generation. Even today we feel obligated to explain Harv's unusual attire.

Every family system has its embarrassments, those relatives to whom you "forget" to send wedding and graduation invitations. Yet, these relatives have the uncanny knack of showing up just when you are trying hard to impress others with your refined identity. They have ways of reminding you of your roots when you would rather have them remain hidden.

Those of us from the Holiness and Pentecostal traditions have the dubious distinction of being the "embarrassing relatives" in the

*Cheryl Bridges Johns (Ph.D., Southern Baptist Theological Seminary). Associate Professor of Discipleship and Christian Formation, Church of God Theological Seminary.

"Evangelical clan." For better or worse, we share a marginal or fringe identity with those who position themselves as centrist. In the early 1990's, two books were published that are good examples of this perspective: Richard Kyle's *The Religious Fringe: A History of Alternative Religions in America*, and Mark Noll's *The Scandal of the Evangelical Mind*.[1]

Kyle places the Holiness movement and Pentecostalism in the category of "Christian related bodies." He sees the two traditions as examples of "fringe religions," which arose during the late 19th century and early 20th century. According to Kyle, the Holiness movement spawned a "bewildering profusion of sectarian organizations," and other offshoots such as Pentecostalism. While the Holiness movement itself could not be labeled cultic, it proved to be the fertile soil for many cultic groups. Regarding Pentecostalism, Kyle follows the standard social deprivation/dislocation tract, noting that the movement made its strongest appeal to those who had difficulty coping with the massive changes brought on by modernity. The shift into the modern urban/industrial capitalistic society was especially difficult for individuals in the lower echelons of society. The bizarre practices found in Pentecostalism, such as speaking in tongues, the holy laugh, the holy dance, and on occasions, snake handling, marked the movement as fringe to the mainstream of Christianity.

Most of us are more familiar with Noll's book, which laments the state of Evangelical scholarship. It is Noll's belief that the sorry condition of the Evangelical "mind" is largely the fault of those in the Holiness, Pentecostal, and Fundamentalist traditions. For Noll, the scandal of the evangelical mind seems to be that no mind arises from evangelicalism. The anti-intellectualism of revivalism coupled with Scottish common sense philosophy has undermined any earlier attempt made by Evangelicals to think Christianly about science, art, culture, and history.

The dominant narrative that guides Noll's criticism is that of post-Enlightenment scientific reasoning as mediated in and through the universities. Quoting a section from orthodox scholar Charles Malik's address at the dedication of the Billy Graham center, the ringing challenge of the book is the following:

> Who among the evangelicals can stand up to the great secular
> or naturalistic or atheistic scholars on their own terms of
> scholarship and research? Who among the evangelical schol-
> ars is quoted as a normative source by the greatest secular
> authorities on history or philosophy or psychology or soci-

---

[1] Richard Kyle, *The Religious Fringe: A History of Alternative Religions in America* (Downers Grove, IL: InterVarsity Press, 1993); Mark A. Noll, *The Scandal of the Evangelical Mind* (Grand Rapids: Eerdmans, 1994).

ology or politics? Does your mode of thinking have the
slightest chance of becoming the dominant mode of thinking
in the great universities of Europe or America which stamp
your entire civilization with their own spirit and ideas? . . .
Even if you start now on a crash program in this and other
domains, it will be a century at least before you catch up with
the Harvards and Tübingens and the Sorbonnes.[2]

Noll confesses that Evangelicals were taken to the woodshed by Malik.
So, standing out in the woodshed is a wounded and shamed Noll. Having
already internalized the narrative described by Malik, his humiliation is
deep. Looking around for someone to blame for the spanking, he turns to
the embarrassing relatives and attempts to take them out to the woodshed
for a thorough going over. The shame is not relieved, but surely he must
feel better.

The Wesleyan Theological Society made *The Scandal of the Evangelical Mind* a subject for discussion at its 1996 annual meeting. Three
of the presentations from this meeting were later published in the *Wesleyan
Theological Journal.*[3] Each of the reviewers of Noll's book pointed out
the hermeneutical errors found in Noll's interpretation of the three movements blamed for the scandal.

However, outside of a few places such as the WTS, Noll's *Scandal of
the Evangelical Mind* received positive, if not rave reviews. Those of us
in the Wesleyan/Holiness or Pentecostal traditions were again marginalized
by reviewers who felt little need to defend their embarrassing relatives.
Perhaps the most disturbing to me was a review in *Prism*, the magazine
published by Evangelicals for Social Action. Surely this group of people,
defenders of the marginalized, would offer a rebuttal to the scandalizing of
some of the very people who make up the editorial board of *Prism.* However, the editors of *Prism* chose David A. Hoekema, Academic Dean and
Professor of Philosophy at Calvin College, to review Noll's book. Needless to say, the review offers no challenge to the basic thesis. Although
Hoekema acknowledges that Noll's characterization of evangelical scholarship will seem unfair to some readers, he fails in any way to defend those
who are slandered by Noll. The review ends with the observation that the
Evangelical community "has been enriched and strengthened by this broad-
side against it."[4]

---
[2]Noll, *Scandal*, 26.
[3]See David Bundy, "Blaming the Victim: The Wesleyan/Holiness Movement in
American Culture;" Henry H. Knight, "John Wesley: Mentor For An Evangelical
Revival;" William Kostleby, "The Dispensationalists: Embarrassing Relatives or
Prophets Without Honor: Reflections on Mark Noll's *The Scandal of the Evangelical Mind," Wesleyan Theological Journal* 32:1 (Spring 1997).
[4]David A. Hoekema, "The Scandal of the Evangelical Mind," *Prism* (May/June
1995).

I. Two Approaches to Our Scandal

The works by Kyle and Noll are but two recent examples of how our movements are marginalized. Like it or not, we are the embarrassing relatives. There are at least two approaches we can take to our commonly scandalized identity. In the first approach, we can continue to internalize our oppressors, offering a form of apologetics that attempts to prove that we are not marginal. This approach accepts the so-called centrist reading on reality and offers explanation after explanation, rebuttal after rebuttal, with the hope of convincing critics that we are more like them than they realize. "Yes, we do have a mind," we counter, "just look at all of our educational institutions." "No, we don't handle snakes. Our denomination never did." "Our worship is not that much different from yours." "If you let us participate in your projects, we promise that we will try hard not to embarrass you." Like abused children, we keep submitting to the beating in the woodshed, actually believing that if we become "good enough" the abuse will stop.

In addition, our shame has caused us to believe the dominant narrative which marginalizes us. As in the case of Noll's work, many from our movements, in order to receive a higher education, internalized the Enlightenment myth of scientific reasoning to the degree that they achieved a comfortable, critical distancing from the traditions of their origin. They became some of our best critics, applying with zeal the tools of analysis learned in the universities. It has been difficult to have the Enlightenment mind and the Holiness or Pentecostal faith. Like oil and water, they do not mix. Therefore, many in previous generations had to choose between criticism and faith, between acceptance or rejection. Their choices were difficult, and the consequences created many broken relationships.

It is also the case that victims who internalize the oppressors have a way of turning on each other. We resent being lumped into the same category of those we consider more marginal than we. Thus, our attacks on our "inferiors" often prove to be more vicious than those from the center. As a result, we focus on our differences rather than on our common heritage, and we scandalize our closest relatives. Pentecostals are an embarrassment to many in the Wesleyan/Holiness tradition. Oneness Pentecostals are an embarrassment to the rest the movement. And we all are scandalized by those snake handlers who continue to be objects of fascination and inquiry!

The second approach to our scandalized identity can be illustrated by a snake handling story. Bill Leonard, a Southern Baptist historian, is a regular faculty member of Appalachian Ministries Resource Center

(AMERC). As part of his course on Appalachian religion and culture, Leonard would take seminary students to a snake handling service.[5] A few summers ago, during the time of the Southern Baptist Church's most vicious fighting, Leonard, after attending the Southern Baptist Convention, found himself deeply wounded by his denomination's division. He recalls that he began his AMERC teaching drained and spiritually depleted. When he arrived at the snake handling service (which was held outdoors), Leonard approached the pastor and asked permission once again to observe the service. The pastor, commonly called "Brother Bob," grabbed Leonard in a huge bear hug and said, "Brother Bill, wherever I am, you are welcome."

These words and the embrace by the pastor had a dramatic effect on Leonard. He notes that he was "saved" at that moment, meaning that he received a deep healing from his wounds and received a renewed faith in Christ.

Bill Leonard allowed the shameful to embrace him, and in doing so he found salvation and healing. His response is the key to the second approach to marginalization. Rather than internalizing that which marginalizes, participating in further shaming or blaming of the victims, the second approach calls for embracing the scandal. It calls for pushing into the embarrassing and not standing back at a critical distance.

There is a biblical precedent for the second approach. For at the very point of scandal is salvation. This is the mystery of the scandal of the cross, and it is the mystery of the scandal of our calling and identity. The very symbol of our shame becomes the way to overcoming our shame. To embrace the cross is to be overtaken by the very thing which embarrasses us.

The second approach is a way of celebrating marginality rather than worshiping an elusive center. It is a form of apologetics which, instead of internalizing a totalizing meta-narrative, offers its own testimony without apology into a discourse of narratives.

II. A Postmodern Opportunity

The dawning of the postmodern era has opened a door for the logic of the second approach. Gone is the understanding of the "mind" as the seat of humanity, which guides history apart from any contextual construction. This dualism, which has been the central mark of modernity, effectively scandalized all forms of knowing that did not submit to its standards. It

---

[5]Leonard had to stop taking students to snake handling services because of AMERC's insurance requirements and it is now illegal in Kentucky to handle snakes.

put both liberals and Evangelicals into "epistemological straight jackets," in which the Christian mind had to submit to the demands of decontextualized abstract propositions. But now, with the demise of the Enlightenment mind, the straight jacket has been removed, allowing the insanity it contained to turn on itself. It is a "mind" that is now being scandalized by its own critical power.

All knowledge is now viewed as being historically conditioned, and there is the abiding suspicion regarding any claim to truth. What was once seen as science is now to be regarded as one more tribal tradition or a set of tribal traditions. Such an epistemological landscape is fraught with dangers and despair; however, it does open a door for those marginalized by the metanarratives of modernity to speak on their own terms.

Returning to Noll's analysis of the Evangelical mind, we must ask, "Just what particular, historically conditioned mind is being scandalized?" According to Noll, the collapse of Evangelicalism's synthesis of American ideals, common-sense Baconian science into a populist style of reasoning (mediated in Fundamentalism, the Holiness Movement and Pentecostalism), effectively abandoned the "mind" to the secular realm. What these three movements did was to empty Evangelicalism of the little bit of intellectual capacity it had before the Civil War. What is left are forms of mind such as Creation Science, which Noll calls "a misguided Baconianism." The Creationists are criticized for undermining a true Christian investigation of the world, and being locked in history with a particular historical form of science.

However, Noll fails to acknowledge that he is utilizing one historically conditioned form of mind to criticize another historically conditioned mind. Failing to criticize the mind that guides his analysis or even to acknowledge that it is only one form of Christian mind, he offers it as an "objective critic." Noll defines his mind as the ability "to think within a specifically Christian framework across the whole spectrum of modern learning."[6] It is "to think like a Christian about the nature and workings of the physical world, the character of human social structures like government and the economy, the meaning of the past, the nature of artistic creation, and the circumstances attending our perception of the world outside ourselves."[7]

"To think like a Christian" is given a generic quality throughout most of the book, without any attempt to define the particular brand of Christian. We are told however, what it is not. To think like a Christian, to praise God with the mind, is not to think like a Wesleyan Holiness person. To think like a Christian is not to think like a Pentecostal. To think like a Christian is not to think like a Fundamentalist.

_____
[6]Noll, *Scandal*, 7.

Finally, toward the end of his book Noll comes clean regarding the ideological assumptions which define a good Evangelical "Christian mind." He sees signs of an awakening of the Evangelical mind in forms of post-fundamentalism as evidenced in the thinking of Harold John Ockenga, Edward John Carnell, and Carl F. H. Henry. Furthermore, Noll cites the establishment of an Evangelical intellectual network with certain well-fixed reference points in the United States, Great Britain, Canada, as well as other parts of the world:

> The extended connections of British InterVarsity, the insights of Dutch Reformed confessionalists, ethical prodding from the Mennonites, literary stimulation from the Anglicans like C.S. Lewis and Dorothy L. Sayers, a common valuing of the classical Protestant heritage, and an ingrained respect for an even broader range of historic Christian expressions have all improved the quality of evangelical intellectual life over the last five decades.[8]

So the Christian mind is a particular form of mind. The "acceptable" Evangelical Christian mind contains particular, historically-conditioned frames of reference. Those of us left out of the landscape should note that Noll is offering only one form, a tribal form of the Christian Evangelical mind. It is his tribe, his narrative, his language, and it is just a mind among many minds that may call themselves Evangelical. It may be scandalized by some, and it may be a scandal to others. In the most despairing of postmodern thought, Noll's version of mind is but a text, which victimizes some and is victimized by others.[9]

Rather than victimizing or attempting to scandalize Noll's version of mind, we do have the opportunity to allow the minds scandalized by Noll to speak for themselves on their own terms. In order to do so we must push into the embarrassing rather than pull away in shame. Space limits me from fully exploring the Wesleyan/Holiness and Pentecostal minds. However, I would like to begin a discussion by offering brief reflection upon two of Noll's criticisms, which seem to reflect the heart of his embarrassment with us:

> In my case, as one who does not believe that the distinctive teachings of dispensationalism, the Holiness movement, or Pentecostalism are essential to the Christian faith, it is not surprising that I find the intellectual consequences of these theologies damaging . . . . With respect to Holiness theology,

---

[7]Ibid.
[8]Ibid., 219.
[9]See Mark Taylor, *Erring: A postmodern a/theology* (Chicago: University of Chicago Press, 1984).

I believe that Christians grow in grace through following God
into the world, embracing their vocations as gifts from God,
and not by "letting go and letting God."...With respect to
Pentecostalism, I believe that every believer, as an essential
element of being a Christian, is baptized with the Holy Spirit
and that it is not necessary for believers to seek the extraordinary sign gifts.[10]

III. "Let Go and Let God"

For Noll, it is the responsibility of the Christian to follow God into the
world as a historical subject. The Holiness Movement's belief that Christians should "let go and let God," or "lay all on the altar," and the admonition to be "clay in the potter's hand," reflected a flight from this responsibility. Just what were the Holiness believers meaning with these phrases?
What do they reflect regarding belief about selfhood and the Christian's
vocation in the world?

The meaning of selfhood as it came to be defined following the Enlightenment was that of the human as a self-grounded subject over an
object-manipulative world. This is reflected in Descartes' dictum, "I think,
therefore I am." The human came to be understood as possessing a "consciousness deceptively pure and an identity deceptively secure."[11] It was
within the power of human reason to control history. The human was thus
grounded in his/her own self-presence needing no other foundation for
identity.

Those within the Holiness movement, as they critically reflected upon
the status of humankind, came to realize that these foundationalists'
pretentions were deceptive. They came to understand that the human
subject was incapable of fulfilling its historical vocation apart from a re-
grounding. Humankind would never achieve the totality for which it
grasps.

Alongside of the Holiness revival came radical social critiques. These
social critiques were grounded in an understanding that social injustice
could only be overcome through radical reorientation. For Phoebe Palmer,
it was the power of Pentecost which enabled women and men to be equal.
For Luther Lee, it was the radical reformatory nature of the gospel, which
declared the "supremacy of the Divine Law over against human law."

"To let go and let God" was therefore a statement announcing the
death of the subject. If death is too strong of a word, perhaps we could
say that the statement called for the decentering of the subject. "To be

---

[10]Noll, *Scandal,* 142.
[11]David Tracy, "Literary Theory and Return of the Forms for Naming and
Thinking God in Theology," *Journal of Religion* 74 (1994): 302-129.

clay in the potter's hand," was to acknowledge that the human was incapable of making its own history. It did in no way imply a disregard for the historical vocation of the Christian. Rather, it called for a yielding, an eclipse, of the human will for that of the Divine.

Also, unlike the self of modernity, what is primary regarding historical action is not the critical side but the participatory side, "the taste of the good that is also the goal." According to Paul Valliere in his analysis of the meaning of Pentecost, the primacy of participation, "allows for the structuring of action in a way that transcends the ethics of means and ends more or less alienated from each other for an ethic based on free participation in the Spirit."[12] To let go and let God is therefore to participate in the righteous transformation of self and world. It means to give up totalizing desire for righteous desire.

Such a call is indeed a scandal in modernity's eyes. It means we acknowledge that our "minds," however sharp and critically astute, are not capable of objectifying reality in order to know it. The subjective is always present, getting in the way, creating desire for totality and power. The holiness folk knew that all knowledge was a reflection of power-based interests. One had to give up this desire for totality and power in order truly to know the world.

The call to "let go and let God" is not only a call from the past. It is a call for the emerging postmodern era. While in today's world the self has been decentered or the subject has been slain, there is no place for it to go. Released from its own self-grounding, it is nomadic, ever wandering in search of an identity. Ours is a world in which people have been forced to let go of control of history, but, as a result, one in which people feel out of control. Knowledge is no longer power. It is powerlessness. Thus, to "let God" is a call to recenter, to regain a sense of vocation and calling. It is a call to receive an identity that is grounded in something more than an image or a sign system. It is to find a home for the homeless mind.

Therefore, it is my contention that the scandal of letting go and letting God is the most intellectually respectable position available. It is to acknowledge the pretentiousness of the critical scientific mind, the despair of the postmodern "Protean mind," and to call for the participatory mind. This mind, participating with the good that is also the goal, is free to be even more critical because it allows self-criticism. It is even more free to explore all areas of human existence. The participatory mind is a form of the Christian mind able to take us into the next century, a time in which we will be called upon to discern the truth and test the spirits.

---

[12]Paul Vallarie, *Holy War and Pentecostal Peace* (New York: The Seabury Press, 1983), 25.

IV. "Be Filled With the Spirit"

For Noll, it is not necessary to seek the extraordinary sign gifts. Who needs extraordinary signs of the Spirit's presence? Kyle's analysis of the religious fringe supplies the answer given by centrist Evangelicals. He views such people as dissappointed and frustrated. Since Pentecostal gatherings were emotion-filled, those on the "fringe" gained a sense of relief from oppression.[13]

Apparently, those people who are not oppressed, frustrated, and bewildered can do well without the bizarre demonstrations of the Holy Spirit. However, for those people who are unable to control their lives as historical beings, the extraordinary sign gifts provide some form of relief and escape.

Certainly there has been a lot about Pentecostalism to cause concern. In an age that valued reason and control, in which Protestant worship and ministry were characterized by order and reasoned discourse, Pentecostal worship was known for promoting chaos. The movement's radicalization of "letting go and letting God," and "laying all on the altar" became an affront to decent, controlled people.

Pentecostalism is by its very nature a disturbing movement, even to those within its ranks. There are mysterious complexities and frightening paradoxes of our spirituality that even those of us within Pentecostalism are afraid to analyze. Sometimes we are a scandal to ourselves. We find ourselves behaving in scandalous ways, even when we do not intend to.

Given the brief nature of this essay, I will explore only one of the aspects of our scandal, namely its radically deconstructive nature. This side of our movement is that which is most frightening and disturbing to the modern mind. There have been few theological constructs available to interpret its meaning. Some of us have dialogued with liberation theology, with its radical challenges to the power interests of modern theology, but have found that its language is inadequate; it leaves intact the human subject and its power to name the world. Pentecostalism leaves nothing intact.

Surprisingly, I have found the deconstructionists to be helpful dialogue partners in exploring the *via negativa* of Pentecost. Their assessments of the nature of knowledge and human discourse parallel in a remarkable manner the critiques inherent in Pentecostalism regarding the modern project. Both deconstructionism and Pentecostalism are consummatory, apocalyptic movements, which dismantle the "cathedral of modern intellect" and mock all forms of anthropological reductionism.[14] Both mock the modernist conceit that humanity can construct a liveable habita-

---

[13]See Kyle, *The Religious Fringe.*
[14]Carl A. Raschke describes deconstruction as a "consummatory, apocalyptic

tion utilizing the skill of rational analysis and problem solving. For the most radical of the deconstructionists, such as Mark Taylor, reality is nothing more than a "festival of cruelty." Within the landscape of multiple discourses, multiple meanings, and multiple texts, we find the act of interpretation becoming a dangerous game in which there is no longer spectator or spectacle, but festival. In the space of festival, distance between the subject/object is closed. A person becomes both actor and spectator, both object and subject, and loses all sense of individuality. The subject/object thus becomes a clown whose "motley dress and shifting masks create a constantly changing play of forms that borders on the utter chaos of formlessness."[15]

For Taylor, the self is empty of everything except its own material presence. Furthermore, Taylor notes that the "book" that is the modern age, with its ordered narrative and sense of history, has been turned into an endless labyrinth. Like a carnival fun house, it is haunted by uncanny sounds, senseless cacophonies, verbal jumbles, and incoherencies. The labyrinth is filled with countless mirrors, whose play is without end, reflecting an infinity of signifiers. At the carnival we are left without a book, a narrative, or a canon to guide us through the maze. The only alternative is to wander and play. The self becomes nomadic, in search for a presence that saves. In such as situation, the wilderness becomes, in the words of Thomas J. J. Altizer, a way of "mazing grace."[16]

In many ways, Pentecostalism acknowledges the reality of the "festival of cruelty." It is a movement that has arisen and continues to grow among the victims of the festival, whose reality is nothing more than an endless labyrinth. It takes seriously the fact that persons are often victimized as objects in someone's historical process. It affirms the need for a presence that saves. Pentecostalism speaks into the festival of cruelty, offering the festival of Pentecost as an alternative.[17]

Furthermore, Pentecost provides a way out of the maze of endless wanderings by providing a way toward the Free City. It is a festival which announces God's saving presence. But beware of this presence! It is a presence that overwhelms and negates the presentness of the modern project. It radicalizes the call to "let go and let God" to the degree that it deconstructs the self, leaving little intact.

---

movement inside Western thought and discourse," which "is the revelation of the inner vacuity of the much touted 'modern outlook.'" See his "The Deconstruction of God," in Thomas J. J. Altizer, Max Myers, Carl Raschke, *Deconstruction and Theology* (New York: Crossroad, 1982).

[15]Taylor, *Erring,* 165.

[16]Thomas J.J. Altizer, "Eternal Recurrence and the Kingdom of God," in D. B. Allison, ed. *The New Nietzsche: Contemporary Styles of Interpretation* (New York: Delta, 1979), 245.

[17]It should be noted that Pentecostalism does not represent the full measure of

As the self is decentered, as it relinquishes the desire for totality, it becomes a newly constituted self, one that has been resurrected from its own deconstruction into a newly configured "I am" found within a matrix of relationships in Trinitarian fellowship. The reconstructed self has a newly formed sense of identity. It is no longer a passive victim of destructive and manipulative forces. As a reconstituted agent, the subject/object becomes a historical actor whose identity is fused with the Spirit in a holy passion for the kingdom. The mind that arises from such an experience is one that participates in the passion of God for the world.[18]

The reconstructed self is not the self in the modernist sense in which it makes its own history, neither is it the nomadic wanderings of the festival of cruelty. Rather, for the self of Pentecost, history becomes mission.[19] Persons are thrust upon an "a-mazing journey" of walking in the light of the Holy Spirit, which guides them through the maze. As "selves on the way," persons participate in holy anarchy, celebrating the coming of the Free City.

The aspect of Pentecostalism that has been the most disturbing to the modern mind is its subversion of language. The speech of Pentecost is that which signifies the presence of "*theos*" within "*logos*." As Frank Macchia observes, in Pentecost language becomes a *prodigium,* "an outstanding sign."[20] This "outstanding sign" can be most profoundly seen among those whose speech has been silenced by the modern *logos*. It is speech that "speaks God," closing the gaps between the sign and the signifier.

In its most mystical and radically deconstructive form, Pentecostal speech becomes glossolalia. It is this deconstructive power that Walter Hollenweger describes as "defying the tyranny of words," in worship and dismantling the privileges of the educated and the literate, allowing the poor and the uneducated to have a voice.[21] Macchia points out that "in glossolalia is a hidden protest against any attempt to define, manipulate or oppress humanity."[22] Pentecostal speech thus becomes a "cathedral of the poor," providing a world fit for the habitation of God among people.

---

the meaning of Pentecost. Rather, I see the movement as possessing "signs of Pentecost." The gifts and calling of Pentecostalism are best seen as an offering to the whole church of these signs of Pentecost festival.

[18]See Steven J. Land, *Pentecostal Spirituality: A Passion for the Kingdom* (Sheffield: Sheffield Academic Press, 1994).

[19]Ibid., 69.

[20]Frank Macchia, "Sighs too Deep for Words," *Journal of Pentecostal Theology* 1 (1992): 47-73.

[21]Walter Hollenweger, *Geist und Materie, Interkulturelle Theologie,* vol. 3, Munich, 1988, 31-45.

[22]Macchia, "Sighs too Deep," 61.

Glossolalia is an unclassifiable, free speech in response to an unclassifiable, free God. Such language is described by Macchia as *Coram Deo*. In the face of God, language breaks down. There are gaps too large for language to bridge and depths too deep for words. Tongues indicate what the postmodernists have aptly noted, namely that the discovery of meaning is often found in the gaps of the unconscious and that language hides as much as it reveals.

The "Pentecostal mind," with its call to a radical "letting go and letting God," is indeed a scandalous mind. It is a mind, which arises from among the victims of the festival of cruelty, giving them hope for a way out of the maze. While it has traditionally been understood that this mind appealed only to the poor, the socially deprived, what we are now realizing is that the "homeless mind" is present everywhere. As Harvey Cox has aptly noted, "Whether middle class or poor, by the last decade of the twentieth century more and more people in every part of the world felt uprooted and spiritually homeless. Whether it was poverty or geographical dislocation or cultural chaos that caused it, all sensed the loss of a secure place in a world where whirl was king."[23] For Cox, Pentecostals are only the visible crest of a very large wave of post-industrial spirituality.

The mind that so scandalizes Noll now represents over 400 million Christians. In a strange way, it turns on its heels the criticisms of Malik, which Noll echos: "Does your mode of thinking have the slightest chance of becoming the dominant mode of thinking in the great universities of Europe or America, which stamp your entire civilization with their own spirit and ideas? . . . Even if you start now on a crash program in this and other domains, it will be a century at least before you catch up with the Harvards and Tübingens and the Sorbonnes."[24]

There indeed may be a lot of catching up to do, but it may not be from our side. No, the Pentecostal mind is not the mind at Harvard, Tübingen, or Sorbonne. It still is found most often among the uneducated. Yet, it remains to be seen what its full import upon civilization will be. This relatively new religious movement, "spawned" out of the Holiness tradition, is leaving its own stamp upon entire cultures with its spirit and ideas.[25]

---

[23]Harvey Cox, *Fire From Heaven: The Rise of Pentecostal Spirituality and the Reshaping of Religion in the 21st Century* (Reading, MA: Addison-Wesley, 1995), 107.

[24]Noll, *Scandal*, 26.

[25]For an analysis of the power of Pentecostalism to transform culture see David Martin, *Tongues of Fire: The Explosion of Protestantism in Latin America* (Oxford, UK: Blackwell, 1990).

V. A Look Toward the Future

I wish to end this essay with some musing regarding the future out-look of Wesleyan and Pentecostal scholarship. My reflections may best be explicated by posing the question, "What seem to be the issues sur-rounding the next generation of scholars in our traditions?"

First, it appears that those students currently enrolled in Ph.D. pro-grams are less burdened by the scandal of their religious identity than those of us in previous generations. They are being given more freedom to contextualize their research and to construct creatively new theological paradigms. If this trend continues, and I think it will, the future is pregnant with possibilities and has the potential to yield some thoughtful and cre-ative scholarship. Because these scholars will not be approaching the theological task with a heavy shame-based identity, they will feel less constrained to defend themselves over against the established paradigms.

Second, as we move more toward a "post-denominational future," there should be more opportunities for Wesleyan and Pentecostal schol-ars to interact freely with the broad range of the Christian tradition. In particular, the Evangelical-Reformed paradigm should have less of a ty-rannical influence over our own work. We will have other partners with whom we can dialogue.

Third, the continued globalization of our movements will contribute to a greater freedom for creative and thoughtful scholarship. Non-North American scholars, who do not have the history of American Evangelical-ism, will feel less bound by the standard paradigms that have governed our own work. Without this "baggage" they can help lead us to learn how to "drink from our own wells."

Fourth, my greatest concern or dread for the future of the Wesleyan and Pentecostal "minds" centers around the fact that the North American context of upward mobility is pushing against our ability to read adequately the human condition. We are thus in danger of having a "mind" much like those who currently criticize us. In other words, we are in danger of having our theological reflections separated from the sufferings of the poor. In some circles I see an ever increasing disdain for the poor and for the religious expressions found among them. Indeed, the great ecumeni-cal divide of the future will not exist between faith traditions. Rather, it will be found within traditions themselves, within the ever widening gaps between the have and the have nots.

Lastly, let me make a final appeal for us to face the future with courage, knowing that we may indeed be on the crest of a wave of new forms of Christian spirituality and theology. Perhaps we can be a small part of the next Christian Reformation that is only now beginning.

The Sacramental Nature of Pentecostal Theological Education

Bob R. Bayles[*]

The primary purpose[1] of this article is to explore the ways in which theological education might be sacramental in nature. Obviously, a need exists to define what both sacrament and theological education mean, a task that cannot be completed in this short essay. It is hoped, however, that this essay will be a springboard for further dialogue about the issues.

The thesis underlying this chapter is the possibility that theological education, at its best, is sacramental in nature. Possibility is used, rather than proof. Previous literature surrounding the nature of transformational adult learning theories indicates that education for adults should move beyond the perception (or reality) of being information dissemination.[2] It

---

[*]Bob R. Bayles (Ph.D., Trinity Evangelical Divinity School). Assistant Professor of Christian Education, Lee University.

[1]While the primary purpose of this article is to explore the idea of the sacramental nature of theological education, it also has a very important secondary purpose—to honor a man who has spent his life devoted to theological education in both the academy and the church. He has invested his time and talents into training ministerial students for almost forty years. In many ways, he has singularly defined the discipline of Bible and Theology at Lee University in Cleveland, Tennessee. The name of Don Bowdle immediately surfaces when thinking of theological education within the Church of God in general, and specifically at Lee University. A personal word of thanks to you, Don, for the many years of trailblazing you have done to make my teaching ministry easier, and to your oft sought after and given advice.

[2]Jack Mezirow. *Transformative Dimensions of Adult Learning* (San Francisco: Jossey-Bass Publishers, 1991). This represents the most comprehensive work currently available in the field of adult education regarding the transformative dimensions of adult education. Application of Mezirow's work to theological education is a developing area of study within theological education.

must be more than the transmission of certain skills deemed necessary to complete tasks.

Too often, it is unclear what is meant by theological education.[3] For some, it must be defined as an academic pursuit entrusted to the ivory towers of the great theological institutions around the world. To others, studying theology represents a threat, a barrier to faith and true spirituality. Between these two extreme poles lies a variegated continuum of beliefs about the nature and purpose of theological education.

Therefore, theological education that strives to be transformational will possess renewing characteristics. It will move us beyond disseminating information, however important that may be. Theological education, at its best, ushers us into the presence of God. There, it fulfills its ultimate purpose in creating within us both the cognitive capacity and the affective ability to respond in worship of God. However, care should be exercised in not drawing a false dichotomy between the cognitive and affective dimensions of learning.

I. The Sacramental Nature of Pentecostal Theological Education

One possible avenue to further our understanding of theological education is to propose that it might be sacramental in nature. Research does not yet easily lead to the conclusion that theological education should be elevated to the level of sacrament (such as the Eucharist). Yet theological education, properly defined and lived out, is a means of grace for it brings us into intimate contact with God, forming and transforming the individual.

Theological education that is sacramental in nature will have a formative and transformative quality to it. It can be formative by helping individuals to construct categories of understanding God and holy things. It can be transformative in that it changes, renews, and recreates within a person the image of Christ. Jack Mezirow, a leading theorist in adult education, speaks of meaning schemes and meaning perspectives; structures that

---

[3]Theological education is currently a hotly debated topic, especially concerning its nature and purpose. For further reading see, Robert W. Ferris, *Renewal in Theological Education: Strategies for Change* (Wheaton, IL: The Billy Graham Center at Wheaton College, 1990); Norma H. Thompson, ed., *Religious Education and Theology* (Birmingham, AL: Religious Education Press, 1982); H. Richard Niebuhr, et al., *The Advancement of Theological Education* (New York: Harper & Brothers, 1957); Edward Farley, *Theologia: The Fragmentation and Unity of Theological Education* (Philadelphia: Fortress Press, 1983); John L. Elias, *Studies in Theology and Education* (Malabar, FL: Robert E. Kreiger Publishers, 1986); Mary C. Boys, *Educating in Faith: Maps and Visions* (San Francisco: Harper and Row, 1989).

help people organize information. Meaning schemes are individual sets of information about a topic or concept. Meaning perspectives are the over-arching belief systems. Significant reorganization of these schemes (meaning schemes and meaning perspectives) is what Mezirow identifies as 'perspective transformation.'[4] Theological education that is sacramental will allow for the construction, deconstruction, and/or reconstruction of the structures (meaning and perspective) we use to understand God. For some, Eucharist is a meaning scheme—for others a meaning perspective. In either view rests the possibility of transformation through the sacraments.

Frank D. Macchia[5] has proposed that tongues represent the presence of God here and now. He states:

> ... for Pentecostals, glossolalia signified God's presence ... [it] represented a heightened awareness of God's presence such as one normally finds in response to the eucharist in sacramental communions. As a linguistic symbol of the sacred, tongues says, "God is here."[6]

Macchia also notes that recent trends in Catholic sacramental theology view sacraments as an occasion for personal encounters between God and the believer.[7] Concerning Macchia's proposal and the new sacramental theology proposed by Karl Rahner, Macchia makes this note:

> Rahner does not locate sacramental efficacy in some kind of material causation necessitated by the elements as elements. Rather, he deals with the question of sacramental efficacy only in the context of the *sign value* of the sacrament. This redefinition does not mean that Rahner holds to a simplistic understanding of "sign" as an intellectual reference to some other reality yet to be experienced. For Rahner, the reality signified becomes present and is experience through the visible sign in the process of signification .... Through sacramental signification, the eschatological presence of God is realized among believers.[8]

Macchia, at least, seems to be opening our understanding of sacrament to include elements of mystery and strangeness through traditionally

[4]Jack Mezirow. "Understanding Transformation Theory," *Adult Education Quarterly* 44(4) (1994): 222-32.
[5]Frank D. Macchia. "Tongues as a Sign: Towards a Sacramental Understanding of Pentecostal Experience," *PNEUMA: The Journal of the Society for Pentecostal Studies* 15/1 (1993):61-76.
[6]Ibid., 61.
[7]Ibid., 62.
[8]Ibid., 62-63.

Pentecostal modes of worship and expression (for example, glossolalia). It seems reasonable to apply this understanding to theological education.

The discussion of sacrament here is limited to that of Eucharist.[9] This is not to suggest that there is a lack of importance that other sacraments may offer. To include discussion on all sacraments would be to go beyond the scope and purpose of this particular essay. Neither is a theology of Eucharist being attempted by this research. What is being described is the sacramental nature of theological education with the Eucharist as a pattern for understanding. The Eucharist presents to us a way that takes participants into the presence of God through faith and grace offered in the elements, typically identified as bread and wine. Theological education presents a way the participants are taken into the presence of God through faith and grace when these participants engage, and are engaged by, the Holy.

II. Theological Approaches to Understanding the Sacraments

There are many approaches (voices) to understanding the sacraments. Four have been chosen, which at least offer the reader a platform from which to survey the field. None of these four is complete in themselves, nor do they offer a comprehensive overview when combined. These do represent a beginning point for dialog.

Karl Rahner

The first approach to Eucharist comes from Catholicism, primarily through the understanding of Karl Rahner. For Rahner, the concepts of Church and Sacraments are intimately linked. He believes that a better understanding of both is discovered when they are studied relationally.

Rahner's understanding of Eucharist's importance is stated in this way:

> It cannot simply be put on a level with other sacraments and listed along with them . . . there is not only a sacrament but also a sacrifice of the new covenant . . . the celebration of the Eucharist is an absolutely central event in the church.[10]

---

[9]The etymology of the English word sacrament is interesting to trace. It is derived from Latin, which in turn is derived from the Greek, *mysterion*. For an excellent overview of how we came to use the word sacrament and what it has meant over the centuries, see G. Bornkamm, *Theological Dictionary of the New Testament*, vol. 4, ed. Gerhard Kittel (Grand Rapids: William B. Eerdmans, 1964), 802-28.

[10]Karl Rahner, *The Church and the Sacraments* (New York: Herder & Herder, 1963), 9-10.

He continues by adding:

> The sacraments . . . are expressions of the life of the Church
> . . . . They make the Church eschatologically, historically and
> socially present and actual as the visible reality of God's
> promise of himself to the world . . . . *They are not simply*
> *distributed by the Church. They are an event of the Church*
> [italics added].[11]

This reflects his Roman Catholic understanding of the nature of the Church. For Rahner, the Church is more than a religious institution or a spiritual welfare organization. The Church is associated with the Old Testament concept of the "people of God."[12] Rahner believes that " . . . the church is not a mere eternal welfare institution, but the continuation, the perpetual presence of the task and function of Christ in the economy of redemption . . . ."[13]

For Rahner, the Sacrament of Eucharist is of primary importance. The value of Rahner's statement for Pentecostals lies, in part, with the connection between a fuller understanding of the nature and purpose of the Church and the nature and purpose of Sacrament. Pentecostals should continue to refine/define our ecclesiology. Taking a cue from Rahner, more thought should be given on how Christology impacts all of theology, thereby providing a more integrative approach to all branches of theology as suggested by the use of narrative theology.

John Calvin

In the *Institutes of the Christian Religion*, Calvin begins his discussion of sacraments in general with the following observations:

> It seems to me that a simple and proper definition would be
> to say that it is an outward sign by which the Lord seals on
> our consciences the promise of his good will toward us . . . one
> may call it a testimony of divine grace toward us, confirmed
> by an outward sign . . . [this] does not differ in meaning from
> that of Augustine, who teaches that a sacrament is a 'visible
> sign of an invisible grace'. . . .[14]

Calvin posits the idea that the number of sacraments is fixed at only two.[15] Calvin seems to indicate that other possibilities exist, which might

---

[11]Karl Rahner, ed., *Sacramentum Mundi* (New York: Herder & Herder, 1970), 1486.

[12]Rahner, *Church and Sacraments*, 11.

[13]Ibid., 13.

[14]John Calvin, *Institutes of the Christian Religion,* ed. John McNeill, trans. Ford Battles (Philadelphia: Westminster Press, 1960), IV.14.1.

[15]Ibid., IV.18.19.

be declared as sacramental. He uses the analogy of unrefined and refined silver. Both are the same until one is given a new value by imprint.[16] He states that sacrament apart from the Word is meaningless since both have the same intention—to transform the believer and impart grace.[17]

For Calvin it seems possible to distinguish act from element in sacrament. What actually happens in communion is an act of grace, which cannot be seen with physical sight, though it does have physical representation. Calvin would not accept the idea of elements merely as symbolic, or the Roman Catholic position of transubstantiation in which the elements are transformed. There seems to be for Calvin a very real way in which Christ is present spiritually. He states:

> Now, the first point is that the sacraments should serve our faith before God; after this, that they should attest our confession before men . . . . the sacraments have effectiveness among us in proportion as we are helped by their ministry sometimes to foster, confirm, and increase the true knowledge of Christ in ourselves . . . the sacrament is a worthless thing if it be separated from its truth . . . [there are] two vices to be avoided. The first vice is for us to receive the signs as though they had been given in vain . . . the second vice is by not lifting our minds beyond the visible sign . . . [the benefits of Christ] are conferred through the Holy Spirit, who makes us partakers in Christ . . . .[18]

In exploring ways that Pentecostal theological education might be sacramental, Calvin makes one final observation that is pertinent. Calvin believed:

> . . . *the Lord teaches and instructs us by his Word* . . . He confirms it by the sacraments . . . *He illumines our minds by the light of his Holy Spirit and opens our hearts for the Word and sacraments to enter in* . . . but the sacraments properly fulfill their office only when *the Spirit, the inward teacher,* comes to them, by whose power alone *hearts are penetrated and affections moved and our souls opened for the sacraments to enter in. If the Spirit be lacking, the sacraments can accomplish nothing* more in our minds than the splendor of the sun shining upon blind eyes . . . I make such a division between Spirit and sacraments that the power to act rests with the former, and the ministry alone is left to the latter— a ministry empty and trifling, apart from the action of the

---

[16]Ibid., IV.14.18.
[17]Ibid., IV.14.3-4, 17.
[18]Ibid., IV.14.13-16.

> Spirit, but *charged with great effect when the Spirit works within and manifests his power* [italics added].[19]

The educative components to sacraments are illustrated in the italicized portions above. The sacrament separated from the Word is useless and results in a worthless and meaningless religious exercise. The same is true for theological education, which strives to be sacramental. Theological education that is sacramental cannot exist as an end to itself.

The value of Calvin's thinking for Pentecostals is rich. We are able to appreciate the relationship(s) between Word and sacrament; the instructional nature of sacraments; that a real, physical representation of the sacraments are present (Christ is very real and very present in Calvin's understanding of the Eucharist); and that without the empowerment of the Holy Spirit the sacraments are empty and trifling.

John Wesley

Wesley was firmly committed to the idea that sacraments were instituted by Christ, accompanied by outward means.[20] These sacraments were means of grace, which, as Wesley stated, he understood in this manner:

> By 'means of grace' I understand outward signs, words, or actions, ordained of God, and appointed for this end, to be the ordinary channels whereby he might convey to men, preventing, justifying, or sanctifying grace.[21]

Wesley held to his Anglican roots by believing that a sacrament is an outward sign of an inward grace, and is the means by which we receive grace. He stated:

> . . . [the phrase 'means of grace'] has been generally used in the Christian Church for many ages—in particular by our own Church [the Church of England], which directs us to bless God both for the means of grace, and hope of glory; and teaches us, that a sacrament is an outward sign of inward grace . . . .[22]

Wesley also insists that, separated from the presence of the Word and the empowering of the Holy Spirit, the means of grace is worthless:

> We allow, likewise, that all outward means whatsoever, if separate from the Spirit of God, cannot profit at all, cannot

---

[19]Ibid., IV.14.8-9.

[20]John Wesley, *Works of John Wesley,* vol. 5 (Grand Rapids: Zondervan, 1958), 185.

[21]Ibid., 187.

[22]Ibid., 187-88.

conduce, in any degree, either to the knowledge or love of God
. . . all those who desire the grace of God are to wait for it in
searching the Scripture . . . the same truth . . . is delivered, in
the fullest manner that can be conceived in the words . . . 'all
Scripture is given by inspiration of God'. . . .[23]

Those branches of Pentecostalism that are rooted in Wesleyan theology
can appreciate the sense of association with the Reformation renewal
understanding of the connection between Spirit and Word, a point very
important to Wesley. Also, without the Holy Spirit and his empowerment,
the sacraments are useless. And finally, for Wesley, the sacraments are
more than symbolic. This is particularly important in that some Pentecostals
view the sacraments as merely symbolic—that nothing actually 'happens'
in the Eucharist.

The Society of Friends

The rationale for inserting a Quaker understanding of sacraments is
simple. The Quakers open a unique vein of thought for many, including
Pentecostals, to reexamine a sometimes narrow understanding of
sacrament. The Society of Friends does not define sacrament with the
usual identification of a liturgical ceremony wherein a physical object (i.e.,
bread and wine) changes spiritually. Trueblood states that ". . . [the]
Quaker insistence is that the miracle of the recognized presence can occur
in connection with common bread and in the midst of common life."[24] The
Quaker position provides an intriguing interpretation that all of life is
sacramental. Even in the common, daily occurrences of education, we
should look for the Holy.

III. Current Trends Impacting Pentecostal Theological Education

The research of three contemporary educators contributes to a better
understanding of Pentecostal theological education. First, Parker Palmer
offers insights from his Quaker background reflecting concepts of

---

[23]Ibid, 188-93. For further reading on Wesleyan Theology, see David L. Smith,
A Contemporary Wesleyan Theology, ed. Charles Carter (Grand Rapids: Francis
Asbury Press, 1983); Thomas A. Langford, *Wesleyan Theology: A Sourcebook*
(Durham, NC: Labyrinth Press, 1984), especially 122-26 where Langford traces
the Catholic, Lutheran, and Calvinist positions of Eucharist; John E. Rattenbury,
The Eucharistic Hymns of John and Charles Wesley (London: The Epworth
Press, 1948).
[24]Elton D. Trueblood, *The People Called Quakers* (New York: Harper & Row,
1966), 147. See also, Douglas V. Steere, ed., *Quaker Spirituality: Selected Writ-
ings* (New York: Paulist Press, 1984); Jessamyn West, ed., *The Quaker Reader*
(New York: Viking Press, 1962).

education as a spiritual journey, engaging the knower and the known in a radically transforming way. Second, Marianne Sawicki offers an emphasis from the Catholic tradition on sacramental catechesis. Finally, Cheryl Johns offers an emphasis on Pentecostal catechesis.

Palmer outlines four primary components of what he identifies as a "Gospel Epistemology."[25] First, Truth is personal, by which he means that truth is a 'Who' not a 'what' mandating a personal engagement with truth—the intersection of Big Story with our story. Second, Truth is communal; there is not one truth for you and one for me. Third, Truth is transcendent and alive in that every community is gathered around some transcendent thing, and as such we are brought face to face with great truths. Last, Truth is transformational. These arguments challenge the objectivist model—one that seeks to keep the knower and the known separated—and posits the idea that the subject is looking back at us to transform us radically.

Marianne Sawicki, a Roman Catholic scholar, believes that we have three means of contact with the historical Risen Christ—narrative, sacrament, and the poor.[26] Sawicki believes that sacraments are best understood in context, that is, in a traditioning or faithing community. Tradition is the handing on of something, and sacrament is one of the means of tradition. She states:

> A sacrament is a communications phenomenon . . . through verbal and nonverbal channels . . . effectively interpreted through song, gesture, story . . . [and] the person participating must have a certain receptivity and faith.[27]

Sacrament is conveyed through educational means (such as teaching) that involves both a leading out and a leading into, from which we get the concept of initiation.[28] She goes on to state that sacramental liturgy "adapts." By this she means that sacrament is a historical reality in the person of Jesus Christ, reinterpreted and engaged in concrete settings of particular lives.[29] Historically, narrative and the poor have been at the heart of Pentecostal theology. It is hoped that Pentecostals will come to

---

[25]Parker Palmer, Audio Tape, April 1998, Coalition for Christian Colleges and Universities National Forum, Indiana. For a fuller treatment of Palmer's thoughts see, *To Know as We Are Known: Education as a Spiritual Journey* (San Francisco: HarperSanFrancisco, 1983); *The Courage to Teach* (San Francisco: Jossey-Bass Publishing Company, 1998).
[26]Marianne Sawicki, *Theological Approaches to Christian Education*, ed. Jack L. Seymour, et al. (Nashville: Abingdon Press, 1990), 43.
[27]Ibid., 46.
[28]Ibid., 48.
[29]Ibid., 61.

embrace more fully the third category of sacrament, particularly in light of the theological contributions by Rahner, Calvin, and Wesley.

Cheryl Johns offers Pentecostals an inside perspective on the issue of how education should be transformative. In a series of articles, Johns seems to identify a template for Pentecostal theological education, which takes into account the idea of the transformational character of theological education—theological education that might be sacramental. This emerging template for Pentecostal theological education has the following features. First, it should be prophetic and subversive.[30] By this she means that theological education should be constantly confronting the group, or ethos, from which it arises. This confrontational nature of theological education functions much the same way as the Old Testament prophet—to bring to the people the voice of God for the purposes of renewal, both corporately and personally. As such, Pentecostal theological education that is prophetic and subversive will also be transformational in character.

Second, it should be an integration of *praxis* and *yada*.[31] Praxis, as a theory of education, is insufficient in and of itself to underpin theological education because it has the ability to be 'self-grounded.'[32] This understanding of praxis eliminates it from being a theory upon which theological education should be constructed. However, if a praxis approach to theological education can be integrated with an epistemology of *yada*, then the grounding of theological education would move from being self-grounded to Other-grounded, specifically in a personal encounter with a personal God. Such encounters are transformational by their very nature (see Isaiah 6; Acts 9).

Third, theological education is immersed in a matrix of orthodoxy, orthopathy, and orthopraxis.[33] This matrix—the intersection where orthodoxy, orthopathy and orthopraxis meet—provides an interpretive lens through which we can construct a worldview that biblically reflects a proper integration of knowing, being, and doing. The integration of these three provides a needed balance for many approaches to theological education that are unbalanced and ill-conceived. Too often, theological

---

[30]Cheryl Johns, "Pentecostals and the Praxis of Liberation: A Proposal for Subversive Theological Education," *Transformation*, 11/1 (1994): 12-15.

[31]Cheryl Johns, "From Babel to Pentecost: The Renewal of Theological Education," World Council of Churches, 1997. See also, Johns, "Pentecostals and the Praxis of Liberation, 12-15; Jackie Johns and Cheryl Bridges Johns, "Yielding to the Spirit: A Pentecostal Approach to Group Bible Study," *Journal of Pentecostal Theology* 1 (1992): 109-34.

[32]Johns, "Pentecostals and the Praxis of Liberation," 13.

[33]Johns, "From Babel to Pentecost," 142.

[34]Ibid., 134-37.

education is either too cognitively based, too affectively based, or too volitionally based. At the point where these three concepts meet, transformation can occur because we see more holistically and in a more balanced way.

Finally, Pentecostal theological education should be about the eclipsing of self and the formation of/transformation into an integrated whole. Modernity (a period from the Enlightenment to the present) has held theological education captive, resulting in theological education being disassociated from formation.[34] Johns states:

> What would be the implications of this fiery Pentecost paradigm for theological education? I believe that under the ongoing sacred canopy of Pentecost, the educational paradigms of both Athens and Berlin are reinterpreted as to their lack of viability for our endeavor to do theological education in the face of the epiphanies of darkness which surround all knowing. Indeed, Pentecost deconstructs these paradigms, revealing them as based upon Babel's towering arrogance more than any of us would care to admit . . . knowledge of God, therefore, is not measured by the information one possesses but how one lives in response to God.[35]

Edward Farley believed this eclipsing of the self has direct impact on the way theological education is perceived. Self-grounded theological education is destructive, trusting in its own powers, and views the world through " . . . a set of unchanging lenses, a fixed set of values, or morals, or doctrines, or traditions . . . no freedom to look at the world any other way."[36]

Diametrically opposed to this self-grounded view of education is one that is focused on living in the Spirit. Farley identified characteristics of this approach to theological education as salvific, sanctifying, and justifying. It allows us to be open to change and struggle, free from fear and open to transformation.[37]

Conclusions and Implications

Pentecostal theological education is about engagement. It is engagement of the heart and the mind. It is an engagement initiated by God for the transformation of the individual and corporate life through the

[35]Ibid., 138.
[36]Edward Farley, "Does Christian Education Need the Holy Spirit?" *Religious Education*, 60/6 (1965): 427, 436.
[37]Ibid., 427-36.

power of the Holy Spirit. It is engagement on the social and religious
levels. It must be personal, communal, alive, and transformational.
    Sacrament is engagement. It is engagement of the heart and mind. It
has visible external elements, yet the profound act of sacrament is spiritual
in nature. Sacrament should bring about transformation of the individual
and corporate community of faith. Sacrament forces us to engage society.
It must be personal, communal, alive, and transformational.
    The fundamental question is, "What is sacramental about theological
education?" Although sacramental and transformational are not
synonymous, they are intricately linked in the process of theological
education becoming sacramental. Theological education is sacramental
in that the learner and teacher confront and are confronted by their
subject—God. Grace is infused into the life of the learner and teacher as
they embrace the mystery and presence of God.
    Just as sacraments have external elements, so too does theological
education. This external physical representation is diverse. It may be
confronting social injustices, earning a diploma, or becoming a teacher. It
will also have an inner representation that is more difficult to "see." Such
inner representations may include a restructuring and/or re-orienting of
belief systems.[38] Such a reorientation is normative when confronted with
a Holy God via theological education. One who has experienced the
sacramental nature of theological education will be compelled to engage
the injustices of the world, confronting fraudulent ways of knowing, being,
and doing.
    Yet, there is also a danger of attempting to name and discover every
mystery of the sacrament in order to use it as a paradigm for theological
education. Such attempts are not only futile, but arrogant stabs to
understand fully the nature of mystery. Sacraments are a mystery and so
is the sacramental nature of theological education. Mystery does not
imply irrationality. Neither does it imply that certain characteristics of
sacramental education cannot be explored and discovered. However,
mystery will frustrate empirically-minded people who seek "proof" for
everything.
    Theological education in general, and Pentecostal theological education
specifically, should create a culture of expectancy—a place where we
expect God to act but simultaneously embrace the pain and the struggle of
mystery. We should anticipate God's surprising us through the process
of theological inquiry. Pentecostals historically have claimed (implicitly
and/or explicitly) to "have all the theological answers." We must rethink
this and now claim it is not only acceptable, but also expected, not to have
all the answers. We must be satisfied with the struggle, realizing the

---

[38]See Mezirow, *Transformative Dimensions.*

mystery of theological education only creates in us more of a desire to peer into depths of God not yet realized. The very nature of mystery compels us to move toward it. As Farley notes, there is a "strangeness" and "peculiarity" that marks anything related to the Gospel of Jesus Christ.[39] Parker Palmer has also raised the same concerns that we not domesticate education and close down learning—his concept of "creating space where truth can be practiced."[40] Theological education that attempts, implicitly or explicitly, to abolish the mysterious is a dead and strangling education. Farley believed that education in and about the Gospel is living and empowering, not stagnating.[41]

Pentecostal theological education should strive to avoid the mentality that theological education is dissemination of information. If truth is really a Person, then theological education is an engagement with Person, namely Jesus Christ. Not all of what happens in Pentecostal theological education, or any other form of theological education, is always transformational. However, one cannot encounter God and not be profoundly and radically changed. This is the point of theological education as sacramental—sacramental in the sense that it brings us into a radical encounter with a holy God—an event that will be transformational.

Something truly gracious happens in a very real sense when learner and teacher alike are confronted by the Subject of their study, and both changed as a result of this encounter. Education is the transmission and living out of that encounter as a way of life that transforms self and community. Geoffrey Wainwright affirms this idea by saying:

> In the sacraments, present realities are evaluated in relation to the ultimate values—and are either rejected, or purified, or affirmed, or enhanced, or transformed, in the sacramental action . . . . In all sacramental action, God is present to transform . . . . The sacraments are but focal instances with the continuing relationship between God and his creatures which is directed towards God's kingdom.[42]

To engage in sacraments is, in a very real sense, to be transported back to Calvary. Real is understood here as spiritual. When one engages in the task of theological education, one really, spiritually, stands before the Cross. This encounter will result in two reactions. The first is repentance, an aspect Sawicki fails to identify. One is confronted with the

---

[39]Farley, "Christian Education," 432.
[40]See Palmer, *To Know As We Are Known*. Also included in Palmer's works, Audio Tape, April 1998; *The Courage to Teach.*
[41]Farley, "Christian Education," 433.
[42]Geoffrey Wainwright, *Doxology: The Praise of God in Worship, Doctrine and Life: A Systematic Theology* (New York: Oxford University Press, 1980), 83.

reality of his/her sinfulness and the vicarious atonement of Christ's death. Such a confrontation will elicit a broken spirit.

In the same event, there is also celebration—celebration that Truth is seeking me for personal relationship (Parker Palmer). In this same sense, theological education that is truly Christian will cause one to repent and celebrate; repentance, when faced with truth as it is revealed, exposing prejudices and erroneous world/life views; celebration that Truth is seeking me for a personal, transformational relationship. This celebration is not to be viewed in contemporary understanding—the ultimate party. As James Loder states:

> Celebration in transformation is not an isolated outburst; it is not temporary self-indulgence in random selection of instinct gratification, but the repeated awakening to and profound appreciation of the fundamental but hidden order of all things undergoing transformation into the glory of God.[43]

Pedagogically every Christian teacher must rethink her/his view of what happens in the classroom. Theological education that strives to be sacramental does not begin the first day of class, but rather in the heart and mind of the professor in pre-syllabus construction. What does she/ he wish the learner to know? What is it that the Spirit wishes to happen in the learning process? As such, it will force revisions in syllabi construction, impact methodologies, and change assessment. Theological education that strives to be sacramental can be intentional, and indeed should be. Education is leading out and leading into. It is leading out of ways and practices that constrict and hinder learning; it is leading into a life in the Spirit—a life of freedom. Life in the Spirit does not imply an absence of struggle—quite the contrary. However, as Jerome Boone notes,[44] it makes the painful process of theological education possible. The multi-dimensional aspects of the educational task (such as underlying educational philosophy, teacher, learner, outcomes, assessment, curriculum) will all be transformed.

There is a transformative power to the educational process that is too often ignored in the day to day grind of higher education. Scholars referenced throughout this research seem to be speaking to us to slow down ourselves, the learner, and the process of education, and realize that something wonderful, powerful, and gracious actually does occur in the life of the learner (and teacher) when educational "facts" are transformed

---

[43]James E. Loder, *Theological Perspectives on Christian Formation,* ed. Jeff Astley, et al. (Grand Rapids: William B. Eerdmans, 1996), 282.
[44]Jerome Boone, "Community and Worship: The Key Components of Pente-costal Christian Formation," *Journal of Pentecostal Theology* 8 (1996): 129-42.

and transfigured into eternal truths. Commenting on the grace given in theological education, Loder says:

> . . . grace is God's alone to give and so move one through the dialectic of transformation into the worship and glorification of him, the supreme end of the transforming work of Christ's Spirit. As such, they are signs of the presence and power of the kingdom of God and they belong not to the convicted person but to God's people.[45]

What is truly hoped for is a view of education that will invite the presence of God so that it, and we, can be transformed, affirmed, and purified. Only then can theological education be truly gracious. Only then can theological education be truly sacramental.

---

[45]Loder, *Theological Perspectives,* 283.

Integrity: A Foundational Principle for Ministry

Jerald Daffe[*]

> That, if gold rust, what shall poor iron do? For if the priest be foul in whom we trust, What wonder if a laymen yield to lust?[1]

Let us contemporize this principle from Chaucer's *Canterbury Tales* and apply it to today's churches. Maybe it should read like this: "If God-called and church-ordained ministers overlook the foundational principle of integrity, how can we expect it to be evident among the members and friends of the local congregation?"

We feel comfortable condemning the Pharisees for their legalism and inconsistencies. It is so easy to say "Amen" as we hear Jesus describe them as "whitened tombs, which look beautiful on the outside but on the inside are full of dead men's bones and everything unclean" (Matthew 23:27). But consider this. Any person in ministry who fails to maintain a consistent life of moral integrity falls into the same category.

The American church has been rocked in recent decades by the public revelations of moral failure among denomination and parachurch leaders. How can we forget the photo of a shackled, bowed, distraught Jim Bakker being led into the courtroom? Or what about seeing Jimmy Swaggart looking heavenward with tears streaming down his face and hearing the anguished statement "I have sinned . . . ." Then some ten years later, Henry Lyons stands in court prior to sentencing on charges including

---

[*]Jerald Daffe (D.Min., Western Conservative Baptist Seminary). Professor of Pastoral Ministry, Lee University.
[1]These lines are part of an extended quote on the dedication page of *Ministerial Ethics: Being a good minister in a not-so-good world* authored by Joe E. Trull and James E. Carter *(Nashville, TN: Broadman & Holman,* 1993).

grand theft and racketeering and describes his actions to the judge and courtroom as stinking in the nostrils of both God and the law.[2]

Though these cases brought public shame to the cause of Christ, destruction to individual congregations, and hurt to their families, there is an even greater problem. These are just the tip of the iceberg of ministerial moral failure. The accounts of marital infidelity, homosexuality, substance addiction, and embezzlement are found across denominational lines. No doubt a number of contributing causes may be cited, but in every case there was a point in time when a crack appeared in the foundation principle of integrity. And due to a failure to repair it quickly, the inevitable disaster became a reality.

I. Integrity: Foundational Principles

It is easy to label a particular concept as a foundational principle. The challenge comes in our being able to grasp its meaning and apply its method. Such would seem to be the case with integrity. Repeatedly we hear the calls for integrity in all areas of life and in a breadth of vocations and professions. The clerical ministry is no exception. We are familiar with the principle but may have some difficulty in spelling out the specifics. Part of this would seem to be due to its frequently being cast as one of the traits of character. In his article, "Why Character Counts," Stephen R. Covey provides an excellent example of such a presentation:

> Character is made up of those principles and values that give your life direction, meaning and depth.... They include such traits as integrity, honesty, courage, fairness and generosity–which arise from the hard choices we have to make in life.[3]

The best way to present integrity as a foundational principle is to explore and interact with several varied definitions. Although each comes from a different perspective, together they emphasize the vital importance of integrity in the life of those whom God calls into specific service.

In their book, *Ministerial Ethics: Being a good minister in a not-so-good world*, Trull and Carter define integrity in terms of the minister's

---

[2]Jim Bakker, formerly head of the $129 million PTL empire, initially was sentenced to over forty years in prison. Jimmy Swaggart, head of Jimmy Swaggart Ministries, was defrocked by the Assemblies of God for moral failure. His growing television and education ministries quickly declined. Henry Lyons, recent President of the Nation Baptist Convention, USA, is facing a prison term of at least five years.
[3]Stephen R. Covey, "Why Character Counts," *Reader's Digest* (January 1999): 133.

moral life. They explain integrity as "the integrating element that unifies character, conduct and moral vision into a 'life worthy of the calling you have received' (Ephesians 4:1) as a minister of Jesus Christ."[4] Character is seen as those virtues which have been instilled within us. It is a matter of being. Conduct speaks of our actions, which should be the outward expression of the "habits of the heart" (our character). Moral vision pertains to our composite lifestyle. This becomes the real test of whether or not we are persons of integrity. Are we continuing over a duration of time to live on the outside what we proclaim as our inner being?

This intriguing approach to the definition does not allow a person to take pride or justify himself/herself as an individual of integrity based on one or two actions. Instead, it places integrity as a foundational principle that includes being, doing, and continuing.

Another approach to reviewing the basics of integrity is to consider the following three statements as a practical, working definition:

> Integrity is playing by the rules.
> Integrity is playing by the rules when
>   no one else does.
> Integrity is playing by the rules when
>   you're playing alone.

The first statement assumes we know the biblical principles or virtues that are expected and that our conduct is in accordance. Yet, in itself that does not necessarily constitute integrity, since our actions may be motivated by habit or manipulation of an outward source. The second statement places one in contrast to those surrounding him/her. Merit is evident in not following the general actions of the group. However, once again this does not automatically assume inner being and belief. Knowledge of what is right or fear of consequences may cause action opposite from the others. Remember, someone is there to see. That is why the last statement is so important. It speaks of doing right because of an inner commitment to good even though no one will ever know.

There is no doubt that these three statements may not stand the test of scrutiny in developing a formal, iron-clad definition of integrity. However, not only are they easy to remember, but they also provide a daily check on one's current moral position. And this is both the challenge and necessity for all of us in ministry!

Let us consider a third definition and approach to integrity as presented by Stephen L. Carter in his book, *Integrity*. He defines this principle as "the courage of one's convictions."[5] For this to become a reality in a person's life, there are three required steps. The first is discerning

---

[4]Trull and Carter, *Ministerial Ethics*, 45.
[5]Stephen L. Carter, *Integrity* (New York: Basic Books, 1996), 5.

what is right and wrong. The second is acting on what you have discerned even at personal cost. The third step is saying openly that you are acting on your understanding of right from wrong.[6]

According to this process, integrity is not just the simple adoption of a set of rules or principles one will follow. It is taking the time to reflect on right and wrong, as well as utilizing the necessary emotions and resources to come to a conclusion.[7] Having made the determination, integrity includes acting upon what you believe to be true regardless of the cost. It requires taking a proactive rather than simply a reactive stance. Then the final aspect is voicing the reason for your decisions or actions. They are based on what has been concluded to be right or wrong.

The following three quotes are reflections of what will take place based on Carter's definition and approach to the principle of integrity:

> . . . a woman who believes abortion is murder may state honestly that this is what she thinks, but she does not fulfill the integrity criteria unless she works to change the abortion law.[8]

> . . .integrity is not about winning but about playing by the rules. And sometimes playing by the rules makes it impossible to win.[9]

> It does not promote integrity to ignore or cover-up wrongdoing by a co-worker or family member. And it does not promote integrity to claim to be doing the will of God when one is actually doing what one's political agenda demands.[10]

II. Integrity: A Biblical Overview

The importance of integrity as seen in the Scripture is illustrated best in the narrative of Job and in the example of Joseph, the son of Jacob. However, not to be overlooked are the written statements of David and the negative example of integrity breakdown that he demonstrates on two separate occasions.

Job's integrity initially appears in God's second conversation with Satan after allowing all of this righteous man's goods and family to be taken. God says, "and he still maintains his integrity, though you incited me against him to ruin him without any reason" (Job 2:3; all translations

---

[6]Ibid., 7.
[7]Ibid., 26.
[8]Ibid., 10.
[9]Ibid., 109.
[10]Ibid., 11.

are from the NIV). Later as he suffers physical pain, Job's wife questions him: "Are you still holding on to your integrity? Curse God and die" (Job 2:9).

Twice during the dialog with his friends, Job projects the importance of his integrity. Regardless of their efforts to convince him of his unrighteousness, he holds to the foundation of his integrity. Hear him as he argues: "Relent, do not be unjust; reconsider, for my integrity is at stake," (Job 6:29), and then as he firmly states, "I will never admit you are in the right; till I die, I will not deny my integrity" (Job 27:5).

Job understands the importance of personal integrity. His loss of possessions and family causes him to respond with all the symbols of deepest grief (Job 1:20). The loss of his health forces him to sit in ashes and scrape his body with a broken piece of pottery (Job 2:7,8). But it appears to be even greater turmoil for him to hear his friends emphasize that his personal sins must be the cause of all the devastation upon family and possessions. They are so bound to the concept of judgment following sin that there is no concept of a personal righteousness when surrounded by major negative occurrences.

Job's persistence in declaring his personal integrity indicates a true sense of value. Relationships (family and friends) and possessions are important. However, they rank secondary to one's personal being. For that reason he cannot admit to any sin he has not committed. He understands that if one loses who he/she is, then everything else loses its glamor and value. But more importantly, one loses his/her relationship with God.

Each of the individuals in this narrative have an approach or view of integrity. Job's wife disdains it. Job's friends misunderstand it. Job clings to it. And God honors it.

Then there is that marvelous example of integrity as exhibited by Joseph. Although the word is not in any part of the story, his actions fulfill the definition of integrity. This can be seen in two aspects of his life while he is living in Egypt.

The first extends over a period of approximately forty years of his life. In spite of being hated and sold into slavery by his own brothers, he never takes revenge even when opportunity repeatedly appears. When famine comes to Cannan as well as to Egypt, Jacob sends ten of the brothers to buy grain. Joseph recognizes them, tests them, and then gives them grain with their money returned secretly. He could have retaliated, but it was not part of his character. Later he moves the entire family to Egypt, supplies them with food, provides a separate location for them to live, and helps them get jobs.

Some fifteen years later Joseph's integrity continues to be seen when his brothers fear retaliation after their father's death. Joseph summarizes the whole situation with these words, "You intended to harm me, but God intended it for good to accomplish what is now being done, the saving of many lives" (Genesis 50:20). Integrity enables him to understand the big picture rather than being caught in the emotion of the moment.

The second demonstration of Joseph's integrity comes earlier in his life when serving as the head of Potiphar's household. Here is a handsome, virile young man who is daily being offered a sexual relationship with his master's wife. His integrity enables him to keep his hormones in check, recognize that the opportunity does not justify the relationship, and respect her as being the master's wife. How easy it would have been for him to succumb under the constant pressuring! How easy it would have been to justify an illicit relationship! Not to be overlooked are the immediate consequences. The rebuffed woman falsely accuses him of sexual assault, and he then languishes in prison for a number of years. But he kept his integrity, and God is with him even there (Genesis 39:20-23).

Joseph's holding to his integrity indicates the final or lasting reward that God provides. Though some would see it as binding and restricting, in the long run it is fulfilling and elevating as God honors him.

Our contrast example is David. This handsome psalmist and mighty warrior king demonstrates the consequences of allowing one's integrity to be compromised. He knows the importance of integrity as is revealed in the Psalms. "May integrity and uprightness protect me, because my hope is in you" (25:21). "In my integrity you uphold me and set me in your presence forever" (41:12). But in two situations he fails miserably. David's actions are not consistent with his knowledge.

The first example is David's adultery with Bathsheba and the eventual arrangment of her husband's death to cover the resulting pregnancy. It begins with David's viewing this beautiful woman bathing (2 Samuel 11:2). The issue is not whether or not he could have avoided seeing her. It is what happens once he has! There are times when you cannot avoid being confronted by temptation. Holding to your integrity keeps you from yielding to it. In David's case he had a choice of how long he would stare at this nude woman, what he would think about after seeing her, and what actions he would choose.[11]

Instead of following God's law, David chooses to cast aside his integrity and follow his lustful inclinations. Blinded by desire, he has no concept of how far this sin will take him and the eventual price to be paid. The lack of integrity results in an imbalance in his life, which can only lead to ruin. Surely while standing on the rooftop he never dreamed that in several months he would be purposely sending one of his mighty men, Uriah, to death in an attempt to hide his sin.

---

[11]Jerald Daffe, *Life Challenges for Men* (Cleveland: TN, Pathway Press,1997), 85.

This event in David's life demonstrates the slippery slope on which any person in ministry can find himself/herself once the bulwark of integrity is allowed to be lowered or breached. It also demonstrates how unrestricted sexual attraction for a person other than one's mate can lead to this total breakdown.

The second example of failure of integrity in David's life is completely different. Here it involves taking pride or confidence in numbers. There appears to be no threat necessitating a military census. Even Joab, the sin-laddened commander-in-chief, recognizes the spiritual error of David's directive (2 Samuel 24:3). But David forges ahead only to be conscience stricken upon its completion (2 Samuel 24:4-10). By then it is too late. His relationship with God is fractured, and he will receive God's retribution.

This event can be repeated in various ministries today when anyone becomes attached to the numbers game: attendance figures, monetary receipts, and building size. Instead of emphasizing what God is doing within people, the spotlight focuses on how many, how much, and what kind. More than likely, this type of letdown in one's integrity does not just spring itself on a person, but rather it comes on gradually as one rejoices in growth or is influenced by those who emphasize numbers. Frequently this breakdown of integrity goes unnoticed as it is often seen as the normal activity for success-minded ministers.

These biblical examples demonstrate that integrity is not a matter of age, position or event. Instead, it comes from our inner spiritual beliefs being reflected through right choices at the right time.

III. Integrity: A Practical Application

All of the talk about integrity is nothing more than a waste of words, time, and oxygen unless applied to concrete areas of our personal lives. The proclamation of biblical truth becomes effective only when the messenger demonstrates it in his/her life. As John R.W. Stott states, "Hypocrisy always repels, but integrity or authenticity always attracts."[12] This necessitates our answering three questions: 1) How does an individual become a person of integrity? 2) Why is there such a struggle for many ministers to maintain their personal integrity? 3) What are some areas in which to evaluate one's integrity?

The development of Christian integrity is both an event and a process. Integrity begins with the salvation experience. Justification and regeneration set us on the right path to holiness. Then it becomes our responsibility to cultivate that goodness and righteousness, which God through the

---

[12]John R. W. Stott, *Between Two Worlds* (Grand Rapids: William B. Eerdmans Publishing Co.,1982), 271.

Holy Spirit imparts within us. We then develop integrity through a process of commitment and right choices. It takes shape as we discern right from wrong through commitment to the Scriptures, acceptance of its principle of doctrine and lifestyle, and following the lifestyle of Jesus.

Not to be overlooked is the spiritual dimension in the development of personal integrity. What good does it accomplish to speak of the empowerment of the Holy Spirit without practicing his presence and opening ourselves to his influence. Let us be more specific. The baptism of the Holy Spirit with the New Testament evidence of speaking in tongues provides power for witnessing. One dimension of that witness is a lifestyle of integrity blossoming in the face of everyday choices as well as the occasional difficult situations. The Holy Spirit enables integrity to shine forth even when darkening clouds surround us and satanic foes would attempt to defeat us.

Since integrity is a foundation principle for ministry, it becomes logical to understand that this area will be a personal battleground. Ultimately the struggle for integrity needs to be seen in terms of Satan's desire to render the church's leadership ineffective. When ministers lose or lack integrity, Christianity appears to be no different from any other belief or philosophy. As a result, some unbelievers respond by rejecting the claims of Christ. Even believers may back off and question whether or not their personal commitment is to a genuine belief structure that makes a major difference in people's lives.

Another impact of ministerial indiscretions is the lowering of established standards for Christian living. The laity begin to rationalize the existence of a new, lower standard on the basis of ministerial failure. In all of these settings, the church as a local congregation and as a whole body of Christ loses its luster. The light on a hill dims, and the salt begins to lose its flavoring (Matthew 5:13-16).

This struggle for integrity intensifies as cultural philosophies creep into our thinking. Unless there is both a careful filtering of our thought processes and evaluation of our motives, we subtly may be incorporating them into our decision making. We can publicly lament the encroachment of secularization, pluralism, and relativism, but are we aware of how they may be privately impacting our lives as ministers of the gospel of Jesus Christ?

The struggle for integrity also may come as a result of attempting to maintain a particular image. When the temptation to look good in front of others leads to self-deception, we definitely are struggling with an issue of integrity. When duplicity dominates, we no longer are living under the supernatural direction of the Holy Spirit and the principles of Scripture. In his article, "Are You Pursuing Integrity or Image?" Mike Fehlauer offers these observations:

A life of integrity sweeps away those small and sometimes undetectable areas of compromise—those attitudes that lead to shading of truth in subtle areas and an embracing of double standards. For example, we don't lie, we disinform. We just don't tell the whole truth. Or, when we communicate a story or situation, we always attempt to tell it to put ourselves in the best light.[13]

There is one other aspect in the struggle for integrity. It differs from those previously mentioned. Instead of being internal, it is more of an outward encounter. As the general populace becomes disillusioned with a failing ministry or accustomed to their moral lapses, we are challenged with proving that there still are men and women of integrity. There still are individuals in ministry who are credible and live the life they proclaim from the pulpit or lectern. James Emery White, in his article, "The High Road to Credibility," describes this as follows:

Every week I stand before people who are not Christians and try to tell them about the Christian faith. With most of them, I have one shot to establish any kind of credibility. The pressure intensifies with the knowledge they are actively looking for a way to dismiss me as a messenger, and as a result the message.[14]

Final consideration needs to be given to the evaluation. There are six main areas in which to evaluate our integrity. They encompass our speech, finances, treatment of people, honesty, sexual morality, and commitments. Rather than discuss each, a list of questions to test one's integrity is offered. Needless to say, they do not cover all areas under each of the topics, but they do provide a basic beginning.

1. Does my choice of humor highlight lifestyles that are condemned as sin in the scriptures?
2. Are my illustrations truthful or exaggerated for effect?
3. When I am angry or frustrated, do my words reflect a Christian response or worldly language?
4. If I am unable to pay my bills, do I immediately speak with my creditors or do I disregard them until confronted by them?
5. Do I report untraceable income when filing my income tax?
6. Do I treat people equally without consideration for color, economic class, or personal benefit?
7. When it is my fault (whatever the situation), will I admit

---

[13]Mike Fehlauer, "Are You Pursuing Integrity or Image," *Ministries Today* (May/June 1998): 49.
[14]James Emery White, "The High Road to Credibility," *Leadership* (Fall 1995): 53.

the mistake or "pass the buck"?
8. Will I lie to "save face"?
9. Am I committed to sexual abstinence prior to marriage?
10. Am I continuing my commitment to a monogamous relationship with my spouse?
11. Will I contribute to someone's lack of integrity by "ghost
writing" for him/her?
12. Am I a person of my word in terms of doing what I
commit to and arriving at the time indicated?
13. Will I stand up for truth even when it costs me financially
or hurts my popularity?

The importance of integrity cannot be understated. People in all areas
expect it. Several paragraphs from Vijai P. Sharma's weekly column illustrate this expectation:

> All human beings care very much about integrity. In what
> way? They want everybody else to have it. Integrity is what
> we look for most in the other person. Even a criminal prepar-
> ing to commit a crime wants integrity in his or her accomplice.
> If you join a gang, you have to be a man (or woman) of your
> word. If you are not, gang members might kill you. Bosses
> want absolute integrity in their leaders so they can depend on
> them. And we all want our partners to have absolute integ-
> rity, so we can trust them. But, how many of us earnestly
> work on becoming persons of absolute integrity ourselves?
> And, if everyone didn't work on perfecting his or her own
> integrity, how can we find it in the people around us?[15]

If integrity is of such importance in the secular world, how much more
important is it in the spiritual world as represented by the life of the minister?

The answer would seem to be this. Integrity provides a foundation
principle upon which a spiritually effective ministry can be built and sustained. It enables the Church as a whole and believers as individuals to be
shining witnesses of life-changing power through salvation in Jesus Christ.
No one else can offer that impact to a sinful degenerate world looking for
answers!

---

[15]Vijai P. Sharma, "Integrity is what we look for in another," *Cleveland Daily
Banner* (25 October 1998), 37.

The Importance of Intercultural Competence in Theological Education: A Mandate for the Church

Ridley N. Usherwood*

Introduction

Due to the demographic changes facing American society and the reality that the world is now a "global city," where pluralism, diversity and interculturalism have become operant words, it is imperative that ministerial training institutions take seriously the challenge of preparing future ministers who are interculturally competent. Can ministers whose academic preparation does not include the necessary intercultural and multiethnic skills effectively carry out their ministries with those outside their own cultures? Can ministers who do not understand the symbols, aspirations and problems of their parishioners and who do not have the skills for entering the world of meaning in other cultures be in a position to guide the faith journey of those parishioners? In other disciplines would not such incompetence be deemed unacceptable and unethical?

This problem makes a theological/intercultural and ministerial training approach imperative. The church is theologically a trans-cultural, sociological, and intercultural body. But as soon as the church speaks, it uses cultural language because all human language is embedded in a cultural tradition. How does theology (which wants to mirror this intercultural entity and point to its transcultural reality) operate if theological language is by definition culturally biased language and if this bias is unavoidable?

*Ridley Usherwood (D.Min., Columbia Theological Seminary). Associate Professor of Intercultural Studies, Lee University.

I. "Melting Pot" vs. "Salad Bowl" Paradigm Shift

In some circles social scientists and religious leaders still hold to the "melting pot" analogy for racial and ethnic assimilation and to the notion of American society as a conglomerate of "unmeltable ethnics." In an unprecedented and rare instance of agreement, however, theologians, sociologists, historians, marketers and futurists seem to have reached a consensus on the need to view postmodern American society as a "salad bowl" in which we find different ethnic groups, which are becoming increasingly aware of their unique ethnic identities and of the value that their particular "ingredient" adds to the overall American salad. In a publication written almost twenty years ago, Church of God Director of Hispanic Ministries, Esdras Betancourt, suggested that if nothing else:

> Ethnic studies teach us that there are other ways of living and being, and that to be racially and ethnically different does not mean that one is inferior or superior. An understanding of other groups and cultures helps to create the kind of racial and ethnic harmony the church needs in order to witness effectively to the humanizing aspects of the Gospel of Christ.[1]

Betancourt's challenge was written in 1980 but it would appear that the church has not heeded his advice. Properly understood and intentionally embraced, his ideas could have far-reaching effects.

II. Radical Praxis Implications for Church of God Leadership and Training

Since the paradigm of the melting pot has both served its usefulness and has lost its credibility, the reality is that ethnic groups did not melt into a standard uniform national type. The Church of God must abandon the old paradigm and learn to minister effectively to all people. Betancourt suggests that this could involve at least four major tasks:

> 1. A sociological assessment, which involves an intentional effort on the part of church leaders and educators to understand the history, culture, spiritual needs and political aspirations of ethnic groups in America;

---

[1] Esdras Betancourt, "Ethnic Ministries: Ethnic America's History and Mission," in *The Promise and the Power: Essays on the Motivations, Developments, and Practices of the Church of God,* ed. Donald Bowdle (Cleveland, TN: Pathway Press, 1980), 229-67.

2. A Biblical assessment, that takes seriously a proper view of ethnicity in the Bible and of God's redemptive mission to the nations of the world;

3. A theological assessment, which calls the church to responsibility and accountability for practicing the ethic of hospitality as was spoken of by Jesus when He said: "I was a stranger and you took me in" (Matthew 25:35), or the Apostle Paul's command previously referred to in Romans 15:7 "...Welcome one another therefore just as Christ has welcomed you, for the glory of God . . .";

4. A contemporary assessment, which further calls the church to the urgent imperative of taking decisive steps to help its membership worldwide develop ethnic literacy (or intercultural competency), and particularly better understanding of ethnicity within America in such racially troubled times such as we live.[2]

While I concur with Dr. Betancourt's assessment, I am skeptical of any of the above taking place prior to the whole church repenting of its past sins of racism and its complicity in supporting, aiding and abetting oppressive societal structures. Furthermore, it will also involve a much more radical and fundamental willingness toward embracing biblical Christianity than Betancourt calls for.

When Jesus issued the Great Commission in Matthew 28:19-20, most of his disciples understood the implications of the command. The command was given to a group of Jews, members of a rather exclusive ethnic group, to go to all nations and make disciples, although the pattern for the church was to cross ethnic barriers and to develop an inclusive fellowship. Peter, a leader of that group, was rather slow in coming around to the implications of that mandate. The obvious conflict he faced came to a head in Joppa where he was confronted with the ugliness of his own prejudice and racism (see Acts 10:1ff).

Implicit in the mandate given to the disciples is the command to educate with the concepts Jesus had commanded. In this educational phase, the idea of a continued relationship is assumed—where fellowship, dialogue, sharing and growth will take place across racial and cultural lines (see Acts 8, and Acts 13).

It is my thesis that part of the reason for the illness plaguing contemporary American Christian churches lies in the segregated, monocultural, homogeneous, and racist approach to ministry. Surely a segregated church is a blight to the body of Christ and as such is a perversion of the Gospel, which leaves the body of Christ and thus the family of God divided and

---

[2]Ibid., 230.

deprived of its essential life and enrichment that can come only from a multi-ethnic and cross-cultural witness. Worst of all, such segregation in Christ's body perverts the image of God's love for all people through their incarnational witness. Commenting on this pathology, Sid Smith has rightly stated that, "The healthiness of a church is determined largely by implications from biblical theology, anthropology, and ecclesiology. When a church deviates in understanding and practice from the biblical teaching in these areas disease results."[3] Smith further comments that "historically in America, a chief pathology in American Christianity has been racism, and that racism in the culture has contributed to the practice of 'racial Christianity' which gave rise to an 'immoral morality.'"[4]

It is therefore imperative for those who seek to educate for peace and justice in the congregation, to confront first the pervasive beguilement of racism and to understand its manifestations and ramifications prior to embarking on a healthy inclusive and multi-ethnic ministry.

III. Why the Church Must Address and Confront America's Legacy of Racism

It is a well-known, though often ignored, fact that the United States of America was established as a white society, founded upon the near genocide of one race and then the enslavement of another; thus, America's racial history has affected us all in profound ways, and it is still shaping our national experience and obstructing the fulfillment of our professed values. Its face is dramatically revealed in the continued devastation of native, black, and other communities of color, in the legacy of benefit still enjoyed by most white people, and in the fear and anger felt by many whites facing shrinking economic realities and the temptation of scapegoat racial minorities.

Opening our eyes and ears to the voices of reeducation and transformation becomes an opportunity to explore the meanings of repentance. Biblically, repentance means far more than feeling sorry (and long-suffering people of color deserve more than white guilt feelings). The Biblical meaning of repentance is to turn around. It means to change one's course and one's behavior by heading in a new direction. Jim Wallis in his commentary on the "Legacy of White Racism" argues that:

> In spiritual and Biblical terms, racism is a perverse sin that
> cuts to the core of the Gospel message. Put simply, racism

---

[3]Sidney Smith, "An Analysis of the Transitional Process of Selected Multicultural Churches," (Ph.D. diss., Golden Gate Baptist Theological Seminary, 1973), 150.
[4]Ibid.

negates the reason for which Christ died—the reconciling work of the cross. It denies the purpose of the church: to bring together, in Christ, those who have been divided from one another, particularly in the early church's case, Jew and Gentiles – a division based on race. There is only one remedy for such a sin and any sin for that matter, and that is repentance. When such a repentance is genuine, the fruit of concrete forms of conversion, behavioral change and reparation (restitution) will follow.[5]

Since racism has to do with the power to dominate and enforce oppression, and in North America that power is in white hands, white racism in white institutional structures (including the church) must be eradicated by white people repenting and changing, not just black, yellow, and brown people. Racism seeks to define the being of others and subsequently to deny their God-given humanity based upon skin color and racial designation. Racism calls into question the nature of God and God's creative order. North American churches have for the most part capitulated to this racist ideology—sometimes in its pronouncements, more often in its silence, and most certainly in its institutionalized life and practice, the church has given sanction, blessing, and occasionally theological justification for racism.

George D. Kelsey, writing in *Racism and the Christian Understanding of Man*, describes the "faith system of racism" as follows:

Racism is a faith, a form of idolatry. It is an abortive search for meaning. In its early modern beginnings, racism was a justification device. It did not emerge as a faith. It arose as an ideological justification for the constellations of political and economic power which were expressed in colonialism and slavery. But gradually the idea of the superior race was heightened and deepened in meaning and value so that it pointed beyond the historical structures of relation, in which it emerged, to human existence itself. The alleged superior race became and now persists as a center of value and an object of devotion. Multitudes of people gain their sense of "power of being" from this membership in the superior race. Accordingly, the most deprived white people culturally and economically [are] able to think of [themselves] as better'n any nigger.[6]

It is imperative that the church rise to the challenge and get its own house in order. It is still riddled with racism and segregation. As has been

---

[5]Jim Wallis, ed., *America's Original Sin: A Study on White Racism* (Washington, DC: Sojourners, 1992), 3.
[6]George D. Kelsey, *Racism and the Christian Understanding of Man* (New York: Scribners, 1965), 27.

aptly pointed out by James Cone and other black church theologians, in
the struggle against racism, a sharp indictment exists upon white churches,
which still mostly reflect the racial structures around them:

> The Holy Spirit's presence with the people is a liberating
> experience. Black people who have been humiliated and op-
> pressed by the structures of White society six days of the
> week, gather together each Sunday morning in order to expe-
> rience another definition of their humanity. The transition
> from Saturday to Sunday is not just a chronological change
> from the seventh to the first day of the week. It is rather a
> rupture in time , a *Kairos*-event that produces a radical trans-
> formation in the people's identity. The janitor becomes the
> chairperson of the Deacon board; the maid becomes the Presi-
> dent of the stewardess Board Number 1. Everybody be-
> comes Mr. and Mrs., or Brother and Sister . . . . Black religion
> is by definition the opposite of white religion because the
> former was born in black people's political struggle to liberate
> themselves from oppression in the white church and the soci-
> ety it justifies. Even when black slaves could not actualize
> their experience of salvation in revolutionary struggle, they
> often verbalized the distinction between black and white reli-
> gion.[7]

IV. The Role the Church of God Could Play in Bringing Unity Between White Churches and Black Churches and Dismantling Racism

According to Professor Catherine Meeks of Mercer University, the
African American church was forced to become the guardian of African
American identity and self-esteem because it was the only institution that
was not totally destroyed by racism. The crucial point to remember, says
Meeks, is that whites were always in control on Sunday, just as they were
on every other day.

> It was the white control of the worship, the inability to ac-
> cept blacks (and all other non-whites) as equals, and the nega-
> tion of black personhood that led to the separation of the
> black church from the white church and to the emergence of a
> black religious community.[8]

In the midst of this reality of separation, how do black and white
believers in Jesus find a way to respond? Professor Meeks suggests that

---

[7]James H. Cone, "Sanctification and Liberation in the Black Religious Tradition," *Theology Today* (July 1978): 140, 150.
[8]Catherine Meeks, as quoted by Jim Wallis, ed., *America's Original Sin*, 55.

first of all it is necessary for whites to relinquish their racism, an example of which is the assumption that African Americans choose to worship apart from whites because of a different style and culture. Secondly, it is necessary for both whites and blacks to decide to turn to scripture, such as Galatians 3:28 ("There is no such thing as Jew and Greek, slave and free, male and female, you are all one in Christ Jesus"), to see if it has anything at all to do with the call of God upon their lives.

Both black Christians and white Christians, indeed all Christians of every race, tribe, and tongue must reflect upon the important possibility that God intends all people who have been created in his image to learn to respect each other and thus treat one another as equals. And if one should elevate that principle to a spiritual level, certainly those who call themselves Christians must learn to share their lives, possessions, and power with one another. But as long as we claim that being Jew or Greek, female or male, black or white, are reasons for disunity, segregation, and discrimination, we will remain separate and will insist on protecting ourselves from having to face the deeper issues of our woundedness. Even more importantly it provides a perfect excuse for us to shield ourselves from having to change.

V. The Church Must Acknowledge the Problems of Relating to Racism

The recognition of the link to a racist past

White America lost its own cultural identity and heritage when it built this country on the shoulders of genocide and slavery—a basic anti-Christian foundation and as such an ungodly approach to the *imago Dei* resident in all humans. It is important to explore a new context for white identity. There must first be a rejection of the unabating sin on which white racism was built—a rejection of the five centuries of oppression, which have destroyed people of color and which eroded the very foundation of American society. Today White Racism contaminates virtually every aspect of personal and societal life in our nation and this must be acknowledged by white Christians.

In the words of Joseph Barndt:

> There is no soft, polite way to discuss the problem. The word by which it must be called is white racism. To call it anything else is to avoid the real issue, and there are few problems we try harder to avoid. No less offensive designation is accurate. There is no way of approaching the subject indirectly. It is the unique problem of white America. It is white racism . . . We not only hold the power of racism in our hands, but we are unable to let it go. We are prisoners of our

own racism . . . that hurts and destoys people of color and
destroys us as white people.[9]

In light of the above, it is also extremely important that all Americans
realize the fact that people of color have resisted racism. Despite the
indescribable suffering, degradation and death of millions of people, Native Americans, African Americans, and Hispanic Americans have
struggled against oppression, and they have survived. White racism has
definitely not been triumphant in its attempt to destroy them, and people
of color have not lost the hope and vision of overcoming racism. Equally
important is the fact that many white people have subjected themselves to
threats, physical violence, and even death in the struggle against racism.
It is a cause of hope and challenge to all Americans; buried beneath the
pages of recorded history are uncounted acts of dissent on the part of
many whites whose heritage and anti-racist identity are not marred by
racism and whose history cannot therefore be painted with the same brush
as that of the majority of white Americans.

The tragedy of the European invasion of the Americas is that the
immigrants did not become identified as European Americans with a specified gift to give to the Americas as did other cultural and racial groups;
instead, they became white Americans and thus planted the seeds of
separation from their sisters and brothers of color, and to a certain degree,
because of the painful limitations of whiteness, forfeited any claim of their
identity as members of the family of God—the one universal human race.

White Americans' claim to a cultural identity is that they most always
use the word white, with everyone else noted as an exception: African-
American, Latin American, Asian American, Native American. Even the
riches that are the basis of white power cannot be claimed as legitimate
experiences of cultural identity but only experiences of white skin privilege since to celebrate with pride and accomplishments the history of our
national heroes is also to celebrate the genocide and destruction upon
which the foundation of our nation has been built.

Therefore, the problem with racism is not just what it has done to non-
whites but what it has done to whites also. It has limited and distorted and
dehumanized whiteness, and until racism is completely dismantled, white
identity will always be attached to the color white. Brandt, therefore,
suggests that:

>...The search for a new cultural identity begins with rejecting
>a racist white identity, along with the power and privilege that
>come with it...Perhaps a parallel illustration will be helpful.
>The term African-American has recently been popularly

[9]Joseph Brandt, *Dismantling Racism: The Continuing Challenge to White America* (Minneapolis: Augsburg, 1991), 40-41.

accepted as a more accurate name and description of those who, throughout the centuries, have been designated by others in terms of their color, i.e., "black," "negro," or "colored." There is not such a thing as "black culture," anymore than there is a white culture. The term African American, however, has a clear meaning, designating a people's way of life and cultural identity that has been created out of a past heritage and a present experience. In the same way, a transformed (anti-racist) European-American cultural identity will be built upon a new examination of our history and present experience.[10]

The challenge of doing theology from an intercultural perspective

A process of re-education will eventually lead to a new cultural identity for European Americans, which was lost 500 years ago when Europeans did not become assimilated as other ethnic groups did and thus became known as "White Americans" instead. "Whiteness" had some inherent sacredness, it was thought.

The above realities call for a radical paradigm shift in how we do theology in the academy, and forces faculty and students to embrace a theological orientation which is thoroughly intercultural.

Professor Walter Hollenweger, former Chair of the Department of Missions at University of Birmingham in England, discusses this paradigm shift in terms of an Intercultural Theology:

> i.) The first step for such intercultural theology would be to acknowledge its limits. Intercultural theology is that academic discipline, which operates in a given culture without absolutizing this culture. If theology is not just a rationalization of our own cultural biases (i.e. sectarian theology or worse a theologically-defended cultural imperialism), then it must attempt to be open to this universal and sacramental dimension of the Christian faith.

> ii.) The methods by which this is achieved have to be chosen on the basis of their suitability. The North Atlantic tradition cannot be given priority as the only way of doing theology, or even the most important one, unless one has arguments which disqualify the great stories of the Bible, including the parables of Christ, as theology. It cannot conform to the *stoichea tou kosmou*.

> iii.) Intercultural theology is not a form of 'pop-theology,' it does not make our task easier but makes it more difficult. It

---

[10]Ibid., 162.

does not mean that we give up our critical scholarship, but we apply it not only to the content of our discipline but to the whole process of communication.

iv.) Intercultural theology is not only concerned with the dominant cultures but also—following the example of the early theologians of our tradition—with 'oral cultures' and 'oral theology,' which is not necessarily 'unwritten theology' but which follows other patterns of thinking and communication than the 'literary cultures.'

v.) If, however, theology is that process which reflects critically on its own tradition within the cultural contexts of the people of God, then we need pontifices, bridge-building theologians, theologians who make the critical dialogue possible between 'oral' and 'literacy;' 'female,' and 'male,' 'black' and 'white.'

vi.) If the Church succeeds in organizing an intercultural dialogue, then, for the first time in world history, a global communication would emerge without giving a privileged position to any one culture of our globe. This would be the translation of the theological concept of conciliarity into cultural categories, and it could defreeze potentials and insights both in the 'old' and in the 'new' cultures.[11]

The above concerns are critical, especially when considering that the present ethos, concerns, issues, and questions emanating from our Bible Colleges, Christian Liberal Arts Institutions, and Seminaries are based on a philosophical and epistemological framework which is Euro-centric, and thus not necessarily representative of a global or intercultural perspective.

I have been a missionary-educator for twenty-six years, and have lamented the fact that until recently churches have sent missionaries abroad with little or no preparation in language or cultural studies, much less an understanding of the challenges of contextualization. The same can be said for ministerial preparation of those who will pastor parishes with a large population of non-Europeans in the USA and Canada.

---

[11]Walter J. Hollenweger, "The Roots and Fruits of The Charismatic Renewal in the Third World," a lecture given at Birmingham University, UK, November 1979.

VI. Major Demographic Changes Present Enough Challenges for a Radical Paradigm Shift in How We Prepare Ministers for the 21st Century

The Immigration Challenge

A recently published report by the Southern Baptist Home Missions Board states that "two-thirds of the world's immigrants are coming to the United States and that America's mosaic of people represents 500 ethnic groups communicating in 636 languages and dialects."[12] In the February 1999 issue of *Time Magazine,* Farai Chideya asks the penetrating question, "Will race provide the midcentury crisis?"[13] He continues:

> We have some hard decisions to make in the next few decades. America has a track record of turning against minorities in tough economic times. By the year 2050, whites will be a demographic minority but not a political or economic one. If we don't open up opportunities equally to all Americans, we could see a rising level of resentment among the nonwhite majority. Americans love to fight. The question is whether we will fight one another for parts of the economic pie or fight together to raise the standard of living and opportunity for all Americans.
>
> Finally, we have to realize that we are responsible for teaching the next generation about race. The young Americans I met who were racist had parents who taught them to be so; those who were open to the changes this country faces were taught to be that way as well. Racial progress should be a part of the American Dream, the dream that we can live our lives better than our parents lived theirs. Fortunately, and unfortunately, it's entirely up to us.[14]

The above mentioned reports describe a reality called "the browning of America."[15] According to the Census Bureau, by 2070 the 21 million Hispanics legally in the U.S. today (there are estimates of up to 10 million here illegally) will have multiplied to 57 million, making them the largest minority in the U.S. Currently, in some Texan cities, Hispanics make up the majority (in Laredo, 95 percent; in El Paso, 68 percent; and in Corpus Christi, 51 percent), and in some important regions they make up a

[12]*America's Ethnicity of the 90's: 1994 Edition.* Compiled by Oscar I. Romo, Director, Language Church Extension Division, 1994 Home Mission Board, Southern Baptist Convention, 3.

[13]Farai Chideya, "Shades of the Future," *Time Magazine* 1 February 1999, 1.

[14]Ibid., 2-3.

[15]*America's Ethnicity of the 90's: 1992 Edition,* 92.

substantial number of residents (37 percent of Los Angeles County and 24 percent of California). In the 1970s, the Hispanic population grew by 61 percent, says the U.S. Department of Commerce, while the entire U.S. population grew only 11.5 percent. In the 1980s, the Hispanic growth rate was 34 percent.[16]

This "Latin Explosion" affects every sphere of mainstream American life, from Jews in Skokie, Illinois, humming "La Bamba" to yuppies dancing away their stock portfolio monies to the "Conga Beat" in Miami. Everyone is eating tacos, and political candidates such as former President Bush will go to any extreme to court the Hispanic vote (such as when he referred to his Mexican grandchildren as "his little brown ones"). Madison Avenue is quite keen to get its piece of the $130 billion Hispanic purchasing pie, and one company thought nothing of spending $30 million in 1990 to advertise to Hispanics, while companies such as Proctor and Gamble, Anheiser Busch, Campbell's, and a host of other companies spent $628 million in 1992 targeting Hispanic pocketbooks. With two Hispanic TV networks, 145 Spanish-language magazines, 30 bilingual or English publications and 450 Spanish radio stations, and the overall growth of the Hispanic population, some politicians are fearful and advocate that the United States Government declare English to be the official "United States language."

It is also quite obvious that this trend is affecting the Christian church, too. According to Oscar I. Romo of the Southern Baptist Mission Board, "browning of the church" is also taking place since by far the fastest growing Protestant ethnic group in the United States is the Hispanic church.[17] In Southern California alone, Hispanic Protestant congregations are reported to have jumped from 320 in 1970 to 1,022 in 1986, to 1,450 in 1990.[18] Defections from the Roman Catholic Church to Protestant denominations in the U.S. are also said to be occurring at a rate of 60,000 per year or as much as one million in 15 years.

Roman Catholic Theologian Allan Deck, among others, has also suggested that Hispanics will comprise the majority of Catholicism in the U.S. by the year 2000. It was no coincidence that on his second visit to the United States in 1987 Pope John II made stops to three cities with significant Hispanic population. These included Miami, San Antonio, and Los Angeles.[19]

---

[16]Ibid, 29-42.

[17]Ibid., 42.

[18]For a fascinating account of the development of two rather different theological positions on social issues see *Missionalia,* 21:1 (April 1993), 40-56, where William Saayman traces the development of the Pentecostal social consiousness in South Africa.

[19]*America's Ethnicity of the 90's: 1994 Edition,* 94.

Oscar Romo also suggests that three very important factors that have always served the immigrant community well are also at work in influencing the growth of Hispanic Protestantism. They include intimacy, opportunity, and expression. It is therefore natural to conclude that due to these factors—intimacy, opportunity, and expression—the churches with the greatest Hispanic growth are the pentecostal churches, the Southern Baptists, and American Baptist churches. As a matter of fact, many pentecostal churches who now boast phenomenal growth cannot point to Euro-American church growth methods as a reason for such growth but as a result of the intensity and fervency of Hispanic evangelism. Jesse Miranda explains that, "While Anglos are afraid of emotion, for us it is a way of life . . . . Sermons by Hispanics have a level of intensity that speaks to the Latin heart."[20]

With such tremendous church growth, one would assume that within the evangelical section of the church, the issue of racism would have been solved in Christ. However, as all other immigrant groups before them, Hispanics experience prejudice in many evangelical churches. "Anglo churches are receiving Hispanics with open arms, but then they are asked to serve in the kitchen rather than in decision-making committees," says Pastor Espenoza. Jesse Miranda sums up the feeling of many Hispanics when he comments that "often, dwindling white urban congregations look to Hispanics as a means of paying the gas bill rather than seeing the need to build a Hispanic church."[21] Surely, this challenge also faces the Church of God, which in most cases still sees ethnic ministries as commodities, another marketing target group or in the now familiar phrase "reaping the ethnic harvest." Of course, what was said about Hispanics can also be said about Asian-Americans and especially African-Americans in the Church of God.

Only the Holy Spirit can predict the valuable impact that interculturally competent pastors and laypersons will have as they assist the global Church in her endeavor to provide meaningful ministries well into the 21st Century.

VII. The Intercultural Identity of the Church of God

Since its humble Appalachian beginnings in 1886, the Church of God has become one of America's fastest growing denominations. Worldwide, the church serves 136 countries, sponsors 19,568 congregations,

---

[20]Jesse Miranda, as cited in Romo, *America's Ethnicity of the 90's: 1992 Edition,* 95.
[21]Ibid.

4,084 missions and preaching stations, has over 25,000 licensed or ordained ministers, and a membership of approximately 6 million.[22]

The church is to be commended for this phenomenal and impressive
growth, but like most North American and European based denominations operating a foreign missions department, the Church of God as a
whole has not always demonstrated a readiness or willingness to allow its
North American constituency to benefit from the rich diversity of perspectives and ministry gifts that the international sector of the church has
to offer. We may be "international" on paper and have token representa-
tives here and there, but the ethos of Church of God missionary endeavor
and policy is still very much white, male, Southern and culturally ethno-
centric.

A leading Church of God minister now deceased was quite accurate
when he remarked eighteen years ago that the reality of internationalization is only a superficial platitude, that in reality "the Church of God
remains a North American denomination with a missions department."[23]

With the increased immigration to the United States during the past
decade and the multiplicity of cross-cultural congregations whose language of worship is not English, the opportunities for developing a truly
international or global consciousness are indeed remarkable. Likewise,
the possibilities for intercultural ministry exist in unprecedented dimensions for the present and future generations of church leaders. If the
Church of God is to meet the challenges of multi-ethnic ministry adequately
as we enter a new millenium, then its leadership and constituency must
give serious attention to the need for training future ministers and lay
persons to become interculturally competent. Without an intentional commitment to use this opportunity to become congruent so that our actions
match our words insofar as internationalization is concerned, then we will
become a truly unworthy vessel, and as such, a scandal in the church
world.

Despite the aftermath of the Rodney King verdict, the Richard Denny
verdict, the deepening ethnic, racial and socioeconomic divisions at home
and abroad, and despite the reality that as a denomination we have not
always allowed our voices to be heard on the unpopular topic of institutional racism and individual racial prejudices within our own camp, the real
irony is that the church is nevertheless in a most favorable position to
give leadership and praxis to cross-cultural and intercultural competency.

---

[22]"Reach 21: Reaching into the 21st Century" provides the five-year ministry
strategy of the Church of God (Cleveland, TN: Church of God General Headquar-
ters, September 1999).

[23]Rev. David Lemons (message given during the 1984 Church of God General
Assembly).

As a denomination, the Church of God has in place the facilities, resources, and the men and women of goodwill who could become a tremendous force for reconciliation and healing in multicultural America and among the nations of the world. Although our own history predates the Azusa Street outpouring under William Seymour, as a part of "classical Pentecostalism" our multi-ethnic heritage places the church in an ideal position to give leadership in all of the aforementioned areas. A radical paradigm shift is needed if we are to embrace a missionary philosophy, which is inclusive of an intercultural and multi-ethnic emphasis.

For a long time the church has labored under the assumption that its rapid growth and expansion is an indication and measure of a good philosophy of missions while failing to look objectively at itself and critically assess its growth in light of its world-wide mission. A study of such materials as writings, correspondence, organizational structure, budgets, and statistics reveals a significant contrast between its biblical mandate and its practical execution of that mandate. There is, therefore, a need to evaluate this assumed philosophy, test it in the light of biblical revelation, restate such a philosophy clearly and bring it in line with the contributions of modern missiology.

The Church has adopted uncritically a theory of mission whose only merit lies in the fact that such theory has been the guiding light for many missionaries and mission agencies in our time. In a paper written by members of a task force set up to consider the need for a philosophy of mission, the authors concluded that the Church has simply adopted from others their theory of mission: 1) Mission is service; 2) Mission is witness; 3) Mission is the promotion of the Great Commission; 4) Mission is Christianization of culture; 5) Mission is raising and spending money; and 6) Mission has as its chief aim the salvation of souls. These aforementioned churchmen seemed to have simply adopted the above list, and—without regard for the intercultural or cross-cultural implications of the items on the list—proceeded to make them the controlling and guiding principles in the church's mission. There is, therefore, a need to base the church's mission on a correct and sound exegetical interpretation of scripture.[24]

In the past twenty-four years, the church has been emphasizing the fact that it is an international church and that world evangelism is the very essence of its mission, but its use of personnel and methods of spending money, as well as its programs and ogrganization, are not directed to reach such a goal, but rather to perpetuate a form of religious colonial imperialism.

---

[24]See, e.g., David J. Bosch, *Transforming Mission: Paradigm Shifts in Theology of Mission* (MaryKnoll, NY: Orbis Books, 1991), 7-12.

Professor Walter Hollenweger stated:

> By and large, the aim of most American and European
> pentecostal mission is to expand its own brand of Christian-
> ity with its liturgy, music, church vestments, church architec-
> ture, theology, understanding of the Bible and understanding
> of political values, and very often where an indigenous
> pentecostal movement, e.g. Romania, West Germany, Chile,
> Holland, Brazil is found, irrespective of the fact that it may be
> numerically and spiritually much more important than the
> American home base, the tendency is to try by hook or crook
> to link such indigenous pentecostals to an American funded,
> American directed, American educated Headquarters.[25]

Indeed, the Church of God speaks of itself as being international, but
in reality such internationality is no more than that of Coca Cola or the
CIA; that is to say, it operates in manÿ countries, but its leadership is
either or almost entirely American supported. What the Gospel is in Germany, Jamaica, India, Ghana or Korea, is decided not in the locale, but in
Cleveland, Tennessee.

Across the United States and Canada, the Church of God operates
6,700 predominantly white congregations, 981 black congregations, and
an additional 636 multicultural and/or language congregations of other
cultures conducting worship weekly. According to the Reverend Billy J.
Rayburn, Director of Church of God Cross-cultural Ministries, "the Department has been mandated by the General Church to discover and help
to meet the needs of this growing section of the Church of God . . . . We are
thus making available all of the benefits and ministries of the larger church
body to the millions of immigrants who will come in the future. . . ."[26]

Although its objective to establish churches among those of other
cultures in the United States and Canada is a noble one, the church appears
to have borrowed the "separate but equal" philosophy from segregation
days and still insists that language, dress, style of worship, type of music,
architectural design, and Christian education methodology are valid
reasons to keep these cultures apart, rather than seeing differences as
important bridges for enrichment through which a diversified body of
Christ learns different approaches to ministry from each other. The Church
should look beyond merely seeing these immigrant Church of God ministers
and members with their distinctive culture and language as *evangelistic
resources* "to help evangelize a diversified and pluralistic American

---

[25]Walter Hollenweger, "Intercultural Theology" (lecture given at Overstone
College, England, 1983).
[26]Adapted from Billy J. Rayburn's *North America's Mission Field: a manual
for establishing multicultural and language ministries* (Cleveland, TN: Church of
God Department of Cross-Cultural Ministries, 1993), 5-12.

continent."[27] As Professor Edward Wimberly of the Interdenominational
Theological Center points out:

> The ethic of hospitality expressed in the early church was
> rooted firmly in the idea of God's covenant with God's people
> represented in the Sinai Covenant of the Old Testament. The
> household of God is made up of people who self-consciously
> have responded to God's welcoming of them to God's salva-
> tion drama. These persons have seen themselves as hosts and
> hostesses and as guests. They have come to the household of
> God broken, battered, oppressed, rejected and victimized.
> They have come to be healed, mended, and redeemed.[28]

Adhering rigidly to the conservative stance of the 1966 Wheaton Declaration and 1970 Frankfurt Declaration on the direction Christian mission
should be taking, evangelical and pentecostal churches are able to speak
boldly against the brutalities of the Gestapo in Germany, the evils of homosexuality, abortion, and the need to bring religion back into the schools.
But the brutalities of the C.I.A. in Chile, or in Central America, or ethnic
cleansing in Bosnia or Kosovo are never mentioned; the havoc wreaked
by the sin of racism, the now defunct system of Apartheid in South Africa,
and the general condition of the poor and unemployed are not mentioned.

As a Church, we must carefully scrutinize a missiology that contains
inescapable philosophical elements, which relate to American imperialism
and cultural arrogance, white American Fundamentalism's opposition to
radical social change, and resistance to justice issues. When a philosophy of mission perpetuates a racist concept of biblical history and pre-
vents other cultural perspectives from influencing the church, we must be
open-minded enough to embrace elements of the ideological and theological correctives in both the African-American religious experience and
that which other non-white ethnic cultural groups could bring are hin-
dered from having an impact on the church. If permitted free development
and expression within a predominantly Euro-American structure, these
diverse contributions from other perspectives could mean the very salvation of the Church. Failing to do this, the present global movements
toward cultural diversity and inclusiveness could see many internationals
leaving the Church of God for more intentionally intercultural, multi-ethnic, and hospitable denominations.

A viable philosophy of missions demands that the Church become
more precise in what it means by mission. Rolland Allen, an Anglican

---

[27]Billy Rayburn, *Planting Chuches Crossculturally* (Cleveland, TN: Church of
God Department of Cross-Cultural Minstries, 1994), 12.

[28]Edward Wimberly, *Language of Hospitality: Intercultural Relations in the
Household of God* (Nashville, TN: Abingdon Press, 1989), 13.

missionary working in China under the Society for the Propagation of the Gospel, became convinced that the modern mission organization, whether separate society, or a department within the Church, was an inconvenient and unbiblical addition. There is obvious confusion between the mission of the Church and what is commonly referred to as "missions" by the Church of God. People are termed missionaries by the simple fact that they were appointed by the Mission Board; a country is referred to as a mission field because it lies outside the United States' borders.

The fact that missionary expansion would create new problems and require new personnel trained in the cross-cultural experience has only recently become evident to some of the leaders of the Church. It is my conviction that intercultural competence should by this time be achievable, and that in our varied approaches to evangelism and church planting, wherever diverse cultures and multi-ethnic situations are found, our automatic response should be to make them become bridges over which the checkered, multicultural, and ethnically different peoples of God have an opportunity to cross-fertilize each other. One would think that after more than one hundred years of international and cross-cultural ministries, the church would be in a position now to lead others in showing the importance of achieving multicultural competence for training these leaders.

If it is true that "the United States is a nation made great by the contributions of its various groups that compose 'the American mosaic,'" then there must be some intentionality on our part to insure that we also benefit from the contributions that the various Church of God ministries and members bring to the United States and Canada, and thereby become a greater racial and culture-friendly church than we are now. How fitting was Paul's instruction to the Roman Church: "...Welcome one another therefore just as Christ has welcomed you, for the glory of God" (Rom 15:7). As a denomination we must seek to live out in the international, national, and local church ministries the vision of the inclusive community Paul calls the house churches in Rome to manifest. They were instructed (commanded) to welcome strangers as Christ has welcomed them, and thus identify with Christ's reconciling love. Religious organizations and institutions play a major role in preparing people to live, cope, and succeed in a diverse and pluralistic society. In this regard, the Church of God must be actively engaged in creating an ecclesiastical environment that not only tolerates but welcomes the many differences found among its membership.

In a recent ASHE-ERIC report, pluralism is defined as a "social condition ... in which several distinct ethnic, religious, and racial communities live side by side, willing to affirm each other's dignity, ready to benefit from each other's experience, and quick to acknowledge each other's contribution to the common welfare."[29]

The above definition comes very close to what I believe to be the crucial task of Bible colleges and theological seminaries, which wish to embrace pluralism in the Christian sense. It involves understanding, appreciating, and celebrating diversity. As an ideal community of worshippers and learners, churches and church training institutions must assume the leadership role in vigorously confronting the problems of racism, anti-Semitism, and other types of prejudice and discrimination. This confrontation is a necessary starting point, as we take seriously the second step of developing competency in those we train to do multi-ethnic and inter-cultural ministries.

Conclusion

With the above considerations, a new day is ahead for all Americans. With a reclaimed heritage, a transformed view of history and a faith-based commitment to dismantle racism, Euro-Americans can create art and music that express a new ability to love themselves and others. New dance forms will express a new freedom of movement and willingness to reach out and touch. A new understanding of politics and power will reflect a desire for true participatory democracy. The self-constructed walls and ghettoized white prisons can then give way to freedom. Euro-Americans can then emerge from behind their suburban walls and well-guarded city apartment doors, and in the process become free of guilt, fear, self-protection, and with self-confidence reach out to embrace others.

Perhaps the most productive and nurturing aspect of the new anti-racist European-American cultural identity will be the commitment and ability to participate at the multicultural table. The decisions of a new anti-racist American must take place in a truly inclusive multicultural setting. Such multiculturalism must be intentional in its commitment to inclusiveness and diversity to the degree that the dismantling of racism in all institutional structures become its first and guiding principle. This will be different from the superficial and often white-male controlled attempts at accommodating diversity.[30]

---

[29]*Opening Windows and Doors: Comprehensive Planning for Ethnic and Racial Diversity.* Compiled by Deborah L. Bailey and Dianne M. Stewart, Christian College Coalition Office of Racial/Ethnic Concerns, Washington, DC., June 3-6, 1992.

[30]Jim Wallis, ed. *America's Original Sin,* 77; Joseph Brandt, *Dismantling Racism,* 78.

Lessons on Spiritual Leadership for a New Millennium

Charles W. Conn[*]

I. The Divine and Human

From the beginning, God has relied upon human participation for the establishment of his kingdom on earth. God has done so because it is necessary for communication of divine purpose to the human mind. I recall the story of a scientist who, with no understanding of divine purpose, watched a body of ants at work. From his height and perspective, he saw a way to make their work easier for them, and attempted to communicate to the ants by tracing lines in the sand and nudging the insect army toward a better direction. After long frustration, he realized that the only way he could ever communicate with them was to become one of them. That awareness started the scientist on a gradual understanding of the incarnation—why God came to earth in Jesus Christ.

When his life on earth ended, Jesus left his mission to the hearts and hands of mortals. Flawed and imperfect as the disciples and future believers might be, there was no other plan. It is the same today as it has been in every generation—a divine work is dependent upon human faith and faithfulness. This does not suggest that there is an equation of the two——only God is divine, and all on earth are merely mortal. But the result of God's plan has been a continuous spread of Christian faith during the last two thousand years.

This essay is not a survey of past generations, but it proposes to be a look at the present generation and its opportunities. It should be pointed

*Charles W. Conn (Litt.D., Lee College). President emeritus, Lee University; Historian of the Church of God; former General Overseer of the Church of God (1966-1970).

out, however, that there are strong similarities between the present time and the earliest days of the Christian faith. A welcome consequence has been an immediacy with the divine in our time not always experienced in earlier times. Rise of what is variously known as the Pentecostal Revival, the Charismatic Renewal, and other designations, has been a largely grass-roots movement. It contained elements of emotional expression and immediacy with spiritual matters not always found in earlier renewals. The result brought an intimate awareness of the divine to some believers, and in others, but less frequently, an almost casual familiarity with the divine. While such intimacy has been reassuring to many, it has presented serious problems to others.

Early Christianity appealed to the common masses with its simple message of faith in Christ, and the assurance of his continued presence with them even after his death. Christ's divine works continued at the hands of apostles who had physically been with him and had been directly taught by him. Those who heard them had no difficulty sensing his presence with them. In such a state of mind, ritual played little part in their spiritual expressions. That personal directness of the early church has been effectively replicated in our century. Also reminiscent of the early church, we have been blessed with gifted leaders and teachers. What the first century church had in the apostles, we have had in an equally anointed preaching of God's Word.

II. Toward a New Millennium

The world is presently approaching the beginning of a new century and a new millennium. The last time such a thing happened (AD 1000) the world was in the midst of something historians have called the Middle Ages—or, questionably, the Dark Ages. Throughout that first millennium after Christ (pre-1000), the spread of Christianity was the principal force on earth for most of Western Civilization. Even though superstition and traces of paganism continued during much of that millennium, the faith of Christ gradually overspread much of Europe.

The second millennium after Christ (AD 1000 to the present) began with apprehension and dread, because the future was so uncertain. About halfway through that period (c. 1400), the Church's spirituality came to be questioned, and its domination of people's lives became so absolute that the Protestant Reformation resulted (c. 1500). It was also a time when human knowledge advanced so greatly that the period is known as the Renaissance.

The last century of this millenium saw the rise of a revival called Pentecostalism, which began as a reassertion of the pristine faith and works of Christ and his apostles. For a century, Pentecostalism has enjoyed the vitality of youth, when there were only blue skies and a hopeful future for the movement. Now, however, Pentecostalism has both a past and a future, and must reckon wisely with both. Past and future must merge now into one continuum, where the past provides the future with balance and a measuring rod; when it must serve as tutor to the present and the future.

Equally, the future will be both heir to and judge of the past. It must be wise enough to adhere to all that is good and advance with new strength in the course it inherits. What the past gave promise of, the present and future should be beneficiary of. In the same way, the future should be wise enough to recognize failures and flaws of the past, and avoid them with the same spiritual balance with which it assumes its inheritance. The past and future must yield with grace to all that the other brings to the continuum.

As an octogenarian, deeply a part of the past with equal appreciation of and confidence in the future, I rejoice in the truth that those who can face the past unashamed can face the future unafraid. We must know in the new century and millennium that it is as true now as it was in the past that advancement of any worthy cause depends greatly upon the quality of leadership we provide or accept. For that reason, we should look carefully at the elements of spiritual leadership that will influence our future—and observe the multiple examples we inherit from the past.

III. Biblical Roots of Leadership

The elements of human leadership are as diverse as the circumstances that bring them forth, and are not always as we fondly imagine them to be. In spiritual matters, it is vital to realize that fact. Paul said to the Corinthians, "There are different kinds of service, but the same Lord" (1 Cor 12:5). Numerous biblical examples of spiritual leadership underscore that truth.

For our first understanding of a "leader" we must look at God. In him we see clearly what a leader is and does—he is one who leads or guides another, or others, from something or to something. Thus we read of God's leading the Israelites out of bondage in Egypt, through the wilderness, into Canaan (Deut 8:2; 29:5). The Psalmist adds the element of teaching to the function of a leader: "Show me your ways, O Lord; teach me your paths. Lead me in your truth and teach me..." (Ps 25:5). Among those whom God teaches are sinners and they who fear the Lord. Carried into the New Testament, the image of God as a leader remains kind and paternal: "Do you despise the riches of his goodness, forbearance and long-suffering, not knowing that the goodness of God leads you to repentance?" (Rom 2:4).

The same projection of a leader as a guide and protector was extended to shepherds of flocks, as when David said, "He leads me beside quiet waters; He guides me in the paths of righteousness for His name's sake." So benevolent was the nature of such a leader that those who followed him were given a sense of safety and well being. That understanding so established the basic sense of spiritual leadership that the leaders were called "pastors"—those who led the flock of God to good pasture. Similarly, those who fell short of it were repudiated sternly in Ezekiel 34, as caring for themselves more than for the people. In John 10, Jesus called such leaders "hirelings"—mere hired hands whose greatest interest is in themselves. There have always been religious persons who have no real care for the flock of God, whose sole motivation is the advancement of their own interests.

Appropriate to his life, however, Jesus was that "Good Shepherd" who cared enough for the flock that he gave his life for it. He was the ultimate shepherd, therefore the ultimate leader and pastor. (Although there is little chance today that any will have his leadership so severely tested, it is mentioned only to stress that a leader's personal welfare should not be his first concern.) The scriptural leader is usually quite different from the world's image of leaders.

IV. Old Testament Leaders

There is no single quality or type of leader. Leaders are as varied as the circumstances that require or reveal them. In early Hebrew history, the leaders were patriarchs that gained recognition through personal distinction. Their leadership was highly individual and paternal. The greatest of these were Abraham, Isaac, and Jacob, who were legendary in their region. God's call to them was direct, and their leadership was principally over their own nomadic or tribal families. They were Israelites, but there was no nation of Israel for them to lead or rule.

In later times the leaders were judges that arose in times of national peril to lead the people in resistance against their enemies. These judges did not remain in a continuing leadership role, but returned to their normal lives within their own tribes when the peril was past. Of the fifteen persons who led Israel in that time, a few stand out for their differences. One of these was Samson, who was renowned for his extraordinary physical strength. And yet he never lived up to what he might have achieved. Samson was so individually exceptional that he never did the things a true leader should do. Instead of rallying the people of Israel behind him, he did individual exploits that gained him wide attention but never overcame the Philistine enemies. He single-handedly took away the gates of Gaza (Judg 16:3), killed a thousand Philistines (Judg 17:15), and other feats, but the greater part of his life was spent fraternizing with the Philistines. His type of heroics is seen all too often in contemporary times, where personal exploits often garner attention but hinder needed cooperative achievement. Samson's life ended in what was probably the most significant achievement of his life—destroying the Temple of Dagon. In his death he achieved more than he did in his lifetime (Judg 16:30); his death was a redemptive act that gained him a place in the listing of faith in Hebrews 11.

Another disappointment among biblical leaders seems to have been Lot, kinsman of Abraham and a member of that illustrious patriarchal line. Strife with Abraham tempted Lot to a selfish decision that led him into Sodom, where "the men were exceedingly wicked and sinful against the Lord" (Gen 13:6-13). Amid the debaucheries of Sodom, Lot lost his own family—even their respect. When Sodom was divinely destroyed, and God, for Abraham's sake, sought to spare Lot and his family, Lot's married children scorned him (Gen 19:12-14), his wife was lost—and his two surviving daughters perpetrated an incestuous fraud that gave birth to the Moabites and Ammonites (Gen 19:30-38).

More admirable were the prophets that arose frequently throughout Israel's history. Their strength and leadership did not come from birth or position, but from conscience and courage, which is appropriately translated as divine calling. They often performed their ministries in the face of imminent and capricious danger, without official acclaim or ecclesiastical stipend. Yet in the record of Hebrews 11 they, of whom the world was not worthy, are said to have subdued kingdoms and wrought righteousness. Probably more than any other, it was their leadership that extended beyond their time even to our own. No less than sixteen books of the Old Testament came from their illustrious ministry.

V. New Testament Leaders

The New Testament presents inexhaustible insight regarding spiritual leadership. The twelve men Jesus chose to be his disciples provide a great variety to show us aspects of what a leader should or should not be. In fact, Jesus used his three years with them for the purpose of instructing them. It is an inescapable truth that he did not attempt to make them identical to each other. The opposite is what we see. In his last contact with them, we see him encouraging each to fill his own place in service (John 21:20-24). Later efforts to make Christians through some assembly-line method came from persons other than Christ. His guidance was to make each of the twelve the best person he was capable of being, not a carbon copy of another. The only time he even mildly drew a comparison between individuals did not regard the company of the disciples, but two sisters when one (Martha) complained to him that the other (Mary) was not doing her share of their work (Luke 10:38-42).

The leadership wealth of his circle was one of the greatest treasuries the world has ever seen. With the exception of Judas Iscariot, all of the twelve possessed qualities that would unite to launch the Christian faith into all the world.

The case of Barnabas and Paul gives an interesting view of diversity in spiritual leadership, for they were alike in basic ways, yet different in important ways. Both became ardent in the cause of Christ without being a part of his disciples. It is not likely that either of them ever saw Jesus in his lifetime. The elder (Barnabas) was a prosperous citizen of Cyprus and Antioch; the younger (Paul) was a citizen of Tarsus and a scholar in Jerusalem. Each became passionately committed to the lordship of Christ. The labors and accomplishments of Paul were legendary, and even today are the subject of books, travel tours, college or seminary studies and sermons. All of that is well deserved, for Paul was one of the greatest of all leaders. Less is recorded about Barnabas, but in vital ways his importance to the Kingdom of God equaled Paul's. They were colleagues and friends, and that friendship would bring their leadership styles and personality differences to surface.

Barnabas and Paul were early missionary partners, whose relationship was strained by a youth named John Mark, who accompanied them on a distant and dangerous trip. Mark returned home, an action which Paul regarded as desertion (Acts 13:13). Later, when Barnabas thought to include Mark on another journey, Paul opposed it adamantly: "Then the contention became so sharp that they parted from one another" (Acts 15:36-39). Barnabas took Mark with him and Paul chose Silas as his partner. That breakup of one of the earliest missionary teams revealed much about both men. Barnabas, whose name means "Son of Consolation," was a nurturing leader. He was the first of the Jerusalem Christians to accept Paul himself after his conversion. While all of the apostles were afraid of Paul, Barnabas accepted him (Acts 9:26-27). Then, after others had ignored Paul for eight years, it was Barnabas who went to Tarsus to recruit Paul for his first missionary journey (Acts 11:25).

John Mark, who ultimately became a protege of Peter, became important in the Christian faith according to tradition; it was he who wrote the Gospel of Mark. Before Paul died as a martyr in Rome, he urged Timothy to come to him: "Be diligent and come to me quickly . . . . Get Mark and bring him with you; for he is useful to me for ministry." The Christian world can thank God for Barnabas and other nurturers like him. Barnabas believed in and encouraged both Paul and Mark until they could appreciate and benefit each other. More will be said about nurturing leaders.

VI. Renaissance Models

Essentially, today as in the past, a leader is apt to be one who knows almost instinctively what to do in time of need. That is as true in spiritual matters as in others. A real leader is one whose skills, while generally specialized, may extend over a range of circumstances. A name given to such persons is "Renaissance Man" because the cultural Renaissance saw numerous persons with skills in such diverse fields as art, architecture, basic science and even medicine. Such breadth of ability is not uncommon in Christian ministry. It is likely that a gifted speaker will also be a good writer. Often a talented musician will also be a knowledgeable pastor. The Christian faith has been advanced for centuries by such multiple-gifted persons as Martin Luther, David Livingston, John Newton and Albert Schweitzer.

In an era of specialization, that exciting phenomenon is possibly less apparent than in previous times, but it is seen often enough to remind us that God can dispense his creative and leadership gifts when he will to whom he will.

VII. The Old and the Young

The final, and probably finest, demonstration of good leadership comes in the transition of power from one to another, especially from one generation to another. As in a relay race, the smooth passing of the torch from one runner to the next is the key to a victorious run. In that regard, spiritual leadership possibly has an advantage over political or secular leadership. Because the goals are more spiritually centered, the ego should become a less troublesome factor. As long as leadership remains mindful of its divine direction and humanitarian purpose, there is less danger of its veering off in a destructive, selfish direction. But, even so, there is a strong addictive danger in power and authority, and many once fine leaders become susceptible to it. The past century has been witness to the addiction of control that appears in people at every level of human leadership.

Leadership has gone awry when its greatest purpose and energy is a determination to keep itself in power. When a one-time productive, creative leadership is reduced in the end to holding on to its seat of control, that is an addiction fully as binding as any substance abuse that exists. It is fully as pathetic and even more injurious because its harm to the abuser is multiplied by the damage it does to the household of God. A glaring example of the disease is that of King Saul. He was so terrified of being replaced by David that his ability to lead became erratic and destructive. Saul's condition has been repeated many times in human history, even by those in religious robes.

One of the strengths of a good leader is self-confidence. It is not pride for anyone called of God to believe that he is capable of achieving legitimate goals for God. The Apostle Paul said, "I can do all things through Christ who strengtheneth me" (Phil 4:13). That is a safe confidence as long as the "through Christ" portion is truly retained. When it is omitted, danger enters. And yet some leaders have come to an arrogant belief that they can do whatever they wish because they are so special to Christ.

There are other qualities in good leaders that provide balance and strength, such as humility, compassion, honesty, and truthfulness. Good leader must always remind themselves that they are in spiritual warfare where they are the most visible, valuable, and vulnerable target.

The final product of leadership is something called legacy. That is where the old and the young are ultimately face to face. Only when leaders leave something of themselves in a younger heart, can they continue to bless others after they are gone. That is why some persons are remembered more widely than they were noted when alive—they left something of themselves with others. That begins with a nurturing heart, when an elder person takes interest in younger persons and ripens in them their latent potential. The one assumes the role of instructor and the other of protege. It is life's greatest teaching strategy and has been practiced since ancient times. Active, busy leaders often brush aside the wealth of opportunity that lies fallow around them. I was blessed with numerous instructor friends—such as G. R. Watson, A. H. Batts, E. J. Boehmer, R. P. Johnson—who once enriched my life and now continue to live within my life.

VIII. The Future of Informed Pentecostalism

The present century has experienced a varied and sometimes profound spiritual renewal. To counter or moderate the immoderation of certain periods of the century, there was a desire for personal relationship with God that resulted in an outpouring of the Holy Spirit reminiscent of the apostolic Day of Pentecost. Included in that revival was the Church of God, of which I am a part. As the revival spread over the world, there came churches, colleges, universities, and a vast following of believers. The revival had been led by leaders equal to those of any other century before them. In the course of events it became necessary to learn distinctions essential to spiritual maturity. Because it is so easy to mistake for a leader one that is really a pied piper, it became essential to understand that leadership is not rabble-rousing or spell-binding. There is always a rabble eager to be roused and insecure souls willing to be bound.

So we come back to the premise of this essay—spiritual leadership is leading from danger to good pasture. True shepherds or leaders always guide, protect, and provide for God's flock. Whatever one's ecclesiastical title or academic assignment may be, its purpose is spiritual. Such leaders do not fit the generally held image of some military and highly visceral leaders. Yet that view of leadership is so fixed in some minds that they equate spiritual and secular leadership. But God does not choose worldly standards or strong-man tactics that dominate or control others. God chooses leaders who are persons of love, peace, longsuffering, and gentleness. I have known, worked with and followed such men—and I always think of them with reverence.

I am equally gladdened by the emerging younger leaders who will take an informed Pentecostalism into the new century and millennium. Leaders such as Donald N. Bowdle, in whose honor this *Festschrift* is published, with his colleagues and contemporaries, are prepared to guide us into that promising new era. They are better equipped, equally ready, and as fully committed to the cause as their elders were. Dr. Bowdle is a distinguished theological scholar and professor at Lee University, where he has been a pillar of the faculty since 1962. When he earned a Ph.D. in New Testament Text and Theology in 1961, he became the first Church of God member with a doctorate in religion. He earned a Th.D. in 19th Century American Social and Religious Thought from Union Theological Seminary in Virginia in 1970. At Lee he is a perennial faculty favorite with the students and has been awarded the Excellence in Teaching and Excellence in Scholarship Awards.

As a senior faculty member, he is both a role model and a champion of younger teachers. In a recent video interview with me he expressed a belief that Lee University will become one of the foremost Christian colleges, particularly in the disciplines of theology and religion.[1] The scholarship and commitment of his proteges and colleagues indicate that he may be right.

---

[1] I became acquainted with Dr. Bowdle in the early 1960s and worked closely with him when I was president of Lee (1970-1982). The range of his skills was so broad that he was considered for administrative assignment, but his love of teaching and effectiveness in the classroom was, and remains, his first love. On April 21, 1999, I interviewed him for posterity in an oral history project I call "Conversations on Camera."

It was scholars like Bowdle and those associated with him that C. S. Lewis addressed at Oxford University during the critical days of World War II:

> To be ignorant and simple now—not to be able to meet the enemies on their own ground—would be to throw down our weapons, and to betray our uneducated brethren who have, under God, no defence but us against the intellectual attacks of the heathen. Good philosophy must exist, if for no other reason, because bad philosophy needs to be answered. The cool intellect must work not only against cool intellect on the other side, but against the muddy heathen mysticisms. Most of all, perhaps, we need intimate knowledge of the past. Not that the past has any magic about it, but we cannot study the future, and yet need something to set against the present, and to remind us that the basic assumptions have been quite different in different periods and that much which seems certain to the uneducated is merely temporary fashion.[2]

---

[2]C.S. Lewis, *The Weight of Glory* (New York: The Macmillian Co., 1949), 50-51.

Bibliography: Donald N. Bowdle

Books and Chapters in Books

Redemption Accomplished and Applied. Cleveland, TN: Pathway Press, 1972.

"Oasis or Crucible?" in *The Promise and the Power: Essays on the Motivations, Developments, and Prospects of the Ministries of the Church of God*, ed. Donald N. Bowdle. Cleveland, TN: Pathway Press, 1980, 87-118.

"Holiness in the Highlands: A Profile of the Church of God in Appalachia" in *Christianity in Appalachia: Profiles in Regional Pluralism*, ed. Bill J. Leonard. Knoxville, TN: University of Tennessee Press, 1999, 243-56.

Books Edited

Ellicott's Bible Comentary: In One Volume. Grand Rapids: Zondervan Publishing House, 1971.

The Promise and the Power: Essays on the Motivations, Developments, and Prospects of the Ministries of the Church of God. Cleveland, TN: Pathway Press, 1980.

Thesis and Dissertations

"A Comparative Evaluation of the Augustinian and Thomistic Doctrines of Authority and Hermeneutics of Scripture." Th.M. thesis, Princeton Theological Seminary, May 1962.

"A Determination of the Exegetical Significance of the Greek Perfect Tense to the Christology of the New Testament Epistles." Ph.D. diss., Bob Jones University, May 1961.

"Evangelism and Ecumenism in Nineteenth-Century America: A Study in the Life and Literature of Samuel Irenaeus Prime, 1812-1885." Th.D. diss., Union Theological Seminary in Virginia, May 1970.

Professional Papers

"Augustine on Authority and Hermeneutics of Scripture"; Southern Section of the Evangelical Theological Society, Lee College, April, 1963.
"Theology: The Teacher and the Task"; European Pentecostal Theological Association, Berea Bible College, Erzhausen, Germany, 8 November 1980.
"Philip Schaff's Assessment of the Development of a National Character: *America,* 1855"; Joint Meeting of the Departments of Ecclesiastical History for the Ancient Universities of Scotland (Edinburgh, Glasgow, St. Andrews, and Aberdeen) at Perth, 11 February 1989.
"Pragmatism or Providence? A Case Study in Ecumenism in Nineteenth-Century America"; Department of Ecclesiastical History, New College, University of Edinburgh, 10 May 1989.
"Components of the Human Psyche Discernible in the Continuities of a National Character"; Zaporozhye State University, Ukraine, 5-6 October 1993.
"Toward a Pentecostal Theology"; Han Young Theological University, Seoul, Korea, 19 March 1997.

Articles: *Church of God Evangel*

"A Concept of Communion: A Study in the Theology of Renewal." 59, no. 4 (31 March 1969): 9-11.
"Access to the Holiest: Thoughts on the Priesthood of the Believer." 64, no. 16 (28 October 1974): 12-13, 27.
"But What is He Doing Now?" 68, no. 1 (13 March 1978): 16-17. Sermon delivered at Cleveland, Tennessee Community Sunrise Service, Easter Sunday, 1977.
"Comments on King James: Putting the Authorized Version in Perspective." 65, no. 16 (27 October 1975): 5-6.
"Emmanuel—God With Us." 52, no. 42 (24 December 1962): 4-5.
"Happiness is . . . Sins Forgiven" 70, no. 18 (24 November 1980): 16-17. Sermon delivered during the Summer Ecumenical Worship Service held at First Christian Church, Cleveland, Tennessee, 1980.
"Keep It Holy." 65, no. 12 (25 August 1975): 14-15.
"Lee College: Division of Religion." 67, no. 10 (25 July 1977): 23.

"Metamorphosis: A Case for Personal Religion." (26 May 1969): 12-13.
Sermon delivered at Watts Chapel, Union Theological Seminary,
Richmond, Virginia.

"Oasis or Crucible?" 70, no. 20 (22 December 1980): 16-17. Extract from
chapter in *The Promise and the Power.*

"On Being a Servant." 58, no. 39 (9 December 1968): 12-13, 20.

"One in Baptism." 69, no. 18 (26 November 1979): 16-17. Sermon delivered
at the Summer Ecumenical Worship Program service at the Broad
Street United Methodist Church, Cleveland, Tennessee, 1979.

"Power for Service: The Pentecostal Distinctive." 57, no. 9 (8 May 1967): 7,
13.

"Sanctification: God's Will for You." 66, no. 10 (26 July 1976): 16-18.

"The Fullness of Time: Events Preempting the Reformation." 55, no. 34 (25
October 1965): 4-5, 14, 22.

"The Future Resurrection." 64, no. 3 (8 April 1974): 12-13.

"The Holy Spirit in Regeneration." 55, no. 30 (27 September 1965): 18-19.

"The Priesthood of the Believer." 53, no. 34 (28 October 1963): 16-17.

"The Reformation Rediscovery of True Worship: A Contemporary
Appraisal." 57, no. 32 (23 October 1967): 12-14.

"Theological Training Leads to Meaningful Lay Involvement." 59, no. 43
(12 January 1970): 17.

"Thus It is Written: The Resurrection of Jesus in the Old Testament." 69,
no. 2 (26 March 1979): 2-3.

"Toward Christian Maturity." 67, no. 1 (14 March 1977): 16-18. Sermon
delivered at the Michigan Camp Meeting, 1976.

"When Jesus is Lord." 64, no. 23 (10 February 1975): 16-17. Sermon
delivered at the Mississippi Camp Meeting, 1974.

Articles: *Academic Forum*

"America's Christian Heritage." *Academic Forum* 1, no. 2 (1 June 1971): 3-
4.

"The Making of a Commentary." *Academic Forum* 1, no. 4 (16 October
1971): 13-14.

Journals Edited

Bowdle, et al, edited the *Academic Forum,* vol. 1, no. 1 through vol. 4,
no. 3 (1971-1973).

Journal Reviews: *Religious and Theological Abstracts*

Union Seminary (NY) *Quarterly Review*
1972 (vol. 27, no. 4)	3 reviews
1972 (vol. 28, no. 1)	11 reviews
1973 (vol. 28, no. 2)	6 reviews
1973 (vol. 28, no. 3)	3 reviews
1973 (vol. 28, no. 4)	7 reviews
1973 (vol. 29, no. 1)	4 reviews
1974 (vol. 29, no. 2)	3 reviews
1974 (vol. 29, nos. 3,4)	12 reviews
1974 (vol. 30, no. 1)	4 reviews
1975 (vol. 30, nos. 2-4)	15 reviews

Journal of Religious Thought
1970 (vol. 27, no. 3)	6 reviews
1971 (vol. 28, no. 1)	6 reviews
1971 (vol. 28, no. 2)	6 reviews
1971 (vol. 29, no. 1)	6 reviews

Book Reviews: *Richmond* (VA) *Times-Dispatch*   **(1967-1982)**

A Biography of Adlai E. Stevenson, by Kenneth S. Davis. (10 December 1967).

The Emergence of the New South, 1913-1945, by George Brown Tindall. (14 January 1968).

The Trouble with Marx, by David McCord Wright. (21 January 1968).

To Seek a Newer World, by Robert F. Kennedy. (28 January 1968).

The Concerns of a Citizen, by George Romney. (4 February 1968).

The New American Commonwealth, by Louis Heren. (3 March 1968).

The Origins of American Diplomacy: The International History of Anglo-America, 1492-1763, by Max Savelle. (17 March 1968).

Politics Battle Plan, by Herbert M. Baus and William B. Ross. (24 March 1968).

Gulliver's Troubles, or the Setting of American Foreign Policy, by Stanley Hoffmann. (24 March 1968).

The Pendergast Machine, by Lyle W. Dorsett. (7 April 1968).

The Degeneration of Our Presidential Election: A History and Analysis of an American Institution in Trouble, by Jules Abels. (5 May 1968).

Benjamin Harrison: Hoosier President (The White House and After, 1889-1901), by Harry J. Sievers. (19 May 1968).

McCarthy, by Roy Cohn. (30 June 1968).

Twelve Years a Slave, by Solomon Northup, edited by Sue Eakin and Joseph Logsdon. (30 June 1968).
Contemporary Politics and Economics in the Caribbean, by Sir Harold Mitchell. (8 September 1968).
The Mooney Case, by Richard H. Frost. (17 November 1968).
1976: Agenda for Tomorrow, by Stewart L. Udall. (22 December 1968).
The Gathering Storm in the Churches, by Jeffrey K. Hadden. (6 April 1969).
Years of the Golden Cockerel: The Last Romanov Tsars, 1814-1917, by Sidney Harcave. (27 July 1969).
Russia in the Twentieth Century: The View of a Soviet Historian, by Albert P. Nenarokov, translated by David Windheim. (3 August 1969).
Hellenism and the Rise of Rome, edited by Pierre Grimal. (17 August 1969).
Rule of Terror: Russia under Lenin and Stalin, by Hellmut Andics, translated by Alexander Lieven.
Europe in the Age of Imperialism, 1880-1914, by Heinz Gollwitzer, and *The Reluctant Imperialists: British Foreign Policy, 1878-1902*, by C. J. Lowe.
Democracy in the Old South and Other Essays, by Fletcher Melvin Green, edited by J. Isaac Copeland.
Liberalism in the New South: Southern Social Reformers and the Progressive Movement, by Hugh C. Bailey. (25 January 1970).
Odyssey of a Friend: Whittaker Chambers' Letters to William F. Buckley Jr., 1954-1961, edited by William F. Buckley Jr. (22 February 1970).
Cornwallis, the American Adventure, by Franklin and Mary Wickwire and *Wellington: The Years of the Sword*, by Elizabeth Longford. (17 May 1970).
The Fear of Crime, by Richard Harris. (24 May 1970).
Confirm or Deny: Informing the People on National Security, by Phil G. Goulding. (7 June 1970).
Report from Wasteland: America's Military-Industrial Complex, by William Proxmire. (14 June 1970).
The Imperfect Union: A History of Corruption in American Trade Unions, by John Hutchinson. (14 June 1970).
Essays on Recent Southern Politics, edited by Harold M. Hollingsworth.
The Governor Listeth: A Book of Inspired Political Revelations, by William F. Buckley, Jr.
Cherokee Tragedy: The Story of the Ridge Family and the Decimation of a People, by Thurman Wilkins.
American Convictions: Cycles of Public Thought, 1600-1850, by Charles A. Barker.

Theodore Roosevelt and the Art of Controversy: Episodes of the White House Years, by Willard B. Gatewood, Jr.

1919: Red Mirage. Year of Desperate Rebellion, by David Mitchell.

A Biographical History of Blacks in America Since 1528, by Edgar A. Toppin. (5 September 1971).

Governor O. Max Gardner: A Power in North Carolina and New Deal Washington, by Joseph L. Morrison.

The Grundrisse, by Karl Marx, edited and translated by David McLellan.

Harmony Hall: A Romantic Historical Novel of the American Revolution, by Jane Meredith. (12 September 1971).

Kennedy Justice, by Victor S. Navasky. (26 December 1971).

Adam by Adam, autobiography of Adam Clayton Powell, Jr.

McGovern: A Biography, by Robert Sam Anson. (23 April 1972).

Liberation in Middle America, by Gabriel J. Fackre. (9 July 1972).

The Drug Hang-Up: America's Fifty-Year Folly, by Rufus King. (13 August 1972).

The Papers of Adlai E. Stevenson, Vol. 2, edited by Walter Johnson and Carol Evans. (15 April 1973).

The Kennedy Neurosis, by Nancy Gager Clinch. (22 April 1973).

Enemy at the Gates: The Battle for Stalingrad, by William Craig. (27 May 1973).

Lloyd George: A Diary of Frances Stevenson, edited by A. J. P. Taylor.

Flight and Rebellion: Slave Resistance in Eighteenth-Century Virginia, by Gerald W. Mullin.

The New Left Today: America's Trojan Horse, by Phillip Abbott Luce.

Black Frenchmen: The Political Integration of the French Antilles, by Alvin Murch.

New Converts to the American Dream? Mobility Aspirations of Young Mexican Americans, by Celia S. Heller.

The New How to Win an Election, by Stephen C. Shadegg.

What You Don't Know Can Hurt You: A Study of Public Opinion and Public Emotion, by Lester Markel.

Eve's New Rib: Twenty Faces of Sex, Marriage, and Family, by Robert T. Francoeur.

So Help Me God: Religion and the Presidency, Wilson to Nixon, by Robert S. Alley.

The Megastates of America: People, Politics, and Power in the Ten Great States, by Neal R. Peirce.

The Washington Pay-off: An Insider's View of Corruption in Government, by Robert N. Winter-Berger.

The Pathology of Politics: Violence, Betrayal, Corruption, Secrecy, and Propaganda, by Carl J. Friedrich.

Inside the Colonels' Greece, by "Athenian," translated by Richard Clogg.

The Great Coalfield War, by George S. McGovern and Leonard F. Guttridge.

Merger Politics: Local Government Consolidation in Tidewater, Virginia, by David G. Temple.

Journey Between Two Chinas, by Seymour Topping.

The Fighting Quaker: Nathanael Greene, by Elswyth Thane.

Meany: The Unchallenged Strong Man of American Labor, by Joseph C. Goulden.

Harry S. Truman, by Margaret Truman.

Right From the Start: A Chronicle of the McGovern Campaign, by Gary Warren Hart.

Out in the Midday Sun: Singapore, 1941-45—The End of an Empire, by Kate Caffrey.

Who Makes War: The President Versus Congress, by Jacob K. Javits.

The Price of Vision: The Diary of Henry A. Wallace, 1942-1946, edited by John Morton Blum.

Memories II, by Julian Huxley.

Plain Speaking: An Oral Biography of Harry S. Truman, by Merle Miller, and *The Awesome Power: Harry S. Truman as Commander in Chief*, by Richard F. Haynes.

Jefferson the President: Second Term, 1805-1809, by Dumas Malone.

To Conquer a Peace: The War Between the United States and Mexico, by John Edward Weems.

The Papers of Adlai E. Stevenson, Vol. 3, edited by Walter Johnson and Carol Evans.

The Papers of Adlai E. Stevenson, Vol. 4, edited by Walter Johnson, et al.

Richard Lion Heart, by James A. Brundage.

Kissinger, by Marvin Kalb and Bernard Kalb.

The President is Calling, by Milton S. Eisenhower.

Winston Churchill, by Henry Pelling.

The Papers of Adlai E. Stevenson, Vol. 5, edited by Walter Johnson, et al.

Political Animals: Memoirs of a Sentimental Cynic, by Walter Trohan.

White House Witness, 1942-1945, by Jonathan Daniels.

Breach of Faith: The Fall of Richard Nixon, by Theodore H. White.

Making Democracy Safe for Oil: Oilmen and the Islamic East, by Christopher T. Rand.

From the Diaries of Felix Frankfurter, edited by Joseph P. Lash.

Ralph Bunche, UN Peacemaker, by Peggy Mann.

Executive Eve—And Other Contemporary Ballads, by William F. Buckley.

Special Envoy to Churchill and Stalin, 1941-1946, by W. Averell Harriman and Elie Abel.

Solzhenitsyn's Religion, by Niels C. Nielsen, Jr.

Bonhoeffer: Worldly Preaching, by Clyde E. Fant.

Lyndon Johnson and the American Dream, by Doris Kearns.
Creativity and Conflict, Vol. 6 of *The Journals of David E. Lilienthal*.
Blind Ambition: The White House Years, by John W. Dean III.
Kissinger: The European Mind in American Foreign Policy, by Bruce
Mazlish.
The American Police State: The Government Against the People, by
David Wise.
The Natural Superiority of Southern Politicians: A Revisionist History,
by David Leon Chandler.
How Jimmy Won: The Victory Campaign from Plains to the White House,
by Kandy Stroud.
*The Abuse of Power: The Permanent Government and the Fall of New
York*, by Jack Newfield and Paul Du Brul.
John L. Lewis: A Biography, by Melvyn Dubofsky and Warren Van Tine.
The Oswald File, by Michael Eddowes.
Mother R: Eleanor Roosevelt's Untold Story, by Elliott Roosevelt and
James Brough.
*Decent Interval: An Insider's Account of Saigon's Indecent End Told by
the CIA's Chief Strategy Analyst in Vietnam*, by Frank Snepp.
Panama Canal: The Crisis in Historical Perspective, by Walter LaFeber.
Grassroots: The Autobiography of George McGovern, by George
McGovern.
*The War That Hitler Won: The Most Infamous Propaganda Campaign in
History*, by Robert Edwin Herzstein.
Mao and the Perpetual Revolution by Franz Michael, and review of *Chou:
An Informal Biography of China's Legendary Chou En-Lai*, by John
McCook Roots.
Education, Lawlessness, and Political Corruption in America, by Harold
H. Punke.
Yankee From Georgia: The Emergence of Jimmy Carter, by William Lee
Miller.
In Search of History: A Personal Adventure, by Theodore H. White.
America Revisited: 150 Years After Tocqueville, by Eugene J. McCarthy.
History of the Westward Movement, by Frederick Merk.
A Hymnal: The Controversial Arts, by William F. Buckley, Jr.
Farewell the Trumpets: An Imperial Retreat, by James Morris.
The Terrors of Justice: The Untold Story of Watergate, by Maurice H.
Stans.
Illustrissimi: *Letters from Pope John Paul I*, by Albino Luciani.
Herbert Hoover: A Public Life, by David Burner.
The Heart of Matter, by Pierre Teilhard de Chardin.
The Four Gospels and the Revelation, by Richmond Lattimore.
Billy Graham: A Parable of American Righteousness, by Marshall Frady.

A Time to Heal: The Autobiography of Gerald R. Ford, by Gerald R. Ford.

Jimmy Carter: The Man and the Myth, by Victor Lasky.

The Papers of Adlai E. Stevenson, Vol. 8, edited by Walter Johnson.

The Bureau: My Thirty Years in Hoover's FBI, by William C. Sullivan, and *The Man Who Kept the Secrets: Richard Helms and the CIA*, by Thomas Powers.

Life Sentence, by Charles W. Colson.

Among Friends: Personal Letters of Dean Acheson, edited by David S. McLellan and David C. Acheson.

Pilgrimage of Peace: The Collected Speeches of John Paul II in Ireland and the United States, Authorized Edition.

Go Quietly . . . Or Else, by Spiro T. Agnew.

Of Kennedys and Kings: Making Sense of the Sixties, by Harris Wofford.

Tip: A Biography of Thomas P. O'Neill, Speaker of the House, by Paul Clancy and Shirley Elder.

The Age of Surveillance: The Aims and Methods of America's Political Intelligence System, by Frank J. Donner.

The Present Danger, by Norman Podhoretz.

George Bush: A Biography, by Nicholas King.

The Court Years, 1939-1975: The Autobiography of William O. Douglas, by William O. Douglas.

Frank Porter Graham: A Southern Liberal, by Warren Ashby.

Louis D. Brandeis and the Progressive Tradition, by Melvin I. Urofsky.

For the Record: Selected Statements, 1977-1980, by Henry Kissinger.

Memorandum for the President: A Strategic Approach to Domestic Affairs in the 1980's, by Ben W. Heineman, Jr. and Curtis A. Hessler.

The Prime Ministers, by George Malcolm Thomson.

On a Field of Red: The Communist International and the Coming of World War II, by Anthony Cave Brown and Charles B. MacDonald.

Raleigh's Lost Colony, by David N. Durant.

Eden Seekers: The Settlement of Oregon, 1818-1862, by Malcolm Clark, Jr.

A Life in Our Times: Memoirs, by John Kenneth Galbraith.

The History of American Wars From 1745-1918, by T. Harry Williams.

Destination Peace: Three Decades of Israeli Foreign Policy—A Personal Memoir, by Gideon Raphael.

The Gate of Heavenly Peace: The Chinese and Their Revolution, 1895-1980, by Jonathan D. Spence.

Bismarck, by Edward Crankshaw.

316 The Spirit and the Mind

Book Reviews: *Church History*

From Pentecost to the Present: A Short History of Christianity, by James B. North. *Church History* 53, no. 4 (December 1984): 545-546.
Eerdmans' Handbook to Christianity in America, edited by Mark A. Noll, Nathan O. Hatch, George M. Marsden, David F. Wells, and John D. Woodbridge. *Church History* 53, no. 4 (December 1984): 559.
The Conversion Experience in America: A Sourcebook on Religious Conversion Autobiography, by James Craig Holte. *Church History* 65, no. 2 (June 1996): 315-317.

Book Reviews: *Journal of the Evangelical Theological Society*

The Mystical Way in the Fourth Gospel: Crossing Over Into God, by L. William Countryman. *Journal of the Evangelical Theological Society* 40, no. 1 (March 1997): 129-130.
Studying John: Approaches to the Fourth Gospel, by John Ashton. *Journal of the Evangelical Theological Society* 40, no. 3 (September 1997): 468-469.

Book Reviews: *The Pentecostal Minister* **(1981-1989)**

Designing the Sermon: Order and Movement in Preaching, by James Earl Massey, and *The Preaching Tradition: A Brief History*, by DeWitte T. Holland, and *The Sermon as God's Word: Theologies for Preaching*, by Robert W. Duke.
Five Smooth Stones for Pastoral Work, by Eugene H. Peterson.
Planting Churches Cross-Culturally: A Guide for Home and Foreign Missions, by David J. Hesselgrave.
In Search of C. S. Lewis, edited by Stephen Schofield.
Early Christians, by John Drane.
Paul and *Jesus and the Four Gospels*, by John Drane.
Harper's World of the New Testament, by Edwin Yamauchi.
Autobiography of God, by Lloyd John Ogilvie.
Paul, Apostle of Steel and Velvet, by James Dyet.
Peter, Apostle of Contrasts, by James Dyet.

Expositions of Scripture

Youth Teacher's Quarterly, Church of God Publishing House, 1962-1966.
Evangelical Sunday School Lesson Commentary, National Sunday School Association, 1971-1974.

Citations and Acknowledgments

"Books: Church Ministry, Part I," *Christianity Today* 25 (24 April 1981): 62.

Boone, R. Jerome, ed. *The New Chronological Bible.* Nashville: E. E. Gaddy & Associates, Inc., 1980, p. ii.

"Choice Evangelical Reprints of 1971," *Christianity Today* 16 (3 March 1972): 30.

Conn, Charles Paul. *Father Care: What It Means to Be God's Child.* Waco: Word Books, 1983, pp. 10, 78.

Conn, Charles W. *Like a Mighty Army: A History of the Church of God, 1886-1995.* Definitive edition. Cleveland: Pathway Press, 1996, p. 277.

Jones, Loyal. *Faith & Meaning in the Southern Uplands.* Urbana: University of Illinois Press, 1999, pp. 22-23, 129, 158.

Sims, John A. *Missionaries to the Skeptics: Christian Apologists for the Twentieth Century: C.S. Lewis, E. J. Carnell, and Reinhold Niebuhr.* Macon: Mercer University Press, 1995, p. ix.

"Some Significant books of 1971; Part 1, The Bible as a Whole: Commentaries," *Christianity Today,* 16 (18 February 1972): 10.

"VIETNAM'S LEGACY: Yale Divinity School ...," *The Wall Street Journal* (28 February 1985).